Achieving Biodiversity Protection in Megadiverse Countries

This volume systematically analyses why legal doctrines for the protection of biodiversity are not sufficiently effective. It examples implementation in Australia and Brazil, two megadiverse countries with very differing legal and cultural traditions and natural environments.

Substantial effort goes into the development and interpretation of legal doctrines for the protection of biodiversity in national and international law. Despite this, biodiversity continues in steeply decline. Nowhere is this more evident than in megadiverse countries, such as Australia and Brazil, which possess the greatest number and diversity of animals and plants on Earth. The book covers a wide range of topics, including farming, mining, marine environments, indigenous interests and governance. *Achieving Biodiversity Protection in Megadiverse Countries* highlights specific causes of underperformance in protecting diverse terrestrial and marine environments. It provides proposals for more effective implementation in these two jurisdictions, relevant to other megadiverse territories, and for biodiversity protection generally. Each chapter was written by teams of Australian and Brazilian authors, so that similar issues are considered across both jurisdictions, to provide both country-specific and generalisable insights.

Achieving Biodiversity in Megadiverse Countries will be of great interest to students and scholars of environmental law and governance and biodiversity conservation, as well as policymakers, practitioners and NGOs working in these fields.

Paul Martin is the Director of the Australian Centre for Agriculture and Law at the University of New England in Australia, and a member of the Research Committee of the IUCN Academy of Environmental Law. He has conducted extensive research on the implementation of biodiversity protection in a number of countries.

Márcia Dieguez Leuzinger is an Environmental Law Professor at Brasilia University Centre – UniCEUB, and a State Attorney for Parana. She has undergraduate, masters and doctoral degrees in Sustainable Development from Brasilia University – UnB and leads the Environmental Law and Sustainable Development Research Group at UniCEUB.

Solange Teles Da Silva is a Law Professor at Mackenzie Presbyterian University. She graduated in Law at Sao Paulo University and has a PhD in Environmental Law at Paris I – Pantheon Sorbonne University. She has a CNPq Research Productivity Fellowship in Brazil, and is the Leader of the Research Group on Law and Sustainable Development. She is actively involved in the IUCN Academy of Environmental Law.

Gabriel Leuzinger Coutinho is an electrical engineer with an MBA in Project Management from the Fundação Getúlio Vargas, and an MSc in Sustainability Policy and Management from the University of Brasília (UnB). He is currently a PhD student at UnB's Center for Sustainable Development, and is a coordinator of the environmental law and sustainable development research group at UniCEUB.

Routledge Studies in Biodiversity Politics and Management

Concepts and Values in Biodiversity
Edited by Dirk Lanzerath and Minou Friele

The Politics of Knowledge and Global Biodiversity
Alice Vadrot

Governing Biodiversity through Democratic Deliberation
Edited by Mikko Rask and Richard Worthington

The Intergovernmental Platform on Biodiversity and Ecosystem Services (IPBES)
Meeting the Challenges of Biodiversity Conservation and Governance
Edited by Marie Hrabanski and Denis Pesche

Economic Valuation of Biodiversity
An Interdisciplinary Conceptual Perspective
Authored by Bartosz Bartkowski

Achieving Biodiversity Protection in Megadiverse Countries
A Comparative Assessment of Australia and Brazil
Edited by Paul Martin, Márcia Dieguez Leuzinger, Solange Teles da Silva, and Gabriel Leuzinger Coutinho

Achieving Biodiversity Protection in Megadiverse Countries

A Comparative Assessment of Australia and Brazil

Edited by Paul Martin, Márcia Dieguez Leuzinger, Solange Teles da Silva, and Gabriel Leuzinger Coutinho

First published 2020 by Routledge

2 Park Square, Milton Park, Abingdon, Oxon OX14 4RN

605 Third Avenue, New York, NY 10017

Routledge is an imprint of the Taylor & Francis Group, an informa business

First issued in paperback 2021

© 2020 selection and editorial matter, Paul Martin, Márcia Dieguez Leuzinger, Solange Teles da Silva, and Gabriel Leuzinger Coutinho; individual chapters, the contributors

The right of Paul Martin, Márcia Dieguez Leuzinger, Solange Teles da Silva, and Gabriel Leuzinger Coutinho to be identified as the authors of the editorial material, and of the authors for their individual chapters, has been asserted in accordance with sections 77 and 78 of the Copyright, Designs and Patents Act 1988.

All rights reserved. No part of this book may be reprinted or reproduced or utilised in any form or by any electronic, mechanical, or other means, now known or hereafter invented, including photocopying and recording, or in any information storage or retrieval system, without permission in writing from the publishers.

Trademark notice: Product or corporate names may be trademarks or registered trademarks, and are used only for identification and explanation without intent to infringe.

Publisher's Note

The publisher has gone to great lengths to ensure the quality of this reprint but points out that some imperfections in the original copies may be apparent.

British Library Cataloguing-in-Publication Data
A catalogue record for this book is available from the British Library

Library of Congress Cataloging-in-Publication Data
A catalog record has been requested for this book

ISBN: 978-0-367-26527-4 (hbk)
ISBN: 978-1-03-217291-0 (pbk)
DOI: 10.4324/9780429296239

Typeset in Bembo
by codeMantra

Contents

List of figures	xi
List of tables	xiii
List of contributors	xv
Foreword	xix
Preface	xxi
List of acronyms and abbreviations	xxxiii

1 The issues, methods and evidence   1

Introduction 1
Biodiversity governance in Brazil and Australia 6
   Biodiversity governance in Australia 9
   Biodiversity governance in Brazil 12
Initial investigations 14
Book structure 16

2 Controlling the biodiversity impacts of agriculture   25

Introduction 25
The impact of agriculture 26
   Expansion and habitat loss 32
   Invasive species 32
   Contamination 34
Financial constraints 35
Public programmes 36
Water, climate and biodiversity 37
Socio-ecological issues 38
Overview 39

3 Biodiversity risk management in mining   47

Introduction 47
Governance frameworks 48
Mine approval in Australia 50
   The Bulga case 50

viii *Contents*

Adani Carmichael case 52
Mine disasters in Brazil 53
Conclusions and implications 61

4 Creating and managing marine protected areas   67
Introduction 67
Marine biodiversity conservation and international agreements 68
Australia's marine governance 70
Brazil's marine governance 74
Implementing Brazil's protected areas 75
Implementing Australia's protected areas 82
Conclusions 84

5 Social justice and the management of protected areas   88
Introduction 88
Brazilian Indigenous and Traditional people's stewardship 89
  The Rio de Janeiro Law *2.393/1995 94*
  Serra do Mar State Park 95
  Contributions to conservation 95
Co-management in Australia 96
  Native title and statutory rights 96
  Uluru-Kata Tjuta National Park 98
Comparing Australia and Brazil 100
Conclusions 101

6 Low impact recreational use and biodiversity protection   105
Introduction 105
Surfing reserves and conservation innovation 106
Surfing reserves and biodiversity 107
Australian surfing reserves 109
Brazilian surfing reserves 111
Perspectives on surfing reserves 112
Conclusions 117

7 Partnered governance of biodiversity   125
Introduction 125
Cotton case studies 130
  Australia 131
  Brazil 131
Sugar case studies 132
  Australia 133
  Brazil 133

Contents ix

Beef case studies 134
  Australia 134
  Brazil 135
Dairy case studies 136
  Australia 136
  Brazil 137
Receptiveness to partnered arrangements 138
Conclusions 140

8 Biodiversity intelligence from satellites 148

Introduction 148
The need for low-cost precision 149
Satellites technologies 150
Murray-Darling Basin case 152
Monitoring habitat loss 153
  Mato Grosso land clearing 154
  Queensland land clearing 158
Discussion and conclusion 160

9 The challenge of using drones 168

Introduction 168
Drone technology evolution 169
Expanding uses 171
Incremental adoption and learning 173
Governance challenges 174
  Human impact risk 174
  Social interests 176
  Lethal drones 177
  Biodiversity impacts 178
  Intentional damage 179
  Drones and data 180
Conclusion 180

10 Funding biodiversity conservation 188

Introduction 188
Resource limitations 190
The funding gaps 191
Funding strategies 193
  Brazil 195
  Australia 198
  Protected areas funding 204
Conclusions 205

x   Contents

11 Governing the governance system

Introduction 210
Key terms 211
Meta-governance 212
The governance challenge 213
Biodiversity strategies 214
Australia's meta-governance 219
Brazil's meta-governance 223
Conclusions 229

210

12 Strategies to improve outcomes

Introduction 236
Politics and regression 237
Undermining existing laws 239
Architectures, not just instruments 241
Weak accountability and continuous improvement 245
Citizen participation arrangements need improvement 247
Meta-governance is inadequate 249
Looking to the future 251

236

Appendix A: legislation list   257
Appendix B: international material   261
Appendix C: cases   264
Index   265

Figures

2.1	Agricultural production, constant US$'000 1961–2016	26
2.2	Agricultural land, '000 ha, 1961–2016	27
2.3	Adult agricultural employment, '000, 1961–2016	27
2.4	Number of 40-CV tractor equivalent in use, 1961–2016	28
2.5	Synthetic fertilizer use, metric tonnes, 1961–2016	28
4.1	Estuarine biodiversity issues identified by workshop participants, east coast of Australia	70
4.2	Management council of federal marine conservation units	81
4.3	Management plan of federal marine and coastal conservation units	81
8.1	Left: Mato Grosso's location in South America; Right: Mato Grosso's biomes	154
8.2	Deforested areas of the Amazon Forest and the Cerrado biomes in Mato Grosso by year	156
9.1	Composite evolution of drone technologies	171
10.1	Commonwealth whole of government projected expenditure 2001–2002 to 2010–2011	202

Tables

1.1	Comparison of *CBD* relevant statistics Brazil–Australia	8
2.1	Comparative agricultural statistics – Australia and Brazil	30
2.2	Largest agricultural landholders in Australia	30
3.1	Characteristics of the Mariana and Brumadinho mine disasters	54
3.2	Federal agencies (Brazil) regulating mining	55
4.1	Treaties relevant to protect marine biodiversity to which Australia and Brazil are parties	71
4.2	IUCN Protected Areas Classification and MPAs in Brazil	80
5.1	Number of interfaces present in each category of full protection conservation unit	92
5.2	Percentage of conservation units with interfaces in each category	92
5.3	Estimated number of individuals (for Indigenous peoples) or families (for Traditional populations or family farmers) living inside full protection conservation units	92
6.1	National Surfing Reserves of Australia	111
6.2	World Surfing Reserves	113
7.1	Importance of four selected farm sectors to Brazil and Australia (per annum values)	128
7.2	Overview of four selected agricultural industry sustainability initiatives – international, Brazil and Australia	129
8.1	Examples of satellite programmes utilised for earth observation	151
10.1	Comparison of Australia and Brazil based on 2017 data	192
11.1	World Bank Governance Indicators for Australia and Brazil (2019)	216
11.2	Australian and Brazilian examples of policy instruments for the environment	217

Contributors

Romana Coêlho de Araujo has Bachelor degrees in Economics and Law and an MSc in Environmental Economics. She has worked extensively on economic valuation and is an author of a well-known book: Economic Valuation of Environmental Damage in Public Civil Inquiry. She is a member of the UNICEUB Research Group on Environmental Law and Sustainable Development.

Boyd Dirk Blackwell is an applied economist with specialist skills and experience in resource, environmental, ecological and institutional economics. His PhD was on the economics of coastal foreshore and beach management and he has an ongoing research interest in coastal and marine issues including surfing.

Paulo Campanha Santana holds a Masters and PhD in Law. He coordinates the Law course and leads the Law and Sustainable Development Research group, and is a member of the Research Ethics Committee (CEP) of the Federal University Center (UDF). He coordinates the Environmental Law and Sustainable Development research group from the University Center of Brasilia (UniCEUB).

Larissa Suassuna Carvalho Barros holds a Master's degree in Law from the University of Brasilia (UnB), Brazil. Her post-graduate study was in Constitutional Law at the Anhanguera–Uniderp University, Brazil. She is a graduate in Law from the Federal University of Pernambuco (UFPE), Brazil, and is a member of the IUCN World Commission on Protected Areas and World Commission on Environmental Law.

Amy Cosby is a researcher with the Australian Centre for Agriculture and Law at the University of New England. During this time she has had research input into a number of programmes over a range of topics including natural resource governance and managing conflict over natural resources.

Gabriel Leuzinger Coutinho is an electrical engineer with an MBA in Project Management from the Fundação Getúlio Vargas, and an MSc in xvi *Contributors*

Sustainability Policy and Management from the University of Brasília (UnB). He is currently a PhD student at UnB's Center for Sustainable Development, and is a coordinator of the environmental law and sustainable development research group at UniCEUB.

Donna Craig is a specialist in international, comparative and national environmental law at Western Sydney University, Australia, with a research focus on Indigenous biodiversity governance. She has worked extensively with Indigenous people in Australia and Canada.

Mauricio Duarte Dos Santos holds a Ph.D. in Economic and Political Law from Mackenzie Presbyterian University, São Paulo – Brazil. He is a Postdoctoral Researcher linked to the Brazilian National Postdoctoral Program (CAPES Fellowship) and the Mackenzie Presbyterian University Postgraduate Program in Political and Economic Law (2019–2020). He is a member of the Mackenzie Research Group on Law and Sustainable Development.

Carolina Dutra holds a PhD in Political and Economic Law at Mackenzie Presbyterian University, and a Masters in Environmental Law. She has held scholarships from Mackenzie Presbyterian University and São Paulo Research Foundation – FAPESP. University She is a Graduate and postgraduate lecturer in law. She is a member of the Mackenzie Research Group on Law and Sustainable Development.

Marcia Fajardo Cavalcanti de Albuquerque is a law graduate from the University Centre of Brasilia, with a University Diploma on sustainable development and land management at the Université de Montpellier I. She holds a Masters in environmental law (University of Paris 1 and 2, Panthéon/Sorbonne); and is a PhD candidate (Sorbonne University and Mackenzie University). She is a member of the Mackenzie Research Group on Law and Sustainable Development.

Larissa Ribeiro da Cruz Godoy is an environmental analyst at the Ministry of the Environment. She holds a Masters in Law and Public Policies form the Brasilia University Centre – UniCEUB, and is an environmental management specialist at Catholic University of Brasilia. He is a member of the UniCEUB Research Group on Environmental Law and Sustainable Development.

Jane Gudde is a PhD candidate with the Australian Centre for Agriculture and Law, researching sustainability assurance schemes in Australian agriculture. Prior to this she worked in natural resource management planning for agricultural landscapes, biosecurity regulation and aquatic biology.

Evan Hamman is a lecturer in law at the Queensland University of Technology. His expertise includes environmental regulation and governance, and the role of law in biodiversity conservation. He has a particular interest in the implementation of international environmental law in a domestic context.

Andrew Lawson, is a researcher at the Australian Centre for Agriculture & Law at the University of New England, Australia. His research focuses on sustainable agriculture and the governance of agriculture's impacts on the environment. His research includes work on stewardship programs for farmers.

Márcia Dieguez Leuzinger is an Environmental Law Professor at Brasilia University Centre – UniCEUB, and a State Attorney for Parana. She has undergraduate, masters and doctoral degrees in Sustainable Development from Brasilia University – UnB and leads the Environmental Law and Sustainable Development Research Group at UniCEUB.

Nathalia Lima has a Masters in Political and Economic Law from Mackenzie Presbyterian University and is Professor of Environmental Law, Human Rights and Public Law at in the School of Law of the Brazcubas Education University Center. She is also Legal Advisor at the Secretariat of Green and Environment of the City of São Paulo. She is a member of the Mackenzie Research Group on Law and Sustainable Development.

Siva Barathi (Sharl) Marimuthu teaches in the areas of Corporate Law and Civil Procedure at the Law School, University of New England. Her research explores how law and governance can facilitate sustainable use of natural resources and food production.

Paul Martin is the Director of the Australian Centre for Agriculture and Law at the University of New England in Australia, and a member of the Research Committee of the IUCN Academy of Environmental Law. He has conducted extensive research on the implementation of biodiversity protection a number of countries.

Vivek Nemane has studied researched law and institutional issues related to biodiversity protection in India, Australia, the USA and Europe. His doctoral dissertation on invasive species management and innovation in peri-urban areas was awarded the prestigious Chancellor's Doctoral Research Award at the University of New England and other prizes.

Jorge Madeira Nogueira is the Senior Professor of Environmental Economics at the Department of Economics of University of Brasília (ECO/UnB), Brazil. He is the Director of two research centres – the Centre for Studies on Agricultural and Environmental Economics (CEEMA) and the Centre for Territorial Ordering (CIORD).

Davi Rossiter is the Chief Legal Officer (CLO) at Bank of Brasília. He is a lawyer and a Civil Engineer and is studying for his Masters in Law student at Centro Universitário de Brasília – Uniceub. He is a member

xviii *Contributors*

of the research group in Law & Sustainable Development which involves UniCEUB, Mackenzie University and University of New England).

Leticia Rodrigues Da Silva graduated in law and as a Public Health and Toxicology Specialist, holds a Masters in Regulatory Toxicology and a PhD in Public Policy. She works in environmental law with topics such as pesticides, agriculture and sustainability, and is a member of the research group of the UFPR on the development and evolution of technical systems

Solange Teles da Silva is a Law Professor at Mackenzie Presbyterian University. She graduated in Law at Sao Paulo University and has a PhD in Environmental Law at Paris I – Pantheon Sorbonne University. She has a CNPq Research Productivity Fellowship in Brazil and is the Leader of the Research Group on Law and Sustainable Development. She is actively involved in the IUCN Academy of Environmental Law

Lorene Raquel de Souza is an analyst for the Environmental Institute Brasília – IBRAM. She is a graduate in Law, and holds a Masters in Law and Public Policies, and is a coordinator of the Environmental Law and Sustainable Development Research Group.

Kip Werren is a lecturer and course coordinator in Law at the University of New England. He is qualified in law and accounting, and holds a PhD in law from the University of New England. He has conducted extensive research into the funding of rural natural resource management, including the potential role of innovative taxation arrangements.

Foreword

Paul Martin

This book is the result of a massive effort by many people, who volunteered time and expertise with one purpose: to help make the laws and other instruments intended to protect biodiversity more effective. Improving the performance of domestic and international biodiversity governance is essential if the next generation, and those that follow, are to be able to enjoy the bounty of nature that our generation and those before have enjoyed. Sadly, despite many international agreements, domestic laws and other initiatives, biodiversity continues to decline alarmingly.

It is clear that some things must change for biodiversity governance to become more effective, but what is less clear is exactly what must change. There are many proposals to improve the governance system, such as advocacy for new international instruments or domestic laws, proposals for more market instruments, or simply more investment in the environment. These are all potentially important tactical interventions, but without an objective diagnosis of the performance of the biodiversity governance system as a whole, it is neither possible to understand how these tactics will come together to fundamentally improve the system nor to understand what other impediments need to be overcome for these tactics to work.

Driven by a passion to improve biodiversity and social outcomes, teams from Australia and Brazil have looked in detail at what is actually happening with the implementation of the many governance instruments that governments and NGOs have created in these two countries. They have analysed what is happening at the front line of implementation, to understand why the outcomes fall so far short of what is needed to protect the biological inheritance that future generations should be able to enjoy.

The results make it clear that many things have to be aligned for international and domestic governance instruments to form the basis of an effective system of governance. These include resources to implement instruments, arrangements to ensure implementation happens with integrity, and effective and transparent oversight and public reporting on the performance of biodiversity governance, to hold those with responsibilities accountable.

In this book, we present factual evidence of what is actually happening with biodiversity governance. The evidence points to an inevitable conclusion: more sophisticated tactical instruments alone are not likely in themselves to form an effective system of biodiversity governance. All of the essential elements of implementation must be in place, within a robust meta-governance framework that ensures implementation is feasible, tightly coordinated, inclusive and transparent.

In both of the countries we have investigated, local arrangements to implement the commitments made under the 1992 Convention on Biological Diversity (the CBD) and related international instruments have been put in place. These have made an important but insufficient contribution to protecting native biodiversity and the interests of Traditional and Indigenous people. Neither country has systematically institutionalised all of the commitments made under the CBD, and neither country has a strong meta-governance framework that will ensure effective implementation of their domestic arrangements. As a result there are serious failings of implementation, which translate into biodiversity losses and continuing social disadvantage. Though we have not carried out similar comprehensive analysis in other megadiverse countries, there is clear evidence that these deficiencies are not unique to Australia and Brazil.

Many of the deficiencies can be fixed. There is increasing international awareness that implementation of the CBD has to improve substantially, and we hope that our work will contribute to both the evidence that the need is urgent, and to proposals for how substantial improvement will be achieved. Above all, we hope that it will help shift attention to the need for effective systems of implementation to be put in place, to be implemented with integrity, that are more transparently accountable than are current arrangements.

Preface

Paul Martin, Márcia Dieguez Leuzinger, and Solange Teles da Silva

Abstract

This preface outlines why there is a need for more objective evidence-based, detailed analysis of the structures and dynamic of implementation of the Convention on Biological Diversity. It outlines the increasing number and variety of biodiversity instruments that have been created, and the evidence that the instruments and strategies being used are inadequate to prevent the continuing loss of species and ecosystems. It introduces the purpose and the approach to the research that underpins this book.

This book is the result of an examination of the implementation of fundamental principles and commitments to the *Convention on Biological Diversity* (*CBD*) and associated international instruments. The *CBD* has three stated purposes: the conservation of biological diversity; the sustainable use of the components of biological diversity and the fair and equitable sharing of the benefits arising out of the utilisation of genetic resources. It has been in existence for a quarter of a century.

In pursuit of these principles its articles commit States Parties to implement: strategies to protect the environment (art. 6); a robust system of *in-situ* protection of biodiversity (art. 8); *ex-situ* species preservation (art. 9); governance of biodiversity resources for sustainable use (art. 10); a system of incentives to protect biodiversity (art. 11); systematic impact assessment (art. 14) and funding for the purposes of the convention (art. 20). Under article 26, states are obliged to track and report on their implementation performance (Le Prestre, 2017). Other international instruments, including the *Cartagena Protocol on Biosafety*, the *Nagoya Protocol*, the *Nagoya-Kuala Lumpur Protocol*, and performance review metrics, such as the United Nations' Aichi Biodiversity Targets and the more recent Sustainable Development Goals (SDGs), add further requirements.

Underlying the text of the *CBD* is the intention that State Parties to the convention will implement comprehensive environmental governance systems. This binding commitment is indicated by the combination of the *CBD* articles 6, 8, 9–11, 14 and 20 that require states to create national biodiversity strategies, *in-situ* and *ex-situ* arrangements to preserve biodiversity, xxii *Preface*

systematic consideration of incentive systems, comprehensive development impact assessment and a national funding strategy. In general, articles 6–20 contain the substantive provisions of the *CBD*; nevertheless, because individual principles are often considered without examining how they interact as a whole, the obligation to implement viable governance systems is often overlooked. It is also important to note that the convention commitments are not limited to the actions of government, because the intent of the convention cannot be realised without multi-actor involvement. The requirements for realignment of incentives and other economic matters and, for example, only the development of impact assessment would also make little sense unless they embrace the actions of citizens, including Indigenous and Traditional communities, and enterprises in more effective governance.

Observations

Three observations explain the purpose of this book. First, there is significant human concern for biodiversity loss. Second, the past few decades have seen an explosion of government and non-government instruments that aim to control this loss. The third, detailed below under the heading 'insufficient effectiveness', is that biodiversity loss continues at alarming rates even given concern and instruments.

People all over the world from all levels and roles in society care for the earth's habitats and species. The millions of people who invest resources and effort to conserve or restore biodiversity include environmental stewards in their everyday lives; political activists; volunteers and philanthropists; politicians and public servants who pursue sustainability through public policy; environmental scholars and researchers and citizens who strive for sustainability through how they vote and how they spend their money. Even the people and organisations who harm biodiversity may declare that they are committed to protecting nature and take positive steps to do so. All these people and their efforts constitute a significant political and economic force for sustainable use and conservation of biodiversity.

The second observation, which arises from this commitment to nature, is the 'explosion' of strategies and instruments designed to ensure that human exploitation of nature does not destroy diversity. We use the term environmental or biodiversity governance in this book to refer to the many arrangements to govern (control, direct, limit, motivate, encourage, etc.) people and organisations in their relationship with the environment. Environmental governance refers to:

> [S]ystem for shaping behaviour to socially useful ends, involving many participants serving various roles. Those involved in this system include government officials, legal authorities, self-governing organisations and non-government actors, such as citizens, industry stakeholders, those being governed and those who are affected by governance. The actors involved

Preface xxiii

in natural resource governance can also pursue objectives that are inconsistent with environmental sustainability and social justice, such as advancing harmful economic developments or socially exploitative activities.

(Martin, Boer, & Slobodian, 2016)

Governance methods include public policies and laws, private rules and arrangements, economic instruments and social action. Governance also involves coordinating, evaluating or improving interventions, using strategies and administration, and information flows for monitoring and measurement and communications. In this sense, the *CBD* lays down institutional arrangements in order to monitor its progress and improve developments to achieve its objectives. There are three institutions: the Conference of the Parties (COP), the Subsidiary Body on Scientific Technical and Technological Advice (SBSTTA) and the Secretariat. The COP has established other subsidiary bodies that can make recommendations to the COP, such as the Working Group on Protected Areas.

The term 'meta-governance', examined in Chapter 11, concerns how systems of governance are themselves managed to ensure that they are effective and accountable. As well as government regulation, there has been an increase in non-state and non-regulatory instruments involving the public and the private sector. For example, the OECD (n.d.) database on environmental instruments details many (primarily government-led) taxes, fees, charges, tradeable permits, deposit-refund systems and environmental subsidies from many countries. It also provides information on voluntary programmes, primarily industry/government partnerships, which are only a fraction of voluntary conservation schemes.

Many instruments are used to improve protection of biodiversity, and their number and variety are increasing. The Ecolex (n.d.) database of legal instruments for the environment records more than 15,000 international instruments and treaty decisions; almost 16,000 laws from many countries and over 25,000 legal decisions and a large body of other jurisprudence (see also UNEP, 2019). The database is an incomplete inventory because it does not count every instrument from every jurisdiction, nor policies, rulings, plans and other subordinate instruments. There are calls for new environmental laws as well as for implementation of those that exist, exemplified by *Environmental Rule of Law: First Global Report* (UNEP, 2019) and UN General Assembly resolution proposing a Global Pact for the Environment (UN, 2018).

Governments increasingly use privatised interests in the environment to achieve environment, economy and social groups goals, primarily through market-based environmental instruments (as well as command and control instruments) such as payments for ecological services (Salzman, 2018) and tradeable rights instruments and many more (see also Pirard, 2012). Market instruments can be used to pursue combined eco-social and economic outcomes, exemplified by the UN Collaborative Programme on Reducing Emissions from Deforestation and Forest Degradation in Developing Countries xxiv *Preface*

(REDD and REDD+) scheme (for details and examples, see UNDP, n.d). This uses a socially and environmentally enhanced version of tradeable carbon credits, requiring that forest management achieve social goals. The overall aim is to protect biodiversity, address climate change and reduce poverty in developing countries. This is one of many government-enabled market instruments to address carbon and climate, water conservation, forestry and pollution and environmental economic growth and human welfare interests in the environment.

Another increasingly important approach is environmental branding of consumer products. This harnesses the purchasing and political power of environment-oriented consumers. The Eco-label index reports 463 ecolabels in 199 countries spanning 25 industry sectors (.eco, www.ecolabelindex. com/resources/ ..."Global Ecolabel Monitor 2010 Towards Transparency" http://www.ecolabelindex.com/resources/). This is an indication of the very many 'responsible consumption' initiatives, such as the substantial organics industry and environmentally motivated vegetarianism. Many corporations have environmental citizenship programmes (Chiabotti, 2004), and industries have environmental codes to govern their members or embark on hybrid arrangements with government (discussed in Chapter 7). Supply chains increasingly impose environmental stewardship requirements on suppliers, because some companies (particularly large firms) respond to consumer environmental expectations and the desire to justify their social licence.

Though government funding is fundamental to biodiversity protection, private environmental standards and brands, volunteer action and philanthropy, including private conservation reserves and covenants over private lands, are increasingly important to how biodiversity protection is funded. Sometimes private protection initiatives can implement costly biodiversity conservation initiatives governments cannot afford (Kamal, Grodzińska-Jurczak, & Brown, 2015). Historically, public and private governance initiatives have not been well coordinated due to institutional silos and the lack of the unified architecture for environmental governance that the *CBD* implies. However, public/private partnerships for environmental and social objectives are increasing, offering the potential for closer integration to provide greater impact.

Environmental protection and social justice issues are often interwoven because: marginalised groups may rely on nature for their living and welfare; the knowledge of people living with nature can facilitate protection and restoration; the welfare and cultural ties between Indigenous and Traditional peoples and biodiversity deserve to be valued; exploitation of nature often causes poverty and dispossession and other welfare injuries and some biodiversity protection strategies, such as exclusion from habitats or prohibition on uses can cause welfare problems. Such concerns for social justice have led to the blending of social and environmental interests in environmental governance. This is exemplified in the *CBD* with principles for equitable and sustainable use of biodiversity, concerning the interests of Indigenous and local communities, women and disadvantaged groups (Knox, 2017). The *Nagoya*

Protocol expands on this theme, and the Aichi Targets and the SDGs national commitments give effect to these principles. The Aichi Target 2 links biodiversity values to development and poverty reduction strategies; and Strategic Goal D aims to 'enhance the benefits to all from biodiversity and ecosystem services' with provisions for protecting ecosystems that provide human services, particularly for women, indigenous and local communities and poor and vulnerable people. The goal also mandates implementation of the *Nagoya Protocol*. Aichi Target 18 seeks respect for the cultural and knowledge connections of Indigenous and local communities, and their full and effective participation in biodiversity governance.

The 17 SDGs frame concern for biodiversity within the ambition to tackle poverty, sustainability, peace and prosperity. Countries undertake to pursue specific outcomes to address social ills, including poverty and hunger, deficiencies in health and education and equality. Within these social interest context, environmental goals are set for urban sustainability (Goal 11), responsible consumption and production (Goal 12), climate (Goal 13) and sustainable marine, coastal-marine and terrestrial ecosystems (Goals 14 and 15). There are many interactions between these goals that cannot be underestimated (Lim, Jørgensen, & Wyborn, 2018).

Achieving social and environmental goals, whether separately or combined, is proving elusive, as Sachs et al. (2019) note:

> Four years after the adoption of the SDGs and the Paris Agreement no country is on track to meeting all the goals. We are losing ground in many areas, as underscored by recent reports of the Intergovernmental Panel on Climate Change (Masson-Delmotte et al. 2018) and the Intergovernmental Science-Policy Platform on Biodiversity and Ecosystem Services (IPBES 2019). One million species are threatened with extinction, and IPBES notes that 'we are eroding the very foundations of our economies, livelihoods, food security, health and quality of life worldwide'. Our report concurs: high-income countries obtain their worst ratings on SDG 14 (Life Below water) and SDG 15 (Life on Land). Young people around the world are taking to the street to protest the lack of environmental action by governments and businesses.
>
> At the same time inequalities are rising around the world, driving calls for deep changes in the policies of developed and developing countries. Our report shows that some countries, including in sub-Saharan Africa, are progressing rapidly towards ending poverty, but extreme poverty remains entrenched in some parts of the world.
>
> (p. viii)

Insufficient effectiveness

There is much evidence about declining biodiversity around the world as well as in the two studied jurisdictions. The IUCN Red List (n.d.) provides detailed data on biodiversity loss by species and by country, and highlights

xxvi *Preface*

that the world is facing an 'extinction crisis'. At the time of writing, there are 28,000 species facing extinction, more than a quarter of all those that have been assessed. Some 'highlights' are mammals 25 per cent, conifers 34 per cent, birds 14 per cent, sharks and rays 30 per cent; reef corals 33 per cent and selected crustaceans 27 per cent. One study has found that 'current extinction rates are 1,000 times higher than natural background rates of extinction and future rates are likely to be 10,000 times higher' (De Vos et al., 2014). It is impossible to truly determine how many species have already disappeared since many species exist without having been catalogued and may have/will disappear without notice.

Apart from the IUCN red list, there are many other sources of data relevant to the outcomes of biodiversity protection. Examples include the Big Data for Biodiversity dataset (GBIF, n.d.); the Biodiversity Indicators database (BIP, n.d.) or the Global Register of Introduced Invasive Species (GRIIS, n.d.). It is possible to find descriptive information about biodiversity governance structures and strategies, and about institutions and institutional integrity from sites such as the CBD portal (n.d.) and the OECD (n.d.) *Policy Instruments for the Environment* database). What is lacking is systematic analysis of how international arrangements and national systems operate in practice, a necessary step to understanding environmental policy causes and effects at a national and international level, and to improve system performance.

There is an increasing awareness of the need for objective diagnosis of the implementation and effectiveness problem. Lack of properly conducted analysis of the effectiveness of legal norms in improving outcomes can lead to better designs of legal norms and legal strategies to create more effective governance systems (Leroy, 2011). The 2014 *Global biodiversity outlook 4* (Secretariat of the *CBD*, 2014) stated, for example:

> Extrapolations for a range of indicators suggest that based on current trends, pressures on biodiversity will continue to increase at least until 2020, and that the status of biodiversity will continue to decline. This is despite the fact that society's responses to the loss of biodiversity are increasing dramatically, and based on national plans and commitments are expected to continue to increase for the remainder of this decade. This may be partly due to time lags between taking positive actions and discernible positive outcomes. But it could also be because responses may be insufficient relative to pressures, such that they may not overcome the growing impacts of the drivers of biodiversity loss.
>
> (p. 4)

The need to shift the focus from creating more instruments towards far more effective implementation was clearly signalled in the Rio+20 (2012) document, *The future we want*:

> 19. We recognize that the twenty years since the Earth Summit in 1992 have seen uneven progress, including in sustainable development

and poverty eradication. We emphasise the need to make progress in implementing previous commitments. We also recognize the need to accelerate progress in closing development gaps between developed and developing countries, and to seize and create opportunities to achieve sustainable development through economic growth and diversification, social development and environment protection. To this end, we underscore the continued need for an enabling environment at the national and international levels, as well as continued and strengthened international cooperation, particularly in the areas of finance, debt, trade and technology transfer, as mutually agreed, and innovation, entrepreneurship, capacity-building, transparency and accountability. We recognize the diversification of actors and stakeholders engaged in the pursuit of sustainable development. In this context, we affirm the continued need for the full and effective participation of all countries, in particular developing countries, in global decision-making.

(p. 4)

Recognition of the need to pay attention to the effectiveness of governance systems was also signified with the IUCN Natural Resource Governance Framework, discussed later, which aims to create a 'basket of governance tools' including methods to objectively review and improve the quality of legal arrangements to support more effective and fair natural resource governance. It was this programme that was the genesis of the research reported in this book (see Commission on Environmental, Economic and Social Policy, n.d.).

The need for objective diagnosis

The Chief of Staff of the Organisation of American States (OAS) Secretary General, announcing a new initiative with the UNEP said 'it is our hope that this agreement will contribute to addressing the greatest challenge of our century: implementation' (De Zela, 2014). Despite such awareness of the importance of implementation, there have been relatively few attempts to comprehensively evaluate CBD underperformance (Young, 2011; see also UNEP, 2010).

The Secretariat of the CBD (Subsidiary Body on Scientific, Technical and Technological Advice. (2017) observes:

The available literature on evaluating effectiveness suggests that there are multiple documented options and approaches for assessing the effectiveness of measures. These approaches have different strengths and weaknesses and require varying levels of resources to implement. Given the different approaches that exist, Parties can choose the most appropriate approach for assessing the effectiveness of measures taken in line with their national biodiversity strategies and action plans. In fact, many Parties, in their fifth national reports, indicate the need to undertake assessments of effectiveness or note that plans were already underway to do so.

(para. 21)

xxviii   *Preface*

Differing perceptions about the performance of legal/political instruments and the causes of outcomes naturally lead to different views about possible solutions to the problems. Economic commentators will tend to point to pricing and market institutions and propose reforms of markets or new market instruments; biophysical scientists will often see gaps in data and analysis as major impediments to biodiversity protection; lawyers and politicians will suggest the need for new legal instruments to fill perceived gaps; citizen interest groups can be expected to highlight problems of insufficient resources and political activists may blame political failures. There is an implicit trade-off when allocating resources to any of the possible solutions, and an obvious potential for fragmented effort and wasted resources through pursuing competing paradigms or shifting between them. The lack of rational consensus limits the opportunity for coordination and clear accountability.

The rationale for this book

In summary, there is a strong social impetus to achieve sustainable use of nature; very many innovative governance arrangements are in place to achieve this but, overall, we are not achieving sufficient sustainability outcomes. The sustainability performance of countries depends on variables including the state and vulnerability of its remaining biodiversity, and many social, economical, institutional and political factors (Swanson et al., 2004) as well as international drivers that are largely beyond the control of any particular country. Transboundary issues include climate change, international air and water pollution, international fishing and the transboundary movement of invasive species. Governing environmentally harmful business activities can be difficult partly because free trade rules and political pressures limit how governments deal with foreign corporations. National sovereignty can also limit the enforcement of international agreements, and international arrangements largely rely on politically negotiated agreements.

This book examines effectiveness and implementation using a transparent, evidence-based approach to propose how biodiversity governance might be improved. This is a heroic go because many complex variables intersect to create the outcomes from any international principle or commitment and because there are so many instruments, articles and principles as well as cultural and historical issues involved.

This book focuses on legally binding international commitments. The 1992 *CBD*, ratified by Australia and Brazil, has its provisions incorporated into the national legislation of both these megadiverse countries. The convention principles are generally interpreted with reference to the 1972 *Stockholm Declaration*, which contains 26 principles for sustainability and development, and *the Rio Declaration* of 1992, which contains 27 principles for implementing the *Stockholm Declaration*. There is an emphasis on sustainable development obligations that are generally considered to be elements in applying the *CBD*.

As noted above, the convention articles impose stewardship obligations on the States Parties; the *Rio Declaration* of 1992, in particular, is an aid to interpreting the convention. The desires of so many people, and the existence of many governance instruments, should give confidence that a viable balance between human use of nature and natural biodiversity can be achieved. However, despite encouraging examples where protection and restoration have saved species and habitats, many studies show continuing declines in biodiversity. This could justify a pessimistic view that environmental governance cannot overcome the strong pressures for destruction of biodiversity. The more optimistic view, which informs this book, is that the effectiveness problem can be cured by learning from experience, to design and implement more effective strategies and instruments.

This book is a step on a journey. Following on from concerns about the effectiveness of environmental governance, there is an awakening interest in objective assessment of the performance of biodiversity instruments and governance systems. The *Environmental Rule of Law: First Global Report* (UNEP, 2019) is one step along this path. Our approach differs substantially from the methods used for that report because it aims to delve into the day-to-day dynamics of implementation, to explain in detail what works and what does not and why.

One fundamental conclusion we derive is that, while legal instruments are fundamental to effective governance, they are very far from sufficient. They are communicative instruments, to which meaning is attached (or not) by those to whom they are addressed. As the evidence in this book amply demonstrates, what happens after an instrument is created depends on many social, economic and political variables; and effective governance requires many complementary things to be in place to motivate and enable the behaviours sought through the instruments. This book will contribute to the dialogue that has now commenced.

Our gratitude

There are many people who have made a significant contribution to this work, and the work which preceded it.

The impetus for the initial work on these issues came from Justice Antonio Benjamin and Prof. Ben Boer from the World Commission on Environmental Law, and Dr. Alejandro Iza and Lydia Slobodian from the IUCN Environmental Law Centre. It relied on the support of many collaborators, in particular those who led the evaluation projects in the different countries, most of whom who have continued to contribute substantial effort: Karen Bubna-Litic, Solange Teles da Silva, Trevor Daya-Winterbottom, Qin Tianbao, Evan Hamman and Elmien Du Plessis. There have been many volunteers who contributed enormous effort and skill to carry out the work under this leadership.

There are, of course, the people who volunteered to work on the research that led to this book. Not all of them were able to continue that commitment

xxx *Preface*

through to the finished product, but their contribution was very important (and their companionship a boon).

Finally, the editors cannot heap enough praise on the head, Dr. Miriam Verbeek, our indefatigable, thorough, lovely and greatly talented editor. Her contribution went well beyond what an editor should be expected to do, and we really do appreciate it and value her for it.

References

BIP (Biodiversity Indicators Partnership) (n.d.). *Home page.* Retrieved from https://www.bipindicators.net/

CBD (Convention on Biological Diversity). (n.d.). *Home page.* Retrieved from https://www.cbd.int/

Chiabotti, T. J. (2004). *Evaluating corporate environmental strategy: A case study of six multinational companies.* (Masters Thesis). University of Florida.

Commission on Environmental, Economic and Social Policy. (n.d.). *Natural resource governance framework.* IUCN. Retrieved from https://www.iucn.org/commissions/commission-environmental-economic-and-social-policy/our-work/knowledge-baskets/natural-resource-governance

De Vos, J. M., Joppa, L. N., Gittleman, J. L., Stephens, P. R., & Pimm, S. L. (2014). Estimating the normal background rate of species extinction. *Conservation Biology, 29* (2), 452–462. doi: 10.1111/cobi.12380

De Zela, Hugo. (2014, November 10). *OAS and UNEP sign agreement on environmental rule of law and sustainable development.* Organization of American States (Press release). Retrieved from https://www.oas.org/en/media_center/press_release.asp?sCodigo=E-506/14.eco. (n.d.). *Ecolabel index.* Retrieved from http://www.ecolabel index.com/

Ecolex. (n.d.). *The gateway to environmental law.* Retrieved from https://www.ecolex.org

GBIF (Global Biodiversity Information Facility). (n.d.). *Free and open access to biodiversity data.* Retrieved from https://www.iucnredlist.org

GRIIS (Global Register of Introduced and Invasive Species). (n.d.). *Home page.* Retrieved from http://www.griis.org/

IUCN Red List. (n.d.). *The IUCN red list of threatened species.* Retrieved from https://www.iucnredlist.org/

Kamal, S., Grodzińska-Jurczak, M., & Brown, G. (2015). Conservation on private land: A review of global strategies with a proposed classification system. *Journal of Environmental Planning and Management, 58* (4), 576–597. doi: 10.1080/09640568.2013.875463

Knox, J. H. (2017). *Report of the Special Rapporteur on the issue of human rights obligations relating to the enjoyment of a safe, clean, healthy and sustainable environment: Biodiversity report.* (A/HRC/34/4) United Nations Human Rights Council.

Le Prestre, P. G. (Ed.). (2017). *Governing global biodiversity: The evolution and implementation of the convention on biological diversity.* London, UK & New York, NY: Routledge.

Leroy, Y. (2011). La notion d'effectivité du droit. (The notion of effectiveness of law). *Droit et société, 79* (3), 715–732. Retrieved from https://www.cairn.info/revue-droit-et-societe1-2011-3-page-715.htm

Lim, M. M. L., Jørgensen, P. S., & Wyborn, C. (2018). Reframing the sustainable development goals to achieve sustainable development in the Antropocene: A system approach. *Ecology and Society, 23* (3). doi: 10.5751/ES-10182-230322

Martin, P., Boer, B., & Slobodian, L. (2016). *Framework for assessing and improving law for sustainability: A legal component of a natural resource governance framework.* Bonn, Germany: IUCN Environment Law Centre.

OECD. (n.d.). *Database on policy instruments for the environmental.* Retrieved from http://www2.oecd.org/ecoinst/queries

Pirard, R. (2012). Market-based instruments for biodiversity and ecosystem services: A lexicon. *Environmental Science & Policy, 19–20,* 59–68. doi: 10.1016/j. envsci.2012.02.001

Rio+20. (2012). *The future we want.* (A/CONF.215/L.1*). UN.

Sachs, J., Schmidt-Traub, G., Kroll, C., Lafortune, G., & Fuller, G. (2019): *Sustainable development report 2019.* New York, NY: (SDSN).

Salzman, J. (2018, March). Global market for ecosystem services surges to $ 36 billion in annual transactions. *Legal Planet.*

Secretariat of the Convention on Biological Diversity. (2014). *Global biodiversity outlook 4: Summary and conclusions.* Montréal, Canada.

Subsidiary Body on Scientific, Technical and Technological Advice. (2017). *Tools to evaluate the effectiveness of policy instruments for the implementation of the strategic plan for biodiversity 2011–2020: Note by the executive secretary.* (CBD/SBSTTA/21/7). UNEP.

Swanson, D., Pinter, L., Bregha, F., Volkery, A., & Jacob, K. (2004). National strategies for sustainable development: Based on a 19-country analysis. doi: 10.1080/09669589808667311

UNDP. (n.d.). *REDD program.* Retrieved from https://www.un-redd.org

UNEP (2010) *Auditing the implementation of multilateral environmental agreements (MEAs): A primer for auditors.* Retrieved from https://www.eurosai.org/de/databases/products/Auditing-the-Implementation-of-Multilateral-Environmental-Agreements-MEAs-A-Primer-for-Auditors/

UNEP (2019). Environmental rule of law: First global report. Nairobi: UNEP. Retrieved from https://wedocs.unep.org/bitstream/handle/20.500.11822/27279/Environmental_rule_of_law.pdf?sequence=1&isAllowed=y

Young, O. R. (2011). Effectiveness of international environmental regimes: Existing knowledge, cutting-edge themes, and research strategies. *PNAS, 108*(50), 19853–19860. doi: 10.1073/pnas.1111690108

Acronyms and abbreviations

ABR	Algodão Brasileira Responsável – Responsible Brazilian Cotton
ABSF	Australian Beef Sustainability Framework
ACT	Australian Capital Territory
ADIC	Australian Dairy Industry Council
ALMG	Legislative Assembly of Minas Gerais
ANA	National Water Agency (Brazil)
ANM	National Mining Agency (Brazil)	
APP	Permanent Preservation Areas
ASPG	Guarda do Embaú Preservation and Surfing Association
BCI	Better Cotton Initiative
BFS	Brazilian Forest Service
BMP	Best Management Program
CETEM	Mineral Technology Centre (Brazil)
CIF	Inter-Federation Committee
CNRH	National Council of Resources – Water Resources (Brazil)
COAG	Council of Australian Governments
CONAMA	National Council for the Environment
CONABIO	National Biodiversity Commission
CPRM	Mineral Resources Research Company
DNPM	National Department of Mineral Production (Brazil)
DSF	Dairy Sustainability Framework
EDO	Environmental Defenders Office ||
EIA	Environmental Impact Assessment
ES	Espírito Santo
EU	European Union
ETEPs	Espaços Territoriais Especialmente Protegidos (especially protected special spaces)
FAO	Food and Agricultural Organization
FEPALE	Pan-American Dairy Federation (Federacion Panamericana de Lecheria)
GBR	Great Barrier Reef
GDAA	Global Dairy Agenda of Action
GM	Genetically modified

xxxiv *Acronyms and abbreviations*

GMO	Genetically modified organisms
GRI	Global Reporting Initiative
GTPS	Grupo de Trabalho da Pecuária Sustentável (Brazilian Roundtable on Sustainable Livestock)
HACZ	Historical Anthopological Cultural Zone
IBAMA	Brazilian Institute of Environment and Natural Renewable Resources
ICAC	NSW Independent Commission Against Corruption
ICMBio	Chico Mendes Institute
IFCP	International Forum for Cotton Promotion
ILUAs	Indigenous Land Use Agreements
IPAs	Indigenous Protected Areas
ISO	International Sugar Organization
ITMF	International Textile Manufacturers Federation
MT	Mato Grosso
MDBA	Murray Darling Basin Authority
MG	Minas Gerais, Brazil
MMA	Ministry of the Environment (Brazil)
MME	Ministry of Mines and Energy (Brazil)
MP	comprises MPY and public prosecutors offices of member states
MPA	Marine Protected Area
MPF	Federal Public Attorney's Office (Brazil)
MPs	Management Plans
MPU	Federal Prosecutors (Brazil)
NGO	Non-government organisation
NP	National Park
NRGF	Natural Resource Governance Framework
NRM	natural resource management
NSRs	National Surfing Reserves
NSW	New South Wales, Australia
NT	Northern Territory
NWI	National Water Initiative
OECD	Organisation for Economic Co-operation and Development
PA	Protected area
PES	Payment for Ecosystem Service
PNRH	National Policy for Water Resources
PPP	Polluter Pays Principle |
PRONAF	National Program for the Strengthening of Family Agriculture
PRP	Polluter Recipient Principle
QLD	Queensland, Australia |
REDD+	Collaborative Programme on Reducing Emissions from Deforestation and Forest Degradation in Developing Countries
SA	South Australia

SDG	Sustainable Development Goal
SEMAD	Secretariat of Environment
SGM	Secretarial of Geology, Mining and Mineral Transformation (Brazil)
SISNAMA	National Environmental System of Brazil
SOE	States of the Environment
TTAC	Transaction and conduct adjustment agreement (Termo de Transação e de ajustamento de conduta)
UCs	Conservation Units
VE	Voluntary Easement
VIC	Victoria
WA	Western Australia
WSRs	World Surfing Reserves

1 The issues, methods and evidence

Paul Martin, Márcia Dieguez Leuzinger, and Solange Teles da Silva

Abstract

This chapter explains the background, methods and overall content of this book. It discusses why an evidence-based policy research method is best suited to conduct objective analysis of environmental law and policy issues; and it outlines the steps in the development and application of this approach. It provides an overview of the contents of this book.

Introduction

Human progress is more reliable when it is based on empirically grounded, peer-validated theory. Deduction based solely on transparent analysis of empirical data is the 'gold standard' of scientific objectivity. Architectural (as distinct from tactical) governance design should reflect objective, evidence-based understanding about what combinations of institutions, organisational arrangements, strategies and implementation activities are likely to work.

Governance implementation involves factual, subjective and political variables that are often not objectively measurable. A purely data-based deduction is often not feasible and innovative research methods are required to ensure objectivity and integrity (Martin & Craig, 2015). Biodiversity governance issues can involve many complex social, ecological, economic and political systems and politics, community values and socio–ecological dynamics are often important to what happens (see e.g. Calatrava & Martínez-Granados, 2017; Martin, Boer, & Slobodian, 2016; Phromlah, 2013; Stavins, 2001; Young, 2011). Concepts of justice and fairness require consideration of values, and strategy involves judgement about future conditions that cannot be empirically tested until they happen. The many potential impediments to implementation of environmental programmes, including natural causes, failures of political will, pressure from interests, weak governments (including parliaments) and cultural factors (among others) (see, e.g. Bovens & Hart, 1996; Howes et al., 2017; Martin & Williams, 2010), should also be considered.

2 *Paul Martin et al.*

Complexity and subjectivity limit the investigators' ability to use purely deductive, data-driven, methods. This does not, however, eliminate the need for objectivity, transparency and reliance on sound theory.

> Legal governance of the environment involves many instruments, often reflecting apparently competing social purposes such as seeking to protect the environment at the same time as producing wealth from natural resources. The resulting complexity reflects the diversity of modern society, but it frustrates simple deductive analysis. An additional consideration is that effectiveness is multi-dimensional, involving considerations such as the receptiveness of society, the economic capacity of communities and governments, and the dynamics of power. Proving causal links between a law and an outcome is sometimes impossible and always complicated. Best practice evaluation aims to rely only on objective facts, rather than subjective information. However legal aspects of governance do involve subjective values. Concepts like justice and fairness cannot be ignored because of analytic difficulties, and legitimate differences in views, or political realities, should not be trivialised. For many performance variables, objective data is not available, or it is costly and difficult to obtain.
>
> (Martin et al., 2016, p. 3)

An evidence-based policy approach is used in public policy research to cope with such complexities. The analysis often involves multiple methods and thus relies on diverse types and sources of data to generate and evaluate evidence. Evidence from different sources is 'triangulated' to provide a reliable basis for inferences when pure deduction is not feasible. The significant differences between an evidence-based policy approach and pure science are the ability to accommodate non-objective considerations (such as values and political trade-offs); the use of transparent assumptions to infer probable facts when complete data are not available and reaching conclusions based on both data and the investigators' judgement. Good practice in evidence-based policy research requires that the conclusions are firmly based on evidence, that the evidence is available to be interrogated and that the judgement is transparent. These are essential integrity requirements in research, regardless of what methods are used (see Jensen, 2013; Majchrzak, 1984; Martin & Craig, 2015).

Evidence-based approaches are consistent with legal traditions. Judges in law courts apply standards of likelihood, such as 'beyond reasonable doubt' or 'on the balance of probabilities', to factual evidence to arrive at judgements. These often must involve non-objective considerations, such as values and beliefs, and consider the effects of context. Transparency is possible by disclosing evidence and the rationale for judgements – though judges are not universally transparent or rational, as explained by Rodriguez (2013) in terms of 'zones of autarchy' in their judgements. Critical peer review occurs because judgements are scrutinised by the legal profession and scholars.

In this book we analyse data from Australia (a wealthy common law country) and Brazil (a developing civil law jurisdiction – but with elements of common law jurisdiction) to find evidence concerning the implementation of governance of various terrestrial and marine biodiversity issues. The data we reviewed included domestic and international law and policy materials, biodiversity databases, technologies and discussions with key informants. Our discussion is broad-ranging though it recognises data gaps, including those caused by databases that have disappeared from public access in Brazil as we finalised this book. We triangulated the various sources of data to provide the evidence that support our conclusions.

Under its 2013–2016 programme, the International Union for the Preservation of Nature (IUCN) initiated a programme to develop a Natural Resource Governance Framework (NRGF) in response to concerns about the effectiveness of biodiversity protection. The NRGF was led by the Commission on Environmental, Economic and Social Policy. Alongside other investigations The World Commission on Environmental Law, the IUCN Secretariat (Social Policy, Nature-based Solutions & Rights Group) and Environmental Law Centre commenced a sub-project on the legal aspects of the NRGF. The focus of the sub-project was developing and testing a method to evaluate the implementation and effectiveness of principles from the Convention on Biological Diversity (*CBD*). The stated intention was:

> [T]o develop, using an inclusive and collaborative process, methods to measure whether environmental and natural resources law as implemented is supporting progress toward the IUCN vision of 'a just world that values and conserves nature'. Objective evaluation of the performance of environmental law must be at the heart of any credible process for systematic improvement in the effectiveness of governance. Whilst best practice evaluation aims at measurement of verifiable facts to the maximum degree possible, governance (and in particular the legal aspects of governance) involves many subjective values. Even apparently objective facts will reflect subjective choices and power relationships. Many aspects of legal governance, and therefore the evaluation of governance, are contestable. This is why systematic evaluation of the legal aspects of governance is likely to require new methods and new data, and it may involve challenges to established beliefs about the role and effectiveness of legal institutions.
>
> (Martin, Boer, Byrner, & Greiber, 2013, p. 3)

The method was developed and documented. Volunteer collaborators drawn from members of the IUCN Academy of Environmental Law agreed to participate, with teams of volunteers conducting evaluations within Australia (two investigations), Brazil, New Zealand, South Africa and China (one

4   *Paul Martin et al.*

each). These trial evaluations were restricted to the participation (community engagement) and precautionary principles. The final report was published in 2016 (Martin et al., 2016).

The investigations demonstrated the value of a disciplined evidence-based method, and generated four propositions related to the *CBD*.

1   Faithful translation of broad principles from international environmental conventions into clear and feasible laws within a jurisdiction is not certain. Governments can be selective in what they adopt into local policy and law, and reinterpret principles for political and administrative purposes. This can undermine implementation. The report suggested that successful implementation would be more likely if, at the design stage, the tangible purpose and operation of a norm, and how it should be implemented through the law, was specified.
2   How implementation instruments and arrangements fit with domestic socio-economic and institutional contexts is important to effectiveness. The six investigations identified jurisdiction-specific issues about institutions, culture and feasibility that limited effectiveness. The evaluation suggested the need for three forms of alignment: fit with the biophysical context; with the social-economic, political and cultural context; and with the total system of natural resource governance in the jurisdiction.
3   The feasibility of implementation may be a problem for implementing agencies and for citizens or organisations who are the objects of governance. Regardless of rules or incentives, if an actor does not have the resources to do what is required, effective action cannot happen. The authors highlight that economic issues are fundamental, confirming that the weight of resources for or against environmental values will substantially shape governance outcomes. The evaluations indicate that environmental instruments should aim to 'tilt' economic and social resources towards supporting sustainability. They also suggest that more attention needs to be paid to fiscal and other resourcing issues in implementation of legal governance (Martin, Boer, and Slobodian 2016, pp. 117–118).
4   Arrangements to ensure the integrity of implementation by government agencies are critical to ensure disciplined and effective implementation. This includes systems to monitor agency compliance with administrative and substantive provisions and safeguards against 'agency capture' by powerful interests. In none of the jurisdictions examined was there a sufficiently strong independent body exercising effective oversight of implementation.

The study concluded:

> [N]orms for protecting and restoring the environment compete with norms that encourage its exploitation. This highlights the need to focus on the balance between harm-doing and protection in legal arrangements for natural resource governance, rather than focusing only the

protective aspects of governance. Governance instruments (whether legal or otherwise) are essential but are only part of what is needed. They will not work well if conditions are hostile, or if implementation resources are not available to those responsible for implementation or people 'at the front line'. This suggests the need for more attention to economic and political feasibility issues, affecting those governing and for those being governed, in implementing legal governance.

(Martin et al., 2016, p. 113)

The in-country team leaders subsequently decided to extend evaluation to the full set of *CBD* commitments made by countries to provide an independent 'report card' on implementation. The method was modified to facilitate comparisons and a consolidated view of implementation. Twelve questions based on the text of the *CBD*, supplemented as appropriate by the *Rio Declaration*, were used to focus on specific commitments.

1 Is the signatory state implementing sound strategies to protect the environment (art. 6), considering intergenerational equity (Rio principle 3)?
2 Does the signatory state have a reliable biodiversity monitoring system (art. 7)?
3 Does the signatory have a robust system of *in-situ* protection of biodiversity (art. 8)?
4 Does the signatory have a system to manage *ex-situ* species preservation (art. 9)?
5 Is there a reliable system to govern biodiversity resources for sustainable use (art. 10)?
6 Does the signatory have a system of incentives to protect biodiversity (art. 11), including application of the polluter pays principle and appropriate economic structures (Rio principle 16)?
7 Is the signatory implementing a reliable system of environmental impact assessment (art. 14)?
8 Are there suitable mechanisms that provide adequate funding for the purposes of the convention (art. 20)?
9 Does the signatory state have a viable environmental Impact assessment and protective regime (Rio principles 4 and 17)?
10 Does the signatory state have an effective system of environmental laws/ governance (Rio principle 22)?
11 Has the signatory state addressed patterns of production and consumption and trade (Rio principles 8, 12–14)?
12 Based on the available evidence, is the signatory state meeting its obligation to incorporate the precautionary principle into its resource governance system (*CBD* Preamble and Rio principle 15)?

In the *CBD* itself, Indigenous people and women's interests are given limited attention, but the *Rio Declaration* supplements this, and later international

6   *Paul Martin et al.*

instruments emphasise this aspect of biodiversity protection. Three matters indicate implementation of the commitment to recognise/protect people's biodiversity interests, including in genetic material.

1   Whether the state has a system that ensures respect for Indigenous and Traditional people's interests, ensuring equitable benefit sharing and cultural respect for their interest in genetic resources (*CBD* Preamble, *CBD* art. 8, 10, 15 and Rio principle 22).
2   Whether the state has a system to ensure respect for women's interests in biodiversity (*CBD* Preamble and *Rio* principle 20).
3   Whether the state has a reliable system for citizen participation in managing biodiversity (Rio principle 10).

This study has not yet been completed, but the framework shows how to consolidate a comparative research of the *CBD*'s implementation.

Biodiversity governance in Brazil and Australia

The need for a richer understanding of the dynamics of implementation suggested the need for more detailed qualitative investigation of the dynamics and results of the implementation of the *CBD* before going deeper in the study that described above. Professors Martin (University of New England – UNE, New South Wales, Australia), Leuzinger (Centro Universitário de Brasília – UniCEUB, Brasília, Brazil) and Teles da Silva (Universidade Presbiteriana Mackenzie – UPM, São Paulo, Brazil) recruited a team of collaborators from within and outside their institutions: from Australia, the UNE, Queensland University of Technology, University of South Australia and Western Sydney University and from Brazil, the UniCEUB, UPM, Universidade de Brasília and Universidade do Distrito Federal. This book reports on that research.

An initial desktop comparative study (Martin, Leuzinger, & Teles da Silva, 2016) was carried out to scope out the proposed research. It identified:

> In both jurisdictions, governments have demonstrated a willingness to put in place various laws and other institutional arrangements with the intention of meeting biodiversity objectives. In both countries much can be said that is positive about this formal step.
>
> In both jurisdictions, economic and political pressures for farming expansion (in particular) have resulted in severe compromises of implementation. In both countries the contest between environmental protection and farm economics continues to be the main feature of the implementation of biodiversity protection law. Traditional regulation is substantially impeded by both this contest and the underlying economic and social problems of attempting to enforce the law. It is clear that the effectiveness of biodiversity protection laws is well short of what is needed, and that the causes for failure are complex. This suggests that the types of instruments

and strategies being used are ill suited. A lot more innovation and probably a lot more resources are needed for effective implementation.

In both countries, political commitment is not followed by resourcing to fulfill that commitment, and in both countries the reports on implementation of the *CBD* are not characterised by rigorous independent analysis. Political rhetoric over rides the type of objective scientific and governance scrutiny that is needed. Issues of social justice are deeply embedded in these problems. The issues are slightly different because of the differing history, but in both poverty and Indigenous people's (and, in Brazil, also Traditional communities) issues are important variables that both complicate the achievement of biodiversity objectives but also offer the potential to combine environmental protection with social justice improvement.

(p. 37)

Table 1.1 provides summary data on the two jurisdictions.

The initial scoping identified that, in both countries and across diverse environmental issues, effective implementation of biodiversity protection is not being achieved. There were indications of patterns consistent with what was tentatively concluded by the 2016 trial of the evaluation method. The scoping study provided a list of possible topics for research to ensure coverage of different biophysical and social environments (e.g. terrestrial, marine, public and private lands) and situations (e.g. different types of resource uses, user categories, resource competitions, disasters and conflicts). The next step was to conduct further preliminary studies of selected topics in each country, with the intention to then carry out parallel and/or comparative investigations reported in this book.

The scoping study demonstrates that Brazil and Australia often have contrasting approaches to otherwise common biodiversity issues. Both countries host substantial agricultural, mining and fishing industries that are export oriented, and have Indigenous and Traditional peoples whose welfare is interwoven with nature. They are of roughly equivalent size, have a tri-level federal government system, sit in the same hemisphere and have parallels in terms of climate and the state of natural conditions – though species and other biophysical differences are significant. These similarities provide the opportunity for conducting a comparative analysis that contrasts biodiversity protection under different laws and socio-political cultures and different legal traditions.

The 17 listed megadiverse countries have unique species, jurisprudential traditions and ecological, social and economic systems (for details see Biodiversity a to z, n.d.). With the exception of the US and Australia, they are economically developing, which limits their economic and institutional capacity. The Group of Like-Minded Megadiverse Countries was formed in 2002, to pursue shared environmental, economic and social goals. Membership is not co-extensive with the generally identified list of megadiverse countries (see LLMC, 2014). Brazil and Australia are among these 'megadiverse' countries.

8 *Paul Martin et al.*

Table 1.1 Comparison of *CBD* relevant statistics Brazil–Australia

	Brazil	*Australia*
Surface area (2018)	8,515,770 sq km	7,741,220 sq km
Population (2018)	209 million	25 million
Gross National Income per person (2018)	US$32,099	US$71,609
Forest cover (2016)	59% of landmass	16% of landmass
Economic equality (Gini co-efficient, 0 = equality)	53.9	34.7
Environmental Performance indicators, biodiversity and habitat protection (2018)	60.7 score Ranking 69th	74 score Ranking 21st
Species under threat (2018)	80 mammal species 558 higher plant species 93 fish species 175 bird species	63 mammal species 108 higher plant species 93 fish species 52 bird species
Protected areas (2018)	17.2% of landmass 26.6% of marine area	16.25% of landmass (10 008 areas) 36.2% of marine area (300 areas)
Governing structure	Federation, with 26 states + Federal District and 5.570 municipalities. Environmental governance responsibilities are divided between national, state and municipality bodies (all those entities integrate the SISNAMA (National Environmental System).	Federation, with 8 states and territories. Environmental governance responsibilities are divided between national, state and 565 local councils, with 56 regional natural resource management organisations.
Biodiversity Convention Ratification year	1994	1993

Source: Updated from Martin, Leuzinger, and Teles da Silva (2016).

Brazil and Australia follow different legal systems. Australia is a British common law jurisdiction. The common law is, in effect, based on the consolidation of English customary laws extant at the time of the Norman conquest (of England) in 1066, which has evolved through judicial interpretation and the jurisprudence of precedent (see Hathaway, 2003; Stone, 1964). In common law countries, many legal rules derive from historical legal precedents. Constitutional change through parliamentary process is, at least in Australia, US and the UK, relatively rare. Constitutional change under the common law is largely driven by the 'accident' of what issues are litigated as courts, particularly the highest courts provide an evolutionary mechanism through statutory interpretation and common law doctrine.

Brazil, following the Portuguese tradition, is a Civil Law country. Public servants and agencies can only act when a law authorises their action (principle of legality). Although some lacunae in legislation can be remedied by judicial decisions, legislation has a central role in public governance. For this reason, the political arrangements between the Executive and the parliament determine what government will or will not be able to do. In the last decade, because farming interests have been strong in the Brazilian parliament, environment protection legislation has been undermined to reduce constraints on agriculture. The courts have had a significant role in preserving environmental protections through interpretation of legislation, following decisions made by superior courts; thus, even though Brazil has a civil law legal system, the adoption of the *New Code of Civil Procedure of 2015* (*Federal Law no. 13.105/2015*) brought to the legal system elements of common law, that is, the use of precedent in courts.

The mechanisms for change in environmental law, including how international arrangements are implemented in domestic law, vary in their detail, but both countries rely on the combination of statutes, administrative rules and judicial interpretation. Many rules have evolved along parallel lines, reflecting an international *zeitgeist* ('spirit of the age'). In both countries, implementation of convention obligations involves not only laws but also public funding, communication and political persuasion. Though there are competing definitions of and perspectives on what environmental governance is, all involve the characteristic of governing (i.e. managing, controlling, regulating) individual or collective human behaviours that impact on nature (see Jessop, 2003; Kaufmann, Kraay, & Zoido-lobatón, 1999); Leach et al., 2007; Torfing, Sorensent, & Piel Christensen, 2003; Weiss, 2000). Within the governance mix, legal implementation can involve regulation, administrative decisions, judicial decisions and implementation actions such as policing and enforcement. Private law is also involved through contracts and property rights, which also rely on public law. An example of this intersection is marketised rights to the environment, such as biodiversity banking, water trading and implementation of the REDD+ initiative (Freeman & Kolstad, 2007; OECD, 2007; Pirard, 2012).

Biodiversity governance in Australia

A credible assessment of the outcomes of Australia's biodiversity protection is provided by national state of environment reports (SOEs). Prepared every few years by a government appointed group of scientists, a number of reports provide an independent scientific evaluation of the biophysical state of the environment. Supporting resources, including a great deal of data, are also accessible (Department of the Environment and Energy, n.d.). The Overview of state and trends of biodiversity from the 2016 State of Environment Report (Australia: State of the Environment, 2016a) states:

> [T]he status of biodiversity in Australia is generally considered poor and deteriorating … Grazing in the extensive land-use zone of Australia is considered a major threat to biodiversity … considered a key pressure on

northern Australian mammal populations ... Birds show variable trends, but some groups ... are in significant decline ...

Very limited information is available to assess the state and trends of reptiles, amphibians and invertebrates, except for a few high-profile species.

As at December 2015, the numbers of threatened species and threatened ecological communities listed under the EPBC Act stood as follows:

- 74 ecological communities, of which 31 were listed as critically endangered, 41 as endangered and 2 as vulnerable; 27 of these are new listings since 2011 ...
- 480 animal species, including 55 listed as extinct or extinct in the wild, an increase of 44 species since 2011 ...
- 1294 plant species, including 37 species listed as extinct ... Movements within the list include an increase of 31 species in the critically endangered category, and a decrease in the number of species in the endangered and vulnerable categories because of (listing changes) ...

The condition of terrestrial habitats in Australia has been influenced by historical land clearing, degradation and fragmentation ... 24 broad vegetation communities ... have lost at least 20 per cent of their original extent, and ... 9 per cent ... have lost more than 40 per cent of their original extent ... Although clearing rates have mostly stabilised, habitat fragmentation continues ... Small patches are more likely to be cleared and are susceptible to deterioration of condition.

The SOE (Australia: State of the Environment, 2016b) evaluations do not diagnose governance systems or implementation of international obligations. They do, however, provide general opinions about the effectiveness of environmental protection.

In the past 5 years (2011–2016), environmental policies and management practices in Australia have achieved improvements in the state and trends of parts of the Australian environment. Australia's built environment, natural and cultural heritage, and marine and Antarctic environments are generally in good condition ... However, a number of key challenges to the effective management of the Australian environment remain:

- An overarching national policy that establishes a clear vision for the protection and sustainable management of Australia's environment to the year 2050 is lacking. Such a programme needs to be supported by ... specific action programmes and policy to preserve and, where necessary, restore natural capital ... complementary policy and strengthened legislative frameworks ... efficient, collaborative and complementary planning and decision-making processes ... with clear lines of accountability.
- Poor collaboration and coordination of policies, decisions and management arrangements exists across sectors ...
- Follow-through from policy to action is lacking.

The issues, methods and evidence   11

- Data and long-term monitoring are inadequate.
- Resources for environmental management and restoration are insufficient.
- The understanding of … cumulative impacts is inadequate …

Meeting these challenges requires:

- integrated policies and adaptive management actions …
- national leadership
- improved support for decision-making
- a more strategic focus on planning for a sustainable future
- new, reliable sources of financing.

Australia's fifth national report on implementation of the *CBD* (Department of the Environment, 2014) draws on the 2011 SOE for indicators of changes to the state of the environment. The sixth report is under preparation. Unfortunately, the *CBD* Secretariat requirements do not require performance-improvement self-review, or independent peer assessment of country reports. It is possible, for example, for a national government to lodge convention reviews (compliant with Secretariat instructions) that mask where public initiatives or non-government actions have failed or have had little effect on major biodiversity issues. Though countries are required to have a national biodiversity strategy and to report on its implementation, the Parties are not required to report implementation against each *CBD* requirement, nor review the performance of their biodiversity governance system *per se*.

Australia's fifth national report illustrates these limitations. It provides a description of the legal arrangements and biodiversity protection mechanisms put in place by the Australian government. Reading these reports gives an optimistic sense about implementation, and, by inference, effectiveness of the convention in Australia. In particular, progress on a network of protected areas and a suite of laws and government programmes indicates a serious commitment to the convention (Department of the Environment, 2014, Parts II & III). The discussion of biodiversity outcomes provides a less positive and more qualified picture.

The tone and content of the report is illustrated by the following extract.

Recent State of the Environment reports and previous national reports, including those submitted to the CBD, have expressed moderate to high levels of concern about the decline in many groups of fauna in Australia. These reports frequently acknowledge that data is inadequate to draw firm conclusions about which groups may be declining and by how much. Many of the concerns stem from known pressures and their effects on biota rather than reliable data on the distribution and abundance of the species themselves … In many cases, it is not possible to draw conclusions about trends in the state of animal species groups and sometimes it is not possible to draw confident conclusions about the state of the taxon itself.

(Department of the Environment, 2014, p. 10)

12 *Paul Martin et al.*

A reader would not find a diagnosis of why biodiversity loss continues at such a pace, despite the many national government initiatives. They would not find, for example, analysis of state or local government actions, nor of the role of private actors and private governance, nor discussion of resourcing challenges. The report provides information, but little useful intelligence about how to improve outcomes.

Commentaries by non-government experts are more critical of Australia's implementation of the CBD and other instruments, suggesting opportunities to improve governance to meet CBD commitments (see Chapter 11). While it is understandable that government will not be openly self-critical, a more reflective approach could facilitate improvement and provide a clearer indication to the public about how the management of natural assets is performing.

Biodiversity governance in Brazil

The last Brazilian National Report on implementation of the CBD was released in 2015 (MMA, 2016). The major threats to biodiversity are listed as: (1) disorganised expansion of agriculture, (2) invasive species, (3) deforestation, (4) fire, (5) climate change, (6) threats to marine and coastal habitats and (7) pollution. Government plans to protect biodiversity are: (1) review of legislation, (2) creation of protected areas, (3) restoration of vegetation, (4) sustainable forest management, (5) integrated landscape management, (6) conservation action plans, (7) sustainability of agricultural production and (8) use of native biodiversity.

It is interesting to note that the Report lists the primary threat to biodiversity as the 'disorganised expansion of agriculture' but that sustainability of agricultural production is low down in the list of actions. A review of legislation is listed as a primary action but, since 2003, when agricultural interests achieved political dominance of environmental policy in the Brazilian parliament, Brazilian policy has become far less protective of biodiversity, as well as Indigenous and Traditional people's land interests. For example, the replacement legislation for the *Biosecurity Law* (*Federal Law No. 11.105/2005*) removes authority over environmental licensing of GMOs from the environmental agency. The *National System of Conservation Units Law* (*SNUC Law*) (*Federal Law no. 9.985/2000*) now allows transgenic plants in some conservation units and the 1965 *Forest Code* (*Federal Law no. 4.771/1965*) has been replaced by the 2012 *Forest Code* (*Federal Law no. 12.651/2012*) which is less restrictive of commercial exploitation of protected areas.

The stated priorities of the Brazilian government give cause for concerns: even though land clearing and water pollution from agriculture and other agricultural risks are a major threat to biodiversity, addressing the biodiversity impacts of agricultural production is a low priority for the government. Modifications to environmental protection legislation since 2003 indicate that legislative reform is focused on 'red tape' reduction and weakening constraints on agriculture.

The issues, methods and evidence   13

Expanding protected areas, the second listed priority, has been pursued, though there are problems of effectiveness, as discussed in Chapters 2, 5, 8 and 10. The area of conservation units (a category of protected area) has increased, but progress has been gradual and not all biomes and marine areas are represented. For example, according to the Ministry of the Environment, between 2010 and 2016 there were no increases in protected areas in the caatinga, pampas, pantanal and marine biomes (MMA, n.d.).

For the Aichi targets, though few indicators are available, the Brazilian Fifth National Report provides an indication of implementation based on various data. The report shows that, of the 46 elements that compose the 20 Aichi Targets, 37 are progressing towards the target but at insufficient rate to meet it by 2020; three have not shown significant progress; five are on track to meet the target by its deadline and only one is expected to meet the target before 2020. Quantitatively, only 13 per cent of the targets are expected to be met on the set deadline.

At the start of 2019, it was expected that the target to reduce the loss rate of native environments (compared to the 2009 rates) in at least 50 per cent in the Amazon region would be achieved. Recent increases in deforestation of the Amazon make this unlikely. Brazil's National Institute for Space Research reported a 29 per cent increase in deforestation rates from August 2015 to July 2016, with clearing of more than 3,000 square miles of rainforest (see, further, Chapter 8). The President of Brazil continues to encourage further exploitation, promoting forest clearing for agriculture and mining even in protected areas (Phillips, 2019a). Expansion has been facilitated by re-structuring and de-funding environmental protection agencies and removing public servants and scientists considered to be opponents to this.

A consequence of this government was the extremely tardy response to the oil spill that has affected the northeast coast of Brazil in 2019. This disaster is the worst oil disaster the country has ever faced, affecting coastal and marine biodiversity, including mangroves, beaches and coral reefs, many in coastal protected areas, as well as Traditional Peoples (or populations). It required the Brazilian's Federal public prosecutor to request the courts cause the government to activate the national plan to minimise environmental and social damages (Phillips, 2019b).

The Aichi targets that are unlikely to be met include: (1) sustainable management practices incorporated into forestry, ensuring the conservation of biodiversity; (2) conservation of 30 per cent of the Amazon region by protected areas; (3) increased resilience of ecosystems and contribution of biodiversity for carbon stocks through conservation and recovery actions in the Amazon; (4) strengthening of science and technologies to provide knowledge about biodiversity, its values, trends and the consequences of their loss; (5) finalisation of the compilation of the existing records of fauna, flora and micro biota, aquatic and terrestrial, made available in free access permanent databases. Of the 51 National Targets for Biodiversity, only two targets were achieved, with progress in 14 others (MMA, 2016, p. 157). In common with Australia, Brazil's 5th National Report does not diagnose the performance shortfalls

14 *Paul Martin et al.*

of its biodiversity strategy, nor assess the value or durability of the reported achievements.

Initial investigations

As explained above, our intention was to use a detailed evidence-based investigation to better understand how the structures and dynamics of biodiversity protection in the two countries create the unsatisfactory outcomes being achieved; and on this basis recommend matters for further investigation or action that should improve the effectiveness of international arrangements. The underlying commitment was to scientific standards of objectivity and transparency but using a method that accommodates the unavoidable constraints of investigations of very complex public policy matters.

To enable transparency and objectivity we 'triangulated' evidence, conducting multiple investigations in both countries, to identify common phenomena and issues to support reasonable inferences. Mickwitz (2003) notes, in relation to policy evaluation that

> [f]our types of triangulations can be distinguished: multiple methods; multiple data sources within one method; multiple analysts; and multiple theories. The many methods that could be used include statistical analyses of data at different levels of aggregation, qualitative analyses of documents, questionnaires and thematic interviews.
>
> (p. 429)

In this book, we present evidence about many biodiversity governance situations in two countries. Though the evidence about particular instances will often not be complete or sufficient to support heroic inferences about biodiversity governance, the accumulation of examples and data provide a basis for confidence in the conclusions we have reached. At the very least, we have provided valuable evidence and clear arguments that will enable objective debate about the conclusions we have reached – the reader does not have to rely on our judgement, there is enough provided for them to exercise their own.

Twenty-eight researchers from Australia and Brazil, mainly from legal backgrounds, examined biodiversity governance issues in each jurisdiction identified in an initial scoping study. Over approximately eight months, individual investigators gathered evidence on specific issues, following the four level hierarchy set out in Martin et al. (2016). Individual reports were prepared and circulated for discussion. These were later published in Leuzinger, Martin, Santana, and de Souza (2019).

The researchers then participated in a five-day workshop in Australia in November 2017. The investigations were grouped around roughly analogous facts or governance issues. Each investigator presented their preliminary data and findings, which were discussed by the larger group. Ample time was also allowed for informal discussion between the researchers.

The issues, methods and evidence 15

Subsequently a synthesis workshop took place to identify patterns from the evidence that had been obtained. The workshop involved three sub-groups, with bilingual team members distributed throughout to assist communication. After the sub-groups had completed their deliberations, they proposed the patterns that they had identified. A final consolidation generated 11 indicative propositions, intended for further investigation.

1 Different interpretations of (and approaches to applying interpretation of) *CBD* principles shape biodiversity governance. The application of *CBD* principles reflects a country's political and legal approach, for example whether rights are legislated or constitutionalised. This reflects historical traditions and the influence of political and economic power-holder views about biodiversity (and their interests in biodiversity).

2 Different approaches to protected areas are possible given interpretations of the application of the IUCN Protected Area categories (see also Farrier et al., 2013). Many variables affect the extent and types of habitat protection, the rate at which representative habitat protection is achieved and the integrity of protected areas and strategies. Fiscal arrangements are particularly important to protection.

3 Compromises to the integrity of the implementation of *CBD*-related policies often occur, even if rules are embedded by law. Sources of implementation compromise can include political dynamics, economic interests, mismanagement and corruption and agency choices about what is feasible or desirable to implement.

4 The accountability arrangements used by governments to monitor and report on, and hopefully improve, implementation of the *CBD* are important for biodiversity protection. Strong meta-governance is particularly important when there are significant economic and political pressures against conservation.

5 Constitutional, jurisdictional and organisational arrangements including, for example, civil or common law traditions create different approaches to biodiversity governance. However, legal architectures do not seem to be fundamental to the dynamics of biodiversity protection when compared to politics, funding and the quality of public agencies.

6 Diverse land uses, including agriculture, mining, conservation and recreational uses and Indigenous or Traditional people's uses, have an impact on governance. This diversity complicates biodiversity protection, partly due to behavioural differences between diverse stakeholders pursuing different activities and, partly, because having to manage many interests with many impacts puts pressure on agencies.

7 Participation and consultation processes, including those involving special interest or disadvantaged groups in management, planning, development approval and sharing of benefits, are politically and operationally important. Variations in engagement approaches and in their effectiveness are due partly to formal institutions (e.g. mandatory consultation

16 *Paul Martin et al.*

requirements) and also to implementation considerations including resources and the ability of those conducting the processes.

8 Increasing competition for natural resources, particularly for farming and minerals, and incompatible uses of the landscape, creates governance pressures. It can cause compromises of protective regimes and undermine biodiversity protection.

9 Effective governance of rural land use and rural production systems, where biodiversity conservation and farm production connect, is complex and is essential. Though the impacts of 'industrial' farming are often highlighted in biodiversity loss, all of the impacts of agriculture and mining on the environment, including all the communities who are involved, need to be well managed.

10 Many existing or potential innovations could affect governance effectiveness. These include technologies for monitoring and sensing (sensors, drones, satellites), transactional innovations (e.g. internet enablement, 'blockchain' contracts) and management innovations (e.g. market-based instruments or private biodiversity protection, industry self-governance, public/private hybrids or co-regulation). Some technologies are likely to increase pressures on nature. How well innovation is used will be significant to governance in the future.

11 Funding is fundamental for effectiveness, for government agencies and citizens. Economic concerns include the pattern of incentives (for harm-doing or harm-reduction), including penalties or compensation from the government or from markets. A lack of funds and labour impedes desirable action for the environment, whether by government, business, NGOs or individual citizens.

Book structure

Ultimately, ten teams were established to examine the issues identified through the above-described process. The team members were primarily researchers who participated in the detailed scoping stage, but with some changes due to unavailability or the need for specialised skills or topic knowledge.

The structure of this book reflects three core themes. The first theme was analysis of what happens in practice with the implementation of generally accepted principles for biodiversity protection. The bio-social issues authors focused on were agriculture (Chapter 2), mining (Chapter 3), marine areas (Chapter 4) and Indigenous and Minority people's interests (Chapter 5). A second theme explored innovations in biodiversity protection: the teams considered an example of new forms of protected areas (Chapter 6), public/private hybrids in environmental regulation (Chapter 7) and using satellite (Chapter 8) and drone technologies (Chapter 9) to facilitate biodiversity protection. The third theme considered how governance itself is governed (Chapter 10), including how governance and compliance are resourced, and mechanisms to ensure the integrity of, and continuing improvement in, biodiversity governance (Chapter 11).

Intact biodiversity is most likely to be found away from centres of industry and population, which is, of course, where agriculture happens and where Indigenous and Traditional communities maintain connections to nature. In most megadiverse countries, agriculture is economically important at a national and community level. It employs people and produces commodities for consumption and trade. Corporatisation, farm aggregation, farmland expansion, technology and the dynamics of international commodity trade increasingly contribute to biodiversity loss and the marginalisation of vulnerable people. Managing the tensions between production and biodiversity, and issues of social justice in rural areas is one of the 'vicious' problems of biodiversity governance. Many of the Sustainable Development Goals (SDGs) have an agricultural aspect (particularly SDGs 1–3, 6, 8, 10 and 12–17), as do all four of the Aichi Targets. Almost all of the principles and commitments in multilateral arrangements apply to rural areas and agricultural industries. In Australia and Brazil, rural biodiversity protection is politically fraught and difficult in practice, which frames the implementation challenges that are particularly analysed in Chapters 2, 10 and 11.

Mining is an important industry in both countries, and it continues to create apparently intractable governance challenges. For Chapter 3, the team focused not on the core function of extracting resources from the earth but on two aspects of risk governance: how mining approval processes implement governance requirements for objective environmental impact assessment and the use of the precautionary principle and the extent to which the Polluter Pays Principle is applied when controls do not prevent mining disasters. The chapter highlights the dynamic interaction between the legal requirements in both countries, economics, administrative processes, politics and public/private interests bargaining. It looks at the tactics that are used, and how the law creates a basis for principled and transparent environmental governance principles, but how sophisticated tactics (ostensibly compliant with legal procedures) can compromise those principles in practice.

The fourth chapter, on governing marine protected areas, focuses on progress on international commitments to create a network of biologically representative protected areas. That chapter suggests that significant progress has been made by governments to meet these commitments in a formal sense, with a significant increase in declared marine environment protection areas in recent years. Where government action has been less encouraging in both jurisdictions is how protected areas, both marine and terrestrial, are managed. Effective protection is compromised by the flow of harms into marine environments, (e.g. climate change, fishing trespass and oil spill); the accommodation of activities that cause biodiversity loss and by a lack of resources for effective management. The chapter demonstrates that meeting the quantified goal (areas protected) is necessary but far from sufficient for

18 *Paul Martin et al.*

substantive marine conservation. The chapter underlines the importance of a generally under-appreciated commitment within the *CBD,* that

> [e]ach Contracting Party undertakes to provide, in accordance with its capabilities, financial support and incentives in respect of those national activities which are intended to achieve the objectives of this Convention, in accordance with its national plans, priorities and programmes.
>
> (art 20(1))

Increasingly, biodiversity and social justice issues are interwoven, particularly concerning the cultural and livelihood interests of Indigenous people and Traditional peoples. The *CBD* and the *Nagoya Protocol,* and the 2007 *UN Declaration on the Rights of Indigenous Peoples,* reflect this. Historically, protected areas practice sought to exclude people, including those with traditional connections, from areas dedicated for biodiversity. More recently, partly due to international developments, protected areas management has evolved towards inclusion of people whose traditions are interwoven with those areas. Mechanisms range from consultation, involvement in managing biodiverse areas, and co-management or Indigenous management. Chapter 5 considers different models of this involvement. It particularly considers how article 7 of the *CBD,* which juxtaposes protected areas and recognition of customary use and traditional practices, and the recognition of customary knowledge, is being addressed and how this intersects with other international human rights and social justice instruments.

It is interesting to note that, though Australian Aboriginal and Torres Strait Islander peoples have not had the benefit of constitutional rights, a radical act by the High Court catalysed changes to law and practices which has had many implications for biodiversity, whereas, in Brazil, the legislated arrangements for Indigenous and Traditional peoples have had variable legal effects. New forms of co-management for environmental protected areas, a form of hybrid governance, are complicated for political as well as practical reasons, demonstrated by the regression from Indigenous and Traditional peoples' rights occurring in Brazil.

Chapters 2–5 demonstrate successes and many practical difficulties in the application of biodiversity protection commitments and principles from international law. They indicate that adopting agreed commitments into domestic laws and putting these laws into practice, faces serious institutional and other impediments. Competing interests and political compromise, insufficient resources, compromised commitments, resistance and practical problems constrain implementation even when legal and other instruments have been created.

Einstein purportedly said that 'doing the same thing over and again and expecting different results each time, is insanity' (though there is little evidence that he actually said this). What is true is that, generally, it is foolish

The issues, methods and evidence   19

to expect radically better results by repeating the same approach to a difficult problem. Better outcomes for biodiversity protection require innovation in policy instruments, technologies, behaviour management, resourcing and coordination and oversight. But innovation comes with various types of risks: that it will fail, that it will be misused or that it will cause unintended consequences. Four chapters discuss types of innovations currently being used to achieve better outcomes.

Good management and adequate resources are necessary for protected areas to safeguard habitats and species. Thus, through the lens of bio-social issues, Chapter 7 discussed partnership innovations between government and civil society to manage protected areas to deliver both environmental protection and better outcomes for people with ancestral connections to nature.

In Chapter 6 the authors investigate the potential for an innovative type of protected area, using the economic and political power of surfers who value surf breaks and the unspoiled environment. The chapter illustrates how harnessing stakeholder self-interest in low impact uses of nature might provide an economic and political basis for special purpose conservation reserve, helping to overcome some of the constraints of conventional protection. There are many types of private conservation reserves, some with a long history (such as private hunting and fishing estates, and lands voluntarily managed for conservation or low impact enjoyment). Conservation NGOs already use private funding for managed biodiversity conservation reserves, and many private landholdings have informal or legally covenanted conservation zones (Kamal, Grodzińska-Jurczak, & Brown, 2015; Merenlender, Huntsinger, Guthey, & Fairax, 2004)). Examination of this innovative concept highlights that innovations in private conservation may help overcome some of the constraints on government where social and recreational interests in nature align well with biodiversity protection.

Another form of innovation is hybrid approaches to promote landholder good stewardship. Chapter 7 builds on ideas introduced in Chapter 2 (the challenges of protecting biodiversity from agricultural harms) and Chapter 5 (partnered governance involving indigenous and traditional users). Hybrid governance (sometimes termed co-regulation, or collaborative governance) blends private codes and standards with government regulation. Industry environmental standards have long existed, though their effectiveness in protecting the environment is variable. The chapter considers how some agricultural industries have adopted co-regulation in their approach to domestic and international markets. The chapter documents tangible progress but considers the risks that industry codes may simply be attempts to avoid regulation without being genuinely committed to better stewardship, or be ineffective. Collaborative governance may involve government making an industry code mandatory, or regulating that compliance with industry standard is *prima facie* compliance with a law, or delegating investigation or enforcement to a non-government body. The chapter primarily considers examples of collaborative governance in both countries in primary sectors. The evidence in the

20 *Paul Martin et al.*

chapter suggests a largely untapped potential for collaboration between the private sector and government to promote better stewardship while facilitating commercial outcomes. It also points to the need for strong mechanisms to ensure the integrity and the effectiveness of these approaches. The integrity aspect of governance is explored further in Chapter 11.

Governance relies on information, which is the 'feedstock' for decisions and the essence of communication. Indeed, flows of information and of resources largely determine how any social system works (Martin & Verbeek, 2006). Often, the cause of the failure of any type of transaction (including those in regulation, market instruments, social interventions, or any other governance approach) is deficient information flows. The economic concept of transaction costs highlights that impediments to the free flow of information, including the costs of gathering it and moving it, can result in inefficiencies. In environmental governance, transaction costs are implicated in difficulties in gathering evidence about nature, or about wrongs such as covert pollution, damage to the environment and about creatures in remote areas. Many new technologies for sensing, recording and transmitting signals from nature can help reduce this problem. Chapters 8 and 9 consider using satellite data to reduce the inefficiency and costs of monitoring habitat and the destruction to habitat in remote areas, and the use of drone technologies to gather intelligence and carry out tasks.

The number and the sensor capabilities of satellites are increasing exponentially, and private entrepreneurs (e.g. Elon Musk with Space X) are pushing development further. A great deal more satellite data will become available at relatively low cost in the next few years. The chapter highlights how satellite data has allowed low cost and precise tracking of habitat destruction, but it indicates that the technology alone is insufficient to ensure better enforcement. The chapter highlights the failure in both countries, even given satellite data providing evidence of breaches of the law, to implement effective controls. Political willingness, resources and legal frameworks (such as rules of evidence) are needed to use this potential. As satellite technology evolves non-government actors are also using it to monitor human activities that impact on biodiversity to identify when government programmes are failing. This aids transparency and allows civil society to pressure governments to implement existing rules, though this is not always effective. The chapter demonstrates how technology, law, institutional arrangements and political phenomena are interwoven, and how the dynamic combination shapes environmental outcomes. Managing one aspect, such as obtaining more precise information faster and more cheaply, will not necessarily improve the outcomes unless the other elements of the system are realigned.

Aerial, submarine and terrestrial drones not only provide data, they can also carry out work. Drones are devices that operate without the direct physical involvement of a human. Basic forms involve a physically distant operator, for example through radio or infrared signals, but, increasingly, devices use some autonomous 'decision-making' allowing them to respond to their

The issues, methods and evidence 21

context. Chapter 9 considers drones for uses, such as sensing and monitoring at relatively low cost or in hard-to-access environments, or for carrying out work (e.g. gathering samples or applying pesticides). Drones have been used by environmental campaigners to record evidence of harm to forests or water bodies from logging, or pollution and contamination, for political purposes or to create pressure for more effective controls.

However, drones can cause environmental harm as well as help with managing the environment, generating concerns about airspace or impact safety, intrusion into people's privacy and trespass over land. These create pressure to regulate the technology or limit the potential for the technology to gather intelligence for environmental enforcement or activism. Chapter 9 looks at the complexities that the dynamics of technology evolution are likely to create for regulators, as well as the diverse biodiversity uses of drone technologies.

Evidence provided in these chapters indicates that international and domestic rules and policies and other instruments are not preventing the losses of species and habitats. Two types of institutional failings are particularly involved: the lack of funds to carry out the necessary work; and the lack of reliable overarching 'meta-governance' institutions to monitor implementation and effectiveness, ensure integrity in implementation and energise continuous improvement. Unless these institutional problems are resolved, it is likely that biodiversity governance will be undermined.

Articles 11 and 20(1) of the *CBD* commit the signatories to ensuring incentives to motivate conservation and to providing resources to carry out this work. A pattern in the cases we have examined is that economic incentives drive environmental harm, and economic resources enable those doing harm to subvert environment protections by compromising biodiversity protection institutions or manipulating the political system. A second recurring pattern is that insufficient financial resources make necessary actions non-feasible. Government agencies responsible for protection or restoration often lack the money to do the job effectively, and the non-government sector is chronically short of resources. Chapter 10 takes examples financial feasibility, and at innovative strategies being used to grapple with this issue. The chapter shows that, in both countries, governments have not implemented the institutional arrangements that can fulfil their article 20 obligations. Innovative economic strategies, though they may not fully fund all that is required, could do a lot more to make better stewardship more attractive and feasible.

For biodiversity protection to be effective, strong institutions to monitor governance performance ensure that what is committed to on paper is carried out in fact. Chapter 11 discusses how these meta-governance issues are addressed in both countries. Unsurprisingly, it demonstrates major deficiencies in this aspect of implementation. The lack of a powerful integrity and accountability structure provides opportunities to undermine or bypass formal norms intended to protect the environment or the people who traditionally depend on biodiversity. Meta-governance weakness sometimes allows a government or its agents to pay lip-service to implementation, even as they are

22 *Paul Martin et al.*

failing to fulfil their obligations. The chapter describes arrangements which are needed to ensure that biodiversity protection is indeed delivered effectively, efficiently and fairly.

The final chapter integrates the strands of evidence and argument presented in the earlier chapters. It distils some patterns observed in biodiversity protection and suggests reforms to make it more likely that the rate of biodiversity losses in each country will be reduced. The conclusions present eight propositions about biodiversity governance, domestically and internationally, and a small number of recommendations.

The body of evidence we have presented about specific examples provide objective support for our conclusions about implementation of *CBD* commitments. They suggest that insufficient attention is being given to the system components of environmental governance essential to make its instruments effective. The book's conclusions can be legitimately extrapolated to the international community; they provide strong support for calls to pay far more attention to ensuring day-to-day implementation of the biodiversity commitments made by countries. At a time when the rate of biodiversity loss is not slowing, making existing commitments work is essential to ensure that present and future generations will not be environmentally impoverished.

References

Australia: State of the Environment. (2016a). *Overview of state and trends of biodiversity.* Retrieved from https://soe.environment.gov.au/theme/overview/biodiversity/topic/overview-state-and-trends-biodiversity

Australia: State of the Environment. (2016b). *Executive summary: Overview.* Retrieved from https://soe.environment.gov.au/theme/overview

Biodiversity a to z. (n.d.). *Megadiverse countries.* UN & WCMC. Retrieved from https://www.biodiversitya-z.org/content/megadiverse-countries

Bovens, M. A. P., & Hart, P. (1996). *Understanding policy fiascoes.* New Brunswick, NJ: Transaction Publishers.

Calatrava, J., & Martínez-Granados, D. (2017). The limited success of formal water markets in the Segura River basin, Spain. *International Journal of Water Resources Development, 34* (6), 1–21.

Department of the Environment. (2014). *Australia's fifth national report under the convention on biological diversity.* Canberra, ACT: Department of the Environment.

Department of the Environment and Energy. (n.d.). *State of the environment (SoE) reports.* Retrieved from http://environment.gov.au/science/soe

Farrier, D., Harvey, M., Da Silva, S., Leuzinger, M. D., Verschuuren, J., … Paterson, A. R. (2013). *The legal aspects of connectivity conservation: Case studies.* Gland, Switzerland: IUCN.

Freeman, J., & Kolstad, C. D. (Eds.). (2007). *Moving to markets in environmental regulation: Lessons from twenty years of experience.* New York, NY: Oxford University Press.

Hathaway, O. A. (2003). Dependence in the law: The course and pattern of legal change in a common law system. *Public Law and Legal Theory, 270.*

Howes, M., Wortley, L., Potts, R., Dedekorkut-Howes, A., Serrao-Neumann, S., ... Nunn, P. (2017). Environmental sustainability: A case of policy implementation failure? *Sustainability, 9* (2), 165. doi: 10.3390/su9020165

Jensen, P. (2013). *Evidence-based policy* (Working paper no. 4/13). Melbourne, Australia: Melbourne Institute of Applied Economics and Social Research.

Jessop, B. (2003). *Governance and metagovernance: On reflexivity, requisite variety and requisite irony*. Manchester, England: Lancaster University.

Kamal, S., Grodzińska-Jurczak, M., & Brown, G. (2015). Conservation on private land: A review of global strategies with a proposed classification system. *Journal of Environmental Planning and Management, 58* (4), 576–597. doi: 10.1080/09640568.2013.875463

Kaufmann, D., Kraay, A., & Zoido-lobatón, P. (1999). Governance matters. (WPS2196). The World Bank Development Research Group Macroeconomics and Growth and World Bank Institute Governance, Regulation.

Leach, M., Bloom, G., Ely, A., Nightingale, P., Scoones, I., Shah, E., & Smith, A. (2007). *Understanding governance: Pathways to sustainability*. (STEPS Working Paper 2). Brighton, England: STEPS Centre. doi: 10.1039/b810642h

Leuzinger, M. D., Martin, P., Santana, P. C., & de Souza, L. R. (Eds.). (2019). *Governance for megadiversity (Brazil/Australia)*. Brasilia, Brazil: UniCEUB. Retrieved from https://repositorio.uniceub.br

LMMC (The Group of Like Minded Megadiverse Countries) (2014). *Welcome to the group of like minded megadiverse countries*. Retrieved from https://lmmcgroup.wordpress.com/2014/03/24/welcome-to-the-group-of-like-minded-megadiverse-countries/

Majchrzak, A. (1984). *Applied social research methods*. Beverly Hills, CA: Sage Publications.

Martin, P., Boer, B., Byrner, N., & Greiber, T. (2013). *Discussion paper: Developing a structure for a legal component for the IUCN Natural Resource Governance Framework*. Bonn, Germany. (unpublished). IUCN.

Martin, P., Boer, B., & Slobodian, L. (2016). *Framework for assessing and improving law for sustainability: A legal component of a natural resource governance framework*. Gland, Germany: IUCN Environment Law Centre Bonn.

Martin, P., & Craig, D. (2015). Accelerating the evolution of environmental law through continuous learning from applied experience. In P. Martin & A. Kennedy (Eds.), *Environmental jurisprudence: Improving governance effectiveness* (pp. 1–23). Cheltenham, UK: Edward Elgar.

Martin, P., Leuzinger, M. D. M., & Teles da Silva, S. (2016). Improving the effectiveness of legal arrangements to protect biodiversity: Australia and Brazil. *Brazilian Journal of International Law, 13* (2), 27–39.

Martin, P., & Verbeek, M. (2006). *Sustainability strategy*. Sydney, Australia: Federation Press.

Martin, P., & Williams, J. (2010). *Policy risk assessment*. Sydney, Australia: CRC for Irrigation Futures. Retrieved from http://www.irrigationfutures.org.au/imagesDB/news/0310_web.pdf

Merenlender, A. M., Huntsinger, L., Guthey, G., & Fairax, S. K. (2004). Land trusts and conservation easements: Who is conserving what for whom? *Conservation Biology, 18* (1), 65–76. doi: 10.1111/j.1523-1739.2004.00401.x

Mickwitz, P. (2003). A framework for evaluating environmental policy instruments. *Evaluation, 9* (4), 415–436.

MMA (Ministério do Meio Ambiente do Brasil). (2016). *5° Relatório Nacional para a Convenção sobre Diversidade Biológica de 2014* (5th national report on the Convention on Biological Diversity for 2014). Brasília. Retrieved from http://www.mma.gov.br/informma/item/10772-quinto-relat%C3%B3rio

MMA (Ministério do Meio Ambiente do Brasil). (n.d.). *Percentual do Território Brasileiro Abrangido por Unidades de Conservação* (Percentage of Brazilian Territory Covered by Conservation Units). Retrieved from http://www.mma.gov.br/informma/item/11276-uc-terrestres

OECD. (2007). *Instrument mixes for environmental policy.* Paris, France: OECD Publishing.

Phillips, D. (2019a, July). Bolsonaro declares 'the Amazon is ours' and calls deforestation data 'lies'. *The Guardian.*

Phillips, D. (2019b, November 7). Oil spill threatens vast areas of mangroves and coral reefs in Brazil. *The Guardian.*

Phromlah, W. (2013). A systems perspective on forest governance failure in Thailand. *GSTF International Journal of Law and Social Sciences, 3* (1), 7–14.

Pirard, R. (2012). Market-based instruments for biodiversity and ecosystem services: A lexicon. *Environmental Science & Policy, 19–20,* 59–68. doi: 10.1016/j.envsci.2012.02.001

Rodriguez, J. R. (2013). *Como decidem as cortes? Para uma crítica do direito (brasileiro)* (How the courts decide? For a critique of the law (Brazilian)). Rio de Janeiro, Brazil: FGV.

Stavins, R. N. (2001). *Experience with market-based environmental policy instruments.* (Discussion Paper). Washington, DC: Resources for the Future.

Stone, J. (1964). *Legal system and lawyers' reasonings.* Stanford, CA: Stanford University Press.

Torfing, J., Sorensent, E., & Piel Christensen, L. (Eds.). (2003). Nine competing definitions of governance, governance networks and meta-governance (Working paper, 2003:1). Denmark: Roskilde University.

Weiss, T. G. (2000). Governance, good governance and global governance: Conceptual and actual challenges. *Third World Quarterly, 21,* 795–814. doi: 10.1080/713701075

Young, O. R. (2011). Effectiveness of international environmental regimes: Existing knowledge, cutting-edge themes, and research strategies. *PNAS, 108* (50), 19853–19860. doi: 10.1073/pnas.1111690108

2 Controlling the biodiversity impacts of agriculture

Paul Martin, Marcia Fajardo Cavalcanti de Albuquerque, Siva Barathi (Sharl) Marimuthu, and Davi Rossiter

Abstract

This chapter considers the relationship between biodiversity and modern commodity agriculture in Brazil and Australia. It provides an overview of the financial constraints on biodiversity protection and the development of public programmes to encourage more sustainable ways of farming, including by small-scale, family farmers. The chapter then focuses on the threats to biodiversity posed by agriculture, including from land clearing, contamination from agro-chemicals and invasive species. The chapter concludes with a discussion of socio-ecological issues and governance of agriculture.

Introduction

Agriculture feeds, clothes and otherwise maintains citizens. Because agriculture often occurs in less populated areas where natural biodiversity persists, it is often a significant cause of biodiversity loss. In areas with vulnerable species and habitats, the impacts of agriculture are likely to be greater than in places where centuries of high impact farming and industry have already reduced biodiversity. In Australia and Brazil, large areas of relatively pristine habitats have continued to exist but are being rapidly lost, with broadacre agriculture being a significant cause.

Agriculture represents approximately 5 per cent of Brazil's GDP and approximately 2.5 per cent of Australia's GDP but percentages vary with market and seasonal fluctuations. Farming uses around 34 per cent of Brazil's landscape and 48 per cent of Australia's (FAO, 2016). The major form of agriculture in both countries is broadacre commodity production, but there is a great variation in what is produced. For example, Brazil produces almost four times as much meat as does Australia and Australia produces almost five times as much wheat as does Brazil. Apart from variations in what is produced, there are differences in how production occurs, partly related to socio-economic characteristics, with labour being far more expensive in Australia. Cattle grazing is the main form of animal farming in both countries, and soy is the dominant broadacre crop in Brazil and grains, notably wheat, in Australia.

In this chapter we analyse the relationship between biodiversity and modern commodity agriculture, considering the development of this activity in Brazil and Australia. First we will discuss the growth and impact of broadacre agriculture in both countries, including a subsection on the impact of broadacre agriculture on habitat loss as well as risks from agricultural contamination and invasive species. The chapter then goes on to present the financial constraints on biodiversity protection and the development of public programmes that can help to drive this activity in a more sustainable way; in addition, we add a section that discusses family agriculture programmes. Completing this overview, we discuss the relationship between water, climate and biodiversity. We conclude with an examination of the socio-ecological issues and an overview of agriculture governance.

The impact of agriculture

Brazil's agricultural economy has grown significantly relative to Australia's, though both countries have seen significant and roughly equivalent increases in farm efficiency. Brazil has more than doubled its farm areas by opening up virgin territory. This has caused biodiversity losses. In Australia, bushland has also been cleared but the overall increase in farmland has been less than for Brazil. Clearing of native vegetation remains a serious problem in both jurisdictions (see Chapter 7). At the same time, Brazil has modernized its agriculture, replacing labour with machinery and massively increasing its use of agro-chemicals.

Figures 2.1–2.5 give a sense of how agriculture has both expanded and increased its production efficiency.

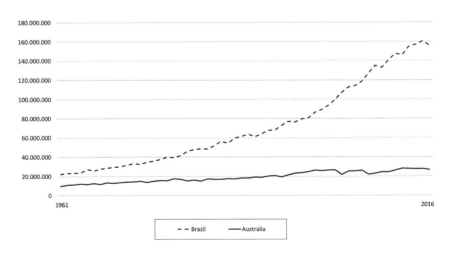

Figure 2.1 Agricultural production, constant US$'000 1961–2016.
Source: Author figure: Data sourced from: USDA. (n.d.). *Agricultural total factor productivity growth indices for individual countries*, 1961–2016.

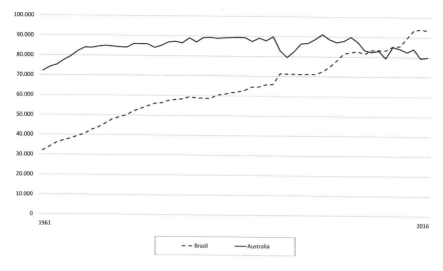

Figure 2.2 Agricultural land, '000 ha, 1961–2016.
Source: Author figure: Data sourced from: USDA. (n.d.). *Agricultural total factor productivity growth indices for individual countries*, 1961–2016.

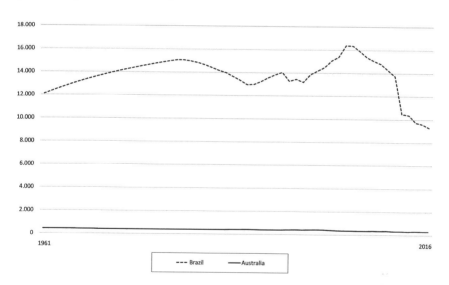

Figure 2.3 Adult agricultural employment, '000, 1961–2016.
Source: Author figure: Data sourced from: USDA. (n.d.). *Agricultural total factor productivity growth indices for individual countries*, 1961–2016.

According to the 2017 Brazilian agricultural census (IBGE, 2017), the country's dominant land use is grazing (45 per cent), 29 per cent of the land is forested and 18 per cent cropped. The FAO reports somewhat different statistics, noting that 58.9 per cent of Brazil's land area is covered by forest

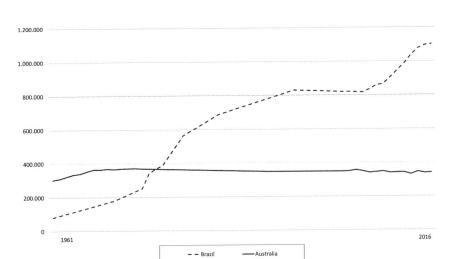

Figure 2.4 Number of 40-CV tractor equivalent in use, 1961–2016.
Source: Author figure: Data sourced from: USDA. (n.d.). *Agricultural total factor productivity growth indices for individual countries*, 1961–2016.

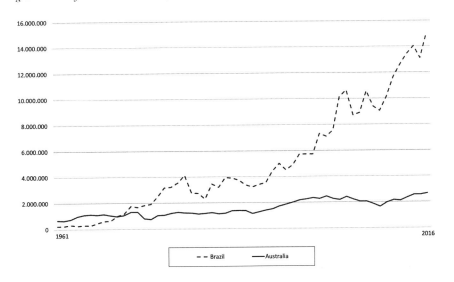

Figure 2.5 Synthetic fertilizer use, metric tonnes, 1961–2016.
Source: Author figure: Data sourced from: USDA. (n.d.). *Agricultural total factor productivity growth indices for individual countries*, 1961–2016.

and 23.45 per cent is covered by permanent meadows and pastures (FA-OSTAT, 2016). The 2006 Brazilian agricultural census showed that over 75 per cent of the agricultural land was used for broadacre cropping (later data is not available). In 2018, the main agricultural exports were soybean, poultry and beef and forest products (Ministério da Economia, Industria, Comércio Exterior e Serviços, 2019). Water use for agriculture has greatly increased since 2000 (OECD, 2015). Brazil's *Fifth National Report to the CDB* (MMA, 2003, 2016) identifies that broadacre agriculture causes habitat loss, fragmentation and reduced diversity due to the land use change and contamination by chemicals. The growing demand to 'open up' more land for agriculture has led to land degradation and loss of biodiversity (Araujo et al., 2014). Recently, habitat clearing and large fires have accelerated the loss of native habitat. Agricultural runoff is a problem in both jurisdictions. In Australia, the main runoff concern is contamination of the Great Barrier Reef (see Chapter 4).

The *Australian State of Environment Report 2016* (SOE 2016) (Metcalfe & Bui, 2017) states that the country's dominant land use is grazing of native vegetation (44.9 per cent) or modified pastures (9.2 per cent). Cropping occupies around 4 per cent. Irrigation is a small percentage of land use but has a significant impact on southern and eastern river systems. Ecological pressures from broadacre agriculture identified in SOE 2016 include extensive clearing of habitat (roughly equivalent to that in Brazil) and exotic pests and weeds and disease (invasive species being those not naturally present). Pollution of waterways, notably coastal and marine catchments, with sediments, animal waste and agricultural contaminants can be a significant biodiversity problem (notably for the Great Barrier Reef, see Craik, 2017).

The most successful farmers operate at a large scale, using technologically advanced production systems, but there are many small 'low-tech' operations. Farmers may often be wealthy on paper because of the land they own but have low and unreliable cash flows. A significant proportion of farmers in both countries suffer socio-economic disadvantage, permanently or periodically, because of climate variability, natural disasters, pests and disease and the volatility of markets. Political traditions in both countries give farmer organisations and agricultural politicians power in political processes that are disproportionate to their numbers. Specialised public agricultural departments promote and support farm productivity, and public programmes are used to reduce social and ecological problems.

Rural biodiversity in both countries is declining alarmingly. Broadacre farming directly affects habitats, soils and landforms and surface and subsurface water, and has indirect impacts through chemicals, biologicals and species escaping farmlands. Dams, transport and processing facilities have major effects on natural systems. Clearing of habitat for farming continues to destroy remaining habitats (see Chapter 8) despite policies and laws. In both countries, disputes over illegal land-clearing result in conflict and sometimes violence. Climate change is affecting rainfall and evapo-transpiration, contributing to drought or flood and seasonal variability. Biodiversity is vulnerable to climate change, particularly with declining water supply and the inability of fauna and flora to find viable replacement habitats. (Qureshi, Hanjra, & Ward, 2013). With the environment and agriculture both placing

30   *Paul Martin et al.*

demands on climate-impacted essential resources, natural systems are increasingly vulnerable (OECD, 2019, p. 84).

In both countries, farm ownership ranges from small tightly held family owned farms, to large properties under domestic and international corporate ownership (Wagstaff, 2019). Concentration and corporatisation, and the marginalisation of the small family farm, is happening in both Australia and Brazil (see Keeffe, 2018; Navarro & Pedroso, 2014). Large, sophisticated farm corporations are often owned by local or international investors. Four Western corporations dominate agricultural trade, and the corporatisation and scaling-up of farms is evident in both Australia and Brazil.

Both countries rely on extensive (rather than intensive) production systems, with very large farms. Australia's farming is more capital intensive with larger holdings, and Australia has a far lower total rural population (though this is a higher percentage of the total population). Table 2.1 highlights these differences.

Table 2.1 Comparative agricultural statistics – Australia and Brazil

	Australia	*Brazil*
Agricultural growth international rank (2007)	195	27
Cereal yield – kg's per hectare (2008)	1649.7	3828.8
Value added agricultural production (2011) US$ billions	$34.78	$100.3
Agricultural Land (sq km 2011)	4.1 m	2.75 m
Arable land – hectares per capita (2011)	2.14	0.365
Arable land in hectares (2003)	49.4 m	59 m
Available farm workers (2008)	443,000	11.65 m
Rural population per 1000 people (2010)	0.273	0.0715

Source: Agricultural Stats Compare Key Data on Australia and Brazil, Nation Master. https://www.nationmaster.com/country-info/compare/Australia/Brazil/Agriculture

To illustrate, the amount of land controlled by major investors, Table 2.2 lists the ten largest agricultural landholders in Australia, whose combined holdings exceed 45 million hectares, corresponding to 6 per cent of Australia's territory, approximately 770 million hectares.

Table 2.2 Largest agricultural landholders in Australia

	Corporation	*Hectares*
1	Outback Beef (S. Kidman and Co)	7,927,300
2	Australian Agricultural Company	6,598,777
3	North Australian Pastoral Company	5,954,468
4	Jumbuck Pastoral	4,937,799
5	Williams Cattle Company	4,652,500
6	Paraway Pastoral Company	4,434,091
7	Consolidated Pastoral Company	3,378,952
8	Hughes Pastoral Group-Georgina Pastoral Company	2,815,500
9	Viv Oldfield-Donny Costello (Crown Point Pastoral)	2,636,500
10	Heytesbury Cattle Company	2,524,100

Source: Wagstaff, J. W. (2019, May 21). Who owns Australia's farms: nation's biggest stakeholders, *The Weekly Times.*

Agricultural demand for land and water continues to drive biodiversity loss (OECD, 2019). Invasive plants and pest animals, introduced by agriculture, are a major biodiversity threat in Australia. There is the risk that genetically modified crops will contaminate natural species or environments, and that runoff of sediment and chemicals will leak into waterways (Dudley & Alexander, 2017).

Farmers often see 'undeveloped', biodiverse areas as potential low-cost farmland to be developed lawfully, or through land invasions or unauthorized habitat removal. Natural biodiversity is, as a result of incremental clearing, increasingly restricted to the ecosystem niches that are least attractive for agriculture, such as rocky areas and regions that have unfavourable climate or rainfall, are too forested, suffer agricultural predation or disease, or are otherwise inhospitable. Species loss has thus been higher in areas that are most attractive to farming.

Technologically sophisticated modern farming is often antagonistic to native species and habitats. Many technologies operate best across large areas where native habitat has been removed and the landscape levelled, and advanced farming systems often involve monocultures based on the use of chemicals, herbicides or pesticides. Modern grain or soy farms may operate large technologically sophisticated planting and harvesting machines, using a field configuration spanning more than a kilometre to maximise efficiency. The operator might be watching a computer screen while operating machines served by robotic 'slave' trucks moving to and from remote silos. An advanced fruit orchard can use 'fertigation' (delivery of fertiliser in liquid form) and not rely on nutrients from the soil; computer systems deliver precise doses of chemicals to the root ball to promote growth, trigger fruit setting and stimulate ripening.

A 'smart' livestock farm can weigh each beast automatically, calibrate its growth against food intake and remotely manage watering points and gates. Though some 'smart farming' technologies do have the potential to reduce some harmful effects through greater precision and fewer inputs, large scale advanced agriculture is often hostile to biodiversity conservation. In Brazil, a massive increase in livestock production has significantly impacted biodiversity in the Amazon. From 2008 to 2014, the government mapped deforested areas in the Amazon and detected that 60 per cent of these spaces were transformed for cattle raising and 25 per cent of the area had been covered by introduced vegetation (INPE, 2016).

Rural infrastructures, such as roads, railways, towns, dams (e.g. for energy and agricultural water) and processing facilities create further environmental impacts. This can be dramatic when agriculture expands into virgin habitat, which happens in both countries (though the destruction of the Amazon attracts the most international attention). For example, in Brazil, new road networks stimulate incursions into forest and Indigenous and Quilombola people's lands (Rocha, 2017); and in Australia, agricultural water infrastructures and demands and introduced species have had disastrous impacts on freshwater ecology, damaged river habitats and restricted Aboriginal traditional uses of rivers, lakes and streams.

32 Paul Martin et al.

Expansion and habitat loss

Removing natural habitat through legal or unlawful clearing for agriculture is a major cause of biodiversity loss. It reduces and fragments habitats (discussed further in Chapter 8). There are consequential impacts from population densification and transport and other infrastructures. For example, the construction of a 1,800 km road connecting the urban areas of Cuiabá to Santarém in the Amazon forest accelerated deforestation, land grabbing, real estate speculation, large farms and extensive cattle raising (Alencar, 2005; Rocha, 2017). The amount of land-clearing fluctuates in both countries and rates of native habitat loss have, in recent years, been similar (Fact check, 2017).

The competition between habitat and land for farming fuels political conflict over biodiversity protection laws in both countries. Though conflicts in the Brazilian Amazon have received international attention, the tension between farming and environmental interests over habitat clearing has been intense in the Australian states of NSW and QLD where the laws that limit landholder destruction of native vegetation have been volatile, and implementation has been unreliable (Hepburn, 2018; Reside et al., 2017). The rate of habitat clearing in Brazil has recently accelerated and rampant fires are increasing biodiversity loss (Spring, 2019).

Both countries cycle between pro-biodiversity or pro-development stances on habitat protection, depending on whether political power is held by worker/ environmental oriented parties or by business/farming interests. Regression from protective laws follows these cycles. For example, in Brazil, a 'legal reserve' is a mandatory area of reserved native vegetation on private property for biodiversity conservation. Consistent with a pro-agriculture agenda, the current government continues to introduce draft bills that will weaken controls over agricultural commodities (such as liberalisation of the use of agrochemicals). In Australia, after a few years of liberalised land clearing laws led to a massive increase in habitat loss, the state of QLD has pivoted towards a more protective regime for native vegetation. However, the adjacent state of NSW moved in the opposite direction, liberalising land-clearing laws, leading to a substantial increase in habitat loss. In both jurisdictions, political volatility, unreliable enforcement and opposition to regulation have created a dynamic that has fundamentally undermined habitat protection.

Invasive species

Biodiversity loss due to invasive species is an increasing international threat. *Aichi* Target 9 aims that, by 2020, 'invasive alien species and pathways are identified and prioritized, priority species are controlled or eradicated and measures are in place to manage pathways to prevent their introduction and establishment', and the Sustainable Development Goal (SDG) 15.8 reinforces this priority. In 2005, 284 alien species had become established in Brazil, threatening biodiversity (179 species in terrestrial ecosystems, 56 species in

Biodiversity impacts of agriculture 33

continental waters and 49 species in the marine zone) (OECD, 2015). In Australia, since European settlement, over 2,800 weeds, 25 mammals, 20 birds, 4 reptiles, 1 frog, 34 fish, between 100 and 400 marine species and an unknown number of invertebrates have been introduced, with major impacts on the environment and on agriculture (Australian Museum, n.d.). The problem is driven by many things, including increasing trade and travel, intentional introduction of exotic species and management failures (Simpson & Srinivasan, 2014). Agriculture is implicated through the use of exotic species as fodder, crops or as farm animals; or accidental introductions (Gong, Sinden, Braysher, & Jones, 2009).

Invasive species displace native species, predate upon them, cause disease and alter habitats. They can cause extinctions. Invasive animal problems are a major issue in Australia, with damaging exotic species such as rabbits and feral pigs thriving in suitable conditions with relatively few native predators, causing disastrous harm to native species and habitats (Low, 2017). Attempts at control sometimes involve the introduction of other exotic species, which may themselves become harmful. An example from Australia is the disastrous introduction of the cane toad to battle the exotic cane beetle in 1935.

When invasive species harm agricultural production there is an economic incentive for control. Public and private funds are often made available, particularly for rapidly spreading, high impact invasive species, including diseases. However, for invasive species that are 'merely' harmful to the environment there is a 'missing market' for control. What control does occur generally involves government staff or volunteers (often with government financial support) but continuing biodiversity loss demonstrates that this investment is inadequate.

Genetic contamination is a recent invasiveness concern; this concern includes cross-breeding between indigenous and exotic species and the potential for invasive genetically manipulated species. In Australia, an example is of the cross-breeding of the native dingoe with the introduced dog, creating fertile hybrids that predate livestock and native animals.

The increasing use of genetically modified organisms (GMOs) is a concern for many, though there is disagreement about the risk (and about how it should be managed). As the use of GMOs increases, so does the risk of GMOs escaping increase, and this, coupled with fundamental disagreement, creates political and regulatory complications (see Department of Health, 2018). In Brazil, between 2010 and 2016, genetically modified (GM) soybean varieties increased by 21.5 per cent, GM corn increased by 33.4 per cent and GM cotton increased 52.3 per cent (Conselho de Informações sobre Biotecnologia, 2017). Genetic engineering of insects and other animals will raise new issues (e.g. Warner, 2018).

One risk is of contamination of natural species with modified genetics, a second is the risk of transferring herbicide or pesticide resistance into native species (making control of organisms for either environmental or economic purposes more difficult) and a third is the potential to contaminate conventional crops with unwelcome GMOs. The *Marsh v Baxter* case (2014), ruled upon by the WA Court of Appeals illustrates this last risk of organic contamination. In that case, contamination of GM canola from an adjoining farm caused a farmer to lose their organic certification. A civil claim failed because the court ruled that the proximate cause of loss was the actions of the organic association in cancelling certification (not the contamination itself). A parallel example is the contamination of organic soy on the state of Rio Grande do Sul in 2004, where farmers had to abandon organic certification (MNA, n.d., Tribuna, 2004). Under Brazilian law, if GMO modified crops are present on a farm, it is assumed this has been planted deliberately and the farmer may be obliged to pay for that material (*Federal Law 9.456/1997*, art. 37).

Contamination

Excess watering can bring salts to the surface and into underground or surface water bodies, contributing to their contamination. Removal of deep-rooted native vegetation (particularly trees) adds to the risk to both agriculture and native habitat. In Brazil, although soil salinisation is a growing concern, most irrigated areas are in regions with good soil drainage and good quality water. This slows the salinisation process. In the drier northeast region, where the soils do not have these characteristics, salinisation is more advanced. In Australia, with a relatively flat and dry landscape and saline soils, salinity caused by land clearing and irrigation is a major problem (Pannell & Roberts, 2010). The policy focus on salinity has decreased in the eastern states in recent years – reflecting improved management and significant reductions in irrigation water. In WA, concern about salinity remains and a report in March 2019 canvassed new directions for salinity management (GHD, 2019).

Pesticides and herbicides reduce biodiversity in cultivated plots and in adjacent areas. They can harm beneficial organisms (such as pollinators) and humans. Chemical harm can be caused by accidents (e.g. wind drift, spills or runoff), unanticipated effects (e.g. bee mortality) and intentional or accidental misuse (e.g. using unregistered chemicals or using chemicals for unauthorised purposes or in an improper manner). Both countries manage contamination risk by requiring approval based on risk analysis before pesticides and herbicides can be registered for use, labelling and compliance with use instructions. These legal requirements are complicated and costly and limit the availability of chemicals.

Brazil is an intensive user of agrochemicals (see Figure 2.5). Some agrochemicals that have been banned from developed countries, including Australia, are still in use in Brazil. Between 2000 and 2014, there was an increase of 135 per cent in the use of pesticides. In Brazil, the agribusiness lobby has pursued *Bill 6299/2002*, to liberalise legislation on pesticides. In 2018, the Normative Instruction no. 40 of the Secretary of Agricultural Defense from the Ministry of Agriculture Livestock and Food Supply granted power to agronomists to tailor mixtures of pesticides and herbicides. Following this move to self-regulation, the government had, by May 2019, released 197 additional pesticides, though many of these are 'follow on' registrations by new suppliers or already registered active ingredients (Brito, 2018). According to the Minister of Agriculture, most of the agrochemicals listed are generic products already sold in Brazil, based on approved ingredients sold under new trademarks (Câmara dos Deputados, 2019). In Australia, the focus is on improving the efficiency of the registration system, particularly for 'minor use' chemicals (Rainbow, 2016).

Financial constraints

In Australia, the authors of the *SOE 2016* report (Metcalfe & Bui, 2017), though reasonably positive about rural governance institutions, indicate that the effectiveness of these is hindered by declining public funding to implement policies. Environmental law experts have expressed a negative opinion about rural legal arrangements and share the concerns that funding to protect rural biodiversity is inadequate (Farrier et al., 2017).

The environmental harms from agriculture and the costs of protection or restoration are not reflected in prices paid for commodities, a form of the 'missing markets' problem (Koller & Bailey, 2017). Commodity agriculture often yields small profits per hectare (though total returns for large enterprises may be substantial) and agricultural commodity incomes are often volatile. Automation, markets and market/natural cycles drive agricultural commodity prices down towards the (declining) marginal cost of production and increase income volatility. This erodes the profits of even efficient producers and further marginalises poorer farmers. The mismatch between funding needed to protect biodiversity and what is available from commodity industries makes it unlikely that rural landholders will ever be able to adequately fund biodiversity. Public funds help to fill the funds-gap but, in Australia and Brazil, public funding for rural biodiversity protection has declined, a trend which is unlikely to be reversed (see Chapter 10).

To reduce costs and income volatility, farmers who can afford to do so pursue greater scale or technological solutions. Consequently, their funds requirements to pay for land and technology, often funded by debt, increase. A failure to meet interest payments or provide a corporate return on investment prejudices enterprise viability, creating pressure to maintain output and cashflow even when natural conditions are deteriorating (experimentally demonstrated by Moxnes, 2000). Economic pressures contribute to job insecurity and low wages. These push farming towards unsustainable practices, with limited economic incentives or capacity to moderate harms.

Many farmers do adopt agricultural methods, such as cell-grazing or minimum-tillage planting, to reduce environmental harm, or engage in projects to repair the land and restore biodiversity. Farming innovations that use fewer or less harmful inputs, restorative practices such as biodiverse or organic farming, or use least harmful methods to control pests and invasive

36   *Paul Martin et al.*

species (e.g. promoting natural predators or other integrated pest management approaches) also reduce impacts.

Substantial investment would be required to protect or restore biodiversity over large farming areas. Though some people will argue that user or polluter pays principles (PPP) (or shared responsibility) mean that agriculture should bear the costs of rural biodiversity protection and restoration, this is often unrealistic. The investment needed is substantial and has to be sustained to be effective, and farming income patterns are hostile to these requirements. The moral and policy question of who should pay is more complex than it appears on the surface. For example, biodiversity harm may have been caused by unrelated prior landholders following ill-advised government policy; and the benefits from protection or restoration may accrue only to the general public and can impose dis-benefits on the farmer (Pannell, 2006). For these reasons even when dealing with private lands' biodiversity, there may often be a principled as well as a pragmatic case for the burden to be shared (Pannell, 2006).

Public programmes

To address rural environmental and social problems often requires government support and there are a variety of approaches. Brazil uses the Food Acquisition Program (established by *Law no. 10.696/2003*) to encourage government agencies to purchase from family farming production, as does the National School Meal Program (established by *Law no. 11.947/2009*)). Public schools must buy at least 30 per cent of school meals from family farmers, prioritising organic and agroecological products. The National Program for the Strengthening of Family Agriculture (PRONAF) was established by *Decree 1946/1996* and provides technical and financial support for family farming. However, because the recipient must demonstrate that the farm is economically viable, this programme can lead to increasing agrochemical use or other harmful practices.

Taking a different approach, in Australia, 56 regional natural resource management organisations develop regional management programmes, provide advisory services to improve agricultural sustainability and administer small grants (Ryan, Broderick, Sneddon, & Andrews, 2010). Though programmes vary across states (and across time), the approach involves collaboration between national and state government agencies, landholders and environmental or other non-government organisations. Australia also has drought and natural disaster schemes but avoids agricultural subsidies beyond (limited) advisory services. Farmer-based programmes, such as Landcare and regional programmes, help to overcome impediments to biodiversity protection; however, these programmes provide far less support than rural biodiversity protection requires (International Fund for Agricultural Development, 2010).

The economic capacity and the incentive for better environmental outcomes could be improved by using market instruments such as farmer Payment for Ecosystem Services (PES) schemes (Alston, Andersson, & Smith,

2013). Internationally, PES schemes have directed billions of dollars towards environmental work (Salzman, 2018). PES schemes, including the international REDD+ scheme, are well known in Brazil, where, of the 26 States and the Federal District, 16 have laws governing PES. In Australia, biodiversity banking instruments have been implemented in some states to protect high value habitats and their potential is recognised but implementation of PES arrangements has been limited to date (Ansell, Gibson, & Salt, 2016). Though gaining increased traction, PES schemes face challenges (Martin, 2017). A fundamental concern is the need for a motivated and financially able purchaser. Finding viable private purchasers for biodiversity services can be difficult and expectations that government will fill this role encounter budget constraints.

Water, climate and biodiversity

Rainfall in Brazil is around 1 to 1.5 m per year with significant variations across the country. Between 2006 and 2014, there was an increase of 36 per cent in irrigated land, with around 20,000 central pivots irrigating an area of 6.1 million hectares in 2014. Irrigation consumes 745,000 litres per second, 67 per cent of national water consumption (ANA, 2017, p. 45). In 1997, a national water management system and criteria for water allocations were established through the National Water Resources Policy. The allocation of water is one of six functions of the National Water Resources Policy which controls water use and access rights to water (articles 5 &11of *Federal Law No. 9.433/1997*). The national and state governments have authority over different categories of water bodies (Section IV, article 4, *Federal Law No. 9.984/2000*) and either the federal or state agencies for water resources grants water resources rights. Since the promulgation of the National Irrigation Policy in 2013, 849 licenses for irrigation have been granted (ANA, 2017).

Australia is a dry continent with a vast inland desert. Its average rainfall is less than half a metre per year, with significant regional variation. Agriculture depends on both surface and groundwater. Many systems are stressed by over-extraction, causing biodiversity loss, risks to agriculture, human welfare problems and economic costs. Key water systems span state boundaries, water demands are increasing, rainfall declining and temperatures increasing. Together, these factors lead to conflict and suboptimal outcomes (Martin & Becker, 2011). The National Water Initiative (NWI) commits all states to economically rational water management for sustainable use but implementation is problematic. The politics of water are intense in the southern states, where over-extraction for agriculture and for industry, mining and urban use is entrenched, creating a need to 'claw back' significant volumes of water. Competition between water for the environment and water for agriculture generates political conflict and has undermined implementation of legislated biodiversity protection (Walker, 2019).

The Northern part of Australia is tropical, with monsoonal rain patterns and sparse population. The Southern part is temperate, with substantial water

38   *Paul Martin et al.*

withdrawals for irrigated agriculture. The Murray-Darling system is Australia's most economically important river, serving four states and one territory and major irrigation districts. Sustainable use principles have been adopted through a federal *Water Act 2008* (Cth), governing the Murray Darling Basin Plan. The legal basis for the *Water Act* is complex because of constitutional issues and institutional arrangements. Around A$13 billion has been committed to implementation of the plan.

This plan has helped reduce over-extraction but what volumes have actually been saved and whether the plan has been effective is not clear (Cosier et al., 2017). There are fundamental disagreements about the science, the effectiveness of investments, the integrity of the institutional arrangements and many other things. In 2019, an extreme drought has highlighted the inadequacies of governance arrangements and compounded political tensions, as well as contributed to further compromises of environmental protection. Future riverine biodiversity protection is far from assured.

The Great Artesian Basin provides groundwater for the sparsely settled inland areas of QLD, NSW and the NT. Significant public and private investments have been made to reduce uncontrolled water waste from untapped bores. This has resulted in water savings but further reductions in extraction are needed to achieve sustainable use (Sinclair Knight Mertz, 2013).

Socio-ecological issues

The economic efficiency of agriculture continues to improve, but prices received for farm product generally move towards that of the most efficient (typically large, industrialised) producers. Industrialisation means that less labour is required for production, and rural communities can suffer unless they have non-farming opportunities. The consequences can include: (1) rural poverty (2) social disadvantage, (3) population loss, particularly of young people and (4) social dislocation (and sometimes conflict).

An important aspect of biodiversity governance is protecting Indigenous and Traditional people's cultural and interests, which have been affected by the expansion of agriculture into traditional lands and by incidental impacts (e.g. contamination, species loss and incursions). They have also been affected by commercialisation of native species without negotiated benefit sharing (contrary to principles of the *CBD*). The problem is compounded when an appropriated species is modified and protected using plant variety or other intellectual property rights. Appropriation of Indigenous and Traditional peoples' interests in biodiversity also occurs when Traditional artistic symbols or artwork, Traditional stories, songs and performance are taken; or when the appropriator claims an affiliation to which they have no right (Stoianoff, 2017).

The *Nagoya Protocol* addresses this issue but does not provide complete coverage. Implementation of protection and benefit sharing has been slow in Australia, and Brazil has not ratified the protocol. Australia uses a limited combination of private intellectual property rights and state laws, with the

Biodiversity impacts of agriculture 39

NT having the most advanced form of protection (see *Australian Government Response to Notification 2011-216 Access to Genetic Resources and Benefit-sharing*, n.d.). Brazil began regulation of the management of genetic heritage and associated traditional knowledge in 2001(*Provisional measure 2.186-162001*) and adopted recently *Federal Law No. 13.123/2015* (revoking the provisional measure). In neither country is the protection of Traditional interests adequate from the viewpoint of Indigenous and Traditional people.

Overview

In 2018, the Australian Panel of Experts in Environmental Law highlighted major structural and implementation issues for environmental law, including for rural and agricultural biodiversity issues. They point to the lack of effective meta-governance of environmental law (discussed in Chapter 11) and to the need for better coordinated landscape governance, completion of a national reserve system, more comprehensive monitoring and evaluation, effective environmental impact assessment and development approval processes, a viable financial investment model for the environment, and more principled treatment of Aboriginal and Torres Strait Islander interests. The plethora of legal instruments (see Ecolex, n.d.) should ensure the protection and sustainable use of agricultural biodiversity but implementation is weak and political opposition limits rural biodiversity protection. The Agriculture Parliamentary Front in Brazil, which opposes legal constraints on agriculture and the implementation of existing laws, has the support of 225 deputies out of 513 and 32 senators out of 81 (*Com 257*, 2019).

A report on implementing the 2030 SDGs, published in 2018 by the Civil society work group for the 2030 agenda, indicated little achievement of the National Biodiversity Targets, which are based on the Aichi Targets. In the first commitment period under the *CBD*, Brazil met only two of its 51 targets. According to the report, 'it is clear that the lack of articulated policies and the continuous threats to Brazilian biodiversity point to the permanence of this scenario in the period that will end in 2020' (Grupo de Trabalho da Sociedade Civil para Agenda 2030, 2018, p. 68). Recent developments have further undermined rural biodiversity protection. This is illustrated by the fact that in his first day in office, President Jair Bolsonaro signed *Interim Measure no. 870/2019* that transferred the management of the Brazilian Forest Service (BFS) to the Ministry of Agriculture. The BFS is responsible for implementing mandatory protected habitat areas on farms and was previously supervised by the Ministry of the Environment. This transfer of responsibility is intended to undermine implementation of the requirement for conservation areas on private land.

Emerging issues will further complicate rural biodiversity protection. Climate change has the potential to increase rainfall and temperature volatility and to fuel rural area disasters. It will strengthen challenges such as invasive plants, animals, insects and diseases that affect natural biodiversity and agricultural production. The explosion of rural technologies and related investments indicates change to almost every aspect of agriculture, such as precision tillage and application of agro-chemicals; new agro-chemicals; CRISPR (clustered regularly interspaced short palindromic repeats) modified genetics; blockchain mediated governance and transactions; and robotics. There will also be changes to what consumers expect, such as new products (e.g. insects as food, or functional foods). This could facilitate environmentally or socially responsible production and processing methods, but to date agricultural innovations have not tended to be beneficial to the environment (see, e.g. AgInnovators, n.d.).

Internationalisation of agriculture and commodification of agricultural products will intensify. Likely effects include increased economic pressures and volatility, more movement of goods and people (affecting trade and invasive species) and capital. Free trade arrangements could restrict how governments respond, though improved implementation of international agreements could strengthen biodiversity protection. Of the 17 SDGs, 12 relate to agriculture and rural community issues. Each country has specific targets against which its performance is measured and reported, and proper evaluation of each country's performance could create international pressure or at least provide more transparency about underperformance. This political dimension is illustrated by the international responses to habitat loss and fires in the Brazilian Amazon, including boycotts of Brazilian leather products by two major international purchasers (HM and the VF Corporation), proposed international trade sanctions from France and the EU, and growing calls for an international consumer boycott of Brazilian products.

A simplistic view of how to manage rural biodiversity loss would focus on the need for farmers and agricultural industries to be more responsible and accountable, and for tighter regulation and stronger enforcement. Though these things are necessary, they are far from sufficient. Both Australia and Brazil experience significant biodiversity loss related to agriculture and both already have laws which, in theory, could improve biodiversity and social outcomes. There are many failures of implementation. Political opposition to environmental protection is often strong, despite the rhetoric of sustainable agriculture. For as long as markets impose few penalties for biodiversity harm or do not provide a premium for good stewardship, commodity producers are unlikely to adequately protect biodiversity. Until market incentives align with policy imperatives, those who might do the right thing will be discouraged by a risk of competitive (costs) disadvantage.

Even where there is political will, there are problems with using the law to protect rural biodiversity. It is cumbersome to monitor large areas, and governance resources are sparse in non-urban areas. Farmer resistance to measures that impede production or add costs can be stubborn, and the farm sector complains about the restrictiveness and economic cost of rural environmental laws (see, e.g. Productivity Commission 2004, 2016). Though better control of environmental 'rogues' and protection of farmland biodiversity are needed, reducing the impact of broadacre farming on biodiversity will also require approaches that do not rely on governments alone.

Private governance arrangements are increasingly important. These include environmental and animal welfare brands and eco-labels, consumer standards, voluntary farming standards and codes, environmental volunteering and NGO activities and private conservation reserves (see, e.g. Ecolabel Index, n.d.; Fitzsimons, 2015). There is a trend towards governance hybrids, or co-regulation, where industry codes are made mandatory or supported by government (see Chapter 7). Some arrangements require primary producers to meet environmental or other standards to access markets.

The organic sector has been a leader in private environmental standards, and there are at least 14 ecolabel systems operating in Australia and 40 in Brazil. In Brazil, agricultural certification mainly applies to export products. International standards such as the European environmental rules on biofuels illustrate that private sustainability standards can have an extra-territorial reach. Private regulation of agriculture is likely to become more important as export/import standards are imposed because of pressure by consumers and voters (Stattman, Gupta, Partzsch, & Oosterveer, 2018). This may lead to sectoral self-regulation that does not depend on government. One concern is the transaction costs of achieving environmental certification, which can be particularly onerous for small-scale and marginal producers. Some Brazilian farmers have formed groups for this purpose. In 2016, in the state of Bahia, 54 farmers were collectively certified and by 2018 this had risen to 200 (Schwarz, 2018).

For environmental laws to be effective requires supporting policies and institutional arrangements, and resources for government agencies and for people to implement these changes at the frontline of agriculture. The examples we have discussed demonstrate that political opposition, insufficient resources and complexities in policy implementation and insufficient safeguards for the integrity of implementation of governance arrangements can erode the effectiveness of laws and international principles. For the objectives of environmental conventions to be met in relation to rural areas and agricultural systems, what is required are better safeguards for the integrity of implementation, stronger economic incentives so that private actors do undertake environmental protection, and sufficient public and private resources to do what is needed. Only then would it be realistic to expect that the remaining valuable species and habitats will be preserved.

References

AgInnovators. (2020). *Innovators: Conceptualizers & change agents.* Retrieved from http://www.wginnovation.com/innovators

Alencar, A. A. C. (2005, December). *Estudo de caso: A rodovia BR-163 e o desafio da sustentabilidade* (Case study: The BR-163 highway and the sustainability challenge). MAPAS. Retrieved from https://ipam.org.br/wp-content/uploads/2005/03/estudo_de_caso_a_rodovia_br-163_e_o_desa.pdf

42 Paul Martin et al.

Alston, L. J., Andersson, K., & Smith, S. M. (2013). Payment for environmental services: Hypotheses and evidence. *Annual Review of Resource Economics, 5* (1), 139–159. doi: 10.1146/annurev-resource-091912-151830

ANA (Agência Nacional de Águas). (2017). *Atlas irrigacão : Uso da água na agricultura irrigada. Brasília* (Irrigation Atlas: Use of water in irrigated agriculture). ANA. Retrieved from http://arquivos.ana.gov.br/imprensa/publicacoes/AtlasIrrigacao-UsodaAguanaAgriculturaIrrigada.pdf

Ansell, D., Gibson, F., & Salt, D. (Eds.). (2016). *Learning from agri-environment schemes in Australia: Investing in biodiversity and other ecosystem services on farms.* Canberra, ACT: ANU Press. Retrieved from http://press.anu.edu.au?p=346093

Calegari, A., Araujo, G., Costa, A., Lanillo, R. F., Casão Junior, R., Santos, D. R. (2014). Conservation agriculture in Brazil. In R. A. Jat, K. L. Sahrawat, & Emir H Kassam (Eds.), *Conservation agriculture: Global prospects and challenges* (pp. 54–88). Wallingford, England: Cabi International.

Australian Academy of Science. (n.d.). *The claws are out.* Retrieved from https://www.science.org.au/curious/earth-environment/invasive-species

Australian Government Response to Notification 2011-216 Access to Genetic Resources and Benefit-sharing. (n.d.). (Ref.: SCBD/ABS/VN/SG/74553). Retrieved from CBD website: https://www.cbd.int/abs/doc/protocol/icnp-1/australia-en.pdf

Australian Museum. (n.d.). *Museum 2 You: Introduced species content.* Retrieved from https://australianmuseum.net.au/learn/teachers/museum-box/introduced-species-the-alien-invaders/

Brito, J. (2018, December 10). *Agrotóxicos proibidos na Europa são campeões de vendas no Brasil* (Europe's banned pesticides are best sellers in Brazil). Publica, Agência de Jornalismo *Investigativo.* (2018). Retrieved from apublica website https://apublica.org/2018/12/agrotoxicos-proibidos-na-europa-sao-campeoes-de-vendas-no-brasil/

Câmara dos Deputados (2019). Ministra da Agricultura diz que aprovação de novos agrotóxicos é técnica e defende uso do glifosato (Minister of Agriculture says that approval of new pesticide is technical and advocates use of glyphosate). Retrieved from https://www2.camara.leg.br/camaranoticias/noticias/AGROPECUARIA/576940-MINISTRA-DA-AGRICULTURA-DIZ-QUE-APROVACAO-DE-NOVOS-AGROTOXICOS-E-TECNICA-E-DEFENDE-USO-DO-GLIFOSATO.html

Com 257 parlamentares, bancada ruralista declara apoio à reforma da presidência (The 257 parliament members of the rural front declares support to pension system reform). (2019, 20 April). *UOL NEWS.* Retrieved from https://congressoemfoco.uol.com.br/economia/com-257-parlamentares-bancada-ruralista-declara-apoio-a-reforma-da-previdencia/

Conselho de Informações sobre Biotecnologia. (2017, November 16). *Qual e a taxa de adoção dos principais transgênicos aprovados no Brasil?* (What is the adoption rate of the main GMOs approved in Brazil?). Retrieved from https://cib.org.br/faq/qual-e-a-taxa-de-adocao-dos-principais-transgenicos-aprovados-no-brasil/

Cosier, P., Flannery, T., Harding, R., Hillman, T., Hughes, L. … Wilder, M. (2017). *Review of water reform in the Murray Darling Basin.* Sydney, Australia: Wentworth Group.

Craik, W. (2017). *Independent review of governance of the Great Barrier Reef Marine Park Authority* (report). Canberra, ACT: Department of the Environment and Energy. Retrieved from http://www.environment.gov.au/marine/gbr/publications/gbr-governance-review

Department of Health. (2018). *Third review of the National Gene Technology Scheme.* Canberra, ACT. Retrieved from https://www1.health.gov.au/internet/main/publishing.nsf/Content/gene-technology-review

Dudley, N., & Alexander, S. (2017). Agriculture and biodiversity: A review. *Biodiversity, 18* (2–3), 45–49. doi: 10.1080/14888386.2017.1351892

Ecolabel Index. (n.d.). Retrieved from http://www.ecolabelindex.com/ecolabels/#C

Ecolex. (n.d.). *The gateway to environmental law.* Retrieved from https://www.ecolex.org

Fact check. (2017). Is Queensland clearing land as fast as Brazil? *RMIT/ABC.* Retrieved from https://www.abc.net.au/news/2017-12-01/fact-check-queensland-land-clearing-brazilian-rainforest/9183596

FAO. (2016). *Country profiles, Australia and Brazil. Retrieved from http://www.fao.org/countryprofiles/en/*

FAOSTAT. (2016). Retrieved from FAO website http://www.fao.org/faostat

Farrier, D., Godden, L., Holley, C., McDonald, J., & Martin, P. (2017). *Terrestrial biodiversity conservation and natural resources management* (Technical paper No. 3). Melbourne, Australia: APEEL. Retrieved from http://apeel.org.au/s/APEEL_Terrestrial_biodiversity_conservation_NRM.pdf

Fitzsimons, J. A. (2015). Private protected areas in Australia: Current status and future directions. *Nature Conservation, 10.* doi: 10.3897/natureconservation.10.8739

GHD. (2019). *A new direction for salinity management in Western Australia: A consultative Review.* (A report for the Department of Primary Industries and Regional Development, Review 6137688). Perth, WA. Retrieved from https://www.agric.wa.gov.au/soil-salinity/new-direction-salinity-management-western-australia-consultative-review

Gong, W., Sinden, J., Braysher, M., & Jones, R. (2009). *The economic impacts of vertebrate pests in Australia.* Canberra, ACT: Invasive Animals Cooperative Research Centre.

Grupo de Trabalho da Sociedade Civil para Agenda 2030. (2018). *Relatório Luz da Agenda 2030 de desenvolvimento sustentável* (Light Report of the 2030 Sustainable Development Agenda). Retrieved from https://artigo19.org/wp-content/blogs.dir/24/files/2018/07/Relatório-Luz-da-Agenda-2030-S%C3%ADntese-II.pdf

Hepburn, S. (2018, March 8). Why aren't Australia's environment laws preventing widespread land clearing? *The Conversation.* Retrieved from https://theconversation.com/why-arent-australias-environment-laws-preventing-widespread-land-clearing-92924

IBGE. (2017). *Censoagro resultados preliminaries* (Preliminary census results). Retrieved from https://censoagro2017.ibge.gov.br/templates/censo_agro/resultadosagro/estabelecimentos.html

INPE. (Instituto Nacional de Pesquisas Espaciais). (2016). *Lançados novos dados do TerraClass Amazônia* (New Terraclass Amazon data published). Brasília, Brazil: Ministério de Ciência e Tecnologia do Brasil. Retrieved from http://www.inpe.br/noticias/noticia.php?Cod_Noticia=4173

International Fund for Agricultural Development. (2010). *Rural poverty report 2011: New realities, new challenges: New opportunities for tomorrow's generation.* Retrieved from http://www.ifad.org/rpr2011/report/e/rpr2011.pdf

Keeffe, P. R. O. (2018). *Creating a corporatized society: Australian agricultural restructuring and the emergence of corporate power.* (Doctoral dissertation). Melbourne, Australia: RMIT.

Koller, T., & Bailey, J. (2017). *When sustainability becomes a factor in valuation.* McKinsey & Company. Retrieved from https://www.mckinsey.com/business-functions/

44 *Paul Martin et al.*

strategy-and-corporate-finance/our-insights/when-sustainability-becomes-a-factor-in-valuation

Low, T. (2017). *Invasive species: A leading threat to Australia's wildlife.* Sydney, Australia: Invasive Species Council. Retrieved from https://invasives.org.au/publications/invasive-species-leading-threat/

Martin, P. (2017). Managing the risks of ecosystem services market. *Ecosystem Services, 29* (March), 404–410. doi: 10.1016/j.ecoser.2017.05.007

Martin, P., & Becker, J. (2011). A tale of two systems: Conflict, law and the development of water allocation in two common law jurisdictions. *International Journal of Rural Law and Policy, 1,* 1–18.

Metcalfe, D. J., & Bui, E. N. (2017). *Australia state of the environment 2016 (SOE 2016).* (Independent report to the Australian Government Minister for the Environment and Energy). Canberra, ACT. doi: 10.4226/94/58b6585f94911

Ministério da Economia, Industria, Comércio Exterior e Servicos. (2019). *Comex: Vis Brasil (Geral)* (Comex: Viz Brazil (General)). Retrieved from http://www.mdic.gov.br/comercio-exterior/estatisticas-de-comercio-exterior/comex-vis/frame-brasil

MMA (Ministério do Meio Ambiente do Brasil). (2003). *Fragmentação de Ecossistemas: Causas, efeitos sobre a biodiversidade e recomendações de políticas públicas* (Ecosystem fragmentation: Causes, effects on biodiversity and public policies recommendations). Brasília: Ministério do Meio Ambiente do Brasil.

MMA (Ministério do Meio Ambiente do Brasil). (2016). *5º Relatório Nacional para a Convenção sobre Diversidade Biológica de 2014* (5th national report on the Convention on Biological Diversity for 2014). Brasília. Retrieved from http://www.mma.gov.br/informma/item/10772-quinto-relat%C3%B3rio

Moxnes, E. (2000). Not only the tragedy of the commons: Misperceptions of feedback and policies for sustainable development. *System Dynamics Review, 16* (Winter), 325–348. doi: 10.1002/sdr.201

Navarro, Z., & Pedroso, M. T. M (2014). A agricultura familia no Brasil: Da promessa inicial aos impasses do presente (Family farming in Brazil: From an initial promise to its current impasses). *Revista Economica NE, Fortaleza, 45,* 6–17. Retrieved from https://ainfo.cnptia.embrapa.br/digital/bitstream/item/158612/1/ren-2014-1-v.2-zander-Pedrozo.pdf

OECD. (2015). *OECD environmental performance reviews: Brazil.* Paris, France: OECD Publishing. doi: 10.1787/9789264240094-en

OECD. (2019). *Environmental review 2019.* Retrieved from https://www.oecd.org/australia/oecd-environmental-performance-reviews-australia-2019-9789264310452-en.htm

Pannell, D. J. (2006). *80 –Public benefits, private benefits: The final framework.* Retrieved from http://www.pannelldiscussions.net/2006/06/80-public-benefits-private-benefits-the-final-framework/

Pannell, D. J., & Roberts, A. M. (2010). Australia's national action plan for salinity and water quality: A retrospective assessment. *Australian Journal of Agricultural and Resource Economics, 54* (4), 437–456. doi: 10.1111/j.1467-8489.2010.00504.x

Productivity Commission. (2004). *Impacts of native vegetation and biodiversity regulations.* (Report no. 29). Retrieved from http://www.pc.gov.au/projects/inquiry/nativevegetation/docs/finalreport

Productivity Commission. (2016). *Regulation of Australian agriculture.* (Report no. 79). Canberra, ACT. Retrieved from https://www.pc.gov.au/inquiries/completed/agriculture/report/agriculture.pdf

Qureshi, M. E., Hanjra, M. A., & Ward, J. (2013). Impact of water scarcity in Australia on global food security in an era of climate change. *Food Policy, 38*, 136–145.

Rainbow, R. (2016). *Delivery of access to AgVet chemicals collaborative system*. (Publication No 17/019). RIRDC. Retrieved from https://www.agrifutures.com.au/wp-content/uploads/publications/17-019.pdf

Reside, A. E., Beher, J., Cosgrove, A. J., Evans, M. C., Seabrook, L., Silcock, J. L., ... Maron, M. (2017). Ecological consequences of land clearing and policy reform in Queensland. *Pacific Conservation Biology, 23* (3), 219–230. doi: 10.1071/PC17001

Rocha, L. R. L. (2017). *Desmatamento e queimadas na Amazônia (Deforestation and burning fires at Amazon)*. Curitiba, Brazil: Juruá.

Ryan, S., Broderick, K., Sneddon, Y., & Andrews, K. (2010). *Australia's NRM governance system: Foundations and principles for meeting future challenges*. Canberra, ACT: Australian Regional NRM Chairs. Retrieved from https://apo.org.au/node/22696

Salzman, J. (2018, March). *Global market for ecosystem services surges to $ 36 billion in annual transactions*. Sustainability. Retrieved from https://sustainabilitycommunity.nature.com/users/85108-james-salzman/posts/31181-global-market-for-ecosystem-services-surges-to-36-billion-in-annual-transactions

Schwarz, F. (2018, June). *Produção orgânica cresce na Bahia com certificação participative* (Certified organic production grows in Bahia). (Press release). Globo Rural. Retrieved from https://revistagloborural.globo.com/Noticias/Agricultura/noticia/2018/06/producao-organica-cresce-na-bahia-com-certificacao-participativa.html

Simpson, M., & Srinivasan, V. (2014). *Australia's biosecurity future: Preparing for future biological challenges*. CSIRO. Retrieved from https://publications.csiro.au/rpr/download?pid=csiro:EP146693&dsid=DS5

Sinclair Knight Mertz. (2013). *Great Artesian Basin sustainability initiative Phase 3: Mid-term review* (GABSI3 future options assessment report). Braddon, ACT: SKM. Retrieved from https://www.environment.gov.au/system/files/resources/8ce555da-281a-4fa8-9430-0c6bc18c4609/files/gabsi-phase-3-midterm-review.pdf

Spring, J. (2019, August 6). Brazil deforestation climbs 67% through July as government attacks data. *Reuters News Service*. Retrieved from https://uk.reuters.com/article/uk-brazil-environment/brazil-deforestation-climbs-67-through-july-as-government-attacks-data-idUKKCN1UV26F

Stattman S. L., Gupta, A., Partzsch, L., & Oosterveer, P. (2018). Toward sustainable biofuels in the European Union? Lessons from a decade of hybrid biofuel governance. *Sustainability (Switzerland), 10* (11), 1–17.

Stoianoff, N. P. (2017). A governance framework for indigenous ecological knowledge protection and use. In R. Levy, M. O'Brien, P. R. Simon Rice, & M. Thornton (Eds.), *New directions for law in Australia: Essays in contemporary law reform* (pp. 231–241). Canberra, ACT: ANU Press.

Tribuna. (2004, December 23). *Lavouras de soya orgânica do RS são contaminadas por transgênicos* (RS Organic soybean crops are contaminated by GMOs). (Press release). Retrieved from https://www.tribunapr.com.br/noticias/lavouras-de-soja-organica-do-rs-sao-contaminadas-por-transgenicos/

USDA. (n.d.). *Agricultural total factor productivity growth indices for individual countries, 1961–2016*. Retrieved from https://www.ers.usda.gov/webdocs/DataFiles/51270/AgTFPindividualcountries.xlsx?v=6612.3

Wagstaff, J. W. (2019, May 21). Who owns Australia's farms: Nation's biggest stakeholders. *The Weekly Times*. Retrieved from https://www.weeklytimesnow.

com.au/agribusiness/agjournal/who-owns-australias-farms-nations-biggest-landholders-of-2019/news-story/4109396defc7e1b4b8961e2dc68f0663

Walker, B. (2019). *Murray-Darling Basin Royal Commission report (MDBA)*. Adelaide, SA: Government of SA.

Warner, B. (2018, October 16). Invasion of the 'frankenbees': The danger of building a better bee. *The Guardian Online*. Retrieved from https://www.theguardian.com/environment/2018/oct/16/frankenbees-genetically-modified-pollinators-danger-of-bulding-a-better-bee

3 Biodiversity risk management in mining

Romana Coêho de Araujo, Jorge Madeira Nogueira, and Paul Martin

Abstract

Mining not only generates economic growth but also environmental impacts that involve risks to biodiversity and vulnerable communities. This chapter discusses the limitations of governance processes in both Brazil and Australia that has led to contentious mines approval processes and mines oversight. The Bulga and Adani mine cases in Australia are examples of the contentious mines approval process, and the Mariana and Brumadinho disasters in Brazil provide examples of the consequences of poor mines oversight. The examples and further discussion in the chapter illustrate the 'realpolitik' of mines governance in both countries and that the implementation of legislation is often less than desired. Therefore there is a need for more robust governance arrangements.

Introduction

Australia and Brazil have extensive mining industries. Mining is approximately 8 per cent of Australia's GDP and 3 per cent of Brazil's GDP (Trading Economics, 2018/2019, Luciano, 2019). In 2010, Australia and Brazil were ranked, respectively, 2nd and 6th in the value of minerals mined; 1st and 2nd largest mines and the 1st and 2nd largest mining firms (Southam, 2012). Mining generates employment, royalties (Deloitte Access Economics, 2019; Luciano, 2019) and welfare through extraction, processing and manufacturing and other activities. Luciano (2019) reports that mining generates 180,000 direct jobs and more than 2.2 million indirect jobs, and corresponds to 25 per cent of Brazil's trade balance in 2017.

Mining involves many actors, conducting processes for extraction, exploration, financing, export, site restoration, processing and investment. Extraction involves violent disturbance of the environment and risks to biodiversity and vulnerable communities, particularly when large mines operate in undisturbed areas, mines and communities co-exist, and mining processes are hazardous. Social tensions exist between the desire for mining products, the wish to control harm and risk and costs and benefits distribution. Managing impacts and risks is technically difficult and can reduce mining profits. Interest negotiations, therefore, involve compromises.

Political systems express social aspirations in policies, rules, structures and processes. These shape the behaviour of people and organisations towards those aspirations but do not necessarily create action, nor do they necessarily deliver desired outcomes. Governance is meant to help inevitable tensions in society by ensuring that decisions are transparent and consistent with rules and policies, and that power is not abused, but it is often poorly implemented. As other authors indicate (Damiens et al., 2017; Martin & Becker, 2011; Williamson, 2000), 'Governance in practice' is politicised and often differs from governance 'on paper'. Political concepts, such as public choice, agency capture, transaction costs and compromise, are all relevant to mining governance.

This chapter uses examples from Australia and Brazil of the dynamics of mining governance in practice. Two Australian examples, which examine the approval processes for the Carmichael and Adani mines, discuss how arrangements were manipulated to favour the mining industry over the less powerful impacted communities and the environment. The failure of mines tailings dams in Brazil, the Mariana and Brumadinho cases, illustrate mining risk and governance difficulties in recompensing mining harms. We begin the chapter with a discussion of governance frameworks before focusing on recent examples to demonstrate the 'realpolitik' of mines governance.

In Australia, contentious mining approvals have affected national and state elections and, in Brazil, mine site disasters continue to have significant consequences. Though the examples are specific to each jurisdiction, there are parallel issues: both countries have contentious mines approvals processes and both countries have mine tailings dams that pose serious risks. Implementation of good governance principles in both countries is compromised by economic and political dynamics and, though mining laws contribute to transparency and biodiversity protection, full implementation with integrity is lacking. Better institutional arrangements are needed to adequately implement *Convention on Biological Diversity (CBD)* principles.

Governance frameworks

In Brazil and Australia, approval power lies with an elected minister, who takes on board the advice of their department and other agencies. Depending on the jurisdiction and the issues, approval may be delegated. In Australia and Brazil, approval can involve both national and state agencies.

The Australian Commonwealth Government's constitutional power to implement international obligations is exercised through the *Environment Protection and Biodiversity Conservation Act 1999* (Cth) (*EPBC Act*). If a development potentially threatens a matter of 'national environmental significance', approval of the Commonwealth Minister for the Environment is required. Major foreign investments require the approval of the Federal Foreign Investment Review Board. Thus, approval processes may involve dual state/national assessments. Where neither international obligations nor foreign investments concerns arise, only state processes apply.

The relevant mining acts for the states are:

- *Land (Planning and Environment) Act 1991* (ACT)
- *Mining Act 1980* (NT)
- *Mining Act 1992* (NSW)
- *Mineral Resources Act 1989* (QLD)
- *Mining Act 1971* (SA)
- *Mineral Resources Development Act 1995* (TAS)
- *Mineral Resources Development Act 1990* (VIC)
- *Mining Act 1978* (WA).

In Brazil, the *Mining Code 1967* (Brazil) is the primary mining regulation. It was revised in 2018 to facilitate investment, strengthen environmental protection and avoid site disasters. Though the jurisdictions have different systems of law, they have Equivalent processes; that is, states and municipalities have rights to approve mining projects and the federal agencies deliberate on environmental licences with state or municipal agencies.

In both countries, non-mining laws and policies (i.e. foreign investment, land use, citizen rights, Indigenous people's rights and environmental protection) are relevant. Private rights (e.g. to compensation for damage or property loss) and administrative law (e.g. development approval appeals) can be involved. Though mining laws emphasise evidence-based governance and community engagement, politics and lobbying are fundamental (Southam, 2012).

There are many complex issues in mining, including the management of: mine spoil, wastes and water, processing (including chemicals) and sites. To be legal, mine operations require government approval and have conditions imposed upon them for ensuring environmental, safety and community concerns (particularly if the mine affects Indigenous or Traditional communities) are met. Conditions may affect site or information access, veto or authorisation rights, royalties and compensation, community facilities and risk mitigation or compensation. Reaching consensus among stakeholders about a mining project involves negotiation over complex issues, and can be conflictual and political. Resolving social conflicts is one function of legal institutions (Luhmann, 1984).

Advocates and opponents or other interests become involved through lobbying or political action, formal processes, mining legislation or general law (constitutional rights in Brazil but not Australia). Citizen engagement and the quality of community participation and rights of appeal vary. Those who prioritise economic benefits characterise regulatory processes or restrictions as inefficient but those concerned about mining impacts and risks prefer 'tight' approval processes. Those concerned with distributing benefits and costs typically value local benefits over benefit to the national or regional economy, employment or profit expectations to motivate mining entrepreneurship. In relation to negotiation about governance issues the *Aarhus Convention* sets global standards for community participation (Andrusevych, Alge, & Konrad, 2011; Ebbesson, et al., 2014) but neither Brazil nor Australia

50   *Romana Coêho de Araujo et al.*

has adopted these. Brazil has signed the *Regional Agreement on Access to Information, Public Participation and Justice in Environmental Matters in Latin America and the Caribbean (Escazú Agreement)*, but has yet ratified the agreement.

Ratification of the *CBD* involves commitments to: rehabilitate ecosystems (art. 8(f)); respect local and Indigenous community interests (with community participation) and implement comprehensive impact assessment (art. 14) using a precautionary approach. Through the *Stockholm Declaration on the Human Environment* (1972) and the *Rio Declaration on Environment and Development* (1992), the precautionary principle, a principle of intergenerational equity and the polluter pays principle (PPP) are part of the *CBD* commitments. PPP requires that the cost of harms be allocated to those who cause them or have the capacity to control them.

> In other words, the cost of these measures should be reflected in the cost of goods and services which cause pollution in production and/or consumption. Such measures should not be accompanied by subsidies that would create significant distortion in international trade and investment.
>
> (OECD, 1972)

The need for economic incentives is reflected in article 11 of the *CBD*:

> Each Contracting Party shall, as far as possible and as appropriate, adopt economically and socially sound measures that act as incentives for the conservation and sustainable use of components of biological diversity.

Mine approval in Australia

Two Australian cases illustrate mines approval practice and associated governance problems: the Mount Thorley-Warkworth coal mine in Bulga, New South Wales (NSW), Australia illustrates state-level mine regulation (see A Kennedy, 2016, particularly Ch. 3); and Adani's Carmichael coal development in Queensland (QLD), Australia, illustrates joint national/state processes.

The Bulga case

Bulga is a community of around 350 residents in a region of high agricultural value. Mining for coal commenced near the community in 1981. Ministerial approval for mine expansion dated from 2003 and was due to expire in 2021. The approval conditions required that biodiversity and landforms be protected collaboratively with the local government. In 2010, an application was lodged to expand the mine, removing a local landform, clearing 700 ha of significant habitat, closing a local road and extending mine operations to 2031. Expansion would bring the mine within 2.6 km of Bulga. The application was approved in February 2012 by the Planning Assessment Commission of NSW, a delegate for the Minister for Planning, with requirements for some offsets for biodiversity loss.

The Bulga community mounted an appeal under the *Environment Planning and Assessment Act 1979* (NSW) aided by the Environmental Defenders Office (EDO), a public interest litigant. They argued for disallowance:

> [By] reason of the Project's significant and unacceptable impacts in terms of: impacts on biological diversity, including on the endangered ecological communities, that are not avoided, mitigated, offset or otherwise compensated; noise impacts and dust emissions on the residents of Bulga and the surrounding countryside; social impacts on the community of Bulga; economic issues including that the full environmental costs are not internalised by the Project; and the public interest.
>
> (Bulga Milbrodale Progress Association Inc v Minister for Planning and Infrastructure and Warkworth Mining Limited (Bulga Case, para. 12))

A right to a merits appeal before a judge arose because of a technicality; that is, the Commission did not hold a public enquiry before its determination. In 2013, Chief Justice Brian Preston of the NSW Land and Environment Court rejected the application for the Mount Thorley-Warkworth mine expansion (see *Bulga case*, 2013 – Appendix C), overturning the earlier approval. The mining industry was outraged and unsuccessfully appealed the decision (*Warkworth Mining Limited v Bulga Milbrodale Progress Association Inc*, 2014 – Appendix C). The mining company then embarked on lobbying, media activities and a public relations exercise, with the industry seeking reforms to facilitate projects and limit the ability of environmental organisations to oppose developments (Kennedy, 2016).

After a public hearing in December 2014, Warkworth's second application, substantially the same as the first, was approved with conditions requiring the rehabilitation of woodland that would be destroyed and a biodiversity offset of 1,500 ha (NSW Planning Assessment Commission, 2015). The decision-making process did not trigger a right for citizens to a court appeal. Around the same time, government funding for the EDO was withdrawn.

Kennedy (2016) studied the governance processes of the disputed mining developments and highlights how disempowerment (leading to injustice) can occur despite apparent environmental and citizen safeguards. She provided several examples (including Bulga) of how economic and political power can undermine the interests of citizens and the environment when the beneficiaries are wealthy and well-connected, and have strong economic incentives (pp. 71–76, 171–186). Institutionalised integrity mechanisms are needed to ensure implementation (see Chapter 12). The Principal Solicitor of the NSW EDO argues that merits appeals can help limit corruption (EDO NSW, 2016; Higginson, 2014) and the NSW Independent Commission Against Corruption argues for merits reviews for the same purpose (ICAC, 2012).

Governance processes can deliver risk-management benefits, providing a mechanism (though imperfect) for citizens to highlight risks and to seek

52 *Romana Coêho de Araujo et al.*

redress. An example of this benefit was a recent case before the NSW Land and Environment Court which endorsed the refusal of a development because consequent emissions would increase atmospheric carbon (*Gloucester resources limited v Minister for Planning*, 2019, para. 525 – Appendix C).

Adani Carmichael case

The Adani Carmichael mine is in the Galilee Basin in QLD. The mine proposes to extract around 20 per cent of the coal reserves in the region and its development is likely to initiate the development of other mines. The mine required state and Commonwealth approvals under the *EPBC Act*. The large, foreign owned Adani development triggered political conflict between those concerned about environmental impacts and long-term economic viability, and those who saw the mine as providing increased opportunities for employment and regional economic activity.

This contested process was pivotal in the 2019 election of a pro-mining federal government. Similar to the Bulga case, it involved legal appeals (successful and unsuccessful) against ministerial decisions (Environment Law Australia, n.d.), multiple development applications, political lobbying and pressure to approve developments. Commonwealth and state approvals were required for the mine, a rail line and an export terminal. Three of the many approval issues are discussed here: groundwater, threatened species and marine impacts.

Central Queensland is drought-prone and the mine could disturb aquifers and damage the environmentally sensitive Doongmabulla Springs (significant to Indigenous people). The company's water impact modelling was rejected by scientific reviewers. Under intense pressure, the national science agency provided a qualified statement that the risks to the springs could be managed (Slezac, 2019). The Minister then issued an approval (Long & Slezak, 2019). Scientific doubts remain about the water modelling and safeguards, and the rush to approval contributed to scepticism (Currell, et al., 2017).

Concerns arose about the impacts on the rare black-throated finch. Management plans were originally rejected by the QLD Government on expert advice but accepted by the Commonwealth. A later plan (coincident with the federal election) was accepted by the QLD Government. Scientific members of the panel who rejected the initial plan have stated:

> There is no excuse for such a poor plan to have been put forward for approval when the company has been aware for almost a decade that the land it wants to mine is home to the largest known remaining population of the black-throated finch.
>
> (Garnett, et al., 2019, pp, 1–2)

> Now the research and monitoring is a hurried add-on with no proof that the threat posed to the finch can actually be solved and an extinction averted.
>
> (Garnett, et al., 2019, p. 5)

Even accepting legitimate differences of opinion between scientists and government agencies, the combination of political and business pressures, limited transparency and criticism from internationally respected scientists does raise a question whether the precautionary principle has been properly applied.

Increases in coal exports from the Adani and other mines created a need to expand the Abbot Point export port, which is within the UNESCO World Heritage Area of the Great Barrier Reef. Dredging would be needed, and it was proposed that the spoil be dumped within the reef area (Advisian, 2015). Three controversial development applications were considered, all mired in scientific and political controversy. Significantly, The Great Barrier Reef Marine Park Authority raised concerns. Nevertheless, the development was eventually approved with spoil to be disposed of on land. Legislative changes (*Environment Legislation Amendment Bill 2013* (Cth)) allowed the Australian Minister for the Environment to ignore scientific evidence when approving a development.

Approval for a 100 km–long pipeline to supply 12.5 billion litres of water per annum to the mine and to expand the associated dam is pending after a court overturned the ministerial approval because of a failure to consider opponents' submissions. Further litigation is likely.

Both the Adani and the Bulga examples illustrate how the political dimension of approval is driven by competing interests. Politics and self-interest are part of democracy and capitalism, foundations of the political systems of Australia and Brazil. Elected governments exercise power conferred by citizens, and capitalists pursue their interests but the law constrains this self-interest, consistent with accepted norms. The examples discussed here raise questions about whether community norms have been overstepped, suggesting the need for stronger rules to implement international commitments.

Mine disasters in Brazil

This section considers two mine disasters in Brazil that occurred when required conditions did not prevent failures. Governance problems arose with the subsequent compensation and restoration arrangements (similar to approaches taken by the Australian firm James Hardie to isolate legal liabilities for the impact of asbestos mining and production) using a structurally separated legal entity.

Brazil experienced one of the world's worst mines environmental disasters on 5 November 2015 when Samarco's (a joint venture of Vale and BHP Billiton) Fundão mine's tailings dam burst, destroying part of the town of Mariana, polluting the Doce River valley, destroying thousands of hectares of vegetation, degrading the water supply of 35 towns and killing 19 people. On 25 January 2019, the Córrego do Feijão iron ore mine near Brumadinho in the state of Minas Gerais also failed causing 259 deaths (11 people are still missing). Table 3.1 summarises the events of both these disasters.

At the time of the Mariana disaster, enforcement of environmental laws concerning mining operations was weak, enabling economic interests

54 Romana Coêho de Araujo et al.

Table 3.1 Characteristics of the Mariana and Brumadinho mine disasters

Date of disaster	Mariana/MG	Brumadinho/MG
	5 November 2015	*25 January 2019*
Company	Samarco Mineração S.A. (joint venture Vale S.A. and BHP Billiton)	Vale S.A.
Mine	Fundão	Córrego do Feijão, 1 Dam
Deaths	19 deaths	269 deaths and 11 missing (to 25 June 2019)
Pollutant released	62 million cubic metres of tailings	12 million cubic metres of tailings
Extent of damage	Destroyed thousands of hectares of native and cultivated vegetation and polluted the Doce River Valley	Destroyed houses, the company's administrative area, a lodge and part of the local community
Water supply impacts	Degraded for 35 towns	Polluted the São Francisco River Basin, affecting cities, Indigenous communities (Pataxós), quilombolas and riverine populations
Legal breaches notified	38 (by FEMA-MG, IEMA-Espírito Santo and IBAMA since 2016)[a]	5 by IBAMA
Dam monitoring	Considered stable by the 2014 inventory[b]	The risk was classified as low probability, with potentially high impact[c]

Source: Authors.

Notes:

a FEMA is the environmental monitoring agency of MG; IEMA is the environmental monitoring agency of the State of Espírito Santo; IBAMA is the federal government's environmental monitoring agency

b A year before the disaster

c According to monitoring agents on September 2018.

to prevail over the interests of those harmed by the disaster. Additionally, mining regulation by federal, state and municipal government agencies led to jurisdictional confusion and fragmentation. Table 3.2 lists the federal agencies that regulate mining. The National Mining Agency (ANM), that replaces the National Department of Mineral Production (DNPM), was created in 2017 to regulate mining rights, reduce transaction costs and increase royalties. The expectation was that it would improve the security of investments, encourage better contracts, ensure transparency and help resolve conflicts by efficient mediation and conciliation (Bastos, 2018). However, as explained below, with the Mariana disaster, mediation and conciliation failed to implement the PPP and has undermined social justice.

Responding to the Mariana disaster, federal and state environment authorities and managers of the Samarco Company signed a Transaction and

Biodiversity risk management in mining 55

Table 3.2 Federal agencies (Brazil) regulating mining

Institution	Role
Ministry of the Environment (MMA)	Formulate, coordinate and implement environmental policies.
Ministry of Mines and Energy (MME)	Formulate and coordinate minerals sector policies.
Secretariat of Geology, Mining and Mineral Transformation (SGM)	Formulate and coordinate mining sector policies.
National Mining Agency (ANM)	Implement mining policy; manage rights and titles; inspections and enforcement; implement precautionary measures and impose sanctions; manage agreements; collect revenues; manage conflicts; issue mining titles; implement regulations.
Mineral Resource Research Company (CPRM)	Provide geological data.
Mineral Technology Center (CETEM)	Develop technologies for the mineral sector.
National Water Agency (ANA)	Implement the National Policy for Water Resources (PNRH) and allocate water.
National Council for the Environment (CONAMA)	Formulate environmental policies.
National Council of Water Resources (CNRH)	Establish criteria, formulate policies and grant rights to water.
Brazilian Institute of Environment and Natural Renewable Resources (IBAMA)	Licenses projects, monitors for environment compliance and implements cave heritage policies.

Source: Adapted by the authors from information available on the ANM (2018) website http://www.anm.gov.br/

Conduct Adjustment Agreement (Termo de Transação e de Ajustamento de Conduta (*TTAC*)) in March 2016 to restore private land protected areas in the Doce River watershed. The agreement was hastily reached but the environmental consequences of the Fundão dam disaster were not yet known. The *TTAC* was welcomed by the Brazilian federal government (MMA/IBAMA), governors of Minas Gerais and Espírito Santo, Samarco Mineração S.A. and its shareholders, Vale S.A., and BHP Billiton Brazil Ltda.

Under Brazilian law, the *TTAC* is a binding agreement to end a dispute. In the Mariana case, a claim exceeding US$7 billion was suspended. Responsibility for the monitoring implementation of the *TTAC* was passed to the Inter-Federation Committee (CIF). A private operator, the Renova Foundation, was created in September 2016 to implement the *TTAC*. These arrangements echo structures used by James Hardie in Australia to manage civil liabilities for asbestosis injuries. In both the Mariana and James Hardie case, there are questions about the legitimacy of arrangements (Lo, 2017).

The *TTAC* outlines a restoration/rehabilitation and compensation programme for the Doce River watershed and the affected population. Restoration/rehabilitation measures address reversible impacts of the event (TTAC, 2016) and affected people can participate in developing and implementing the actions, access information and physical restitution but not compensation.

Compensatory measures fund social, environmental and economic improvements to address impacts that cannot be mitigated, remediated or repaired. Measures must be proportional to the non-remediable impacts and accelerate recovery of the watershed (TTAC, 2016). The CIF created ten advisory Technical Chambers (CTs) under Deliberation no. 07 of 07/06/17, to implement the *TTAC*. Each involves public institutions. Coordination is the responsibility of an institutional member of CIF. Each CT monitors a group of programmes. Of the 41 programmes, 18 are socio-economic and 23 are environmental.

Specific programmes may limit the geographic area, measures or affected groups – including 'specific measures and actions aimed at locations outside the directly affected area, given that these locations are relevant for the impacted population or contribute to effective environmental recovery of water bodies affected directly by the event' (TTAC, 2016, p. 30, author's translation). An example of a programme is the Restoration of Permanent Preservation Areas (APP) and of Reload Areas of Doce River Watershed, and to control erosion processes. APP areas are key structures for biological diversity conservation in Brazil (discussed below). The overall timeframe for implementation is 15 years, though some programmes are shorter. Budget limits are not predetermined, though sometimes there are minimum and maximum estimated expenditures.

In Brazil, the rights of consumers and victims can be exercised through either individual or collective legal action, under the *Code of Consumer Protection and Defense* (CDC) (*Federal Law no. 8.078/1990*). Collective actions (called 'class actions' in common law jurisdictions) are available for diffuse or group interests or rights, or some individual rights or interests laid down in art. 81, item I, II and III of the *CDC*. These situations include: (i) rights shared by groups or categories of persons; (ii) where the harm affects more than the identifiable individual and (iii) if multiple right holders are affected by the same fact situation (see *CDC*, art. 81, item I). These conditions exist with the Mariana tragedy. Thus, under Brazilian law, the *TTAC* is akin to an arbitration or negotiated settlement. According to Grinover, Cintra and Dinamarco (2012), its consensual nature does not exclude the jurisdiction of courts because it is a means to resolve conflicts by reconciliation:

> The civil procedure law expressly admits three forms of self-composition to be obtained in due process (Code of Civil Procedure, art. 269, II, III and V) to give them effectiveness to conclude the process: an agreement among the parties does not require that a judge recognizes it by sentence.
> (Grinover et al., 2012, p. 38, author's translation)

The *TTAC* is criticised as an inadequate response to the disaster at a number of levels. There is no guarantee of timeliness or effectiveness of implementation (Milanez & Pinto, 2015) and implementation can deprive stakeholders of rights they might have under law. Rodrigues (2004) argues that the *TTAC* was proposed by public agencies to limit civil claims. An out-of-court agreement does not prevent later litigation should that agreement fail, but the *TTAC* mandates that the agreement negates recourse to the law through the courts. The *TTAC* lists what is expected of the parties but probably not all requirements will be satisfied because of unforeseen circumstances. The agreement limits mandatory actions to situations/conditions 'when they are possible', undermining legal enforcement. Citizen interests could be defeated if the *TTAC* fails to be effectively implemented and implementation is outside their control.

Milanez et al. (2015) point out that the *TTAC* includes the goal of 'transparency of actions and the involvement of communities in the discussions' but participation mechanisms are not specified. Medeiros (2016) highlights the absence of representatives of the affected population in the development and implementation arrangements. The effective involvement of riparian and estuarine populations, Indigenous and traditional peoples, rural workers, residents, fishermen, farmers, tourism industry and businessmen, etc., is not guaranteed. The Federal Public Attorney's Office (MPF) has challenged the agreement in the courts because it prioritises the company's interests over the affected populations and the environment (MPF, 2016). Milanez et al. (2015) suggest that the *TTAC* negotiation process should be restarted and involve the affected population and the MPF.

Legal concerns have been raised about the CIF and the Renova Foundation. The CIF consists of representatives from the three levels of government (federal, state and local) and monitors implementation of the *TTAC*. Milanez et al. (2016) point out conflict of interest concerns, partly because the companies of the Vale Group were financiers of the election campaigns of the ex-President of the Republic and the Governors of MG and ES.

The Renova Foundation implements the environmental and socio-economic programmes as a private foundation insulated from political pressures, including oversight of its activities. Governance concerns include that the Renova Foundation can select its own auditors and pay for their services under Clause no. 198, Section III, of the *TTAC*. Milanez et al. (2016) point out that the independence of the panel of audit firms is questionable and suggest that Brazilian public agencies were naive in ignoring institutional problems within the agreement. Milanez et al. argue that Clause no. 10 poses a potential problem by removing public authorities from negotiations between the Foundation and the victims; though promising a fair, fast, simple and transparent negotiation, it will occur without government protection. Clause No. 17 of the *TTAC* allowed Samarco to resume operations before private claims were resolved, reducing the negotiating power of victims. The poverty level and political powerless economic dependence and vulnerability of those affected, compared to the power of the company and the Foundation, suggests that protection may be needed.

58   *Romana Coêho de Araujo et al.*

Many legal complexities that could slow down the *TTAC* are indicated by the lawsuits and administrative actions already commenced. Additional to claims filed by the MPF in the Mariana region, 16 collective actions have been lodged. In the region of Governador Valadares, there are 55,000 actions! One of these actions is claiming R$300 million (US$91 million) for future compensation and reconstruction of damages in the region of Governador Valadares. Many actions have been commenced by signatories to the *TTAC*, particularly against Samarco management (Lopes & Werneck, 2017). Thirty-eight fines were imposed by IBAMA totalling R$345.5 million (US$104 million). None has been paid because of unresolved Samarco appeals. The MG Secretariat of Environment awaits payment of more than R$200 million (US$60 million) of which Samarco has paid only R$6.3 million (US$2 million).

In effect, the mining company has, thus far, merely taken palliative measures. Samarco argues they have applied R$2 billion (US$605 million) towards repair and compensation in addition to the resources supplied to the Renova Foundation.

The James Hardie case in Australia reflected many of the same issues as are evident in the Mariana case. Thus, in responding to massive civil claims for injuries due to asbestos, James Hardie established the Medical Research and Compensation Foundation. A payment of A$293 (approx. US$199) million was made to provide for all future asbestos claims. Similar to the *TTAC*, the structure and the amount were negotiated with the company and the government taking lead roles. The James Hardie corporation then relocated to Holland. Subsequently, it emerged that the amounts provided for future compensation were vastly inadequate. A government enquiry in 2004 was very critical of the negotiation, and independent economic analysis identified a massive funding shortfall. Public pressure led to renegotiation. The interest of affected citizens was represented by a team led by a senior union figure, appointed by the state government. Ultimately, in 2007, James Hardie agreed to guarantee a A$4 (almost US$3) billion fund, and successful prosecutions of some James Hardie executives followed.

Are there also reasons to believe that the amounts allocated to the *TTAC* might be insufficient to deal with the damage to society and the environment caused by the Mariana disaster? Under Clause no. 226 of the *TTAC*, Samarco, or its controlling shareholders, must have financed the 41 restoration programmes up to R$4.40 (US$1.34) billion, from 2016 to 2018. There is an additional R$500 (US$151) million for sanitation in affected municipalities. The estimated expenditure by Samarco is R$11.1 (US$3.36) billion by 2030. According to the Renova Foundation, indemnities of R$430 million (US$130 million) had been paid by mid-2017. Is US$84,000 per hectare enough to restore a degraded biologically diverse area in a tropical country, and has enough been allocated to reverse social, financial and economic losses? The *TTAC* requires shareholders to restore the Doce River watershed to the situation prior to the disaster (Reading 23, TTAC) but what defines the *status quo*?

Blignaut, Aronson and De Wit (2014) argue that although conceptual progress has been made in the economics of restoration, insufficient practical results have emerged to be confident in valuation and financing. In their words: "there has been far too little work on how to actually measure and monitor the economic effects of restoration". They note that if restoration scientists and practitioners were to work closely with economists, it would be "increasingly easier to detect the economic effects of future restoration projects, choose economically efficient ones to implement, and demonstrate their economic outcomes" (p. 36). According to Milanez et al. (2016), the proposed socio-economic programmes are generic and vague, while environmental programmes are specific and detailed. The meaning of some of the *TTAC* programmes is unclear (e.g. E.6: Programme to Manage Socioeconomic Programmes; and J.2: National and International Communication Programme). The *TTAC* does not provide mechanisms to ensure sustained tangible outcomes, especially with socio-economic programmes. It is unclear whether the affected regions and people can transform early recovery investment into permanent conservation, and social and economic wellbeing outcomes. These problems and inconsistent deadlines will make it difficult to assess and control performance.

A closer examination of the G2. Programme to Recover Permanent Preservation Areas (APP) and Recharge Areas of the Doce River Watershed and for Erosion Control (the G2 Programme) illustrates the risks. For example, the G2 Programme is influenced by: (a) size of the focal area; (b) scale of estimated costs; (c) relationship with the biodiversity and private land conservation objectives of the *Brazilian Forest Code* (*Federal Law no. 12.651/2012*) and (d) dependence upon a Payment for Environmental Service (PES) scheme for long-term success.

The G2 Programme area is 40,000 ha, which is 0.5 per cent of the Doce River watershed. This is much larger than typical PES schemes in Brazil (Pagiola, Von Glehn, & Taffarello, 2012). Its scale and complexity will demand significant human, material and financial resources. Cost benchmarking for the restoration projects is particularly difficult because of a need to estimate PES payments that should ensure effective voluntary participation. De Groot et al. (2013) note that in some instances of reported cost, a total is provided and in others an average is reported. Sometimes costs include direct financial cost, ignoring in-kind contribution. Often, total cost is mentioned without a reference unit such as area or distance (e.g. kilometres of riverfront restored).

Bernardo (2017), after analysing PES schemes in Brazil, concludes that payments to agricultural producers for environmental services from their holdings are smaller than the opportunity cost of land use, providing little incentive to voluntarily participate. De Groot et al. (2013) point out that though benefits are often reported, the reports seldom show whether the perceived benefits were marketable and, if so, to whom and by whom, or whether they represented economy-wide benefits. In their opinion, a failure to consider the distributional impacts and/or the difference between marketable and economy-wide benefits to society can, and often does, lead to confusion because restoration benefits are often public while the costs are private.

Land uses and people are heterogeneous, environmentally and socially, and payment requirements can vary greatly. How will the programme ensure participants stay in a programme covering 40,000 ha for ten years over 80,000 sq km. If purchaser funding for environmental services is inadequate? Is ten years long enough to ensure the achievement of restoration objectives and efficiencies desirable for implementation? Have the risks of insufficient funding been explicitly considered and contingency plans put in place? How will (inefficient) overpayment be avoided? Such fundamental questions are not answered in the available documents.

To date there has been no answer to the frequently asked question: How was the US$3.4 billion for a 15-year period estimated? Comparing this to restoration costs of other environmental disasters worldwide, US$3.4 billion is low (though comparison is difficult). Making US$3.4 billion the *TTAC* ceiling provides certainty for Samarco. An adequate procedure would involve estimating all damage costs and all restoration costs to at least create transparency.

The issues discussed suggest a credible risk that the *TTAC* will not be effective. This will waste human, material, financial and economic resources and fail to implement the polluter's obligation to restore biological diversity. It would condemn thousands of people to poverty. A failure to implement the PPP will send a counterproductive signal to Samarco, Vale, BHP Billiton and the mining sector that they can avoid full responsibility for harms they cause.

As already noted, the PPP requires the internalisation of externalities by imposing the costs of harm and risk prevention on the accountable entity. This provides a powerful incentive to avoid creating risks without requiring criminality. This is different to rewarding pro-environmental activities, a Protector Recipient Principle (PRP), the basic framework of PES schemes. According to Faganello and Folegatti (2007), any actor who undertakes practices that conserve or protect a natural asset should be paid for that conservation. This might be via compensation, credit or financial transfers from beneficiaries of environmental services.[1]

PRP provides rewards for environmental services rendered voluntarily (Deon Sette & Nogueira, 2012, p. 162). This is different to a situation where environmental investment is a legal obligation. Brazilian law provides for civil liability for environmental harm, holding harm-doers accountable for repairing, eliminating or reducing harm to return the environment asset to the *status quo ante*. If this is impossible, financial compensation is payable. These compensatory and accountability rules reflect the PPP approach. Under the *TTAC* the Samarco Company obtains cash flow for its restoration expenditures that reduce its liability expenditures in the short run, and it benefits from a 30-year payment schedule financed by the exploitation of its mines. This approach compromises PPP accountability with something approximating a PRP.

To understand the case of Brumadinho tailings dam disaster, it is necessary to understand the context in which the dam was installed (Almeida, Jackson

Biodiversity risk management in mining 61

Filho, & Vilela, 2019). This upstream tailing dam was located in the buffer zone of the State Park Serra do Rola Moça (Minas Gerais). It had been deactivated for three years before breaking. The company had adopted strategic choices to derive maximum profit from its mining operation. One of the consequences of that choice was 'to lobby for a softening of the legislation that regulates mining and its environmental and social impacts as well as reduce the level of agencies public oversight and inspection' (Almeida et al., 2019, p. 3, author translation). Thus, the licensing process for the reactivation and expansion of the Córrego do Feijão mine had been approved in a simplified environmental licensing process. TÜV Süd, a Germany company, had certified the structure of this dam before it collapsed in January 2019, spreading toxic mud and causing human tragedy, release of contaminants and irreversible damage to the environment. Note also that in the case of the case of the Brumadinho, as well as in Samarco disaster, 'emergency plans existed only on paper and ... alarm systems were non-existent and ineffective' (Freitas et al., 2019). Many agreements concerning liability and reparation have been approved by the Court of Justice of Minas Gerais with the families of the victims and there are lawsuits in Brazilian courts (and in Germany against TÜV Süd) concerning requirements to repair environmental damage.

There are 717 mining tailings dams in Brazil, categorised by ANM by construction, and a large number are identified as having significant risks. The Mariana disaster triggered the discussion for *State Draft Bill no. 3,676/2016* – also known as 'a sea of mud never again' – in the Legislative Assembly of Minas Gerais. This draft bill became *State Law no. 23,291/2019* (MG) on 25 February 2019 – less than a month after the Brumadinho disaster. Under this law mining companies, whether operating or idle, in MG have 90 days to submit plans to replace upstream tailings dams. After approval by the public authority, each company has three years to migrate to alternative technology. It is prohibited to grant licences for dams that could harm communities. Legally, the mining entrepreneur is responsible for 'whole of life' dam safety.

Federally, upstream tailings dams were prohibited by Resolution 4 of ANM of 15 February 2019 with up to five years for companies to adjust. Companies in the Minas Gerais have three years to implement alternative technology and companies operating in other states have five years. The resolution creates 'auto rescue' zones up to ten kilometres below the dams or, where possible flooding might occur, within 30 minutes. In these zones, dams must be disabled by 15 August 2019.

Conclusions and implications

Examination of two tailings dam failures in Brazil illustrates inadequacies in post-disaster management. Tailings dam disasters of the magnitude experienced in Brazil have not occurred in Australia but do, nevertheless, occur, including one associated with the Adani coal operation. Some failures have disastrous potential (e.g. radioactive leakage from the Ranger uranium mine (ERA radioactive slurry spill, 2016)). Following mine dam disasters in Brazil, the Church of England (2019) launched the Investor Mining and Tailings Safety site which identified 11 Australian dams of high to extreme risk (McGuire, 2019). The Australian mining sector has also grappled with compensation for human injury from mine products, particularly, as noted, from asbestos (Australian Asbestos Network, 2019). The James Hardie case was widely publicised, around the world. The Jackson Enquiry report (2004) alone provides lessons about negotiated settlements of large class claims: negotiating when full facts are not known is unreliable; injured parties should be independently represented and reliance on experts and audit firms retained by the polluter is problematic (Gunz & van der Laan, 2011).

The Brazilian mineral sector faces major governance challenges and further (avoidable) mine dam and other disasters cannot be ruled out. As in Australia, the institutional structures for mining governance structures are fragmented, undermining regulatory credibility with the two major mining related disasters in Brazil having caused significant social and environmental costs. Our examination of the mining governance regimes also reveals the failure of institutional arrangements to promote legal certainty, reduce discretionary power and promote sustainable mining.

A mine disaster is evidence that safety protocols were either inadequate or not complied with or both. Political lobbying creates pressures for 'light touch' regulation. Mine advocates, and some government agencies, will oppose conditions that add costs to mining or complicate operations. Risks may increase as mine activities change and the context of the mine changes without protocols being adjusted. Citizens may have limited involvement and may not know risks are increasing. Safeguards may be implemented poorly and risks may not be predictable or feasibility manageable.

Though Brazil and Australia are far apart, have different legal traditions, and differ in many other ways, similar dynamics in mining governance can be observed. The formal institutions largely reflect environmental and social protection principles in international agreements. These are translated into coherent laws, and organisational arrangements and processes implement these laws. Citizens can use these institutions to protest against decisions which they think are improper and courts will give effect to the rules. Benefits in terms of transparency and accountability are a result and the system should act as a check against egregious abuses of power.

However, the examples demonstrate that implementation often falls short of desirable practice. In both countries, public agencies act in ways that favour the mining sector, following the procedural letter while failing to honour underlying principles. There is evidence that political decisions enable tactics that undermine the public interest rationale of governance. The examples specifically do not show commitment to the PPP.

There is evidence that the methods for deciding to approve mines or to redress harm caused by mines have tended to favour the mining industry. There are many possible explanations, not least being the capacity of those holding economic power to suborn those with political power. In neither jurisdiction is there an independent guarantor of the integrity of implementation of laws nor explicit reporting of their effectiveness. This meta-governance failure affects natural resource governance generally (Chapter 12). A study of Australia's environmental laws suggests the need for politically independent oversight and quality control for environmental governance (Fowler et al., 2017).

What can be learned from the examples discussed in this chapter? Three things stand out. The first is the need for explicit attention to power imbalances. The second is the need for robust mechanisms to ensure implementation of governance arrangements. The third is that more attention should be directed to the analysis used for decisions that have significant impacts on disadvantaged groups and the environment.

Above all this chapter demonstrates that laws and procedures which should ensure governance with integrity and transparency are necessary but not sufficient to deliver that outcome. Rules and procedures can be manipulated; and they can be implemented well or badly. It is necessary to have strong institutional arrangements to ensure that manipulation is limited and decision making and action are credible.

Note

1 This PR Principle has been widely used as the basic theoretical framework for PES schemes for the last two decades. For an overview of its use in Latin America, see the UNEP-WCMC (2016). For a study in Kenya, see Kagombe Kungu, Mugendi, & Cheboiwo (2018). See also Faganello, and Folegatti (2007).

References

Advisian. (2015). *Abbot Point environmental impact statement* (vol. 2). Brisbane, QLD Department of State Development.

Almeida, I. M., Jackson Filho, J. M., & Vilela, R. A. G. (2019). Reasons for investigating the organizational dynamics of the Vale tailings dam disaster in Brumadinho, Minas Gerais State, Brazil. *Cad. Saúde Pública, 35* (4). doi: 10.1590/0102-311X00027319

Andrusevych, A., Alge, T., & Konrad, C. (Eds.). (2011). *Case law of the Aarhus Convention Compliance Committee, 2004–2011* (2nd ed.). Bruxelles, Belgium: UNECE, Resource & Analysis Center, 'Society and Environment'.

Australian Asbestos Network (the). (2019). *Court cases.* Retrieved from https://www.australianasbestosnetwork.org.au/asbestos-history/battles-2/court-cases/

Bastos, M. M. T. (2018). *Governança, desenho institucional e regulação no setor mineral Brasileiro* (Governance, institutional design and regulation in the Brazilian mineral industry). (Unpublished doctoral dissertation). Federal University of Rio de Janeiro, Brazil.

Bernardo, C. T. S. (2017). *Economia ambiental e ecologia: A proximidade se limita ao prefixo?* (Environmental economics and ecology: The closeness is confined to the prefix?). (Doctoral dissertation). University of Brasília, Brazil.

Blignaut, J., Aronson, J., & De Wit, M. (2014). The economics of restoration: Looking back and leaping forward. *Annals of the New York Academy of Sciences, 1322* (1), 35–47.

Church of England. (2019). Investor mining and tailings safety initiative. Retrieved from. https://www.churchofengland.org/investor-mining-tailings-safety-initiative

Currell, M., Werner, A., McGrath, C., Webb, J., & Berkman, M. (2017). Problems with applying hydrogeological science to regulation of Australian mining projects: Carmichael Mine and Doongmabulla Springs. *Journal of Hydrology, 548*, 674–682.

Damiens, F. L. P., Mumaw, L., Backstrom, A., Bekessy, S. A., Coffey, B., Faulkner, R., & Gordon, A. (2017). Why politics and context matter in conservation policy. *Global Policy, 8*(2), 253–256. doi: 10.1111/1758-5899.12415

De Groot, R. S., Blignaut, J., Der Ploeg, S. V., Aronson, J., Elmqvist, T., & Farley, J. (2013). Benefits of investing in ecosystem restoration. *Conservation Biology, 27* (6), 1286–1293.

Deloitte Access Economics. (2019). *Estimates of royalties and company tax accrued in 2017–2018*. Retrieved from Minerals Council of Australia website: http://minerals.org.au/

Deon Sette, M., & Nogueira, J. M. (2012). Tributo Ambiental: Avaliação inicial acerca dos aspectos jurídicos e econômicos (Environmental tax: Preliminary assessment of the legal and economic aspects). Retrieved from Marli Deon Sette website: http://www.marliambiental.com.br/artigos.php

Ebbesson, J., Gaugitsch, H., Jendrośka, J., Stec, S., & Marshall, F. (2014). *The Aarhus convention: An implementation guide* (2nd ed.). Retrieved from https://www.unece.org/fileadmin/DAM/env/pp/Publications/Aarhus_Implementation_Guide_interactive_eng.pdf

EDO (Environment Defenders Office), NSW. (2016). *EDO NSW report:* Merits review in planning in NSW. Retrieved from NSW EDO website https://d3n8a8pro7vhmx.cloudfront.net/edonsw/pages/2998/attachments/original/1467777537/EDO_NSW_Report_-_Merits_Review_in_Planning_in_NSW.pdf?1467777537

Environment Law Australia. (n.d.). *Carmichael coal (Adani) mine cases in the federal court.* Retrieved from http://envlaw.com.au/carmichael-coal-mine-federal-court/

ERA Radioactive Slurry spill: NT Government won't lay charges against miner. (2016, February 12). *ABC News.* Retrieved from https://www.abc.net.au/news/2016-02-12/era-avoids-charges-over-radioactive-slurry-spill/7163560

Faganello, C. R. F., & Folegatti, M. V. (2007). *Fundamentação da cobrança pelo uso da água na agricultura irrigada, na microbacia do Ribeirão dos Marins, Piracicaba/SP* (Rationale for charging for the use of water in irrigated agriculture in the Ribeirão dos Marins, Piracicaba/SP). Universidade de São Paulo, Piracicaba. Retrieved from: http://www.teses.usp.br/teses/disponiveis/91/91131/tde-18072007-101710/

Fowler, R., Wilcox, M., Martin, P., Holley, C., & Godden, L. (2017). *Environmental governance.* (Technical Paper No. 2). Melbourne, Australia: APEEL. Retrieved from http://apeel.org.au

Freitas, C. M., Barcellos, C., Asmus, C. I. R. F., Silva, M. A., Xavier, D. R. (2019). From Samarco in Mariana to Vale in Brumadinho: Mining dam disasters and public health. *Cad. Saúde Pública, 35* (5). doi: 10.1590/0102-311X00052519

Garnett, S., Wintle, B., Lindenmayer, D., Franklin, D., & Wolnarski, J. (2019, May 31). Adani's finch plan is approved, just weeks after being sent back to the drawing board. *The Conversation.* Retrieved from http://theconversation.com/adanis-finch-plan-is-approved-just-weeks-after-being-sent-back-to-the-drawing-board-118114

Grinover, A. P., Cintra, A. C. A., & Dinamarco, C. R. (2012). *Teoria geral do processo* (General theory of process). São Paulo, Brazil: Malheiros Press.

Gunz, S., & Van der Laan, S. (2011). Actuaries, conflicts of interest and professional independence: The case of James Hardie Industries limited. *Journal of Business Ethics, 98*(4), 583–596.

Higginson, S. (2014). *Legal challenges like Bulga a key safeguard against corruption*. Retrieved from NSW EDO website https://www.edonsw.org.au/legal_challenges_like_bulga_a_key_safeguard_against_corruption

ICAC (Independent Commission against Corruption). (2012). *Anti-corruption safeguards and the NSW planning system* (ICAC report 2012). Retrieved from https://www.icac.nsw.gov.au/prevention/corruption-prevention-publications

Jackson, D. F. (2004). *Report of the special commission of inquiry into the Medical Research and Compensation Foundation*. Sydney, NSW: NSW Government. (Jackson Report).

Kagombe, J. K., Kungu, J., Mugendi, Mugendi, D., & Cheboiwo, J. K. (2018). Evaluating the willingness to pay for watershed protection in Ndaka-ini Dam, Muranga County, Kenya. *Civil and Environmental Research, 10* (1), 2225–2514.

Kennedy, A. (2016). *Environmental justice and land use conflict*. London: Earthscan, Routledge.

Lo, S. H. (2017). Piercing of the corporate veil for evasion of tort obligations. *Common Law World Review, 46* (1), 42–60.

Long, S., & Slezak, M. (2019, April 11). Inside Melissa Price's decision to approve Adani's groundwater plan. *ABC News*. Retrieved from https://www.abc.net.au/news/2019-04-11/adani-damning-assessment-turned-into-approval/10990288

Lopes, V., & Werneck, G. (2017). Milhares de ações sobre a tragédia de Mariana se arrastam na Justiça (Thousands of lawsuits of the Miriana tragedy drag on in court). *Press Release*. Estado de Minas Gerais website. Retrieved from https://www.em.com.br/app/noticia/gerais/2017/08/09/interna_gerais,890448/milhares-de-acoes-sobre-a-tragedia-de-mariana-se-arrastam-na-justica.shtml

Luciano, D. (2019). *Da Banana à Prata: Os mistérios desvendados da mineração Brasileira* (From banana to silver: Mysteries of Brazilian mining activities). Rio de Janeiro: Editora Lumen Juris.

Luhmann, N. (1984). *Social systems*. Stanford, CA: Stanford University Press.

Martin, P., & Becker, J. (2011). A tale of two systems: Conflict, law and developing water allocation in two common law jurisdictions. *International Journal of Rural Law and Policy, 1*, 1–18.

McGuire, K. (2019, June). Tailings dams failure risks range from high to extreme in audits by Australian Mining Giats. *ABC Rural*. Retrieved from https://www.abc.net.au/news/rural/2019-06-20/tailings-dam-audit-finds-high-failure-risks-across-australia/11223510

Medeiros, E. (2016). *Longe das vítimas, governo assina acordo sobre desastre de Mariana* (Away from the victims, the Government signs an agreement related to the disaster of Mariana). Agência Pública. Retrieved from http://apublica.org/2016/03/longe-das-vitimas-governo-assina-acordo-sobre-desastre-de-mariana/

Milanez, B., & Pinto, R. G. (2016). *Considerações sobre o termo de transação e de ajustamento de conduta firmado entre Governo Federal, Governo do Estado de Minas Gerais, Governo do Estado do Espírito Santo, Samarco Mineração S.A., Vale S. A. e BHP Billiton Brasil Ltda* (Considerations on the agreement of transaction and of conduct adjustment between the Brazilian Federal Government, the State Government of Minas Gerais, the State Government of Espírito Santo, Samarco Mineração S.A., Vale S.A. and BHP Billiton Brazil Ltda). Retrieved from Research Gate website: https://www.researchgate.net/publication/301219622_Consideracoes_sobre_o_Termo_de_Transacao_e_de_Ajustamento_de_Conduta_firmado_entre_Governo_Federal_Governo_do_Estado_de_Minas_Gerais_Governo_do_Estado_do_Espirito_Santo_Samarco_Mineracao_SA_Vale_S_A_e

Milanez, B., Santos, R. S. P., Wanderley, L. J. M., Mansur, M. S., Pinto, R. G., Gonçalves, R. J. A., & Coelho, T. P. (2015). *Antes fosse mais leve a carga: Avaliação dos aspectos econômicos, políticos e sociais do desastre da Samarco/Vale/BHP em Mariana/MG* (I wish it was a lighter load: Evaluation of the economic, political and social aspects of Samarco's disaster/Valley/BHP in Mariana/MG). PoEMAS. Retrieved from http://www.ufjf.br/poemas/files/2014/07/PoEMAS-2015-Antes-fosse-mais-leve-a-carga-vers%C3%A3o-final.pdf

MPF (Ministério Publico Federal). (2016). Ministério Público questiona acordo entre União, Estados de MG e ES, Samarco, Vale e BHB Billiton (Prosecutor questions agreement between Union, States of MG and ES, Samarco, Vale and BHB Billiton). *Press Release.* Retrieved from http://www.mpf.mp.br/es/sala-de-imprensa/noticias-es/nota-a-imprensa-2013-ministerio-publico-questiona-acordo-entre-uniao-estados-de-mg-e-es-samarco-vale-e-bhb-billiton

NSW Planning Assessment Commission. (2015). *Determination Report: Warkworth Continuation Project SSD6464.* Retrieved from http://www.pac.nsw.gov.au/resources/pac/media/files/pac/projects/2015/05/warkworth-continuation-project--determination/determination-report/1-warkworthdeterminationreportpdf.pdf

OECD (Organisation for Economic Co-operation and Development). (1972). *Environment and economics: Guiding principles concerning international economic aspects of environmental policie: Recommendations C(72)128.* Retrieved from http://www.oecd.org/officialdocuments/publicdisplaydocumentpdf/?cote=OCDE/GD(92)81&docLanguage=En

Pagiola, S., Von Glehn, H. C., & Taffarello, D. (2012). *Experiências de pagamentos por serviços ambientais no Brasil* [Experiences of payments for environmental services in Brazil]. São Paulo, Brazil: Secretaria do Meio Ambiente.

Rodrigues, G. A. (2004). Princípios da celebração do compromisso de ajustamento de conduta em matéria ambiental (Principles for celebration of commitment to environmental conduct adjustment). *Revistas Direito do Ambiente, 7* (13), 67–88.

Slezac, M. (2019, May 14). Adani water plan ticked off within hours despite lack of detail, internal CSIRO emails reveal. *ABC News.* Retrieved from https://www.abc.net.au/news/2019-05-14/adani-csiro-emails-foi-melissa-price/11107276

Southam, J. (2012). *Mining law and policy: International perspectives.* Annandale, NSW: Federation Press.

Trading Economics. (2018/2019). *GDP from mining: By country 2019.* Retrieved from https://tradingeconomics.com/country-list/gdp-from-mining

TTAC (Transaction and conduct adjustment agreement). (2016). *Termo de Transação e de Ajustamento de Conduta* [Transaction and conduct adjustment agreement]. Retrieved from. http://politica.estadao.com.br/blogs/fausto-macedo/wp-content/uploads/sites/41/2016/05/acordo_rio_doce.pdf

UNEP-WCMC (2016). *The state of biodiversity in Latin America and the Caribbean: A mid-term review of progress towards the Aichi Biodiversity Targets.* Cambridge, UK: UNEP-WCMC.

Williamson, O. E. (2000). The new institutional economics: Taking stock, looking ahead. *Journal of Economic Literature, 38* (3), 595–613. doi: 10.1257/jel.38.3.595

4 Creating and managing marine protected areas

Nathalia Lima, Paul Martin, and Solange Teles da Silva

Abstract

The complex, diverse and often-fragile ecosystems fringing the coastlines of Brazil and Australia are impacted by the behaviour or many diverse actors. Marine spatial planning (MSP) and Marine Protected Areas (MPA) are important instruments that governments of the two countries use to protect biodiversity and regulate activities within these ecosystems. This chapter provides an overview of the use Australian and Brazilian government make of MSPs and MPAs and discusses the successes and problems of implementation. Australia's marine protection system is more advanced than Brazil's but the latter has been progressing towards a comprehensive MSP and MPA system, though the system is hampered by a lack of implementation.

Introduction

Oceans cover approximately two-thirds of our planet and the habitats associated with oceans are a complex assemblage of natural and human systems, involving incredible biodiversity and human-nature interactions. Human uses of oceans, seas and marine resources are diverse, as are their impacts. The UNEP-WCMC Ocean Data Viewer (n.d.) provides access to details of many ocean habitats and species distributions, and the UNEP's draft *Proposal for a New Marine and Coastal Strategy for 2020–2030* (2019) highlights the important role of Marine Protected Areas (MPAs) in the conservation of marine biodiversity and for people who depend on marine resources. Such MPAs have been part of marine strategies since the 1980s. The International Union for the Preservation of Nature (IUCN) and the World Wildlife Fund, in their global conservation strategy, recommend that MPAs should be large enough to:

1 ensure the essential ecological processes and functions of the life support system
2 preserve genetic diversity
3 ensure the sustainable use of species and ecosystems.

68   *Nathalia Lima et al.*

According to the *Atlas of Marine Protection* (Marine Conservation Institute, 2019), Australia is the legal steward of 9,025,021.0 km^2 of marine areas, with 1,177 MPAs covering 35.99 per cent of its maritime jurisdiction. More than 0.01 per cent (704.4 km^2) of these MPAs are classified as implemented, that is, having 'demonstrable and ongoing enforceable rules, monitoring, evaluation, adaptive management and conservation outcomes' (Marine Conservation Institute, 2019). In addition to declaring MPAs, Australia has introduced commercial fishing quotas to address fishing overharvesting. The quotas have been partly responsible for causing a reduction Australia's fishery production.

Brazil's marine estate is around one-third of Australia's (Australia is an island, thus having more ocean frontage) at 3,677,598.6 km^2. The atlas (Marine Conservation Institute, 2019) shows that Brazil has 163 MPAs covering 63,630.0 km^2 or 1.73 per cent of the marine jurisdiction as implemented MPAs and 903,090 km^2 of unimplemented MPAs. Fishery statistics have not been produced for Brazil since 2011; it is, therefore, not possible to provide an analysis of current fishery production.

The governance of marine areas is difficult regardless of whether they are large and remote or small and close to heavily populated coastal zones. In this chapter, we discuss the successes and problems of marine biodiversity conservation in Australia and Brazil through the lens of MPAs. We also stress the role of Marine Spatial Planning (MSP) to create an ocean governance system. Neither Brazil nor Australia can claim to have achieved sustainable marine biodiversity, though both have set aside significant areas as MPAs. A declaration of a marine reserve does not automatically indicate good biodiversity outcomes. We begin our discussion by outlining the issues that must be managed by governments to ensure marine biodiversity conservation and list the international agreements that have implications for marine conservation and have been ratified by Australia and Brazil. We then outline the different approaches that Australia and Brazil have taken to marine governance before presenting a discussion on the challenges of creating effective marine protected areas in Brazil compared to the challenges for Australia, particularly highlighting the case of the Great Barrier Reef Marine Park. We conclude by highlighting the role of MSP and its potential to foster ocean governance.

Marine biodiversity conservation and international agreements

Many issues – all to be managed by the governments of respective countries – affect marine biodiversity and some pressures (notably climate change and human) are pervasive. Issues include:

- Species and habitat protection. This includes marine protection zoning and control of maritime environmental crimes (e.g. illegal harvesting; seabed, reef or seagrass destruction; vessel pollution, and control over foreshore mangrove removal and illegal development).

Marine protected areas 69

- Management of in-shore and offshore fisheries. These include amateur, professional and Traditional fishing, aquaculture and the incursions of unlicensed trawlers.
- Inland and foreshore activities that impact the marine environment. These include activities on the foreshore and land clearing or agriculture away from the marine environment, which cause sediment and chemical pollution.
- Protection of iconic species. These include those recognised in international agreements (e.g. cetaceans, turtles, sharks) and other threatened or endangered species.
- Control of extractive activities. These include offshore oil and gas, minerals and resources such as sand and gravel.
- Boating and shipping, which cause harm to seabeds, reefs and seagrasses (from anchoring, 'ploughing' and impact), pollutants (garbage, fuel and contaminated ballast), foreshore activities (pollution, facilities impacts) and marine accidents (cargo overboard, wrecks, pollutants).
- Marine infrastructures including foreshore jetties and moorings, refuelling and other services, boat building and boat wrecking and tourism facilities; and marine structures such as oil-rigs and windfarms.
- Contaminants including sediment from rivers or the foreshores, chemicals, fuel and marine invasive species.
- Legal and political claims, including international disputes over boundaries and marine rights, and domestic claims over, for example, Indigenous or Traditional communities' rights, and marine and coastal protected areas.

Marine biodiversity involves more than waters and submarine habitats. Marine life and systems involve the zone between the waters and the land, and impactful activities from the land: Figure 4.1 illustrates the complexity and the interconnectivity of issues. The issues identified in Figure 4.1 were those highlighted through workshops with some citizens of the South coast of Eastern Australia. The estuaries included sites with MPA status. Larger marine areas with diverse human uses and more industrial or human pressures are more complicated to manage – we also discuss those issues in this chapter.

The figure illustrates the interaction among natural states (left-hand side), pressures from human decisions and actions (right-hand side) and the effects on biodiversity (centre). The illustrated assemblage of issues, decisions and actions highlights many challenges for marine biodiversity governance. There are many (often seemingly unconnected) users and interest groups involved, and some interests conflict. The effects of the resulting political complexity emerge as difficulties in creating effective MPAs in both countries. Proposals for marine reserves are often hotly contested between user and environmental interest groups. This typically results in less than complete protection, and in conflicts and difficulties for environmental and policing agencies in their attempts to implement protective zones.

The diversity of issues and interests means that many government agencies are, or might be, involved. In the example above (Figure 4.1), relevant

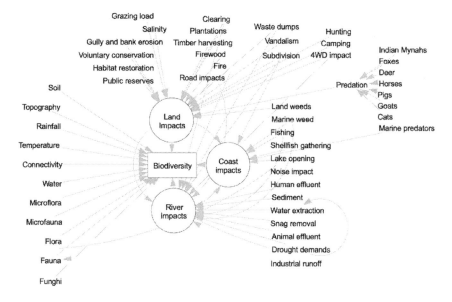

Figure 4.1 Estuarine biodiversity issues identified by workshop participants, east coast of Australia.
Source: Paul Martin.

agencies span all three levels of Australian governments – federal, state and local – with responsibility for environmental protection, MPAs, boating, housing and industrial development, fishing, agriculture and other issues. The interests that are affected and which affect that governance include fishing and boating, environmental science and advocacy, businesses and business lobby groups, citizen NGOs and agricultural interests.

One result is political complications that affect marine governance. A similar political complexity occurs with proposals for marine environmental protection in both countries, which has motivated Australia and Brazil sign a number of international agreements with implications for marine conservation (see Table 4.1).

Australia's marine governance

The Australian government has taken a laudable approach to marine environmental governance. It has an extensive system of commercial fishery licences, and government purchase and cancellation of these licences has reduced excessive fishing pressure on many stocks. Australia has a substantial and growing system of marine parks, though there are imperfections (to be discussed later). Australia demonstrates international leadership for the control of whaling and Australia enforces strong laws against marine pollution.

Marine protected areas 71

Table 4.1 Treaties relevant to protect marine biodiversity to which Australia and Brazil are parties[a]

Year	Convention title	Aspect of marine biodiversity	Commencement date	
			Australia	Brazil
1946	International Convention for the Regulation of Whaling	Conservation of whale stocks and the orderly development of the whaling industry.	1948-11-10	1974-01-04
1971	Convention on Wetlands of International Importance especially as Waterfowl Habitat (Ramsar Convention)	Conservation and sustainable use of wetlands.	1975-12-21	1993-09-24
1972	Convention concerning the Protection of the World Cultural and Natural Heritage	Conservation of nature and preservation of cultural heritage, considering the interaction of them.	1975-12-17	1977-12-01
1972	Convention for the Conservation of Antarctic Seals	Protection, scientific study and rational use of Antarctic seals, and to maintain a satisfactory balance within the ecological system of the Antarctic.	1987-07-31	1991-03-13
1973	International Convention for the Prevention of Pollution from Ships, as Modified by Protocol of 1978 (MARPOL 73/78)	Prevention of pollution of the marine environment by ships from operational or accidental causes.	1988-01-14	1988-04-29
1973	Convention on International Trade in Endangered Species of Wild Fauna and Flora (CITES)	Protect of certain endangered species from over-exploitation by a system of import/export permits. Aims to ensure that international trade in wild marine animals and marine plants does not threaten their survival.	1976-10-27	1975-11-04
1979	Convention on Conservation of Migratory Species of Wild Animals	Protection of migratory species of wild animals and their habitat through action of States where such species spend part of their life cycle or over which they fly.	1991-09-01	2015-10-01
1980	Convention for the Conservation of Antarctic Marine Living Resources	Preservation of marine life and environmental integrity in and near Antarctica.	1982-04-07	1986-02-27
1982	United Nations Convention on the Law of the Sea (UNCLOS)	Preservation of marine environment	1994-11-16	1994-11-16
1991	Protocol on Environmental Protection to the Antarctic Treaty	Affirms Antarctica as a special conservation area, and enhances the protection of the Antarctic environment and dependent and associated ecosystems.	1998-01-14	1998-01-14

(*Continued*)

72   *Nathalia Lima et al.*

Year	Convention title	Aspect of marine biodiversity	Commencement date	
			Australia	*Brazil*
1992	*Convention on Biological Diversity (CBD)*	Conservation and sustainable use of marine and coastal biological diversity.	1993-12-29	1994-05-29
2001	*Agreement on the Conservation of Albatrosses and Petrels*	Conservation of albatrosses and petrels.	2004-02-01	2008-12-01
2004	*International Convention for the Control and Management of Ships' Ballast Water and Sediments (Ballast Water Convention).*	Prevention of the spread of harmful aquatic organisms through standards and procedures for managing ships' ballast water and sediments.	2017-09-08	2017-09 08

Source: (Ecolex, 2019; UN, *Treaty Collection*, 2019).

a   The list does not include regional agreements.

Despite this, the trends for marine biodiversity are 'mixed', as the quote from the *Marine state of environment report 2016* (Evans, Bax, & Smith, 2017):

> Although the overall status of the marine environment is good, some individual species and species groups remain in poor condition. Despite improving management in several sectors, trends in many marine environmental resources and, in particular, many listed species are uncertain, and some populations continue to decrease in size. The lack of coordinated monitoring and management across sectors reduces Australia's capacity to respond to new and increasing pressures and cumulative impacts.
>
> (p. xi)

Australia's 5th report under the *Convention on Biological Diversity (CBD)* (Department of the Environment, 2014) discusses riverine and marine species protection but the report has significant gaps. It does not, for example, consider the important work of state agencies which primarily govern terrestrial and near coastal issues other than for waters under federal jurisdiction; nor does it discuss the private sector's role in biodiversity use and protection (e.g. marine stewardship standards and sustainable fishery initiatives, and managing offshore fish farms). In summary, the 5th report states:

> [I]n comparison to the marine waters of other nations, Australia's oceans are considered as being in good condition; however, there is substantial degradation in the east, south-east and south-west of the oceans surrounding the continent, and ecosystems near the coast, bays and estuaries in these regions are in poor to very poor condition.
>
> (p. 2)

The detailed assessment in the *State of the marine environment report* (Evans et al., 2017, pp. 94–101) on the state of biodiversity concludes with a graphic that indicates continued deterioration is likely, and a summary:

Overall condition of the marine environment is good. A number of pressures on marine species and ecosystems are increasing and reports that some individual species and habitats are in poor condition, including coral reefs, fringing temperate rocky reefs and associated species.

(p. 105)

The later review of Australia's federal marine governance by the Australian Panel of Experts in Environmental Law (APEEL, 2017) came to the more pessimistic view that despite:

[P]olicy commitments to integrated planning and management of marine resources and the coastal zone, current governance approaches are fragmented across various levels of government and sectoral regimes, including those for conservation, fishing, pollution control, biosecurity, and oil and gas and seabed mining.

(p. 3)

That report considers current states, pressures and likely futures. Its discussion of marine governance is complementary to, but more detailed than, the marine commentary within the 5th report (Department of the Environment, 2014) or the *State of the marine environment report* (Evans et al., 2017). It focuses on constitutional issues, sectoral laws, marine planning and MPA, protection outside MPA (including declared threatened or vulnerable marine species), marine bioregional planning and Australia's protection of cetaceans. APEEL's recommendations include the need to clarify national marine goals and priorities; comprehensive MSP; completion of the National Reserve System for MPAs; more effective pollution control; more effective biosecurity; a feasible funding model and more effective engagement with Indigenous stakeholders.

Australia's inability to ensure the sustainability of its marine and coastal environment is partly because of causes to biodiversity loss that are not fully within Australia's control. One such factor is climate change, which will continue to have a significant deleterious impact. Another is activities beyond Australia's territorial waters, such as the use of drift nets and shark-finning. Within Australia's marine territory, conservation is compromised by interest bargaining and politics, with competition between private economic and recreational interests, and environmental protection, as well as competition for funds within government. There is not enough public money to manage Australia's vast marine area, and private funding for marine conservation is limited. Harnessing a consumer preference for sustainable seafood may help address this missing private incentive problem, such as those proposed by organisations such the Marine Stewardship Council (2019) and Dolphin Safe (IMMP, 2019). The costs of supervising marine areas and activities are high, and enforcement often non-viable. Technological innovations can help to overcome this problem. Already, on some Australian fishing vessels, digital log books are linked to automatically activate cameras to record what is caught and how accidental by-catch is treated; and satellite tracking of vessels is sometimes used for fisheries management (including by NGOs such as Global Fishing Watch, 2019).

Brazil's marine governance

Brazil's 5th report (Mattos Scaramuzza, 2016, pp. 46–65) provides a more detailed examination of marine biodiversity than does Australian's report. A large part of the report is an inventory of species and an outline of public governance. Marine issues are discussed as part of broader analyses of biodiversity. Discussion of threats to aquatic and coastal habitats highlights damage to coastal ecosystems, and problems with overfishing and pollution. The report lists 134 of the 144 threatened marine species as affected by fishing, 72 affected by pollutants (including noise), and others suffering various harms (pp. 100–102).

The report's discussion of the effectiveness of public policies highlights the problem of overfishing, and points to institutional fragmentation and complexity as part of the problem, noting:

> The regulation of extractive fisheries activities, however, has proven a challenge particularly at the institutional level, with the creation of new agencies and redefinition of responsibilities, which compound with the still present conflict of assigned duties between the environmental agencies and the agencies responsible for promoting fisheries activities.
>
> (p. 106)

The report notes difficulties with shared public/private management, including:

- Failures to implement precautionary approaches.
- Political complexities, including tensions between agencies and constituencies with competing interests.
- Deficiencies with scientific data.
- Failures of enforcement (largely due to agency capacity issues).

Brazil, like Australia, has taken international action to limit commercial whaling, supporting the proposal for an International South Atlantic whale sanctuary.

Target 6 of Brazil's *National Biodiversity Strategy and Action Plan* is that, by 2020, all stocks of any aquatic organisms will be managed sustainably and recovery plans will be created for fisheries that have suffered overuse. The plan is to afford effective protection for threatened species and vulnerable ecosystems. Many of the general biodiversity targets within the action plan apply to marine biodiversity. These include addressing environmentally perverse economic incentives, partnerships between the public and private sector, increasing MPA to 10 per cent of the marine environment under Brazilian jurisdiction, according to the implementation of the *Nagoya Protocol* (signed but not yet ratified by Brazil) for equitable benefit sharing, participatory processes and stronger scientific foundations (pp. 153–154).

Processes to achieve these goals include sub-national (state) arrangements, and the coordination of implementation of the conventions on climate change

(UNFCCC) and desertification *(UN Convention to Combat Desertification)* with the *CBD* (though marine governance is not specifically discussed in this context). The discussion of transboundary arrangements considers marine issues, including *Law of the Sea (UN Convention on the Law of the Sea)* and migratory species arrangements.

A section within Brazil's 5th report, similar to that in the *Australian State of the marine environment report 2016*, discusses delivery of the *Aichi Targets*. In relation to National Aichi Target 6 concerning marine ecosystems, the report identifies progress on reducing overfishing and reducing significant adverse effects on vulnerable ecosystems. Recent data that can verify this is not provided. It also reports that difficulties in implementing the recovery of damaged ecosystems and bringing fisheries within safe ecological limits are likely to continue. The discussion suggests that, though steps have been taken towards a legal and policy basis for sustainable use, implementation is in its early stages.

Aichi target 11 states that, by 2020, at least 17 per cent of terrestrial and inland water areas and 10 per cent of coastal and marine areas, especially areas of particular importance for biodiversity and ecosystem services, are conserved through effectively and equitably managed, ecologically representative and well-connected systems of protected areas and other effective area-based conservation measures, and integrated into the wider landscape and seascape. In relation to this target, Brazil has substantially increased its protected ocean area from 1.68 per cent (2016) to 26.62 per cent (2018). In 2018, four MPAs were created:

1. Área de Proteção Ambiental do Arquipélago de São Pedro e São Paulo, in the state of Pernambuco (38,450,193.81 acre) – *Decreto Federal no. 9.313/2018.*
2. Área de Proteção Ambiental do Arquipélago de Trindade e Martin Vaz, in the state of Espírito Santo (40,385,419.59 acre) – *Decreto Federal no. 9.312/2018*
3. Monumento Natural das Ilhas de Trindade, Martin Vaz e do Monte Colúmbia (6,769,671.75 acre) – *Decreto Federal no. 9.312/2018*
4. Monumento Natural do Arquipélago de São Pedro e São Paulo (4,726,317.84 acre) – *Decreto federal no. 9.313/2018.*

Two are large MPAs (da Silva, 2019) but no management plans have been adopted, and their protection is largely theoretical. The achievement of the qualitative goals of Target 11 is more elusive than the quantitative goals.

Implementing Brazil's protected areas

The Sustainable Development Goals (UN, 2015) objective 14 recognises the importance of 'conserving and using sustainably the oceans, seas and marine resources for sustainable development'. The 14th Conference of the Parties to

76 *Nathalia Lima et al.*

the *CBD* in 2018, in Egypt, adopted three decisions concerning MPAs and area-based conservation measures (Silva & Leuzinger, 2019):

1 Decision 14/8 invited governments to adopt area-based conservations measures for biodiversity protection and to respect traditional communities' rights.
2 Decision 14/9 establishes criteria for marine areas to be classified as ecologically or biologically relevant:

  a rarity or exclusivity
  b importance for the lifestyle stages of species
  c importance for endangered, threatened or declining species or their habitats
  d vulnerability, fragility, sensitivity or slow recovery
  e biological productivity
  f biological diversity
  g being in a natural state.

3 Decision 14/10 states that voluntary measures for the integration of protected areas and territories with terrestrial and marine landscapes, and good governance and equity, are encouraged.

MPAs are a component of marine biodiversity protection and 'a necessary instrument to re-establish climate stability' (Maestro, Pérez-Cayeiro, Chica-Ruiz, & Reyes, 2019, p. 35). Biodiversity of marine and coastal ecosystems, including the terrestrial areas linked to marine habitats, is under pressure (and most are threatened outside protected areas). MSP is contemporary good practice for integrated biodiversity protection and has been implemented in Australia since around 2012. It requires science-informed strategies at a 'seascape' scale, spanning protected and unprotected areas, reflecting interconnected system characteristics. Five large-scale marine bioregions have been defined for Australia, with a bioregional plan for each. These plans use scientific information to describe the values to be protected, set objectives and provide strategies for that protection (Department of Environment and Energy, 2019). Implementation is reported using report cards which primarily consider pressures on that bioregion. These have not been updated for some years. However marine biodiversity is discussed in national State of the Environment Reports and in reports on particular areas or issues (such as the Great Barrier Reef Marine Park, discussed below).

Australia's extensive system of MPAs is not a complete representation of marine ecosystems and there are legitimate criticisms, but Australian marine parks now cover 3,300,000 km^2, or 36 per cent of the country's marine territory. These are categorised as sanctuaries, marine national parks, recreational use zones, habitat protection zones, multiple use areas and special purpose areas. These categories are roughly equivalent to the protection zonings used in Brazil. They range from very small protected areas (for example the tiny

Shiprock Aquatic Reserve in Port Hacking, NSW) to the Coral Sea National Park that covers 989,836 km^2. The Great Barrier Reef (GBR), the Ningaloo Coast (which includes the marine area) and some islands have world heritage status based largely on their biodiversity.

Australia's 5th report (Department of the Environment, 2014) highlights that, in addition to protected reserves (and other biodiversity and marine protection discussed in the *2016 State of the marine environment report* and the 2018 APEEL analysis), marine bioregional plans have been created to support implementation of the coastal and marine aspects of the *Environment Protection and Biodiversity Conservation Act 1999* (Cth) (*EPBC Act*), which frame the management plans for individual MPAs within those zones.

Brazil's institutional arrangements for protecting its equally rich marine biodiversity are less mature than those of Australia. The Brazilian coastal zone incorporates the Amazonian coastline, includes the great coral reef at the mouth of Amazonas; the coastline to the northeast which is marked by dunes; the southeast coastal habitat of the Serra do Mar and the remnants of the Atlantic Forest and the south coast, which is covered in mangroves. Creating a representative network of protected areas has proven to be difficult, and has faced political and economic challenges. We discuss, below, two large MPAs located in the Economic Exclusive Zone (EEZ).

The *Brazilian Constitution* prescribes:

> [E]veryone has the right to an ecologically balanced environment, which is a public good for the people's use and is essential for a healthy life. The government and the community have a duty to defend and to preserve the environment for present and future generations.
>
> (art. 22)

The article also declares the coastal zone as national heritage to be used 'under conditions assuring preservation of the environment, including use of natural resources'. The constitution prescribes the creation of protected terrestrial and marine areas (art. 225, § 1, III). *Federal Law no. 9.985/2000* created the *National System of Conservation Units (SNUC)*, with 12 different management categories, divided into two groups of conservation units, also known as protected areas and defined as:

> [T]erritorial spaces and their environmental resources including waters under Brazilian jurisdiction, with relevant natural characteristics, legally instituted by the government, with objectives of conservation and defined boundaries, under a special administrative regime, to which are applied adequate guarantees of protection.
>
> (art. 2-I of *SNUC*)

Federal Decree 5,758/2006 (NPPA) also provides that protected areas include conservation units, Indigenous lands and Quilombola (Maroon) territories.

78 *Nathalia Lima et al.*

There are two categories of conservation units: 'full protection' conservation units, which restricts the use of natural resources, comprising Ecological Stations, Biological Reserves, National Parks, Natural Monuments and Wildlife Refuges and 'sustainable use' units, which allows for sustainable use of resources, within the limits established by a management plan, comprising Environmental Protection Areas (APAs), Areas of Ecological Interest, National Forests, Extractive Reserves (Resex), Wildlife Reserves, Sustainable Development and Private Natural Heritage Reserves (*Federal Decree 4.340/2002* – art. 12). Protected areas can be created by federal, state or local authorities and, to ensure their effectiveness, *SNUC law* requires conservation units have a management plan: 'The conservation units must have a management plan, that shall cover the area of the conservation unit, its buffer zone and ecological corridors, including measures to promote its integration into the economic and social life of neighbouring communities' (§ 1°, art. 27). Each conservation unit must also have a council (art. 15, §5°; art. 17, §5°; art. 18, §2°, art. 20, §4°; art. 29; art. 41, §4°).

Though the constitution refers specifically to the protection of the Coastal Zone and specific terrestrial areas, including the Amazon, it does not prescribe protection of the oceanic area along the Brazilian coast, which are referred to as the 'Blue Amazon' and includes the territorial sea, the EEZ and the continental shelf beyond 200 miles. The process that established the outer limit of the Brazilian Continental Shelf was initiated in 2004 with the UN Commission for the Limits of the Continental Shelf, which facilitates the implementation of the *Law of the Sea*. In 2007, the CLCS approved 80 per cent of a proposal by Brazil and endorsed the Brazilian bid for the incorporation of 170,000 km^2 of continental shelf area, in addition to the EEZ (see CLCS, 2019). According to the Brazilian Navy, 'Brazil has the right to explore a large ocean area of about 5.7 million km^2' (Marinha do Brasil, 2019), taking into account international environmental commitments and legal requirements including environmental impact assessment.

Regarding the assessment of the effectiveness of MPAs protected by law in terms of legal instruments for the conservation of marine biodiversity, from a quantitative perspective Brazil's protected marine and coastal areas cover approximately 26.34 per cent[1] of the Blue Amazon (territorial sea and EEZ), achieving the quantitative Aichi goal. Federal, state and municipal authorities have created 228 Conservation Units (MMA, 2018a) to protect, to varying degrees, marine and coastal environments. These cover over a quarter of the Atlantic Ocean under Brazilian jurisdiction.

Typically, these protected areas allow shared use, but no management plans have been created (da Silva, 2019). The shared use management of the marine environment is a great challenge, considering the extensive more than 8,500 km shoreline, one of the largest in the world (MMA, 2018b), and the increasing pressure for extractive and other economic uses.

To assess the qualitative aspect (ICMBio, 2017) of the effectiveness of Brazilian MPAs we have used information provided by the government

Marine protected areas 79

agencies responsible for the creation and management of these protected spaces, the Ministry of Environment (MMA) and the Chico Mendes Institute for Biodiversity Conservation (ICMBio), especially data on the existence of management plans and management councils in these areas.

These sources provide data relevant to three indicators:

1 whether an area is categorised for 'full protection' or 'sustainable use'
2 the existence of management plans
3 the existence of management councils (operational or under development) to ensure public participation

Of the MPAs, 99 are 'fully protected' conservation units and 129 are classified as 'sustainable use' and created at the federal, state and municipal level.

Overall, 56 per cent of Brazilian marine and coastal protected areas are zoned for sustainable use and 44 per cent for full protection. Sustainable use zonings permit the use of resources (e.g. fishing, other harvesting, mineral extraction, tourism, etc.) controlled through management plans. In most cases, management plans have not been developed and so the legal and scientific basis for controlling harm to biodiversity is lacking.

Among 228 protected areas for coastal and marine areas, 90 are federal protected areas:

* 37 'full protection' conservation units: Ecological Stations (8); natural monuments (3); coastal and marine national parks (13); wildlife refuges (5); biological reserves (8).
* 53 'sustainable use' conservation units: Environmental Protection Areas (15); areas of ecological interest (2); national forest (1); sustainable development reserve (1); extractive reserves (26) and private reserves for natural heritage (8).

Table 4.2 describes the approximate equivalence of the Brazilian and IUCN Categories for Protected Areas.

Figure 4.2 illustrates where legally required management councils operate in terms of the number of MPAs and spatial coverage. The majority of these areas have management councils, but spatial coverage is incomplete because the marine conservation units created in 2018 (archipelagos São Pedro, São Paulo, Trindade and Martim Vaz), which represent 23.5 per cent of MPAs, do not yet have management councils.

A similar pattern exists for federal coastal and marine conservation units (see Figure 4.3). Only one-third of these have documented plans. Some management plans are outdated. Less than half of the documented plans (9) have been revised since their formulation; because as implementation occurs, adaptive management will generally be required and so plans that are not updated may not reflect current best management practice, but further in-depth investigation is required.

Eighty-eight per cent of the marine protected areas are categorised as Environmental Marine Protected Area (APA) comprise 88.6 per cent of

80 *Nathalia Lima et al.*

Table 4.2 IUCN Protected Areas Classification[a] and MPAs in Brazil[b]

IUCN categories	Characteristics and main objective	Corresponding status in Brazil and total AMP
Ia	Integral nature reserve: protected for biodiversity, managed mainly for scientific or wilderness protection purposes.	Ecological stations (8), biological reserves (8)
Ib	'Wilderness areas' are usually vast areas that are intact or slightly modified.	
II	National Park: Large natural or quasi-natural areas to protect large-scale ecological processes, and species and ecosystems characteristic of a region.	Coastal or marine national parks (13)
III	Monument or natural element be protected due to the existence of a specific natural monument.	Wildlife refuges (5) Natural monuments (3)
IV	Habitat/species management areas.	Areas of ecological interest (2)
V	Protected terrestrial or marine landscape: areas where the interaction of humans and nature has produced a distinct character, with considerable ecological, biological, cultural and panoramic values; where safeguarding this interaction is vital to protect and maintain the area, emphasising nature conservation and other values.	Environmental protection areas ('Áreas de Proteção Ambiental' – APA) (15)[c]
VI	Protected area with sustainable use to preserve ecosystems and cultural values and Traditional natural resource management systems. They are generally vast and mostly natural, a certain proportion subject to sustainable management of natural resources, and moderate natural, non-industrial and nature-friendly resources.	Extractive reserve

a Source: Dudley (2008).
b Adapted from (IBAMA 2004).
c No APAs fall into this category.

MPAs (ICMBio, 2017), permitting sustainable use. Effective and equitable management of such areas necessarily involves many interests, which may include ports, navigation, mining, fishing, tourism, conservation, traditional peoples and communities and military defence. In addition, the intersection of Brazil's marine boundaries with neighbouring countries and with waters subject to international maritime and conservation rules adds to the complexities. Effective management plans would be challenging to create and implement. By 2017, only 90 of the federal marine conservation units – less than half – had required management plan (ICMBio, 2017).

It is unclear whether the network of use and protection zones will provide an effective protective regime for three reasons: the continuation of permissible uses such as fishing, industrial foreshore activities and mining/

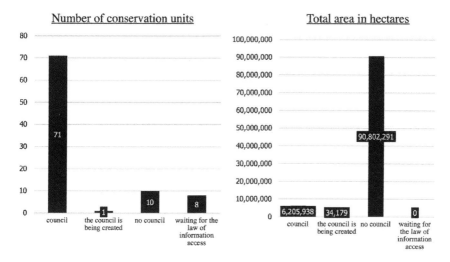

Figure 4.2 Management council of federal marine conservation units.
Source: Nathalia Lima.

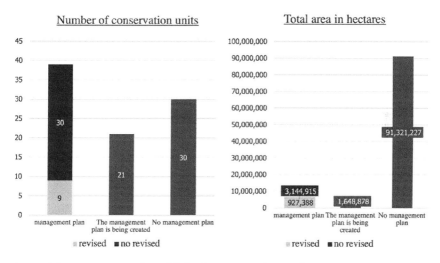

Figure 4.3 Management plan of federal marine and coastal conservation units.
Source: Nathalia Lima.

oil that can compromise environmental protection; political forces leading to environmentally compromised protective zones; and the lack of institutional capacity. Brazil's fishery take continues to increase and there are strong demands to increase offshore oil extraction. Recently, the government released areas for oil exploitation close to the Marine National Park of Abrolhos, the first marine national park created in 1983. Offshore oil extraction

82   *Nathalia Lima et al.*

can have negative consequences for biodiversity conservation. Without well coordinated and resourced marine protection agencies, it will be difficult to deliver effective protection.

The problems of achieving coordinated protection from oil spills have been recently demonstrated. In September 2019 a major oil-spill from a non-identified source reached the northeast coast of Brazil. This is widely considered to be a major marine and coastal biodiversity disaster. However, even 50 days after awareness of this disaster, the government had not activated the National Contingency Plan for Oil Pollution Incidents in Water. This national plan, enacted in October 2013, establishes general provisions and an organisational structure with allocated responsibilities to provide a cooperative framework to reduce the response time for incidents with significant environmental impacts. In this instance, slow response times and failures of coordination suggest (once again) that having a legal instrument in place does not mean that governments can deal effectively with marine biodiversity disasters.

It is hoped that MSP can be well implemented in Brazil, with the participation of artisanal fishers and local communities, to provide a stronger basis for protecting marine biodiversity. However, *Federal Bill no. 6.969/2013* for the protection of the marine biome, which creates the basis for marine special planning, has yet to be approved by the National Congress.

Implementing Australia's protected areas

Australia's longer experience in implementing MSP and large-scale MPAs, including multiple use, illustrates the challenges that must be met and the potential effectiveness of marine protection. The Australian GBRMP provides a good example of the such challenges. Established in 1975, the Great Barrier Reef Marine Park Authority (GBRMPA) administers a marine protected with the following IUCN protective zones:

- Category Ia – Strict Nature Reserve – 859 km^2
- Category II – National Park – 114,309 km^2
- Category IV – Habitat/Species Management Area – 15, 207 km^2
- Category VI – Protected Area with sustainable use of natural resources 213,769 km^2.

The Park was World Heritage listed in 1981, partly because its biodiverse reefs represent around 10 per cent of the world's reefs.

Data about the reef, its management and its challenges are available through the GBRMPA website. The GBRMP enjoys strong political and institutional support (see Australian Government, 2018), substantial scientific research – though scientific data and knowledge remain insufficient, professional management, a strong regulatory framework, demonstrable economic incentives for biodiversity protection (Deloitte Access Economics 2017) and widespread community support.

Marine protected areas 83

Despite laudable aspects of its governance, the biodiversity outcomes are far from ideal and the trajectories are not a cause for optimism. A recent governance review (Craik, 2017) highlighted:

> Despite some positive results from management investments, in 2014 the Great Barrier Reef Outlook Report reported that the overall outlook for the Great Barrier Reef was poor, had worsened since 2009 and was expected to further deteriorate … Coral bleaching in 2016, triggered by record breaking global sea surface temperatures, killed an estimated 29 percent of the Reef's shallow water corals. This was followed by further mass bleaching in 2017. Also in 2017, Tropical Cyclone Debbie, the tenth severe category cyclone since 2005, affected around one-quarter of the Reef.
>
> (p. 9)

This gloomy assessment mirrors what is reported in the *2016 State of the marine environment report* (Evans et al., 2017) and the APEEL discussion paper about marine biodiversity (APEEL, 2017). The state of marine biodiversity depends on many forces acting on the ecosystem, causing non-linear (sometimes 'chaotic') dynamics and harm to biodiversity. The pressures include:

- Climate change – increased water temperature, more and more intense storms, movement of species triggered by water and other ecosystem conditions.
- Navigation – wastes and impacts from vessels, the construction and operation of onshore and offshore navigation facilities. This is illustrated by loading terminals to export minerals and energy, causing damage from construction, spills and vessel impacts.
- Runoff from the land, resulting in poor water quality due to sediment and various chemicals. This is illustrated by the ongoing battle to control sediments and chemicals from land clearing and farming that has harmed corals and other species.
- Changes to the dynamics of natural species, including the movement of species, changed populations and behaviours, illustrated by coral predation by the crown of thorn starfish.
- Direct human action, with accumulating effects including damage to mangroves and wetlands, changes to island ecosystems, fishing and harvesting and the accumulation of plastics and trash.

Government decisions to approve onshore mineral and energy export facilities have compromised the reef, illustrating how economic interests and political dynamics can compromise protection even within protected areas. Such decisions have led to three liquid petroleum gas processing and export plants, dredging and dredge spoil impacts within the Great Barrier Reef Marine Park (GBRMP) and coal sediment damage within park boundaries (see Chapter 3). Responding to these pressures federal and state governments have increased their investment in reef protection and strengthened legal

84 *Nathalia Lima et al.*

instruments but continue to approve developments that pose risks to marine biodiversity.

The competing interests and political compromises that affect reef protection are evident in the 'see-saw' approach to land clearing and farming pollution within the reef catchment, discussed in Chapter 8. Many attempts have been made to address these issues, and the intensive political battles have led to episodic tightening and loosening of controls, and various incentives and other programmes. This history is documented in the regulatory impact analysis for the latest round of agricultural land clearing and runoff management reforms in the reef catchment areas.

The recent *2017 Scientific Consensus Statement: Land use impacts on Great Barrier Reef water quality and ecosystem condition* (Waterhouse et al., 2017) states:

> Key Great Barrier Reef ecosystems continue to be in poor condition. This is largely due to the collective impact of land run-off associated with past and ongoing catchment development, coastal development activities, extreme weather events and climate change impacts such as the 2016 and 2017 coral bleaching events.
>
> Current initiatives will not meet the water quality targets. To accelerate the change in on-ground management, improvements to governance, program design, delivery and evaluation systems are urgently needed. This will require greater incorporation of social and economic factors, better targeting and prioritisation, exploration of alternative management options and increased support and resources.
>
> (p. 6)

Proposed arrangements to manage agricultural runoff involve a cocktail of regulatory, co-regulatory, incentive, compliance and social interventions. Whether these initiatives will be sufficient is unknown, but political conflict over biodiversity protection within this internationally important marine reserve is inevitable.

Conclusions

Marine systems are complex and interconnected. Pressures from within national boundaries and from outside contribute to the loss of marine biodiversity. International arrangements have led to the significant and rapid creation of MPAs in many parts of the world, but this has happened along with an explosion of marine exploitation, including, for example, fisheries and offshore mining and energy extraction, shipping and foreshore development. Protected areas are necessary but they are far from sufficient to protect marine biodiversity. The marine, coastal and onshore system need to be managed as an integrated whole in addition to managing the components to ensure sustainability.

Marine areas offer many ecosystem services to human beings, resulting in significant economic interests and political pressures. There are often powerful forces opposed to aspects of conservation and recovery management; and strong incentives for illegal or non-sustainable action. The remoteness and extensiveness of areas to be managed poses governance challenges, as do the difficulties of direct observation of ocean areas. New technologies (notably satellite supervision and drones discussed in Chapters 8 and 9) coupled with on-vessel and remote monitoring will be used increasingly but the underlying challenges remain difficult to deal with.

Marine management requires governing the behaviours of many actors within a complex socio-economic system, interwoven with a complex marine ecological system. Many aspects of this task are difficult: the transaction costs of supervision by government are high; the incentives to do harm are great; citizen supervision and action is difficult; many issues are transboundary, and political complexities abound.

Both countries have an 'architecture' of legal protection and other actions to protect marine biodiversity, and investment in this aspect of environmental governance continues to increase. Australia's marine protection systems are more advanced than those for Brazil. It has a framework for MSP for its territorial waters and has marine parks that have operational plans and management agencies that are substantially resourced (but always insufficiently) to implement protective regimes. Brazil has taken giant steps towards a comprehensive MPAs system but management arrangements have not caught up. Comprehensive MSP is contemplated but has not been fully established. This will require political and bureaucratic commitment to deal with the scientific and stakeholder complexities, as well as to ensure the participation of Indigenous and Traditional communities who live all along the coastal zone.

MSP can provide a good conceptual framework for the integrated science-informed approaches that are needed, including Traditional knowledge approaches. International conventions and country-to-country treaties deal with many key issues on paper but implementation lags. It may take fundamental changes to incentives to significantly change the trajectory of biodiversity loss, along with strong public governance and action by civil society. The role of the private sector in achieving this is fundamental. There have been some heartening signs but these are weak. An important component that is underdeveloped is pro-conservation economic pressure from the consumer end: tourism, seafood, minerals and energy. That is to say, both domestic and international marine biodiversity protection are focused on government actions and there is insufficient attention to reshaping the underlying incentives and resourcing for effective marine protection.

Note

1 Varied in 2019 by a UN agreement to extend Brazil's jurisdiction.

References

APEEL (Australian Panel of Experts on Environmental Law). (2017). *Marine and coastal issues* (Technical Paper 4). Retrieved from http://apeel.org.au/papers

86 *Nathalia Lima et al.*

Australian Government. (2018). *Reef 20150 long-term reef sustainability plan.* Retrieved from https://www.environment.gov.au/marine/gbr/publications/reef-2050-long-term-sustainability-plan-2018

CLCS (Commission on the Limits of the Continental Sea). (2019). *Outer limits of the continental shelf beyond 200 nautical miles from the baselines: Submissions to the commission: Partial revised Submission by Brazil.* Retrieved from https://www.un.org/depts/los/clcs_new/submissions_files/submission_bra_rev.htm

Craik, W. (2017). *Independent review of governance of the Great Barrier Reef Marine Park Authority* (report). Canberra, ACT: Department of the Environment and Energy. Retrieved from http://www.environment.gov.au/marine/gbr/publications/gbr-governance-review

da Silva, A. P. (2019). Brazilian large-scale marine protected areas: Other 'paper parks'? *Ocean and Coastal Management, 169,* 104–112.

Deloitte, & Deloitte Access Economics. (2017). *At what price? The economic, social and icon value of the Great Barrier Reef.* Retrieved from http://hdl.handle.net/11017/3205

Department of the Environment. (2014). *Australia's fifth national report under the convention on biological diversity.* Canberra, ACT. Retrieved from https://environment.gov.au/biodiversity/international/fifth-national-biological-diversity-report

Dudley, N. (Ed.). (2008). *Lignes directrices pour l'application des catégories de gestion aux aires protégées* (Guidelines for application of management categories for protected areas). Gland, Suisse: IUCN.

Ecolex. (2019). *Marine protected areas.* IUCN, UNEP, FAO. Retrieved from https://www.ecolex.org/result/?q=Marine+Protected+areas&type=treaty&xcountry=Australia&xcountry=Brazil&xdate_min=&xdate_max=

Evans, K., Bax, N., & Smith, D. C. (2017). *Australia state of the marine environment 2016.* In D. J. Metcalfe, & E. Bui (Eds.). *Australia state of the environment 2016 (SOE 2016).* (Independent report to the Australian Government Minister for the Environment and Energy).

GBRMPA (Great Barrier Reef Marine Park Authority). (n.d.). Retrieved from http://www.gbrmpa.gov.au/

Global Fishing Watch. (2019). Retrieved from https://globalfishingwatch.org/

IBAMA (2004). *Atlas de Conservacao da Natureza Brasileira – Unidades Federais* (Brazilian nature conservation atlas – Federal units). Capa dura. São Paulo, Brazil: Metalivros.

ICMBio (Chico Mendes Institute of Biodiversity Conservation. (2017). *Painel Dinâmico de Informações* (Dynamic Panel of Information). Retrieved from http://qv.icmbio.gov.br/QvAJAXZfc/opendoc2.htm?document=painel_corporativo_6476.qvw&host=Local&anonymous=true

IMMP (International Marine Mammal Project). (2019). *Protecting dolphins from deadly fishing practices.* Retrieved from http://savedolphins.eii.org/campaigns/dsf/

Maestro, M., Pérez-Cayeiro, M. L., Chica-Ruiz, J. A., & Reyes, H. (2019). Marine protected areas in the 21st century: Current situation and trends. *Ocean and Coastal Management, 171,* 28–36.

Marine Conservation Institute. (2019). MPATLAS [On-Line]. Seattle, WA. Retrieved from http://www.mpatlas.org

Marine Stewardship Council. (2019). The MSC Blue Fish Tick. Retrieved from https://www.msc.org/en-au/what-we-are-doing/our-approach/the-msc-blue-fish-tick

Marinha do Brasil. (2019). *Bem-vindo a 'Amazonia Azul'* (Welcome to 'Blue Amazon'). Retrieved from https://www.mar.mil.br/hotsites/amazonia_azul/

Mattos Scaramuzza, Carlos Alberto de (Ed.) (2016). *Brasil: 5° relatório nacional para a Convenção Sobre Diversidade Biológica* (Brazil: 5th national report to the Convention of Biological Diversity). Brasília, Brazil: MMA.

MMA (Ministry of Environment). (2018a). *Download geographic data*. Retrieved from http://mapas.mma.gov.br/i3geo/datadownload.htm

MMA (Ministry of the Environment). (2018b). *Coastal zone*. Retrieved from http://www.mma.gov.br/biodiversidade/biodiversidade-aquatica/zona-costeira-e-marinha.html

Silva, S. T., & Leuzinger, M. D. (2019). Os desafios de criação e gestão das áreas marinhas protegidas no Brasil à luz dos objetivos do desenvolvimento sustentável (The challenges of creating and managing marine protected areas in Brazil in light of sustainable development goals). In T. C. F. Mont'alverne, S. T. da Silva, C. C. de Oliveira, & G. R. B. Galindo (Eds.) *Meio Ambiente Marinho, Sustentabilidade e Direito* (Marine environment, sustainability and law) (pp. 121–148). Rio de Janeiro, Brazil: Lumen Juris.

UN. (2015). *Transforming our world: The 2030 agenda for sustainable development*. Retrieved from https://sustainabledevelopment.un.org/post2015/transformingourworld/publication

UN. (2019). *Treaty collection*. Retrieved from https://treaties.un.org/

UNEP. (12 February 2019). *Proposal for a new Marine and Coastal Strategy of UN Environment Programme for 2020–2030*, UNEP/CPR/145/5, Agenda Item 5: Consideration of resolution of UNEP/EA.2/Res.10: Oceans and Seas.

UNEP-WCMC. (n.d.). *Ocean data viewer*. Retrieved from https://data.unep-wcmc.org/

Waterhouse, J., Schffelke, B., Bartle, R., Eberhard, R., Brodie, J., Star, M., ... Kroon, F. (2017). *2017 Scientific consensus statement: Land use impacts on Great Barrier Reef water quality and ecosystem condition*. Retrieved from https://www.reefplan.qld.gov.au/about/assets/2017-scientific-consensus-statement-summary.pdf

5 Social justice and the management of protected areas

Donna Craig, Márcia Dieguez Leuzinger, Lorene Raquel de Souza, and Paulo Campanha

Abstract

Brazil and Australia are rich biodiverse countries occupied by diverse Indigenous and Traditional people. The *Convention on Biological Diversity's* article 8(j) and 10(c) together highlight the important role played by Indigenous and Traditional people in the preservation of biodiversity. Yet, in both countries, protected areas have been created in territories traditionally occupied by Indigenous and Traditional people, often forcing them to leave. This chapter discusses the issues faced by such peoples in Australia and Brazil and a number of joint management initiatives and changes to regulations. Clearly, effective and institutional arrangements must respond to local concerns and priorities, and a single 'model law' is not feasible.

Introduction

The UN Sustainable Development Goals recognise the importance of law and governance (Martin, Boer, & Slobodian, 2016) and the *Convention on Biological Diversity* (*CBD*) addresses governance in many aspects of its work programmes and national action plans. Governance is about power, relationships, responsibility and accountability, including who has influence, who decides what and who is accountable for what.

Biodiversity governance for protected areas (PAs) has received considerable attention. The International Union for the Conservation of Nature (IUCN) (n.d.) provides categories for PAs and creates management principles and guidelines (Dudley, Shadie, & Stolton, 2013). The IUCN categories and guidelines have almost global acceptance and the governance of PAs has changed to reflect their increasingly diverse types, roles in ecosystem management. The categories have also established and recognised emerging norms related to biodiversity conservation, human rights and the rights of Indigenous peoples. Analysis of the deliberations of the World's Park Congresses, held every ten years since 1962, illustrates this.

From the first two congresses (1962 and 1972), the conclusions were that the PAs around the world should be increased and that communities living inside national parks should be removed. The scientific community belatedly

Management of protected areas   89

recognised the importance of Traditional populations for the protection of biodiversity. The dependence of these communities on natural resources found on the lands they traditionally inhabit often caused them to develop methods to sustainably use and protect the resources. As a result, the third World Parks Congress in 1982 affirmed the rights of Traditional populations and recommended that PAs be managed collaboratively. The transition to this 'new paradigm', however, is substantially incomplete (Rights and Resources Initiative, 2015), and both Brazil and Australia face significant challenges with implementation of effective protective zones (Rights and Resources Initiative, 2015, pp. 113–120).

This chapter discusses the biodiversity governance arrangements with regard to Indigenous peoples in light of the constitutional and other legal instruments in Australia and Brazil, taking into account international normative frameworks, such as the *CBD*, *Indigenous and Tribal Peoples Convention (ILO169)* and the *UN Declaration on the Rights of Indigenous Peoples (UNDRIP)*. The comparative approach used in the chapter identifies the strengths and weaknesses of the national approaches and explores better national biodiversity governance approaches that could support Indigenous land ownership and self-determination.

The chapter begins with a consideration of some difficulties with the situation in Brazil and then considers a co-management approach used in Australia which may assist in resolving some of the problems facing protected areas.

Brazilian Indigenous and Traditional people's stewardship

In Brazil, there are two types of Traditional peoples: Indigenous and non-Indigenous. Indigenous peoples are those of pre-Columbian origin who identify as belonging to an ethnic group and whose cultural characteristics distinguish them from the national society (*Indigenous Law – Federal Law no. 6.001/1973*, art. 3). There are 246 Indigenous populations in Brazil with 150 distinct languages, numbering about 800,000 individuals. Most live in rural areas (Brazilian Institute of Geography and Statistics, 2010).

Indigenous populations have greater legal protection than non-Indigenous Traditional populations because the *Brazilian Federal Constitution 1988* (art. 231) established that lands they traditionally occupied belong to the Brazilian Federal Union and is set aside for their permanent possession and exclusive use of natural resources. Those lands are inalienable and the rights are imprescriptible, allowing Indigenous people with demarcated lands to go to court to defend their rights. Six hundred and ninety-nine Indigenous lands have been demarcated by the Federal Government, occupying 115,819,863 ha (13.6 per cent of the Brazilian territory) (see further, Instituto Socioambiental, n.d.).

The non-Indigenous Traditional populations who expressly received protection under the constitution were the Quilombolas, descendants of African slaves who established communities – some formed by fugitive slaves

90 *Donna Craig et al.*

and others by land donations, purchases, inheritance, etc. (Vitorelli, 2012). Though they do not have the same protection as Indigenous peoples, article 68 of the *Constitutional Transitory Dispositions 1988* (part of the constitution) states that their land rights are recognised for lands possessed at the time of the creation of the constitution. These interests are collective property that is inalienable and cannot be divided (*Presidential Decree no. 4887/2003*, art. 17) and refers to the specific place where the community lives and the land they use for agriculture, extractive exploitation, celebrations, etc. The seasonality of activities should be recognised for the purpose of demarcating Quilombola's lands (Gama, n.d; Leuzinger & Lyngard, 2016).

Land rights afforded to the Quilombola are different to those afforded the Indigenous peoples: the latter have guaranteed possession of federal lands and their natural resources while Quilombolas have collective property rights to lands but do not have the rights to sell the land. Demarcating Quilombola's lands is more difficult because of the need to demonstrate occupation at the time of the issue of the constitution. If they had been expelled from the area, they cannot claim land rights. At the time of writing, there are 179 Quilombos (138 recognised by the state governments; 38 recognised by the federal government; three recognised by state and federal governments) occupying 752,797 ha of the Brazilian territory (0.088 per cent). However, there are 1,695 open requests at institution of national colonisation and agrarian reform (Comissão Pró-Indio de São Paulo, n.d.),

For the hundreds of other Traditional populations, including, for example, artisanal fishers, castanheiros (communities involved in the gathering of Brazil nuts), seringueiros (involved in the extraction of latex), there are no specific provisions ensuring their rights to the lands they occupy; though a few laws provide special rights to non-Indigenous Traditional communities, such as the right to stay in a full protection PA until they are transferred to another area (*Federal Law no. 9.985/2000, National Conservation Unit System Law – SNUC Law*), these do not provide the right to land.

The non-Indigenous Traditional populations were formed over many centuries and since colonial times. Some emerged as a result of economic cycles that led to people being transferred between regions to work on specific projects. When the project ceased to be economically viable, the transferred people were simply abandoned. This happened, for example, with people transferred from the northeast to the Amazon Forest to extract rubber during the 'Rubber Cycle' from the late 19th century to the 1960s (Silva et al., 2010, pp. 61–82). Other communities were formed by adapting to the natural resources and cycles of the land they occupied, and many worked together with the Indigenous populations (Arruda, 1999; Leuzinger & Lyngard, 2016).

To be considered a Traditional group, environmental legislation requires the group to adopt sustainable practices that help preserve biodiversity. Thus, a group of miners, even if considered Traditional by anthropologists, will not be eligible for special interests under environmental legislation. In addition, a Traditional group is required to demonstrate characteristics of self-identification, dependence on nature and its cycles, reduced capital accumulation, territoriality, communal possessions and oral transmission of knowledge (Diegues & Arruda, 2001; Leuzinger, 2009; Santilli, 2005; Souza Filho, 2005). Demonstration of such characteristics enables the group to legally carry out certain activities, such as the right to collect firewood or wood for construction from the forest without an authorisation (see further, Bensusan, 2000; Diegues & Arruda 2001; Leuzinger, 2009; Lima & Bensusan, 2003; Posey, 1993; Santilli, 2005; Souza Filho, 2005; Varella & Platiau 2004).

Beyond the benefits listed, Traditional populations do not have the right to acquire the areas they occupy (Traditional areas), although they can practice low capital investment subsistence activities.

Because land rights are not assured for non-Indigenous Traditional populations, the creation of PAs in Brazil by the government can deprive them of resources. This is different from what happens, at least in theory, with Indigenous and Quilombolas groups who have more secure constitutional rights to land. If a PA is created on Indigenous lands, their permanent right will have to be respected. The Brazilian Supreme Court (2009, PET, 3388) decided that, in those cases, the land will be subject to the Indigenous rights to live upon and use the land. For Quilombolas, although there is still debate about this issue, expert commentators propose that the treatment should be the same as for Indigenous peoples because they have the same originating rights on the land (Santilli, 2005; Souza Filho, 2005). However, as already noted, since the adoption of the constitution in 1988, only 179 Quilombola lands have been recognised and 1,695 requests are still pending. When the government creates a PA that excludes Traditional populations from their land, the *SNUC Law*, which created the National Conservation Unit System, must be observed; that is, the population must be reallocated but they can still live and use the land until the transfer.

In Brazil, PAs are a genus of which conservation units (UCs) are a species. UCs, according to the *SNUC Law*, are in 12 management categories administered by the Chico Mendes Institute for Biodiversity Conservation (ICMBio), an environmental agency responsible for federal UCs. Five categories are full protection UCs (equivalent to the IUCN I, II and III categories (IUCN, n.d.)) that do not allow direct use of natural resources: national parks, biological reserves, ecological stations, natural monuments and wildlife refuges.

The first three (national parks, biological reserves and ecological stations) can only be created in public lands and exclude inhabitants, even Traditional populations. Because full protection UCs are usually created in well conserved areas, it generally coincides with areas inhabited by Traditional peoples. According to a study by the Federal Public Prosecutor's Office, in 2012, 39 federal full protection and public domain UCs were inhabited by Traditional groups (Ministerio Público Federal, 2014).

Using the *Access to Information Law (Federal Law no. 12.527/2011)*, the authors sought information from ICMBio about UCs inhabited by Traditional populations to check the figures from the Federal Public Prosecutor's Office

92 *Donna Craig et al.*

study. The agency's response was that a study between 2013 and 2014 verified the existence and quantity of situations called 'territorial interfaces' where the presence of Traditional populations in UCs conflicts with its categorisation or management plan. This data was obtained by ICMBio through a questionnaire to UC managers and does not include units created between 2014 and 2018 (at the time there were 313 federal UCs). The questionnaire only identified territorial interfaces that include housing. Tables 5.1–5.3 were provided by the agency in relation to full protection UCs.

Table 5.1 Number of interfaces present in each category of full protection conservation unit

Presence of interfaces	*Yes*	*No*	*NA*	*Total*	*Responses*
Ecological station	19	10	2	31	29
Natural monument	2	1	0	3	3
National parks	53	16	0	69	69
Biological reserve	17	12	1	30	29
Wildlife refuge	1	4	2	7	5
TOTAL	92	43	5	140	135

Table 5.2 Percentage of conservation units with interfaces in each category

Percentage with interface	*Yes*	*No*	*NA*	*Total*	*Responses*
Ecological station	61.29	32.26	6.45	100	93.55
Natural monument	66.67	33.33	0	100	100
National parks	76.81	23.19	0	100	100
Biological reserve	56.67	40	3.33	100	96.67
Wildlife refuge	14.29	57.14	28.57	100	71.43
AVERAGE	65.71	30.71	3.57	100	96.43

Table 5.3 Estimated number of individuals (for Indigenous peoples) or families (for Traditional populations or family farmers) living inside full protection conservation units

Number of full protection UC with Interface(s)	*94*
With inhabitants	66
With Indigenous inhabitants	7
With Traditional populations inhabitants	55
With both (Indigenous and Traditional inhabitants)	4
Without inhabitants	28
Total estimated of Indigenous individuals living in full protection UC	9.830[a]
Total estimated of Traditional families or family farmers living in full protection UC	9.775[a]

a   The numbers do not include Traditional individuals or groups that use but do not live inside conservation units.

Responses were received from 96 per cent of managers of the full protection UCs. Of these UCs, 59 per cent contained Traditional populations and 11 per cent contained Indigenous populations. This is higher than the percentage reported by the Federal Public Prosecutor's Office (28.5 per cent). This may be because ICMBio's study includes family farmers, often not categorised as Traditional populations. Regardless of the percentage of Traditional peoples living inside UCs, this is a problem that exists and solutions are not simple to find.

There is not a specific article in the constitution guaranteeing the right to land for Traditional peoples: articles 215 and 216 guarantee cultural rights and establish that Brazilian cultural heritage comprises material and immaterial assets that include forms of expression and ways of creating, making and living by Traditional communities. *ILO 169* (ratified by Brazil), applies to non-Indigenous Traditional populations and article 16 of the convention provides that Traditional populations can only be transferred from the areas they occupy in exceptional cases and their return must be guaranteed once the threat is over. There is an obligation for government to protect the fundamental rights of Traditional peoples to a healthy environment and cultural rights, including the right to stay in their Traditional lands. The relocation solution created by the *SNUC Law* does not satisfy either *ILO 169* or articles 215 and 216 of the Brazilian constitution. Relocation itself is difficult to accomplish, partly because it requires government to provide funding and acquire areas where Traditional groups can be settled.

With relocation, cultural rights will be violated unless the vacated area is so fragile that it cannot stand the impact of those groups (Leuzinger, 2009). In this case, relocation will not violate cultural rights because the group would be forced, sooner or later, to leave the lands it traditionally occupies. If this is not the case, notwithstanding the *SNUC Law*, complementary measures should be taken to guarantee fundamental cultural and environmental rights.

One possible approach for Brazil for Traditional peoples involvement in full protection UCs is co-management. This has been successfully implemented in Australia and Canada. However the *SNUC Law* does not authorise this solution as an alternative for these UCs. Because Brazil is a civil law country (unlike Australia which has the flexibility of a common law jurisdiction), the written law has to be followed or an action may be unconstitutional. Though the co-management approach is consistent with *ILO 169* and the *CBD,* the lack of a clear constitutional or statutory framework in Brazil would need to be overcome to adopt a co-management approach.

Nevertheless, co-management is not completely unknown in the management of Brazil's conservation areas. It is used in some types of sustainable use UCs, especially Extractive Reserves (Resex) and Sustainable Development Reserves (RDS), which are conservation categories intended to protect both Traditional populations and the environment. Where used, the land is public but the government signs a contract with the Traditional group called a '*Concessão de direito real de uso*'. This allows them to live and use natural

94　*Donna Craig et al.*

resources within the UC boundaries provided they observe the limits imposed by the management plan. Those reserves are created at the request of the Traditional populations but with the support of government. However, achieving this support can be problematic when there are political and economic obstacles.

The system used in Brazil for Resex and RDS is similar to the joint management arrangements adopted in Australian National Parks, such as Kakadu (Uluru-Kata Tjuta), which are discussed below. The Australian model, however, is more developed and is adapted to each PA.

Full protection UCs inhabited by Traditional populations in Brazil create a human rights problem that needs an urgent solution. The solution given by the *SNUC Law* (relocation) is far from ideal, and the Brazilian government does not have enough funds to relocate populations to newly acquired areas. Traditional populations continue to live illegally inside UCs. Some conservation area managers act oppressively, hoping that the residents will leave the area of their own volition. In some cases, Memorandas of Understanding are signed that allow Traditional populations to stay temporarily in the UCs pending a permanent solution. This has happened in Juruena National Park, located in Mato Grosso State, in the Amazon biome (Instituto de Pesquisas Ecológicas and ICHBio, 2016) but is not a satisfactory permanent solution to the problem.

Modern approaches, such as co-management – perhaps using Terms of Compromise or Coexistence Agreements that are allowed under Brazilian legislation, should be introduced by the environmental agencies to consolidate the protection of the environment and cultural rights as a more viable and principled alternative to relocation.

The Rio de Janeiro Law 2.393/1995

In the State of Rio de Janeiro, the *2.393/1995 law* (RJ), applicable to only state UCs, created a mechanism for Traditional populations to continue living inside a full protection unit if the following requirements are followed: (1) residence in the area for more than 50 years; (2) dependence on local ecosystems for survival; (3) sustainable use of those ecosystems.

If all requirements are met, a contract can be signed that allows permanence inside the UC and the sustainable use of its natural resources for subsistence. The impact caused by the Traditional activities cannot disrupt local ecosystems (Sathler, 2008) and shall comply with the following requirements: (1) the use of endangered species or practices that compromise their habitats are forbidden, (2) exploitation of non-renewable natural resources is restricted to the minimum necessary to maintain the quality of life of the populations; (3) prohibition of practices and/or activities that compromise the natural recovery of ecosystems.

The Rio de Janeiro state legislation is flexible and reflects the Brazilian constitution and the international conventions Brazil has signed and ratified.

However, unlike co-management it does not provide for Traditional group participation in management. It is a better model than was established by the *SNUC Law* but co-management would better respect Traditional interests.

Serra do Mar State Park

In Brazil, national parks' zoning has been introduced since 1979, with *Presidential Decree no. 84.017/1979*. The decree derives from the global movement to consolidate rules for the definition of objectives for the creation and implementation of PAs but does not mention anthropological zones for national parks in which Traditional populations could continue to live. However, São Paulo State recognised, in its zoning of the Serra do Mar State Park, located in the mountain chain that goes from the shore to the plateau in the Atlantic Forest biome, a Historical Anthropological Cultural Zone (HACZ) in the Picinguaba Core to allow the permanent habitation of Traditional communities, classified as Quilombolas and Caiçaras (Traditional groups that inhabit coastal areas).

The zoning is part of the Park's management plan and the HACZ established specific guidelines to reconcile the conservation objectives of the full protection unit with the way of being and living of the Caiçaras and Quilombolas (Lima, 2018).

This is an innovative initiative led by the State Environmental Agency that could become a model to other state and federal parks. The problem is that an extensive interpretation of the *SNUC Law* will be needed, but this is possible if articles 215 and 216 of the constitution are invoked.

Contributions to conservation

The presence of Traditional populations inside UCs involves not only cultural rights but also the conservation of biodiversity. Traditional populations have a close relationship with the environment and depend on natural resources for their physical and cultural survival, leading to knowledge and practices that can advance conservation. Balée's (1994) study of the Kayapó Indigenous tribes showed that, because they are a small population, practice subsistence agriculture, use natural resources sustainably and use technologies whose sources of energy are solar, fire and human effort, they maintain biodiversity in pristine conditions.

Their use of natural resources in a sustainable way is usually what has led governments to create UCs in the area. Their presence can also help with monitoring. In Brazil, this is an important task that the government is often incapable of doing effectively. Even when it comes to UCs, there is only one inspector for every 17,600 ha (Godoy, 2015). There is little, if any, monitoring on other public lands, especially in the Amazon Forest. The significant potential contribution of Traditional peoples in protecting biodiversity should not be ignored. There is ample domestic and international

96 *Donna Craig et al.*

evidence that they can make a valuable contribution, which can help to solve funding and management challenges that would otherwise reduce the effectiveness of PAs.

Co-management in Australia

Indigenous management and co-management of lands, waters, seas and resources are rapidly expanding internationally. Advanced approaches to co-management have emerged in Australia and Canada. Their 'success' is largely anecdotal and reflects informal practices and relationships developed by dedicated participants. The focus has been on practical means of making co-management work on the ground. Much has been gained in this process. However, it should be noted that some fundamental challenges relating to Indigenous rights have often been ignored.

It cannot be assumed that conservation management agendas will align with the aspirations of Indigenous owners and careful attention needs to be given to the contexts and parties involved. Indigenous roles will vary depending on whether co-management is part of human rights-based agendas (i.e. Indigenous rights, poverty alleviation and livelihoods), self- government negotiations or more limited approaches to biodiversity governance, resource management or planning and development frameworks.

To frame the Australian study, we provide an overview of Aboriginal and Torres Strait Islander land rights and legal and institutional developments. Biodiversity governance will primarily be explored through Indigenous Protected Areas (IPAs) and co-management (known as joint management in Australia) of PAs. IPAs are protective arrangements over land owned by an Indigenous group and jointly managed PAs are usually Indigenous owned land 'leased' to an Australian Government national park agency. Uluru-Kata Tjuta National Park (see Section 6.3.2) is an example of a jointly managed PA.

Native title and statutory rights

The 1992 radical judgements of the Australian High Court in the *Mabo case* (*Mabo and others v. Queensland*) recognised the traditional rights of the Meriam people to their islands in the eastern Torres Strait, and that native title existed for all Australian Indigenous people prior to the establishment of the British Colony of New South Wales (NSW) in 1788. In recognising Indigenous people's title prior to Captain Cook's declaration of possession in 1770, the Court held that this title continues over any portion of land where it has not legally been extinguished.

In response, the Australian Government passed the *Native Title Act 1993* (Cth). As stated by the Australian Institute of Aboriginal and Torres Strait Islander Studies (2016, p. 3), under Section 223(1) of this act, 'native title or native title rights and interests' means the communal, group or individual rights and interests of Aboriginal peoples or Torres Strait Islanders in relation to land or waters, where:

- The rights and interests are possessed under the traditional laws acknowledged, and the traditional customs observed, by the Aboriginal peoples or Torres Strait Islanders;
- The Aboriginal peoples or Torres Strait Islanders, by those laws and customs, have a connection with the land or waters;
- The rights and interests are recognised by the common law of Australia.

The 2013 *Akiba v Commonwealth* case characterised native title as a continuing 'bundle of rights' that may also be 'non-exclusive' or partially eliminated by extinguishment of rights within the bundle.

Indigenous Land Use Agreements (ILUAs) are a private law mechanism to modify or determine Aboriginal and Torres Strait Islander land rights. ILUAs can provide for Indigenous management and use of biodiversity. An ILUA can be over areas: where native title has, or has not yet, been determined; entered into regardless of whether there is a native title claim; and part of a native title determination or settled separately from a claim (Craig, 2000, pp. 440–452).

The IPA programme illustrates the use of ILUAs to determine land rights and expand the national reserve system. The Australian Government may settle a land claim provided the claimants agree to manage the land as a IPA (Bauman, Haynes, & Lauder, 2013, pp. 14–17). Alternatively, existing Aboriginal and Torres Strait Islander landowners may donate land to the National Reserve System in exchange for financial support for land management work 'to conserve the lands ecological and cultural value' under international standards and a Plan of Management (Bauman et al., 2013, pp. 14–17). IPAs comprise over 40 per cent of Australia's National Reserve System, substantially managed by government-funded Indigenous ranger groups (Australian Government, 2016). However, the IPA programme is not a statutory programme, so provision of funds is discretionary and subject to policy changes.

There are fundamental differences between land rights and native title. Land rights are rights created by the Australian, state or territory governments. However, native title arises under Australian common law, recognising pre-existing Indigenous rights and interests under Traditional Laws and Customs. Land granted or reserved under statutory land rights regimes does not extinguish native title interests. Dealings in Aboriginal owned land or land reserved for the benefit of Aboriginal people must take into account native title rights to be valid. Land subject to native title rights and interests is inalienable. Estimates suggest that Aboriginal and Torres Strait Islander peoples control access to just over 30 per cent of Australia's land, most of which are in remote areas (see generally SCRGSP, 2016, p. 56; NNTT, n.d.).

The National Reserve System was established by the states, territories and the Commonwealth, NGOs and Indigenous landholders to create an

98   *Donna Craig et al.*

Australian system of terrestrial PAs. It aims to represent all regional eco-systems, in accordance with the Interim Biogeographic Regionalisation for Australia. Uluru–Kata Tjuta National Park (NP) is one of five PAs in the Great Sandy Desert bioregion. Uluru–Kata Tjuta NP is inscribed on the World Heritage List under the *World Heritage Convention* (*WHC*) for its out-standing natural values (1987) and cultural values (1994). The park represents one of the most significant arid land ecosystems in the world and is a Bio-sphere Reserve under the UNESCO Man and the Biosphere Programme.

Uluru–Kata Tjuta National Park

Uluru–Kata Tjuta NP covers 1,325 km^2 and is 335 km south-west of Alice Springs in the central part of Australia. Each year, more than 300,000 people visit the NP. Anangu is the term that *Pitjantjatjara* and *Yankunytjatjara* Aboriginal people (Traditional Owners of the land) use to refer to themselves. Aboriginal people have always been associated with Uluru. The Anangu believe that the landscape was created at the beginning of time by ancestral beings and that they are responsible for 'looking after country'. The knowledge necessary to fulfil these has been passed down through *Tjukurpa* (the Law).

Many Traditional Owners live in the Mutitjulu Aboriginal community, which is the only resident community in Uluru NP, and Parks Australia are largely responsible for services to the growing population. Traditional Owners for the Park also live elsewhere in the Northern Territory (NT), Western Aus-tralia (WA) and South Australia. In 1985, title to the park was transferred to the Uluru–Kata Tjuta Aboriginal Land Trust. The first Board of Management was constituted for Anangu to jointly manage the park with the federal agency: Parks Australia. The joint management of Australian NPs under federal juris-diction provides well known examples of Indigenous peoples joint management of PAs. However, the NP and high visitor numbers on Anangu land raise issues about 'sharing country', governance (principles, resources and methods), com-munity development and livelihoods (Bauman & Dermot, 2007).

Local laws

Freehold title was granted to Uluru–Kata Tjuta Aboriginal Land in 1985. However, Aboriginal owners had to lease the land back to Parks Australia as a condition for joint management. Joint management designates a part-nership between Traditional Owners, relevant Aboriginal People[1] and the Director of Parks Australia, as lessee for 99 years. The park is a proclaimed Commonwealth reserve under Section 343 of the *Environmental Protection and Biodiversity Conservation Act 1999* (*EPBC Act*) (pursuant to the *Environ-mental Reform (Consequential Provisions) Act 1999 Act*). There are various legal arrangements for Australian joint managed NPs under state and territory legislation including Indigenous owned parks that do not involve a lease (Craig, 2002, pp. 199–255).

The majority of the members of Uluru-Kata Tjuta Board of Management must be Aboriginal persons nominated by the Traditional Owners of land in the park (*EPBC Regulation* 2000 (Cth), Section 377(4)). The functions of the Board, in conjunction with the Director, include the preparation and monitoring of management plans (MPs) and advising the Minister. The MP for a Commonwealth reserve has effect for ten years. The *EPBC Act* prohibits certain actions in Commonwealth reserves other than in accordance with the MP. Aboriginal people may continue their traditional use for hunting or gathering except for purposes of sale, and for ceremonial and religious purposes (i.e. exempted from the application of ss.354 and 354A of the *EPBC Act* by s.359A and exempted from the operation of the *EPBC Regulations* by r.12.06(1)(e)). World Heritage, National Heritage and Commonwealth Heritage values of the park must be taken into account (*EPBC Act*, ss. 313 to 324).

The MP must apply the IUCN Management Principles (*EPBC Act,* s. 346) of the IUCN PA Category (Uluru-Kata Tjuta NP is designated as IUCN PA Category II). Access to biological resources in Commonwealth areas is regulated under the *EPBC Act* (ss. 301 & 528) and *EPBC Regulations*, Part 8A. The Uluru-Kata Tjuta NP MP should address the interests of the Traditional Owners, any other Indigenous persons with an interest, and the protection, conservation and management of biodiversity and heritage. After Ministerial approval, a MP becomes a legislative instrument (*EPBC Act*, s. 371). The Director and the Park agency must act consistently with the MP (*EPBC Act.,* s 362(2)). The *EPBC Act* makes provision for resolution when there is a dispute with a land council or Board (*EPBC Act*, s 363 & 364).

Evaluation

Indigenous joint governance of PAs can be effective in protecting natural and cultural biodiversity values, efficiently and fairly (Borrini-Feyerabend, Kothari, & Oviedo, 2004; Ross, et al., 2009). Bauman and Dermot (2007) concluded that PA partnerships in Australia were shaped by histories, environments, legal frameworks and capacities. They further conclude that evaluations should distinguish between the monitoring of the overall success of the management of PAs and the success of the partnerships that are involved.

The institutional arrangements for Uluru-Kata Tjuta NP reflect the current legal framework and demonstrate the intent to recognise and implement Anangu Law. However, tourism interests prevailed over the spiritual and cultural values and Aboriginal Law for 25 years. Tourists climbing Uluru cause deep distress to Anangu and only in 2017 was it decided to phase this out (by October 2019). This suggests an inequity in the partnership.

Progress has been made in ranger training and employment, cultural guidance and interpretation and management practices such as customary fire practices. This reflects the discretionary power of the Minister and of Parks Australia. Best practice would incorporate an adaptive management approach based on trust, joint problem-solving and social learning (Berkes,

100 Donna Craig et al.

2009, pp. 1692–1702). Berkes (2009) argues that integration of biodiversity and human livelihoods and well-being requires a multi-layered approach to governance with multiple objectives. However, this should not imply a weak Indigenous rights framework, because respect for rights and respect for culture go hand in hand (Ross et al., 2009, pp. 242–252).

Comparing Australia and Brazil

Australia and Brazil are rich in biodiversity and have diverse Indigenous and Traditional peoples. In both countries, PAs have often been created in territories inhabited by Indigenous and Traditional peoples, forcing them to vacate the territories even though their presence does not compromise biodiversity and may even contribute to its preservation.

In Australia, the first NP was established in 1879 – The Royal National Park – but concerns about the consequences of removing Aboriginal peoples only emerged in the mid-1970s because of the growing pressure from the international community to recognise the rights of Aboriginal and Torres Strait Islander peoples to the lands they inhabit and their role in conserving biological diversity (Walker, 2010). In Brazil, Itatiaia National Park was the first to be established in 1937, 50 years after Australia had begun its policy of creating PAs and concerns about Traditional populations emerged a decade later in late 1980s with the development of a socio-environmentalist ethos.

The approach that has emerged in Australia, used by most states and the territories in PAs used by Aboriginal and Torres Strait Islander peoples is joint management. This has involved varied arrangements between public entities and Aboriginal and Torres Strait Islander peoples and the evolution of the National IPA programme. The legal basis for co-management began with successful Aboriginal and Torres Strait Islander land claims and state and Northern Territory Aboriginal land rights Acts: *Land Rights Act 1976* (NT), *Land Rights Act 1983* (NSW), *Land Rights Act 1991* (QLD), *Land Rights Act (Traditional Owners Settlement)* 2010 (VIC), *Conservation and Land Management Act 1984* (WA).

Joint-management experiences vary for each state and the NT. The instruments that have been used are: protocols, memoranda of understanding, ILUAs and Lease Back Agreements. Australian experience indicates that conservation and management aims will always be the same as the aspirations of Indigenous owners. An adaptive management approach based on trust, joint problem-solving and a social learning process is important to resolve potential conflict resolution, and creative management is often required. However, joint-management practice continues to evolve and to be aligned with the rights-based approaches that are increasingly the normative standards for best practice.

In Brazil, although categories of UCs have been established to reconcile the protection of biodiversity and Traditional populations, like Resex and RDS, for full protection UCs (IUCN I, II and III categories), no solution to the problem of Traditional people presence has been achieved, other than for Serra do Mar State Park. If 59 per cent of federal full protection UCs contain Traditional peoples or family farmers, as shown by ICMBio's study, feasible solutions to the problem must be found. This is partly because Indigenous and Quilombola's peoples have the right to their lands under the Brazilian constitution. If a UC is established, it must respect constitutional rights, including the right to use natural resources. Co-management can offer a proven, respectful and practical solution to many problems.

Conclusions

This examination of Australian and Brazilian experiences with biodiversity governance by Indigenous and Traditional peoples suggests the opportunity and need for improved implementation of the *CBD*'s articles 8(j) (dependency of Indigenous and local people on biodiversity) and 10(c) (protect and encourage traditional use of biological resources in accordance with Traditional customary use). IUCN comparative research in other jurisdictions (Forest Peoples Program, 2011) has called on state parties to:

1   Take measures to recognise and respect Indigenous peoples' rights to their lands and resources.
2   Recognise the role of Customary Law and Traditional institutions and freedom to use Customary Laws related to biodiversity use rather than rules or laws imposed by others.
3   Recognise the right of Indigenous and local communities to fully and effectively participate in natural resource management and decision-making.
4   Take concrete actions to acknowledge the value of customary practices and Traditional knowledge in relation to biodiversity conservation and sustainable use, for example by reviewing and reforming national policies and laws to make them compatible with and supportive of, the protection of customary use and Traditional knowledge.
5   Ensure that 'free, prior, informed consent' becomes a well-understood and generally applied principle in all matters affecting Indigenous peoples' lands and territories.
6   Address all cases where PAs have adversely affected Indigenous peoples' customary sustainable use.
7   Ensure that educational policies and programmes are culturally appropriate and promote the use and revitalisation of Indigenous languages and Traditional knowledge.
8   Use the *UN Declaration on the Rights on Indigenous* Peoples and related human rights instruments as the basis for the full and effective implementation of article 10(c) of the *CBD*. These provide a framework for respecting fundamental human rights as well as providing a legal and environmental basis for protecting and encouraging customary sustainable use.

102 *Donna Craig et al.*

Civil society organisations are often pivotal to developing legal and institutional bases for collaborative biodiversity governance. They can play vital mediating roles. It is best if these mediating organisations are locally based but connected with international organisations through partnerships and networks.

To be effective and resilient, collaborative biodiversity governance in Australia and Brazil requires sound legal and institutional bases and implementation strategies. Biodiversity governance occurs in plural legal contexts. The legal and institutional bases for collaborative biodiversity governance initiatives are influenced by and should take account of customary and state authority and norms. Customary law on Indigenous owned and co-managed lands should be recognised and implemented to the greatest extent possible.

The social, economic and ecological contexts for collaborative biodiversity governance initiatives in Australia and Brazil differ greatly between locations and jurisdictions. Effective legal and institutional bases for these initiatives must respond to local concerns and priorities, so it is not appropriate to recommend a single 'model law'.

Note

1 Relevant persons means the traditional Aboriginal owners of the park, Aboriginal people entitled to use or occupy the park and Aboriginal people permitted by the traditional Aboriginal owners.

References

Arruda, R. (1999). Populações tradicionais e a proteção dos recursos naturais em unidades de conservação (Traditional populations and the protection of natural resources in conservation units). *Ambiente & Sociedade, 5,* 79–92.

Australian Government. (2016). *Australia's indigenous protected areas.* Canberra, ACT: Australian Government.

Australian Institute of Aboriginal and Torres Strait Islander Studies. (2016). *Native title information handbook.* Canberra, ACT: Australian Institute of Aboriginal and Torres Strait Islander Studies.

Balée, W. L. (1994). *Footprints of the forest: Ka'apor ethnobotany: The historical ecology of plant utilization by Amazonian people.* New York, NY: Columbia University Press.

Bauman, T., & Dermot, S. (2007). *Indigenous partnerships in protected area management in Australia, three case studies.* Canberra, ACT: Australian Institute of Aboriginal and Torres Strait Islander Studies.

Bauman, T., Haynes, C., & Lauder, G. (2013). *Pathways to the co-management of protected areas and native title in Australia.* Canberra, ACT: AIATSIS.

Bensusan, N. (Ed.) (2000). *Seria melhor mandar ladrilhar? Biodiversidade como, para que, por quê?* (Would it be better to have it titled? Biodiversity how, for what, why?). Brasília, Brazil: Universidade de Brasília; Instituto Socioambiental.

Berkes, F. (2009). Evolution of co-management: Role of knowledge generation, bridging organizations and social learning. *Journal of Environmental Management, 90* (5), 1692–1702.

Borrini-Feyerabend, G., Kothari, A., & Oviedo, G. (2004). *Indigenous and local communities and protected areas: Towards equity and enhanced conservation: Guidance on*

Management of protected areas 103

policy and practice for co-managed protected areas and community conserved areas. Gland, Switzerland: IUCN.

Brazilian Institute of Geography and Statistics. (2010), *Demographic census.* Retrieved from http://www.ibge.gov.br/home/estatistica/populacao/censo2010/default. shtm. Accessed in 19 November 2015.

Brazilian Supreme Court. (2009), Petition 3388, [Relator Ministro Carlos Ayres Britto]. Retrieved from http://portal.stf.jus.br/processos/detalhe.asp?incidente=2288693

Craig, D. (2000). Native title and environmental planning: Indigenous land use agreements. *Environmental and Planning Law Journal, 17* (5), 440.

Craig, D. (2002). Recognising indigenous rights through co-management regimes: Canadian and Australian experiences. *New Zealand Journal of Environmental Law, 6,* 199.

Diegues, A., & Arruda, R. (2001). *Saberes tradicionais e biodiversidade no Brasil* (Traditional knowledge and biodiversity in Brazil). Brasília & São Paulo, Brazil: Ministério do Meio Ambiente; USP.

Dudley, N., Shadie, P., & Stolton, S. (2013). *Guidelines for applying protected area management categories including IUCN WCPA best practice guidance on recognising protected areas and assigning management categories and governance types* (Series No. 21). Gland, Switzerland: IUCN.

Forest Peoples Program. (2011) *Customary sustainable use of biodiversity by indigenous peoples and local communities.* England: Moreton-in-March.

Gama, A., (n.d.), *O direito de propriedade das terras ocupadas pelas comunidades descendentes de quilombos* (Property right of the lands occupied by communities of quilombos descendants). Retrieved from https://jus.com.br/artigos/7396/o-direito-de-propriedade-das-terras-ocupadas-pelas-comunidades-descendentes-de-quilombos.

Godoy, L. R. (2015). *Compensação ambiental e financiamento de áreas protegidas* (Environmental compensation and financing of protected areas). Porto Alegre, Brazil: Fabris.

Instituto de Pesquisas Ecológicas & ICHBio (Instituto Chico Mendes de Conservação da Biodiversidade). (2016). *Good practices in the management of protected areas* (2nd ed.). Institute of Ecological Research. Retrieved from http://www.icmbio.gov.br/portal/images/stories/comunicacao/publicacoes/revista_boas_pratica_2016.pdf

Instituto Socioambiental. (n.d.). *Povos Indigenas no Brasil* (Indigenous people in Brazil). Retrieved from http://pib.socioambiental.org/pt/c/terras-indigenas/demarcacoes/localizacao-e-extensao-das-tis

IUCN (International Union for the Conservation of Nature). (n.d.). *Protected area categories.* Retrieved from https://www.iucn.org/theme/protected-areas/about/protected-area-categories

Leuzinger, M. (2009). *Natureza e cultura: Unidades de conservação de proteção integral e populações tradicionais residentes* (Nature and culture: Full protection conservation units and resident traditional people). Curtiba, Brazil: Letra da Lei.

Leuzinger, M., & Lyngard, K. (2016). The land rights of Indigenous and Traditional peoples in Brazil and Australia. *Revista de Direito Internacional, Brasilia, 13* (1), 419–439.

Lima, A., & Bensusan, N. (Eds.). (2003). *Quem cala consente? Subsídios para a proteção aos conhecimentos tradicionais* (Silence is taken as consent? Subsidies for the protection of traditional knowledge). (Série Documentos do ISA; 8). São Paulo, Brazil: Instituto Socioambiental.

Lima, N. (2018). *Gestão de áreas protegidas: Instrumentos para implementação dos direitos socioambientais nos parques brasileiros marinhos costeiros* (Management of protected areas: Instruments for the implementation the socioenvironmental rights in the Brazilian coastal marine parks) (Master's thesis). Universidade Presbiteriana Mackenzie, São Paulo, Brazil.

104 *Donna Craig et al.*

Martin, P., Boer, B., & Slobodian, L. (Eds.). (2016). *Framework for assessing and improving law for sustainability.* Gland, Switzerland: IUCN.

Ministerio Público Federal. (2014). *Territórios de povos e comunidades tradicionais e as unidades de conservação de proteção integral: Alternativas para o asseguramento de direitos socioambientais.* (Territories of traditional people and communities and the full protection conservation units: Alternatives for the assurance of socioenvironmental rights). (6ª Câmara de Coordenação e Revisão). Brasília, Brazil: MPF.

NNTT (National Native Title Tribunal). (n.d.). *Register of native land use agreements.* Retrieved from http://www.nntt.gov.au/searchRegApps/NativeTitleRegisters/Pages/Search-Register-of-Indigenous-Land-Use-Agreements.aspx

Posey, D. (1993). The importance of semi-domesticated species in postcontact Amazonia: Effects of the Kayapó Indians on the dispersal of flora and fauna. In C. M. Hladik, A. Hladik, O. F. Linares, H. Pagezey, A. Semple & M. Hadley (Eds.), *Tropical forests, people and food: Biocultural interactions and applications to development* (Man & the Biosphere Series, vol. 13, pp. 63–71). Paris, France & New York, NY: UNESCO, The Parthenon Publishing Group.

Rights and Resources Initiative. (2015). *Protected areas and the land rights of indigenous and local communities: Current issues and future agenda.* Washington, DC: Rights and Resources Initiative.

Ross, H., Grant, C., Robinson, C., Izurieta, A., Smyth, D., & Rist. P. (2009). Co-management and indigenous protected areas in Australia: Achievements and ways forward. *Australian Journal of Environmental Management, 16* (4), 242–252.

Santilli, J. (2005). *Socioambientalismo e novos direitos* (*Socioenvironmentalism and new rights*). São Paulo, Brazil: Peirópolis.

Sathler, E. (2008). *Populações residentes em unidades de conservação de proteção integral: A competência da lei (rj) 2.393/95 para além do sistema nacional de unidades de conservação* (Resident populations in full protection conservation units: The competence of the law). SNUC. Retrieved from http://www.ambiental.adv.br/poptrad.pdf

SCRGSP (Steering Committee for the Review of Government Service Provision). (2016). *Overcoming indigenous disadvantage: Key indicators.* Canberra, ACT: Productivity Commission.

Silva, A., Silva, A., Paula, J., Silva, J., & Sousa, L. (2010). O processo de des(re)territorialização dos trabalhadores nordestinos no território amazônico durante os ciclos da borracha (The process of deterritorialisation of the Northeast workers in the Amazon territory during the rubber cicles). *Revista Geografar, 5* (1). doi: 10.5380/geografar.v5i1.17782

Souza Filho, C. (2005). As populações tradicionais e a proteção das florestas (Traditional populations and the protection of forests). *Revista de direitos difusos, 31.*

Varella, M., & Platiau, A. (Eds.). (2004). *Diversidade biológica e conhecimentos tradicionais* (Biological diversity and traditional knowledge). Belo Horizonte, Brazil: Del Rey (Coleção Direito Ambiental, 2.

Vitorelli, E. (2012). *Estatuto da igualdade racial e comunidades quilombolas* (Racial equality statute and quilombola communities). Salvador, Brazil: Editora Juspudivm.

Walker, J. (2010). *Processes for effective management: Learning from agencies and Warlpiri people involved in managing the Northern Tanami Indigenous Protected Area, Australia.* (PhD thesis). The Northern Institute, Institute of Advanced Studies Charles Darwin University.

6 Low impact recreational use and biodiversity protection

Mauricio Duarte dos Santos and Boyd Dirk Blackwell

Abstract

This chapter outlines the role that surfing reserves play in biodiversity conservation in Australia and Brazil. Surfing reserves demonstrate the possibility of untapped opportunities to use recreation (and possibly other cultural values) to secure biodiversity conservation in situations where purely environmental concerns are insufficient to obtain and fund protection. Both countries are megadiverse and surfing reserves are an important innovative opportunity to meet biodiversity targets while helping protect social and cultural capital, and to deliver economic benefits. These two countries provide contrasting examples of how surfing reserves have been implemented in conjunction with broader biodiversity measures, and the effectiveness of the various surfing reserve regimes. These cases identify a new International Union for Conservation of Nature category, 'low-impact passive recreation (surfing_ reserve)', that has the potential to deliver positive biodiversity outcomes.

Introduction

The discussion in this book highlights that effective biodiversity protection is unlikely to occur without community engagement in the endeavour. Innovation will be needed to achieve citizen engagement, including for the creation and operation of biodiversity reserves and to align private incentives with the achievement of public-good outcomes.

Innovative citizen-led initiatives play an important part in biodiversity protection and restoration. Non-government organisations deliver political support and activism for better governance; environmental philanthropists and community volunteers deliver important benefits to the environment and good stewardship by individuals is indispensable.

For centuries, conservation areas have existed to satisfy private needs which simultaneously assist biodiversity. These have included game reserves, water catchment areas and scenic areas. In recent years, areas of privately operated conservation reserves have been on the rise (Langholz & Lassoie, 2001). These point to the possibility of innovative ways to align private incentives with public-good conservation.

106 *Mauricio Duarte dos Santos et al.*

This chapter discusses surfing reserves in Australia and Brazil to demonstrate how private recreation can facilitate biodiversity conservation. Both countries have created surfing reserves but in different ways, providing innovative opportunities to meet biodiversity targets and, simultaneously, recreational opportunities and economic benefits.

Surfing reserves and conservation innovation

Surfing reserves are areas of land and sea in the nearshore zone of the coast that conserve its heritage and ongoing use as a special location for surfing. Biophysical factors form an iconic 'surf break' where wave quality is consistently high. Such areas have a unique history of developing surfing 'greats' and a 'hot spot' for surfer congregation, socialisation, competition, culture and economy; the areas are important to surfing and to society in a broader but not commonly known sense (Lazarow, 2007a).

Setting aside areas for recreation and conservation is not new. The evolution of national parks (Clawson & Knetsch, 1966; Frost & Laing, 2013) with eco-use and ecotourism have resulted in eight billion annual visits and expenditures of $600 billion per year (Balmford et al., 2015). Surfing reserves are a late addition and often mere adjuncts to terrestrial and marine protected areas, partly because surfing is on the 'margins' of society. The need for surfing spaces to be protected is demonstrated by hard lessons of losing surf breaks (surf capital) to urbanisation, congestion and contested uses of the nearshore environment. Some activities that harm surf break uses include: the construction of navigational infrastructure, such as boat ramps and seawalls (Blackwell, 2008; Lazarow, 2007b); cruise ship terminals and port facilities (Blackwell, 2017; Lazarow, Miller, & Blackwell, 2009); 'armouring' river mouths with rock and associated property, and canal developments (Blackwell, 2017) and commercial fishing (Lazarow, 2007a). Compared to many of these, surfing is a low-impact use, though its side-effects also need to be managed (e.g., see Towner & Orams, 2016).

We argue that surfing reserves present the case for a new category of protected area, a 'low-impact recreational protected area' where contextual factors and the adverse impacts of heightened human visitation are managed. The first national parks were established largely due to recreational aesthetic use or interests (photography in the case of Yosemite in the US, and hunting in the Royal National Park, Australia). Further evidence for such a case for culture and use-based protection is the novel protective category based on cultural interests in Australia, Indigenous Protected Areas (Department of Environment and Energy, 2019b); These are a significant part of Australia's protected estate (Clark & Johnston, 2016). Surfing reserves are one possible example of expanding the reserve system by harnessing other values and interests. Other cultural and recreational interests include private ecotourism, sustainable hunting, Indigenous or other cultural activities and scenic enjoyment. Surfing reserves provide an example of the opportunities for protected areas innovation and the issues that might arise when blending human use and biodiversity goals.

The Great Barrier Reef is one of Australia's and the world's megadiverse and iconic marine protected areas, forming part of a system of protected areas (Clark & Johnston, 2016). Brazil's iconic megadiversity substantially lies in its inland terrestrial and aquatic protected area and catchment: the Central Amazon Conservation Complex (OECD, 2015, 2018). The offshore 'Blue Amazon' includes significant maritime zones (Fernandes & Oliveira, 2012). In both countries, the coastal zone, particularly close to cities, experiences significant use pressures. The impacts on nearshore surf zones are broadly similar, though adverse impacts are more spread across Brazil's coastline than Australia's because of a more even and densely spread coastal population (ABS, 2018; IBGE, 2011).

In both countries, early environmental harm happened on the coasts where the first settlements and port facilities arose. These forces have created a need for coastal protective regimes that can work in populated and pressured socio-ecological contexts, where the creation of parks and reserves is unlikely to be feasible. The Atlantic Forest, only second to the Amazon in biological diversity, extends from northeast Brazil, south along the Brazilian Atlantic coastline and inland into northeast Argentina and eastern Paraguay (WWF, 2019). Because of population pressures, which are also experienced at adjacent key Brazilian surfing locations, only a small part of the forest remains, protected through measures including world heritage listing (WWF, 2019).

Surfing reserves and biodiversity

Surfing reserves offer complementary opportunities to protect marine and terrestrial environments on the coast, particularly in areas of concentrated population where the pressures are great (Jones et al., 2017). The function of surfing reserves is to ensure that high quality surfing locations and the cultural and natural heritage they embody, are conserved (e.g. Surf Coast Shire, 2015). Farmer and Short (2007) state that the primary purpose of the National Surfing Reserves (NSRs) in Australia is 'to recognise sites of cultural and historical significance in Australian surf culture … acknowledge the surfing way of life and link past, present and future generations with our oceans, waves and beaches' (p. 100). Therefore, recognition of NSRs is to conserve culture, which appears consistent with the special case of the conservation function of Bells Beach SR (Surf Coast Shire, 2015, p. 5). However, Bells Beach SR is different and not recognised as a NSR.

In contrast to NSRs, World Surfing Reserves (WSRs) explicitly address biodiversity conservation, including environmental criteria such as 'recognised hotspot', 'threatened species present', 'protected designations', 'key avenue for legal protection locally', 'provides key ecosystem services' (Save the Waves Coalition, 2015a). Environmental protection is the second of four main criteria for WSRs, the other three are: '(1) Quality and consistency of the wave/s … (2) Culture and Surf history and (3) Governance capacity and local support' (Save the Waves Coalition, 2015a).

Surfing might be viewed as a simple recreational pursuit but it embodies much more. It has evolved over hundreds of years into a component of coastal communities, affecting culture, society, economy and politics. Surfing involves at least 35 million participants (Wales, 2012, p. 71) contributing about $50 billion dollars to the global economy annually (McGregor & Wills, 2016, p. 1).

Surfing and surfing reserves are currently attracting increasing attention by researchers, including studies on the benefits from combining trans-disciplinary systems thinking and adaptive co-management to address environmental issues of surf breaks (Arroyo, Levine, & Espejel, 2019; Silva et al., 2016; Skellern, Peryman, Orchard, & Rennie, 2013), surf tourism development and the disconnection of local communities (Doering, 2018), the conservation potential of coastal surfing resources through legislative protection, the awareness and management of surfing sites (Martin & Assenov, 2015), sustainable surfing tourism development and the empowerment of local people (Ponting, McDonald, & Wearing, 2005), the development and difficulties of protecting remote surfing locations (Orams, 2017), social and economic values of surfing and the negative consequences of developments (Lazarow, 2010; Lazarow, Miller, & Blackwell, 2007, 2009; Usher, 2017), surf site discovery and economic growth, particularly for emerging economies (McGregor & Wills, 2016), relationships between informal property rights and surf quality (Kaffine, 2009) and accessing uncrowded surf locations in Africa (Wales, 2012).

Surfing is different to other marine recreational pursuits because it relies on the natural conjunction of wind, waves, sand, rocks and shore to form waves for riding. It requires the 'surfer' to use skills developed over decades through a typical daily exercise ritual, and resulting mental and biophysical connection with surf sites (Kaffine, 2009) and fellow surfers. However, historical stereotypical perspectives of this recreational activity see it as marginal, unproductive and not mainstream (Thompson, 2011). Surfers spend considerable time identifying which break is suitable, taking the time to check breaks in person and travelling between sites. Because of their often daily participation, they have the potential to monitor the implementation of environmental protection (Brewin et al., 2015; Reineman, Thomas, & Caldwell, 2017).

High quality surf breaks near urban populations are relatively scarce (Skellern et al., 2013). Where they exist, they are predominantly shared open-access (see Hardin 1968; Lloyd, 1833; Ostrom, 1990) and *de facto* common property (see Blackwell, 2003) and, therefore, can become congested and generate conflict because of differing cultures, perspectives and knowledge (Santos, 2018; Stocker & Kennedy, 2009; Thompson, 2007).

Surfing is a 'passive-use' recreation compared with, for example, spear fishing or other extractive marine activities. Nevertheless, surfing and passive-use recreation do not always facilitate environmental conservation; they can cause local impact on beaches beyond recreational carrying capacities (e.g. see Towner, 2016). Supporting built infrastructure can degrade the natural asset by 'loving it to death' (see Blackwell, 2003). These factors, particularly conflict and congestion, combine to stimulate local-to-global community demands to better manage (Ostrom, 1990) and conserve these sites as surfing reserves, particularly iconic sites (Farmer & Short, 2007).

These considerations raise two questions with respect to the role of surfing in the conservation of megadiversity: How can surfing reserves help conserve biodiversity? and How can surfing reserve governance be improved to ensure biodiversity conservation? We respond to these questions by examining the consequences of surfing reserves on biodiversity conservation in Australia and Brazil. We begin the examination by discussing two case study surfing reserves and their conservation outcomes – one in Australia and one in Brazil – and then we consider international perspectives on surfing reserves and biodiversity conservation. We follow this examination with a discussion of innovations and mechanisms that would better protect surfing reserves and their biodiversity, including allowing for a category of 'low-impact passive recreation (surfing) reserve'.

Australian surfing reserves

Australia has 21 NSRs (see Table 6.1). Bells Beach was Australia's first surfing recreation reserve, and 'protected' under legislation of the state of Victoria but, surprisingly, it is not listed as a surfing reserve. The purpose of NSRs is outlined by the NSR (2019)

> National Surfing Reserves are 'iconic' places of intrinsic environmental, heritage, sporting and cultural value to a nation. NSR(s) embrace all peoples to enjoy, understand and protect special coastal environments of universal value to the surfing world. A Surfing Reserve does not attempt to exclude any user group.

This definition highlights that NSRs are designed to protect coastal environments but biodiversity conservation is not an explicit goal; that is, the extent of species diversity in the reserves is not necessarily assessed through the NSR processes. Sites close to dense human populations are less likely to have high biodiversity values and the biodiversity they contain are not likely to be protected without sufficient resources and active management. Stronger protection from the effects of human populations may require the legal status of protected area. The biodiversity conservation outcomes likely to emerge from the NSRs listed in Table 6.1 rank from limited (in highly human affected areas of dense populations) to moderate (in less populated areas with nearby conservation areas such as national parks) and high (where NSRs are remote from population centres which limits human impact). People residing

110 *Mauricio Duarte dos Santos et al.*

near remote NSRs have opposed attempts to use their locations for world surfing competitions because of the environmental and other negative impacts from the visitation these events bring, such as traffic, congestion, waste, excess demands on services and resources and other negative impacts (e.g. see Poulsen, 2018).

New South Wales (NSW), the most populated state in Australia, had planned to provide legislative standing for surfing reserves through the *Crown Lands Act* 1989 (NSW). However, this Act was replaced by the *Crown Land Management Act 2016* (NSW), which does not refer to surfing reserves in either the Act or its Regulations, although there are references to reserves for uses, including recreation use. Bells Beach Surfing Recreation Reserve has legal standing under the *Crown Land (Reserves) Act 1978* (VIC), *Geographic Place Names Act 1998* (VIC), *Coastal Management Act 1995* (VIC), *Western Regional Coastal Plan 2015–2020* (VIC), *Aboriginal Heritage Act 2006* (VIC), and is listed in the *Hertiage Act 1995* (VIC) because of its significant historical and surfing culture status. While Bell's Beach is not listed as a NSR because of the various legislative protections, it has *suis generis* legal status. Anderson (2013) criticises declarations of NSRs as largely symbolic and reports that surfing groups point to the need for stronger protection.

Angourie was among the first NSRs in NSW, cited at the northern tip of the Yuraygir National Park. In addition to the main surfing site, which has a consistent right-hand break, there are two car park entry points with walks and beach and rock platform sites, a spectacular blow hole and two large freshwater swimming holes with rock jumping sites adjacent to the sea, which are particularly popular with youth and family groups.

The coastal heathlands and marine environment of Angourie are beautiful. With heightened visitation, the facilities at Angourie become congested, resulting in undesirable social, cultural and environmental impacts, such as conflict between local residents and some visitors defecating in the nearby heathlands and using the showers of a local recreation club (causing the club's hot water bill to rise significantly – Shop owner, Yamba, 2018, pers. comm.).

These adverse consequences highlight the need for adequate services and management to limit adverse effects. In Australia, NSR day-to-day management rests with local government, which are not as well resourced as state and federal governments. Possible policy responses for obtaining more management resources to manage these out-of-the-local- area visitors include user fees, quota systems, funding from state and national governments and appointment of rangers. One proposal is to establish a camp site with facilities at the local sports ground. However, this may displace local sporting groups and visitors want to continue to camp next to the ocean as they have done in the past (Shop owner, Yamba, 2018, pers. comm.).

The problems faced by the Angourie reserve demonstrate the need for listed NSRs to be well resourced and managed in order for them to be able to meet biodiversity conservation and social objectives. Identifying and planning for such management needs should be part of the preparation for listing.

Recreational use, biodiversity protection 111

Table 6.1 National Surfing Reserves of Australia

	Name	Established date	Location[a]	Biodiversity protection potential
1	Maroubra	Mar 2006	Sydney, NSW	Limited though national ark nearby
2	Angourie	Jan 2007	Northern NSW	High with nearby national park & lower levels of development
3	Lennox Head	Feb 2008	Northern NSW	High with national park nearby and lower levels of development
4	Crescent Head	Jun 2008	Mid NSW	High with national parks nearby and low levels of development
5	Cronulla	Sep 2008	Sydney, NSW	Limited because of development
6	Merewether	Mar 2009	Sydney, NSW	Limited because of development
7	Killalea	Jun 2009	NSW	Moderate because at distance from Sydney but reserve immediately adjacent beach
8	North Narrabeen	Oct 2009	Sydney, NSW	Moderate as further from Sydney human impacts than other Sydney beaches
9	Margaret River	Mar 2010	WA	High because less developed
10	Kallabri	Mar 2010	WA	High because relatively remote
11	Manly-Freshwater	Sep 2010	Sydney, NSW	Limited but National Park nearby
12	Yalingup	Dec 2011	WA	High because less developed
13	Burleigh Heads	Feb 2012	QLD	Limited but National Park nearby
14	Currumbin Alley	Feb 2012	QLD	Limited
15	Snapper-Kirra	Feb 2012	QLD	Limited
16	Daly Head	Jan 2013	SA	High because of its remoteness on Yorke Peninsula
17	Point Sinclair	Jan 2013	SA	High because remote and National Park nearby
18	Phillip Island	Mar 2013	VIC	Moderate as some distance from Melbourne
19	Noosa	Mar 2015	QLD	High with National Park nearby and population controls
20	Bondi	Dec 2017	Sydney, NSW	Limited as Sydney's most iconic and visited
21	Cabarita	Feb 2018	Northern NSW	High because less developed and national parks nearby

Source: OzBeaches (2019).

Abbreviations: New South Wales (NSW), Queensland (QLD), South Australia (SA), Western Australia (WA).

Brazilian surfing reserves

Before the 1970s, *Guarda do Embaú* was a small agricultural village and a place for fishers in the town of Palhoça in the state of Santa Catarina, Brazil. Once surfers discovered the waves, the site became internationally recognised. The village is adjacent to the Serra do Tabuleiro State Park, the largest conservation area in Santa Catarina State, providing a stunning natural environment including the Rio da Madre (Da Madre River) and an intact estuary system (Save the Waves, 2015b). These natural and cultural features resulted in the unique surf break being recognised as the first Brazilian World Surfing Reserve.

In addition to its own natural attributes, the reserve is part of a complex biodiversity area that includes state and federal Conservation Units (UCs), the marine protected area, Environmental Marine Protected Area Baleia Franca (APA Marinha Baleia Franca) and the terrestrial protected area, Environmental Protected Area Entorno Costeiro (APA Entorno Costeiro). In 2009 the state of Santa Catarina passed *Law no.14,661*, reducing the area of environmental protection from 87,405 to 84,130 ha to allow for subdivisions of land, mining, irrigation and an industrial zone. This initiative was found to be incompatible with the *1988 Brazilian Constitution* by the Attorney General's Office and has not been resolved.

Brazil does not have a law to protect its surf breaks or institutions for the protection and management of these natural resources. For the most part, surfing stakeholders are not on the boards of Brazilian's UCs and other specially protected territorial spaces. Certification under the WSR programme is insufficient by itself to protect the reserve; the Guarda do Embaú WSR needs an explicit strategy to ensure its protection.

The Guarda do Embaú Preservation and Surfing Association (ASPG) established a Local Steering Committee to focus on evaluating and communicating the four aspects of the WSR assessment criteria (quality and consistency of wave/s, environmental characteristics, history of culture and surfing and community support) to the three levels of government, non-government entities, media, local associations and sports personalities. The main conflicts to be overcome were urban sprawl, lack of management of tourism, no sanitation, problems of spillover effects of agrochemicals from adjacent rural areas, and the socio-economic characteristics of a developing country.

The Guarda do Embaú WSR committee conducted three workshops focused on finding a solution for its sewage and the lack of sanitation. They expect, through the engagement of a sanitary engineer and information gained in a public hearing called by Palhoça's Mayor, to prepare a report and work to improve sanitation. In January of 2018, the committee initiated the Save the Waves Coalition 'surfonomics' programme to enable the Guarda WSR to assess the economic value of waves and surfing to their local community and to help decision makers understand the importance of coastal conservation (Save The Waves, 2015b). The report was provided in October 2019 at the declaration of the WSR.

Perspectives on surfing reserves

Table 6.2 lists the dedicated World Surfing Reserves (WSRs). Two are in Australia, two in the US, four in Latin America (one in Brazil) and one in Portugal. Two WSRs are approved but not yet dedicated and include Punta Boriquen, Puerto Rico and Noosa, Australia. A requirement of WSR protection is that the reserve category has to be incorporated into national law or a natural resource management frameworks, such as in a Crown Lands Act of a state in Australia. The process for approval of new surfing reserves through

Table 6.2 World Surfing Reserves

Name	Year established	Country	Size	Description	Biodiversity protection potential	Management document
Guarda do Embaú	2019	Brazil	nyk	Left had break over mouth of *Do Madre* River with scenic rocky headland, surf culture and history, artisanal fisherman.	Pristine coastal environment flanked by rivermouths, protected areas and mature sand dune systems	*Strategic Plan*
Punta de Lobos	2018	Chile	0.11 km² but conservation easement could be larger (Fundacion Punta De Lobos, 2017)	Iconic 800m + left-hand point break, country's best surfers honed skills, artisanal fisherman, & iconic film.	Explicit & integral: 'Global biodiversity hotspot'	*Stewardship Plan*
Gold Coast	2016	Burleigh Heads to Snapper Rocks, Central & Southern Gold Coast, Queensland, Australia	Approx. 7.5 km²	Wave quality and consistency, Surf culture and history, environmental characteristics.	Adjacent Burleigh Heads National Park & Currumbin Wildlife park	*Gold Coast Surf Management Plan*
Bahia De Todos Santos	2014	Baja, Mexico	0.5 km²	High quality waves and big wave location year round, birthplace Mexican surf culture,	San Miguel catchment a critical riparian ecosystem; efforts to establish 4 miles as a state natural reserve & park	*Stewardship Conceptual Model*

(Continued)

Name	Year established	Country	Size	Description	Biodiversity protection potential	Management document
Huanchaco	2013	Peru	Approx. 6 km^2	Consistent clean left-hand surf & ancient pre-Columbian seafaring town, earliest known surf crafts, 'caballito de totoras'.	Prevented local trash dumpsite in Buenos Aires, efforts to protect 'totora' reed wetlands & created world's first law in waves protection	*World Surfing Reserve Management Plan Huanchaco, Peru*
Santa Cruz	2012	California, US	Approx. 14 km^2	23 consistent right-hand surf breaks including two world class breaks, first boarding surfing in North America by Hawaiian Princes, marine protected area	Within Monterey Bay National Marine Sanctuary: kelp forests home to diverse megafauna, nutrient rich temperate waters	*Sant Cruz World Surfing Stewardship Plan September 2015*
Manly Beach	2012	Freshwater, Queenscliff & Manly, Australia	Approx. 4 km^2	Australian surfing birthplace, 1st body surfing, legal bathing, surf lifesaving club, surfboat, Duke Kahanamoku's surfing display, & world championships and champions.	'Not take' Cabbage Tree Bay Aquatic Reserve Sthn end & Sydney Harbour National Park Sthn Headland, Southern Right whale migration	*Coastal Zone Management Plan for Manly Ocean Beach* & noted National Surfing Reserve 2010 under *Crown Land Management Act* 2016 (NSW)

Ericeira	2011	Portugal		World class surf zone: beach to reef breaks, ancient Jagoz people lived from the sea, surf tourism destination & annual Quick Silver Pro.	Rich biodiverse waters from upwelling	*Management Plan of the Ericeira World Surfing Reserve* (Azul Ericeira Mag, 2018), & the world's first WSR interpretive centre
Malibu	2010	California, US	Approx. 0.7 km^2 (Pacific Long Boarder, 2018)	Consistent right-hand cobblestone perfect point break, home of numerous surfing legends, setting for iconic Gidget movie.	Malibu Creek State Park, part of Santa Monica Mountains National Recreation Area nearby & Malibu Lagoon State Beach of Santa Monica State Conservancy (recreation & wildlife conservation)	*Malibu Historic District* of the National Register of Historic Places, *National Historic Preservation Act* 1966 (Pacific Long Boarder, 2018)

Sources and notes: Unless otherwise noted, Save the Waves (2015b).
Abbreviations: LTWM = Low tide water mark; nyk = not yet known.

the Save the Waves Coalition creates a *sui generis* arrangement that includes protection of biodiversity. 'Environmental protection' is a key criterion for approval. However, biodiversity conservation might not be implemented within the reserve *per se*; rather, it may require managing adjacent properties through separate legislative and other processes.

When a surfing reserve is established, it may imply that the rest of the nearby coast is not valued or available for surfing. This may (for example) facilitate the approval of a desalination plant, outfall or other degrading coastal activity which destroys a surfing site (Gemmill, J. 2019, pers. comm, 14 March). Often, there will be surfing locations adjacent to a surfing reserve that do not receive protection, leaving them vulnerable. The assumption that one site is reserved may perversely facilitate the loss of biological diversity at non-reserved sites.

Less well-known surf breaks can be overlooked by decision makers because surfers may keep them secret. An uncrowded surf break is preferred by experienced surfers, providing more waves and less competition at the point of entry to the wave. Given populations near the coast, uncrowded breaks will usually only remain uncrowded because of restricted access (e.g., from abutting private property, or restricted crown land potentially containing unexploded ordinance, etc.). Surfers are not likely to reveal secluded, inaccessible and non-congested surf sites (Gemmel, J. 2019, pers comms, 14 March; Jarratt, 2019). A systematic approach to identifying potential surfing reserves and protecting them would maximise recreational opportunities and their potential to conserve biodiversity.

The *Convention on Biological Diversity (CBD)* states that a protected area is 'a geographically defined area which is designated or regulated and managed to achieve specific conservation objectives' (art. 2). National biodiversity strategies and action plans must address: (a) protected areas to conserve biological diversity while promoting environmentally sound development; (b) public participation, particularly when assessing the environmental impacts of development projects that threaten biological diversity; (c) education of people and raising awareness about the importance of biological diversity and the need to conserve it (Secretariat of the Convention on Biological Diversity, 2000, p. 9).

The 10th Conference of the Parties of the CBD in 2000 adopted the *Aichi Biodiversity Targets*, including goals for the marine environment; target 11 provides that at least 10 per cent of coastal and marine areas be conserved through effective and equitable management of well-connected systems of protected areas by 2020 (see Chapter 4).

Though Brazil has formally achieved the Aichi 11 target for open oceans, it has not created effective arrangements to protect the coastal marine zone where surf breaks exist. Brazil needs to improve marine spatial planning (Gandra, Bonetti, & Scherer, 2018; Maes, 2008), ideally with consideration of recreational activities areas like surfing reserves that are compatible with the multiple uses included in the marine area.

Australia has established a range of protected area categories and zones. Its National Reserve System aims to create protected areas to conserve the biodiversity and protection of ecosystems, without these necessarily being locked away or isolated (Department of Environment and Energy, 2019b). Other than Bell's Beach surfing recreation reserve, surfing reserves are not a recognised category of protected areas in Australia. As already noted, the NSW Department of Lands (2008) intended to recognise a new category of Crown Land called a 'Surfing Reserve' through the Regional Reserve Strategy under the *Crown Lands Act 1989* (NSW) (see Farmer & Short, 2007). The surfing site would have been included in the reserve extending from the high-water mark and 500 m seaward. Unfortunately, this did not happen.

At the state level, Local Environmental Plans of local government could be another mechanism for legal protection of surfing reserves (Johnson, C., 2019, pers. comms, 1 Sep, NSW NPWS, Armidale). Whether through state or local law, SRs, whether NSRs or WSRs, are added in a piecemeal fashion, dependent on a jurisdiction's willingness to recognise them explicitly through legislation. In the Bells Beach case, the extent of biodiversity conservation is limited to maintaining cultural and surfing culture and recreational access. The major benefit of surfing reserves is to protect a social asset (Blackwell, Raybould, & Lazarow, 2010) so low impact use becomes a legitimate consideration in managing the coastal zone.

Surfing and other recreational use zones that are consistent with biodiversity conservation present an opportunity to help meet the *CBD* goals. Surfing reserves could help improve the coverage of marine protected areas. However, any recreational use that attracts people to areas in good natural condition may generate harmful impacts: traffic, facilities, adjacent urbanisation, waste and other harms. This is why surfing reserves arrangements should embed effective controls against such harms.

Conclusions

Certifying Guarda do Embaú as the first Brazilian WSR is intended to facilitate governance by the local community. It illustrates how certification can help to integrate coastal management with social, economic and environmental governance, and how public participation can improve the legal framework (Silva, Santos, & Dutra, 2016). However, it also illustrates that detailed issues must be addressed to implement such a scheme, such as: (i) obtaining title to the area; (ii) how the reserve will be managed, including integration with the management of the UCs in which this beach is inserted and (iii) the potential conflicts and overlaps of use.

Surf breaks are multidimensional marine resources within often sensitive marine and terrestrial natural environments and in a unique cultural environment formed by surfers, fishermen and other citizens. Effective governance requires proper monitoring of the site with data, including data provided by the surfing community (e.g., see new data from indicator methods from Ariza et al., 2010: Martin & Assenov, 2015). Good meta governance is required because of the 'difficulty to discern the set of processes by which the rules of the game are imposed and reworked by those who... shape the planning system' (Allmendinger & Haughtonô, 2009, p. 631). Attention must be paid to the institutional arrangements that determine how surfing reserves are planned and managed, including outcomes for biodiversity.

A relevant institutional approach may be that of the International Union for Conservation of Nature (IUCN) under which areas are delineated to meet the objectives of protecting and maintaining 'biological diversity and natural resources and cultural associations' (IUCN, 1994). The IUCN protected area concept espouses that management is carried out using effective legal or other means. Surfing reserves can be an effective mechanism to meet largely complementary objectives, including conserving history, culture and biodiversity (Monteferri, Scheske, & Muller, 2019; Santos, 2018).

The *1988 Brazilian Constitution* is built on the IUCN protected area approach with a category of specially protected territorial spaces (*Espaços Territoriais Especialmente Protegidos* – ETEPs) conceptualising ecology as a human right (Downs, 1993). We argue that the Brazilian National Policy on socio-biodiversity protection could be enhanced by recognising 'recreation (surfing) reserves' as a form of protected area or ETEP, or by protecting surf breaks using existing categories. The former could be done through the legal recognition of 'low-impact passive recreation reserves' as a protected area category. The latter could be done through the legal recognition of specific surfing reserves under land management legislation. The former is likely to have stronger biodiversity conservation outcomes as it involves the legal status of a protected area, while the latter may meet broader objectives but with the likelihood of compromise to biodiversity outcomes, as highlighted in the Angouri case study Australia.

Australia incorporated the IUCN range of Protected Area categories into its legal system (IUCN, 2019). According to the Australian Government, the National Reserve System aims to create protected areas to conserve biodiversity and ecosystems but not to lock away or isolate the systems from other land or water uses (Department of Environment and Energy 2019a). Protected areas are a valued land use, providing social, economic and scientific benefits (Department of Environment and Energy 2019a). Surfing reserves do not fit neatly into the recognised categories. Surfing areas do not always have significant national or global environmental values nor ancient cultural heritage in the environment. A new category of 'low-impact passive recreation reserves' with surfing reserves as a sub-category would enlarge the estate of protected areas, with sustainable use offering revenues to help fund conservation.

The Indigenous Protected Areas (IPAs) discussed in Chapter 5 are a recent Australian innovation in protected areas. They help ensure that Aboriginal and Torres Strait Islander people's heritage and homelands are conserved for cultural and usage reasons. IPAs 'are areas of land and sea country owned or managed by Indigenous groups which are voluntarily managed as a protected area for biodiversity conservation through an agreement with the Australian Government'(Department of Environment and Energy, 2019b). Through state planning mechanisms in Australia, agricultural areas of significant cultural heritage and food security have also achieved special status under some planning regimes to address rapid coal seam gas development (e.g. NSW's exclusive zones for equestrian and wine industries, and QLD's strategic agricultural areas). These examples reinforce that contemporary cultural and non-consumption values can be a sensible basis for protective zoning.

In 2009, the Australian state and territory governments released a *Strategy for the National Reserve System*. This updated strategy identified actions to create a national system of protected areas and reserves and envisaged a substantial extension of marine protected areas.

Concurrently (but not as marine protected areas), Australia has been expanding its surfing reserves. As discussed, the first world surfing reservation was established in Australia as a land-based reserve in the state of Victoria in 1973: the Bells Beach Surfing Recreation Reserve. This signalled a movement in 2005 that led to the NSR Programme. It recognised iconic surf sites of environmental, cultural and historical significance, through a coalition between community and government. Reiblich (2013) argues that surfing reserves largely fail to achieve their goals because their designation is symbolic and lacks legal recognition. Lazarow (2010) highlights that, in addition to the need to protect the surfing area, it is necessary to protect the adjacent land area. Human activities on the adjacent land can adversely affect the seaward environment and biodiversity. We argue that a strong legislative basis is needed for surfing reserves in Australia, including a specific focus on biodiversity conservation objectives. It is also important to plan for managing visitation impacts (similar to Management Plans for National Parks in Australia) and a need to secure funding for management.

Arrangements used in Chile provide a possible model with success in securing funds from philanthropists to conserve the land and sea interface of the surfing reserve (*Fundacion Punta De Lobos*, n.d.). Chile 'aims to design and implement a scalable prototype project for the conservation of Punta de Lobos' (the World Surfing Reserve) landscape and biodiversity through the use of a private model of conservation and working together within the community' (Fundacion Punta De Lobos, n.d.). The model involves specified rules for: (i) public access to the coastline and regulation of tourist activities; (ii) allowing both artisanal fishing and surfing and (iii) guaranteeing that the conservation conditions will be applied regardless of the current land owner. The model involves the use of a voluntary easement (VE) based on the Chilean *Law no. 20.930/2016 (Derecho real de conservación)* regarding property law. It is implemented in four stages: (1) acquire the properties or agree with owners to include their lands in the VE; (2) design the VE; (3) implement the VE and monitor to ensure the restrictions are met and (4) expand the VE to other properties. The land owner voluntarily limits rights over their land to

120 *Mauricio Duarte dos Santos et al.*

ensure that particular ecosystem attributes are protected. The property titles include ongoing restrictions over use of the land to protect its biodiversity.

In addition to the above innovations, local environmental planning may also be an important instrument for recognising and sustainably managing recreational reserves, including those for surfing, to meet biodiversity outcomes (Johnson, C. 2019, pers. Coms, NSW NPWS, Armidale).

In conclusion, there are broader biodiversity implications from the experience with surfing reserves. These highlight that innovative possibilities for protected areas, including using recreational and other uses as part of the mix to provide benefits from biodiversity conservation, exist. They illustrate the potential for beneficial outcomes by creatively harnessing non-biodiversity incentives, but with the need to ensure that adverse impacts are carefully managed.

References

ABS (Australian Bureua of Statistics). (2018). *Census of population and housing: Reflecting Australia – Stories from the Census, 2016* (no. 2071.0). Canberra, ACT.

Allmendinger, P., & Haughtonô, G. (2009). Soft spaces, fuzzy boundaries, and metagovernance: The new spatial planning in the Thames Gateway. *Environment and Planning A: Economy and Space, 41*, 617–633.

Anderson, S. (2013, March 15). Victoria gets its first National Surfing Reserve. *The World Today*. Retrieved from https://www.abc.net.au/worldtoday/content/2013/s3716376.htm

Ariza E., Jimenez J. A., Sarda R., Villares M., Pinto J., Fraguell, R. ... Fluvia, M. (2010). Proposal for an integral quality index for urban and urbanized beaches. *Environmental Management, 45*, 998–1013.

Arroyo, M., Levine, A., & Espejel, I. (2019). A transdisciplinary framework proposal for surf break conservation and management: Bahía de Todos Santos. *Ocean and Coastal Management, 168*, 197–211. doi: 10.1016/j.ocecoaman.2018.10.022

Azul Ericeira Mag. (2018, July 19). Approval of the management plan of the Ericeira World Surfing Reserve. *Waves*. Retrieved from http://www.ericeiramag.pt/en/approval-of-the-management-plan-of-the-ericeira-world-surfing-reserve/

Balmford, A., Green, J. M. H., Anderson, M., Beresford, J., Huang, C., Naidoo, ... Manica, A. (2015). Walk on the wild side: Estimating the global magnitude of visits to protected areas. *PLoS Biology, 13* (2), e1002074. doi: 10.1371/journal.pbio.1002074

Blackwell, B. D. (2003). The economics of coastal foreshore and beach management: Use, safe bathing facilities, erosion and conservation (Doctoral dissertation). St Lucia QLD: School of Economics, The University of Queensland.

Blackwell, B. D. (2008, July 30). *Expert witness report: Beach and coastal foreshore economics* (An expert witness report to the Planning Panels Victoria on the proposal for an open access boat ramp, Bastion Point, Mallacoota, Victoria). Melbourne, Australia: Department of Sustainability and Environment.

Blackwell, B. D. (2017, August, 23). 'Fixing', through hard infrastructure, a naturally dynamic and well functioning estuarine and beach system is crazy, especially where the economics does not stack up, Don't Rock the Maroochy comment, *Facebook*.

Blackwell, B. D., Raybould, M., & Lazarow, N. (2010). Beaches as societal assets: Council expenditures, recreational returns and climate change. In C. A. Tisdell (Ed.), *Handbook of tourism economics: Analysis, new applications and cast studies* (pp. 443–467). London, UK: World Scientific.

Brewin, R. J. W., De Mora, L., Jackson, T., Brewin, T. G., & Shutler, J. (2015). On the potential of surfers to monitor environmental indicators in the coastal zone. *PLoS One, 10* (7), e0127706.

Clark, G. F., & Johnston, E. L. (2016). Coasts. In: *Australia State of the Environment 2016*. Canberra, ACT: Australian Government Department of the Environment and Energy. Retrieved from https://soe.environment.gov.au/theme/coasts

Clawson, M., & Knetsch, J. (1966). *The economics of outdoor recreation*. Baltimore, MD: Resources for the Future.

Department of Environment and Energy. (2019a). *Australia's protected areas*. Retrieved from https://www.environment.gov.au/land/nrs/about-nrs/australias-protected-areas

Department of Environment and Energy. (2019b). *Indigenous protected areas*. Retrieved from https://www.environment.gov.au/land/indigenous-protected-areas

Department of Lands (NSW). (2008). *National Surfing Reserves*. Retrieved from http://www.surfingreserves.org/pdf/National_Surfing_FINAL_web.pdf

Doering, A. (2018). Mobilising stoke: A genealogy of surf tourism development in Miyazaki, Japan. *Tourism Planning & Development, 15*, 68–81. doi: 10.1080/21568316. 2017.1313772

Downs, J. A. (1993). A healthy and ecologically balanced environment: An argument for a third generation right. *Duke Journal of Comparative & International Law, 3*, 351.

Farmer, B., & Short, A. D. (2007). Australian National Surfing Reserves: Rationale and process for recognising iconic surfing locations. *Journal of Coastal Research Special Issue, 50*, 99–103. Retrieved from http://www.jstor.org/stable/26481564

Fernandes, L. P. da C., & Oliveira, L. L. de. (Eds.). (2012). *O Brasil e o mar no século XXI: relatório aos tomadores de decisão no país* (Sea and Brazil into 21st century: Report for the country decision makers). (2nd ed.). Niterói, Brazil: Centro de Excelência para o Mar Brasileiro (CEMBRA).

Frost, W., & Laing, J. (2013). From Yellowstone to Australia and New Zealand: National parks 2.0. *Global Environment, 12*, 62–79. Retrieved from http://www.environmentandsociety.org/sites/default/files/key_docs/ge12_frost-laing.pdf

Fundacion Punta De Lobos. (n.d.). *What we do: Conservation model*. FPL, Pichelmue, Chile. Retrieved from https://www.puntadelobos.org/en/fpl-what-do-we-do/#nuestroModelo.

Fundacion Punta De Lobos. (2017, March 28). *2017 summer actions*. Davenport, CA: Save the Waves Coalition. Retrieved from https://www.savethewaves.org/wp-content/uploads/2017-Summer-Actions.pdf

Gandra, T. B. R., Bonetti, J., & Scherer, M. E. G. (2018). Onde estão os dados para o Planejamento Espacial Marinho (PEM)? Análise de repositórios de dados marinhos e das lacunas de dados geoespaciais para a geração de descritores para o PEM no Sul do Brasil (Where are the data for the Marine Spatial Planning (MSP)? Analysis of marine data repositories and geospatial data gaps for descriptors generators to the Southern Brasil MSP). *Desenvolvimento e Meio Ambiente, 44* [February, Edição especial: X Encontro Nacional de Gerenciamento Costeiro], 405–421.

Hardin, G. (1968). The tragedy of the commons. *Science, 162* (3859), 1243–1248.

IBGE (Brazilian Institute of Geography and Statistics) (2011). *Atlas geográfico das zonas costeiras e oceânicas do Brasil* (Geographic atlas of Brazil's coastal and oceanic zones).

122 *Mauricio Duarte dos Santos et al.*

Rio de Janeiro, Brazil: IBGE, Direitoria de geociências. Retrieved from https://biblioteca.ibge.gov.br/visualizacao/livros/liv55263.pdf

IUCN (International Union for Conservation of Nature). (1994). *Guidelines for protected areas management categories.* Gland, Switzerland: IUCN.

IUCN (International Union for Conservation of Nature. (2019). *Protected area categories.* Gland, Switzerland: IUCN. Retrieved from https://www.iucn.org/theme/protected-areas/about/protected-area-categories

Jarratt, P. (2019, June 5). Reserving judgement. *Surfpolitik.* Retrieved from https://www.swellnet.com/news/surfpolitik/2019/06/05/reserving-judgement

Jones, A. R., Schlacher, T. A., Schoeman, D. S., Weston, M. A., & Withycombe, G. M. (2017). Ecological research questions to inform policy and the management of sandy beaches. *Ocean & Coastal Management, 148,* 158–163. doi: 10.1016/j.ocecoaman.2017.07.020

Kaffine, D. T. (2009). Quality and the commons: The surf gangs of California. *The Journal of Law and Economics, 52* (4), 727–743. doi: pdfplus/10.1086/605293

Langholz, J. A., & Lassoie, J. P. (2001). Perils and promise of privately owned protected areas. *BioScience, 51* (12), 1079–1085. doi: 10.1641/0006-3568(2001)051[1079:PAPOPO]2.0.CO;2

Lazarow, N. (2007a, August 28). What is a surfing reserve and why should surfers care about them? *Coastal Watch, Avalon Beach, Sydney.* Retrieved from https://www.coastalwatch.com/environment/309/what-is-a-surfing-reserve-and-why-should-surfers-care-about-them

Lazarow, N. (2007b). The value of coastal recreational resources: A case study approach to examine the value of recreational surfing at specific locales. *Journal of Coastal Research Special Issue, 50,* 12–20. Retrieved from http://cerf-jcr.org/index.php/international-coastal-symposium/ics-2007australia/496-the-value-of-coastal-recreational-resources-a-case-study-approach-to-examine-the-value-of-recreational-surfing-to-specific-locales-n-lazarow-pg-12-20

Lazarow, N. (2010). Managing and valuing coastal resources: An examination of the importance of local knowledge and surf breaks to coastal communities. (Doctoral dissertation). Canberra, ACT: The Australian National University. Retrieved from https://www.researchgate.net/publication/329142435

Lazarow, N., Miller, M., & Blackwell, B. D. (2007). Dropping in: A case study approach to understanding the socioeconomic impact of recreational surfing and its value to the coastal economy. *Shore and Beach, 75* (4), 21–31. Retrieved from http://www.surfbreak.org.nz/wp-content/uploads/2012/02/Lazarow-paper-2007.pdf

Lazarow, N., Miller, M., & Blackwell, B. D. (2009). The value of recreational surfing to society. *Tourism in Marine Environments, 5* (2–3), 145–158. Retrieved from http://www.valueofwaves.org/uploads/1/1/4/2/11420190/time_2008.pdf

Lloyd, W. F. (1833). *Two lectures on the checks to population.* Oxford, UK: Oxford University. Retrieved from https://archive.org/details/twolecturesonch00lloygoog/page/n6

Maes, F. (2008). The international legal framework for marine spatial planning. *Marine Policy, 32* (5), 797–810.

Martin, S. A., & Assenov, I. (2015). Measuring the conservation aptitude of surf beaches in Phuket, Thailand: An Application of the Surf Resource Sustainability Index. *International Journal of Tourism Research, 17,* 105–117. doi: 10.1002/jtr.1961

McGregor, T., & Wills, S. (2016). *Natural assets: Surfing a wave of economic growth.* (Sydney University Economics Working Papers Series 2016-06, pp. 1–41). Retrieved from http://econ-wpseries.com/2016/201606.pdf

Recreational use, biodiversity protection 123

Monteferri, B., Scheske C., & Muller M. R. (2019). The surf breaks legal protection: An option for conservation and development. In M. R. Muller, R. Oyanedel, & B. Monteferri (Eds.), *Sea, coastal and fisheries: An comparative overview from Chile, México y Perú* (pp. 148–162). Sociedad Peruana de Derecho Ambiental.

National Surfing Reserves. (2019). *About NSR.* Retrieved from www.surfingreserves. org

OECD (2015). *OECD environmental performance reviews: Brazil 2015.* doi: 10.1787/ 9789264240094-en

OECD (2018). *Biodiversity conservation and sustainable use in Latin America: Evidence from environmental performance reviews.* Paris, France: OECD. doi: 10.1787/ 9789264309630-en

Orams, M. (2017). Spot X: Surfing, remote destinations and sustaining wilderness surfing experiences. In G. Borne, & J. Ponting (Eds.), *Sustainable surfing* (Chapter 10). London, UK: Routledge. doi: 10.4324/9781315680231

Ostrom, E. (1990). *Governing the commons: The evolution of institutions for collective action.* Cambridge, UK: Cambridge University Press.

OzBeaches. (2019). *Australian National Surfing Reserves.* Retrieved from https://www .ozbeaches.com.au/pages/national-surfing-reserves-of-australia

Pacific Long Boarder. (2018, February 6). Malibu surfing area added to US 'Register of Historic Places. *Pacific Long Boarder.* Retrieved from https://www.pacificlongboarder. com/news/Malibu-surfing-area-added-to-the-US-Register-of-Historic-Places/

Ponting, J., McDonald, M., & Wearing, S. (2005). De-constructing wonderland: Surfing tourism in the Mentawai islands, Indonesia. *Loisir et Société /Society and Leisure, 28*, 141–162. doi: 10.1080/07053436.2005.10707674

Poulsen, A. (2018, December 20). Kalbarri Board Riders club pushes environmental concerns. *The West Australian.* Retrieved from https://thewest.com.au/news/ midwest-times/kalbarri-board-riders-club-pushes-environmental-concerns-ng-b881044115z

Reiblich, J. (2013). Greening the tube: Paddling toward comprehensive surf break protection. *Environs: Environmental Law and Policy Journal, 37* (1), 45–72.

Reineman, D., Thomas, L., & Caldwell, M. (2017). Using local knowledge to project sea level rise impacts on wave resources in California. *Ocean and Coastal Management, 138*, 181–191.

Santos, M. D. dos. (2018). *Reservas de surfe: Uma análise jurídica da governança do espaço marinho-costeiro. 179 f. Tese (Direito Político e Econômico)* (Surfing reserves: A legal analysis of coastal marine governance. (Doctoral dissertation (Political and Economic Law). Universidade Presbiteriana Mackenzie, São Paulo, Brazil.

Save the Waves Coalition. (2015a). *The process: How to apply.* Retrieved from https:// www.savethewaves.org/programs/world-surfing-reserves/the-process/

Save the Waves Coalition. (2015b). *World Surfing Reserves.* Retrieved from https:// www.savethewaves.org/programs/world-surfing-reserves/reserves/

Secretariat of The Convention On Biological Diversity. (2000). *Sustaining life on Earth: How the Convention on Biological Diversity promotes nature and human well-being.* Retrieved from https://www.cbd.int/doc/publications/cbd-sustain-en.pdf

Silva, S. T. da, Dutra, C., Borges, F. S., Albuquerque, M. F. C., Santos, M. D. dos, & Souza, P. B. de. (2016). Brazil: Participation principle and marine protected áreas. In P. Martin, B. Boer, & L. Slobodian (Eds.), *Framework for assessing and improving law for sustainability: A legal component of a natural resource governance framework* (vol. 1, pp. 33–50). Gland, Switzerland: IUCN.

Silva, S. T. da, Santos, M. D. dos, & Dutra, C. (2016). Reservas de surfe e a proteção da sociobiodiversidade (Surfing Reserves and the protectiona of socio-biodiversity). *Nomos, 36* (2), 345–367.

Skellern, M., Peryman, B., Orchard, S., & Rennie, H. (2013). *Planning approaches for the management of surf breaks in New Zealand.* Auckland, New Zealand: Auckland Council.

Stocker, L., & Kennedy, D. (2009). Cultural models of the coast in Australia: Toward sustainability. *Coastal Management, 37* (5), 387–404.

Surf Coast Shire. (2015). *Bells beach surfing recreation reserve coastal management plan 2015–2025.* Torquay, Victoria: Surf Coast Shire Council.

Thompson, G. (2011). 'Certain political considerations': South African competitive surfing during the international sports boycott. *The International Journal of the History of Sport, 28* (1), 32–46. doi: 10.1080/09523367.2011.525301

Thompson, R. (2007). Cultural models and shoreline social conflict. *Coastal Management, 35* (2–3), 211–237.

Towner, N. (2016). How to manage the perfect wave: Surfing tourism management in the Mentawai Islands, Indonesia. *Ocean & Coastal Management, 119,* 217–226. doi: 10.1016/j.ocecoaman.2015.10.016

Towner, N., & Orams, M. (2016). Perceptions of surfing tourism operators regarding sustainable tourism development in the Mentawai Islands, Indonesia. *Asia Pacific Journal of Tourism Research, 21* (11), 258–1273. doi: 10.1080/10941665.2016.1140663

Usher, L. E. (2017). Sustaining the local: Localism and sustainability. In G. Borne, & J. Ponting (Eds.). *Sustainable surfing.* London: Routledge. doi: 10.4324/9781315680231

Wales, L. (2012, March, 17). Surf economics: Beach rush – Surfers hate crowds and need more waves. Good news for Africa. *The Economist, 402,* 71. Retrieved from https://www.economist.com/international/2012/03/17/beach-rush

WWF (World Fund For Nature). (2019). *Atlantic forests, South America.* Retrieved from https://wwf.panda.org/knowledge_hub/where_we_work/atlantic_forests/

7 Partnered governance of biodiversity

Andrew Lawson, Amy Cosby, Jane Gudde, and Leticia Rodrigues da Silva

Abstract

Agriculture is a major cause of biodiversity loss. International instruments, particularly the *Convention on Biological Diversity* and *the Sustainable Development Goals*, impose obligations on the Brazilian and Australian Governments that can only be satisfied if they engage agriculture in biodiversity conservation. This chapter discusses innovative industry stewardship approaches to biodiversity conservation that use partnered (or hybrid) arrangements between industry and government. To demonstrate the development of this emerging innovative approach, five aspects of hybrid governance are analysed: (1) International farm industry initiatives, (2) Domestic farm industry initiatives, (3) Alignment of international and domestic responses, (4) International alignment of public and private responses and (5) Alignment of public and private responses at the domestic level. These issues are examined within the context of four major agricultural industries in Brazil and Australia: cotton, sugarcane, beef and dairy.

Introduction

This chapter considers innovative industry stewardship approaches to biodiversity conservation that use partnered (or hybrid) arrangements between industry and government. These approaches are emerging in many economic sectors but, in this chapter, we focus on those emerging in agriculture because of the significance of agricultural governance to biodiversity (see Chapter 2); agriculture is a major cause of biodiversity loss and is essential to ensuring connectivity between habitats (Evans, 2016; Dal Soglio & Kubo, 2016; Pulsford et al., 2015). In many countries, farm organisations have implemented stewardship programmes for farmers to voluntarily reduce agriculture's impacts on biodiversity and, increasingly, governments are using these in innovative hybrid arrangements.

In addition to the obligations for *in situ* and *ex situ* biodiversity conservation within the *Convention on Biological Diversity* (*CBD*), signatories commit to:

- Supporting local populations to reverse biodiversity decline (art. 10(d))
- Encouraging co-operation between the government and private sector on sustainable use of biological resources (art. 10(e))

126 *Leticia Rodrigues da Silva et al.*

- Adopting economic and social measures to incentivise biodiversity conservation and sustainable use (art. 11)
- Providing financial support and incentives to implement national biodiversity plans and policies (art. 20).

Sub-goal 17.17 of the Sustainable Development Goals (SDGs) (UN, 2015) also calls on signatories to 'encourage and promote effective public, public-private and civil society partnerships'.

Satisfying these obligations requires more than direct, centralised, command-and-control environmental regulation. Innovative and collaborative forms of governance that engage citizens more effectively than regulation, such as hybrid governance, are required.

Over the past five decades, environmental governance has slowly begun to embrace models that combine or 'hybridise' government and non-government governance approaches (Ayres & Braithwaite, 1992; Glasbergen, 2007; Goldsmith & Eggers, 2004; Gunningham & Grabosky, 1998; Gunningham & Holley, 2016, pp. 283–285; Ostrom, 1990). The interdependence of actors is a key feature of hybrid governance with a 'variety of mutually dependent private and public actors' engaging in 'rulemaking, implementation and enforcement activities' (Ponte & Daugbjerg, 2015, p. 99).

Despite their potential, hybrid arrangements have inherent risks and are notoriously difficult to implement and evaluate (Faure, 2012; Gunningham & Grabosky, 1998; Lawson & Martin, 2018; Wyborn, 2015). Finding ways to 'orchestrate' the actors, options and relationships, and to 'nest' them in a coherent, mutually supportive framework are significant challenges (Gunningham & Holley, 2016; Marshall, 2008; Ostrom, 1990; Williams, Alter, & Shrivastava 2018). Hybridity means there are many components and moving parts for public and private environmental 'governors' to negotiate, which creates significant meta-governance challenges (the 'governance of governance': Torfing, Peters, Pierre, & Sørensen, 2012), addressed in Chapter 11.

Hybrid governance is not only a domestic response to local issues; increasingly, it is relevant to global food, fibre and energy production. Drivers include consumer preferences, political agitation, market access issues, and reputational concerns of multi-national conglomerates operating in a competitive international trading environment.

This chapter examines five aspects of hybrid governance:

1 *International farm industry initiatives* – how farm industries are responding internationally to biodiversity concerns.
2 *Domestic farm industry initiatives*– how Australian and Brazilian farm industries are responding to biodiversity concerns.
3 *Alignment of international and domestic responses* – how Australian and Brazilian farm industry responses are aligning with international counterparts.
4 *International alignment of public and private responses* – how international and national industry responses are aligning with international public law and policy objectives for biodiversity (e.g. *CBD* and *SDGs*).

Partnered governance of biodiversity   127

5   *Alignment of public and private responses at the domestic level* – how Australian and Brazilian governments are creating space in domestic governance systems for industry initiatives.

This chapter analyses stewardship initiatives of four agricultural sectors in Brazil and Australia: cotton, sugarcane, beef and dairy. These are major agricultural sectors in both countries and Table 7.1 summarises their importance. The analysis reveals a variety of international and national industry approaches, summarised in Table 7.2.

This chapter discusses the initiatives in each sector in detail in the following sections but sets the scene here with some broad observations. In the case of cotton and sugar internationally, the key initiatives are multi-stakeholder initiatives rather than industry led, involving producers, industry and environmental and social NGOs, leading to specific sector certification for the global market (Better Cotton Initiative (BCI) and Bonsucro, respectively). Beef is engaged in a multi-stakeholder process that has not yet resulted in a globally oriented assurance scheme. Of the four sectors, only dairy has achieved a unified, industry-led international approach.

In Australia, industry-led cotton and sugar initiatives have taken advantage of international developments by harmonising processes and earning equivalency – Australian farmers attaining credentials in the local industry programmes are regarded as meeting the international industry-specific sustainability standards. The beef sector in Australia has not developed a national certification standard but it now has a high-level policy framework and, in the Australian state of Queensland (QLD), a voluntary self-assessment programme has been operating for a decade. The Australian dairy sector mirrors the international scene with an industry-led policy framework. Dairy has a stewardship programme though, as yet, without verification or certification.

The Brazilian situation is also varied. Unlike in Australia, the Brazilian beef sector has chosen to mirror the international approach by collaborating in a multi-stakeholder process. In cotton, the Brazilian industry – like Australia – has a certification scheme aligned with the international process, allowing BCI equivalency in the global market. The Brazilian sugar sector has not followed this approach, though Brazilian sugar producers can be certified to the Bonsucro standard, and the private energy and biofuel firm, Raízen, has attained equivalency with Bonsucro. To date, the Brazilian dairy sector has not developed a unified sustainability framework.

Observations on recent developments in law and policy in Australia and Brazil indicate the extent to which domestic policy is receptive to hybrid governance. In Brazil, government interest in integrating industry initiatives into environmental governance frameworks is limited but, in Australia, governments are more receptive. There are some indications of possible causes (Lawson, 2017, pp. 296–297).

Reinhardt, Stavins, and Vietor (2008) note that different jurisdictions have different legal and corporate governance cultures, influencing corporate

Table 7.1 Importance of four selected farm sectors to Brazil and Australia (per annum values)

Sector	Brazil	Australia
Cotton	• 2nd largest producer of cotton in the world (2018). • 2 million tonnes; 1.2 million ha (2017–2018). • 2nd largest export industry by value.	• 6th largest producer (2017–2018). • 4.7 million bales (+1 million tonnes); 452,190 ha (2017–2018). • 3rd largest exporter (2017–2018); +AU$2 billion. • Highest yield/ha globally.
Sugarcane	• World's largest producer (2017) • 8.6 million ha; 633 million tonnes of cane (38 million tonnes raw sugar). • Exports: +22 million tonnes sugar (US$6.8 billion in 2018); 1.7 billion litres ethanol (+US$900 million in 2018).	• 7th largest producer of cane (2016). • 380,000 ha; 4,000 farms; 4.8 million tonnes raw sugar. • + 80% raw sugar is exported; almost AU$2 billion.
Beef	• 2rd largest producer and exporter (2018). • 215 million cattle; 147 million ha. • Exports: +20% of production; US$6.57 billion (2018); 1.64 million tonnes; Mainland China and Hong Kong SAR are top destinations.	• 3rd largest producer and exporter (2017). • +26 million cattle; almost 50,000 businesses (2017). • Value of production: AU$11.4 billion (2017–2018). • Value exports: AU$8 billion (2017–2018).
Dairy	• 5th largest producer globally, after India, USA, China and Pakistan; 0.7% global exports. • 1.3 million dairy farms; 10–100 cows per farm.	• 3rd largest agricultural industry in Australia by value/ • 5th largest milk surplus after New Zealand, USA, Germany and France; 2% global exports. • 6,000 dairy farms; 200–300 cows per farm.

Sources: ABARES, 2019; ASMC, 2019; CONAB, 2018; Cotton Australia, 2019; FAO, 2019; Hemme & Otte, 2010; IBGE, 2017; ISO, 2019a; MDIC, 2018; MLA, 2018; USDA, 2019.

Table 7.2 Overview of four selected agricultural industry sustainability initiatives – international, Brazil and Australia

	International	Brazil	Australia
Cotton	• No industry-led initiative • Multi-stakeholder voluntary assurance/certification: BCI – linked to SDGs.	• Industry-led initiative: ABR.	• Industry-led initiative: myBMP.
Sugarcane	• No industry-led initiative. • Multi-stakeholder voluntary assurance/certification: Bonsucro – linked to SDGs.	• No industry-led initiative. Producers can participate in Bonsucro directly, or through corporate intermediaries, such as Raízen's ELO Programme.	• Industry-led initiative: Smartcane BMP.
Beef	• No industry-led initiative. • Multi-stakeholder initiative: GRSBeef.	• No industry-led initiative. • Multi-stakeholder initiative: GTPS.	Industry-led initiatives: • ABSF – linked to SDGs. • (Queensland) GrazingBMP.
Dairy	Industry-led initiatives: • International Dairy Declaration. • [International] Dairy Sustainability Framework.	• No industry-led initiative.	Industry-led initiatives: • ADSF – linked to SDGs. • DairySAT.

130 *Leticia Rodrigues da Silva et al.*

engagement with environmental programmes and corporate social responsibility (CSR) initiatives. In common law, industrialised countries (e.g. US, UK, Canada and Australia), 'CSR is discouraged but permitted' (p. 224), whereas civil law jurisdictions (e.g. France, Germany and Japan) emphasise a stronger role for stakeholders in corporate governance, reflected in law. In some jurisdictions, legal institutions are weak: 'Regulation can go unenforced; agency problems can be a serious issue; and members of the judiciary may be corrupt' (p. 224); the strength of the 'shadow of the law' and the 'stick behind the door' in the hands of public regulators are cited as influential (Alberini & Segerson, 2002; Birks, 2012; Gunningham & Sinclair, 2002; Khanna & Damon, 1999; Paton, 2000; Sharma, 2001).

Differences in the willingness of industry to overcome collective action problems and to lobby governments, and the extent to which governments are susceptible to lobbying, are relevant (Buchanan & Tullock, 1975). The capacity of firms to exploit opportunities for governance innovations are also relevant. Firms used to dealing with command-and-control regulation develop compliance (or evasion) capabilities and, if they are uncertain whether possible hybrid governance arrangement will persist or succeed, may see little value in pursuing innovation (Stavins, 2002, p. 43).

Cotton case studies

Two international groups serve the cotton industry, the International Forum for Cotton Promotion (IFCP) and the International Textile Manufacturers Federation (ITMF). Sustainability and conservation are not major concerns of these bodies (Advisory Committee, 2019a; ITMF, 2014). An intergovernmental body, the International Cotton Advisory Committee (Advisory Committee), provides technical guidance on sustainable production and tools for improved environmental practices – such as soil management – through its Expert Panel on Social, Environmental and Economic Performance of Cotton. The Advisory Committee consists of government representatives from 27 cotton-producing nations. It does not appear to have engaged with international protocols such as the *SDGs* or the *CBD* (Advisory Committee, 2019b).

A US-based NGO, Textile Exchange, actively promotes sustainability and social responsibility in the cotton supply chain. It launched the '2025 Sustainable Cotton Challenge' in 2017, which encourages retailers to commit to acquiring 100 per cent of their cotton from sustainable sources by 2025 and lists 14 certified sustainable sources (Textile Exchange, 2018). Of these, BCI leads in terms of acreage and volume (Tyrell et al., 2017). BCI's principles include minimising the impacts of agronomic practices, water stewardship, soil health, and biodiversity (BCI, 2018). BCI maps its activities to ten *SDGs* (BCI, 2019). BCI is represented on the Advisory Committee and is a partnership between the World Wildlife Fund (WWF) and brands, including Adidas, IKEA, H&M, GAP and Levi Strauss. It was the fastest

Partnered governance of biodiversity 131

growing sustainability certification scheme in any sector between 2015 and 2019. In 2019, over two million certified farmers grew 19 per cent of the global cotton crop for BCI (BCI, 2019). However, in 2016 only 21 per cent of certified sustainably grown cotton was sourced by brands and retailers (Tyrell et al., 2017). The local Australian and Brazilian cotton industry stewardship programmes (myBMP and ABR respectively) are recognised by BCI as equivalents (BCI, n.d.).

Australia

The Australian cotton growers' peak body, Cotton Australia, supports research and development, stewardship, natural resource management and cotton production, and is funded by a levy paid by growers. Its board comprises growers and industry representatives. Cotton Australia is the growers' representative in Cotton Research and Development Corporation (CRDC), funded jointly by grower levies and the Australian Government. The CRDC's research includes sustainability issues such as integrated pest management, water efficiency and reducing the impacts of agricultural chemicals.

In response to concerns about farm chemicals, the cotton industry developed Cotton best management programme (BMP) in 1997 to help growers improve on-farm environmental management using self-assessment tools and education (Roth, 2011). An updated, web-based version, *myBMP*, was released in 2010. Growers can be certified by independent audit. More than 75 per cent of Australian farms participate in *myBMP*, and around 20 per cent of farms are fully certified (Cotton Australia, n.d.).

MyBMP includes practice modules on biosecurity, integrated pest management, pesticide management, soil health, sustainable natural landscapes, and water management (*myBMP*, 2019). Through links between Cotton Australia and the CRDC, industry- and government-funded research informs *myBMP*. Of the four sectors we considered, the Australian cotton industry has made the most in-roads into formal co-regulatory arrangements with government. Cotton BMP was written into the Queensland *Water Act 2002*, enabling participating cotton farmers an alternative avenue for meeting regulatory objectives (Lawson, 2017, p. 289).

Brazil

ABR (Algodão Brasileira Responsável – Responsible Brazilian Cotton) was created in 2005 to promote responsible social, environmental and economic practices to support Brazilian cotton in the growing responsible cotton market. The programme emphasises communication of sustainability practices and continuous improvement.

ABR participants commit to respecting labour laws and rejecting child labour or employment akin to slavery. Producers are also encouraged to

132 *Leticia Rodrigues da Silva et al.*

use practices that combine productivity and environmental preservation. Best practices include protecting springs, watercourses and reserves, preserving biomes, and maintaining air, water and soil quality. ABR cotton producers commit to applying only registered pesticides, using recommended dosage and modes of application. The programme encourages good labour policies that also reduce labour costs; personal protective equipment that also reduces workers' absence from work; and benefits, such as food and lodging, that increase workers' satisfaction, motivation and productivity.

New ABR members have a grace period to meet programme requirements. Farms must be audited to earn ABR certification. ABR certified 1.2 million tonnes of fibre on 244 certified farms, covering 682,000 ha in the 2016/2017 harvest. This equates to 78 per cent of the harvest and 73 per cent of the area planted to cotton (ABRAPA, 2016).

Sugar case studies

There is no international industry peak body for the sugar sector but there is a quasi-governmental body – the International Sugar Organization (ISO) – with representatives from 87 sugar-producing nations. The ISO website (ISO, 2019b) does not indicate any alignment of activities with the *SDGs* or the *CBD*.

Four international voluntary initiatives have been adopted by sugar producers – Organic, Fairtrade, Rainforest Alliance and Bonsucro. Organic and Fairtrade dominated the market up until 2011, when Rainforest Alliance and Bonsucro offered standards addressing the environmental challenges of sugar production (Potts et al., 2014).

Bonsucro is a global multi-stakeholder non-profit organisation formed in 2008 to encourage sustainable production. Single-commodity certification, such as Bonsucro, has grown faster than multi-sector schemes (Potts et al., 2014). Bonsucro is now the largest sugar certification scheme globally, with over 500 member companies and grower associations in 20 nations. One-quarter of the total sugarcane area and one-fifth of sugar globally are Bonsucro certified (Bonsucro, n.d.).

The domestic national schemes, Smartcane BMP in Australia and the biofuel company Raízen's ELO Programme in Brazil, are benchmarked to Bonsucro. Bonsucro has committed to contribute to the SDGs and has a standard for greenhouse gas emissions driven largely by EU requirements for biofuel production. Modelling shows that global adoption of the Bonsucro standard would halve the greenhouse gas emissions of sugar production (Smith et al., 2019).

The production standard includes five core principles for legal compliance, human rights, production and processing, biodiversity and ecosystem impacts, and continuous improvement. A principle on monitoring greenhouse gas emissions applies to biofuel growers. Compliance is verified by annual third-party audits (Bonsucro, 2016).

Australia

Ninety-five per cent of Australian raw sugar is produced in QLD (ASMC, 2019), predominantly from coastal catchments that discharge into the Great Barrier Reef. Two peak bodies represent sugarcane growers in Australia: the Australian Cane Farmers Association and the QLD Canegrowers Organisation (known as Canegrowers). They are voluntary, grower-led organisations offering advocacy and other services to canegrowers in QLD and New South Wales.

Canegrowers manage Smartcane BMP, an industry-owned and managed programme for growers to continuously improve on-farm practices for increased productivity, profitability and sustainability (Smartcane, 2018). Smartcane BMP employs facilitators and provides information to help growers. During its development, Smartcane BMP received funding from the QLD Government, which aimed to limit sediment, nutrients and pesticides in run-off from farms entering the Great Barrier Reef.

Smartcane BMP comprises eight modules, some of which relate to biodiversity, including soil health and fertiliser management, drainage and irrigation, pests, diseases and weeds, crop production and natural systems. Growers benchmark their operations so that improvements can be measured. Records of improvement actions must be kept. When some threshold requirements are met, the operation can be formally certified upon independent auditing. Smartcane BMP has an equivalency with Bonsucro. In 2019, Smartcane BMP had 1,818 farms benchmarked and 4,125 farms accredited, over 10 per cent of all cane farms (Smartcane, 2019).

Brazil

Raízen is one of Brazil's largest companies, a joint venture between Royal Dutch Shell and Cosan (a major Brazilian sugar, ethanol and energy firm). Raízen developed a stewardship programme called ELO in 2014/2015 for its sugarcane suppliers. ELO goals include economic sustainability, environmental responsibility and respect for human and labour rights. The programme achieved equivalency with Bonsucro, and it partners with two international institutions involved in sustainability and fair trade certification: Imaflora and Solidaridad Foundation. Two thousand producers participate in ELO, 89 per cent of Raízen's suppliers (Raízen, 2017).

Raízen is an intermediary between producers/processors and Bonsucro, though producers or mills may be certified to Bonsucro standards directly. The stewardship programmes are applicable to both the sugar and ethanol markets. A driver for certification in the Brazilian sugar sector is compliance with the EU sustainability directive on the promotion of the use of the energy from renewable sources, including biofuels (EU, 2009).

ELO social indicators include working hours, worker infrastructure, minimum age of hiring, safe use of agrochemicals, remuneration, accommodation

134 *Leticia Rodrigues da Silva et al.*

and transportation. The environmental pillar aims for optimisation of natural resources. Certified suppliers have an action plan for improving their performance. A monitoring team promotes training and technical support, assesses progress, and monitors compliance with the rules governing Permanent Preservation Areas (Áreas de Preservação Permanente or APPs), Legal Reserves and illegal deforestation.

Beef case studies

Like cotton and sugar, but unlike dairy, the global beef sector has not developed a unified sustainability framework. However, as with cotton and sugar, it is involved in a multi-stakeholder roundtable initiative, the Global Roundtable for Sustainable Beef (GRSBeef). This involves producers and producer associations, processors, retailers (e.g. McDonalds), civil society (e.g. WWF), national or regional roundtables, allied industries (e.g. textiles), and observers (GRSBeef, 2017). The roundtable's 'five principles and criteria of sustainable beef' address natural resources, people and the community, animal health and welfare, food, and efficiency and innovation. In Brazil, Canada, EU, US, Paraguay and Colombia, the beef industry pursues regional multi-stakeholder roundtable projects. Though the Australian beef sector is represented in GRSBeef, the local industry has had a difficult relationship with the roundtable process.

Australia

A proposal for an Australian Roundtable for Sustainable Beef was scuttled because of objections to the participation of WWF (Farmonline, 2014). The Australian industry substituted a 'square-table' process, excluding the major environmental groups. The end-result was the Australian Beef Sustainability Framework (ABSF), established in 2017, with annual reports released in 2018 and 2019. The framework is funded by levies (ABSF, n.d.a) and developed by partnership of several key beef industry bodies, including the Red Meat Advisory Council (ABSF, 2019).

Red Meat Advisory Council is the 'red meat' (beef, goat and sheep meat) industry peak body, comprising pasture-based and lot-fed producers, processors, retailers and livestock exporters. The Council leads the ABSF project and convenes a Sustainability Steering Group as a 'grassroots group, representative of the beef value chain' (ABSF, 2019, p. 19) to drive development of the framework. The Council supports the *Meat Industry Strategic Plan 2020*, with a vision for the red meat industry to be 'recognised for its environmental credentials' (RMAC, 2015).

ABSF is organised around four themes, 10 priority areas and 23 priorities, six of which have been nominated as 'key priorities'. The most relevant of these to biodiversity conservation are Theme 3 (Environmental Stewardship), Priority Area 5 (Improved Land Management Practices), Priority 5.1

(Minimise nutrient and sediment loss), and Key Priority 5.2 (Balance of tree and grass cover), which receives considerable attention (ABSF, 2019). The ABSF is aligned with nine SDGs (ABSF, n.d.b).

The latest ABSF update expressly highlights that ABSF is not designed for developing measurements systems, accreditation or certification, or prescribing management practices (ABSF, 2019, p. 16). To the extent that these are desired or needed, they must be developed by complementary processes, such as *GrazingBMP*.

GrazingBMP is a self-assessment system for beef producers to demonstrate they are utilising best management practices, achieving animal welfare standards and undertaking environmental stewardship (*GrazingBMP*, 2019). It was developed in 2010 by the QLD Department of Agriculture and Fisheries, Fitzroy Basin Association (a community-based regional natural resource management body) and AgForce (the peak body for broad acre farming in QLD) (*GrazingBMP*, 2019). The QLD Government supported industry to develop a BMP because of the potential impacts of run-off from cattle grazing into the Great Barrier Reef.

GrazingBMP has five modules: soil health, grazing land management, people and business, animal production, and animal health and welfare, which participants complete via webinar, workshop, or teleconference (*GrazingBMP*, 2019). The relationship between industry and government is characterised by mistrust, especially concerning the use of data collected from participants in *GrazingBMP*. Industry partners in *GrazingBMP* have threatened to delete a decade's worth of data gathered via *GrazingBMP*. They are concerned the proposed legislative amendments for protection of the Great Barrier Reef (discussed below) will compel the programme to provide data to the government, potentially for use in prosecutions (Kennedy, 2019).

Brazil

GTPS (Grupo de Trabalho da Pecuária Sustentável – Brazilian Roundtable on Sustainable Livestock) began in 2007 and was formalised in 2009. It is a multi-stakeholder forum and a member of GRSBeef. GTPS's objective is 'to discuss and formulate the principles, standards and common practices adopted by the industry founded on the premise of developing a sustainable, fair, environmentally correct and economically feasible livestock farming value chain' (GTPS, n.d.).

GTPS uses its Guide of Indicators for Sustainable Livestock (*Guia de Indicadores de Pecuária*) and partnerships to encourage responsible production practices. The guide is an evaluation and measurement tool for assessing management, environmental and production system parameters. Data from these assessments inform member training and other support. GTPS report that 494 participants completed the guide's assessment in 2018, including 435 producers, 13 industry groups, 18 community organisations and 11 financial institutions (GTPS, 2019).

Dairy case studies

The 2016 *Dairy Declaration* commits the global dairy industry 'to the sustainable development of the dairy sector to generate widespread benefits for people and the planet' (FAO & IDF, 2016). The Declaration is a partnership between the International Dairy Federation (IDF) and the UN FAO. It is a brief, high-level, one-page document recognising the SDGs. The dairy sectors in 55 countries have endorsed the *Declaration*, including Australia and the Pan-American Dairy Federation (Federacion Panamericana de Lecheria – FEPALE), of which the Brazilian dairy sector is a member (IDF, 2018, p. 30).

The international Dairy Sustainability Framework (DSF) is a programme of the Global Dairy Agenda of Action (GDAA), responding to the FAO's assessment of greenhouse gas emissions from livestock (FAO, 2006). GDAA seeks to comprehensively address industry sustainability issues (DSF, 2014a). The DSF refers to continuous improvement, safe and nutritious products, healthy cattle, preserving natural resources and ensuring decent livelihoods (DSF, 2014b).

Dairy Australia and FEPALE are members of the international DSF and report on behalf of smaller industry groups in Australia and FEPALE's member countries. Members endorse 11 sustainability criteria (including biodiversity) and implement the framework, including prioritising sustainability at a local level, implementing initiatives, continuous improvement and annual reporting (DSF, 2014a). Eleven global criteria have been chosen through a 'highly collaborative' bottom-up approach with the help of a consultant (DSF, 2014a).

Australia

The Australian Dairy Industry Council (ADIC) developed the *Australian Dairy Sustainability Framework* in 2016 (ADIC, 2016) and updated it in 2018 in response to stakeholder feedback (Dairy Australia, 2019, pp. 81–88). The 'Dairy Promise' in the framework makes four commitments on behalf of the industry: commercial rewards, safe and nutritious food, animal welfare, and environmental considerations. The 11 industry goals are arranged around four headings: enhancing economic viability and livelihoods; improving wellbeing of people; providing best care for animals; and reducing environmental impact. These are supported by 52 targets (Dairy Australia, 2019, pp. 13–55). The development of the Australian framework was influenced by international standards and norms, including the UN Global Compact (n.d.), Global Reporting Initiative, and SDGs (ADIC, 2016, p. 43). Stakeholder feedback for the 2018 *Dairy Sustainability Report* was conducted via a 'consultative forum' of mostly commercial industry stakeholders, but engaged environmental, animal welfare and research organisations, such as WWF, RSPCA and CSIRO (Dairy Australia, 2019, p. 79).

Dairy Australia is an independent, industry-owned research and development company set up under the Federal *Dairy Produce Act 1986*, funded through levies and Commonwealth Government funds. The joint-funding reflects a hybrid governance intention. *DairySAT* was launched in 2005 by Dairy Australia; it is a self-assessment tool with ten modules to assess dairy farm sustainability and to meet processors' or retailers' reporting or risk assessment requirements. After self-assessment, *DairySAT* creates an action plan for the farm based on identified risks. The programme is accessible to anyone through the DairySAT website.

The Biodiversity module addresses:

- Whether there is an integrated whole farm plan
- Riparian and wetland management
- Protection of habitat
- Revegetation practices (e.g. providing connectivity)
- Management of local threatened species or habitat

The action plan lists sources of information about identified environmental risks so farmers can improve their environmental outcomes. It does not contain prescriptive instructions or advice. The links are generally to organisations such as regional natural resource management bodies, Landcare, Greening Australia (an Australian NGO focused on regeneration, revegetation and restoration), state government agencies, and industry programmes.

Risk-based programmes are often flexible and adaptable but are criticised for lack of performance standards and for reliance on continual improvement without required monitoring (Cary & Roberts, 2011, pp. 883–884; Higgins, Dibden, & Cocklin, 2010, pp. 173,181). *DairySAT* does not require ongoing monitoring or reporting but does record management for each issue and ongoing progress. For each module, 'good practice' functions as the performance standard. The biodiversity module contains six descriptions of 'good practice' and five of 'innovative practice'. There is not a higher level for those who implement 'innovative practices'.

DairySAT has been integrated into the Australian DSF after a consultative forum in 2018 (Dairy Australia, 2019, p. 87). Dairy Australia envisages *DairySAT* will evolve into 'Sustainable Dairy Products', with improved data collection, capture and reporting capabilities (Dairy Australia, 2019, p. 60).

Brazil

There is no country-wide industry-led dairy sector stewardship programme in Brazil. There are programmes for farmers, generally instigated by the government, in which milk producers can participate. For example, under the Healthy Milk programme, government funds producers in the states with the highest production to implement milk quality improvements (MAPA, 2019).

Under the *National Plan for Low Carbon Emissions in Agriculture (Plano ABC)*, promulgated in 2010, the government provides farmers with low interest

138   *Leticia Rodrigues da Silva et al.*

loans to implement low carbon farming practices (MAPA, 2017). These include no-till agriculture, pasture renovation, agro-forestry, nitrogen fixation, management of manures, and development of integrated cropping-livestock-forestry systems (CGIAR & CCAFS, n.d.; Russell & Parsons, 2014). The initiatives reflect Brazil's commitments to the *UN Framework Convention on Climate Change (UNFCCC)*.

Companies such as Nestlé, part of the UN Global Compact, have programmes for dairy farmers. The company provides technical guidance to implement Nestlé's Good Farm Practices. Farmers are audited for compliance with laws, and environmental and social objectives. Nestlé's programme also monitors water use, protected areas, labour conditions and animal welfare (Nestlé, 2019).

Receptiveness to partnered arrangements

Though some Brazilian agricultural industries engage in sustainability standards and private rulemaking, hybrid governance is not well-established in Brazilian governance processes. A limited exception is the multi-stakeholder approach by the National Environment Council (CONAMA), composed of federal, state and municipal governments constituting the National Environmental System (SISNAMA), with representatives of industry and civil society. However, there is conflict between public and private interests:

> Often, rivalry takes place among the government institutions themselves, from different areas of government, whose interests may not only be conflicting, but frankly opposed and irreconcilable.
>
> (Moura, 2016, p. 37)

President Bolsonaro's administration, coming into office in January 2019, has a clear intention to restrict social participation in environmental policy and to focus on development rather than environmental protection. Brazil decided to leave the *Paris Agreement on Climate Change,* but pressure from the business and agricultural sector, who fear loss of partnerships with developed countries and reprisals to Brazilian exports, caused reversal of the decision. *Decree no. 9.759/2019* extinguishes several councils for environmental protection, requiring a Presidential order to reinstate them and, even if reinstated, it is possible that environmental organisations will be excluded.

The situation in Australia is more promising. Notwithstanding the challenges, Australian governments have pursued novel governance arrangements (Lawson, 2017, pp. 284–294). The 2016 Productivity Commission inquiry into the regulation of Australian agriculture observed 'farmers can bear a disproportionate share of the financial burden of conservation for the benefit of all Australians' (Productivity Commission, 2016, p. 18). In 2018, Dr Wendy Craik (2018) finalised an independent review for the Commonwealth Government of interactions between farmers and the *EPBC Act*, concluding:

> As a regulatory mechanism, [the *EPBC Act*] is largely punitive and based on the prohibition of actions detrimental to the health of MNES [matters of national environmental significance] rather than the incentivisation of actions that maintain or improve MNES health.
>
> (p. 67)

Dr Craik opined that a 'responsive and collaborative approach to regulating the agriculture sector will become ever more important' (p. 30–31), and recommended 'greater adoption of market-based approaches that incentivise farmers to protect and maintain MNES' (p. 67). This was supported by the peak farming lobby in Australia – the National Farmers Federation – which noted a significant proportion of farmers prefer their own industry associations as the conduit for information about their environmental obligations (Craik, 2018, p. 31).

A Bill (*Environmental Protection – Great Barrier Reef Protection Measures – and Other Legislation Amendment Bill 2019*, (the *2019 Bill*)) before the QLD Parliament to regulate activities affecting the Great Barrier Reef (GBR) highlights that government is open to integrating private stewardship initiatives into public governance. The GBR's huge area and its vast series of contiguous river catchments are subject to an array of laws and institutions (see Chapter 4). Sugarcane and cattle enterprises in some GBR catchments are subject to regulations under the QLD *Environmental Protection Act 1994* to control sediments, nutrients and agricultural chemicals entering the Reef (Ch. 4A, ss. 78–105).

Smartcane BMP and Grazing BMP are informally recognised by the government in its GBR governance, and the 2019 Bill (if enacted) would formalise that recognition. The Bill proposes a co-regulatory model that allows non-government programmes to be accredited (ss 318YA–318YF), providing participating farmers with a defence to prosecutions where they are certified under an accredited programme and their conduct complies with the programme (s. 82(3)). The government has Smartcane BMP and Grazing BMP in mind as candidates for accreditation.

Farm stewardship programmes, such as those of the Australian cotton, sugarcane, beef and dairy sectors, are a proactive approach, preparing members for increasingly stringent requirements. However, many are underdeveloped and the market signals are weak, so the regulatory 'shelter' proposed in the 2019 Bill may provide more incentives for voluntary participation. It remains to be seen whether the managers of the stewardship programmes will participate in the co-regulatory arrangements. Trust and data remain vexed issues (Nason, 2019).

Hamman and Deane (2018) conclude that combining regulatory and non-regulatory approaches is required to improve the condition of the GBR.

Weak enforcement has softened the regulatory 'back-up' (the 'shadow of the law': Birks, 2012), reducing the incentive value of regulatory concessions.

Industry-capture and political factors can militate against the effectiveness of partnered governance. Commentators have speculated that the public interest can be strengthened by allowing non-government environmental advocates a stronger role in governance, to become 'surrogate regulators' (Ayres & Braithwaite, 1992; Faure, 2012; Gunningham & Grabosky, 1998). In an analysis of hybrid governance in the European biofuels sector, Stattman, Gupta, Partzsch, and Oosterveer (2018) observed that, of the voluntary standards recognised by the EU's Renewable Energy Directive (EU, 2009), multi-stakeholder arrangements were more stringent. However, since less stringent industry and government standards were permitted, biofuel suppliers could 'standard shop' for the least stringent standard.

In Brazil and Australia, public governance structures do not generally facilitate involvement by civil society. In Brazil, the President and the environmental authorities have proposed reduced sanctions for environmental offenders (Maisonnave, 2019). Incentives for increased self-regulation have been introduced (Salles, 2019) without civil society involvement. The Australian Commonwealth Government has canvassed the removal of legal standing for environmental groups to seek judicial review of government decisions or inaction under s 487 of the *EPBC Act* (Hepburn, 2015). Other proposals include stripping public funding from cash-strapped environmental groups that challenge government decision-making in the courts (Australian Parliament, 2015, pp. 23–24) and restricting their charitable status, affecting their capacity to generate public donations (Australian Parliament, 2016).

In QLD, the 2019 Bill proposes a government-and-industry arrangement and not a tri-partite arrangement involving civil society groups. It is challenging for civil society groups to engage in hybrid governance arrangements while maintaining their independence. The experience of the Australian beef industry highlights that securing trust in multi-stakeholder processes is a potential stumbling block.

Conclusions

Agriculture remains a major cause of biodiversity loss. International instruments, particularly the *CBD* and the SDGs, impose obligations on the Brazilian and Australian Governments that can only be satisfied if they engage agriculture in biodiversity conservation. The inability of existing arrangements to prevent biodiversity loss has spurred interest in alternative approaches involving private schemes and instruments, such as farm stewardship programmes.

Innovations such as hybrid arrangements present opportunities and risks. The stewardship initiatives discussed in this chapter reflect considerable effort by farm industries to create environmental governance approaches at international, national and local levels. They suggest the possibility of novel approaches to environmental governance that rely less on command-and-control regulation and more on collaboration and the economic interests of industries and supply chains. In the best case scenario, global market players who are more aware of worldwide consumer concerns and familiar with international public institutions (such as the SDGs) than domestic sector organisations may pressure domestic governments and industries towards adopting good stewardship standards.

Hybrid models have risks and challenges. These include adequate incentives for participation, and credible accountability and integrity mechanisms. Involving private actors requires patience and trust building since stakeholders usually need to operate via goodwill, persuasion and engagement – 'bringing people along on the journey' (Holley & Lawson, 2015, pp. 251–254). Private governance mechanisms should not be a weaker substitute for public governance. They have a role in sophisticated and robust regulatory frameworks, ideally involving citizen environmental advocates as well as government and industry. Effectiveness, efficiency and integrity of new hybrids require a credible approach to each of the following elements:

1   Strategic alignment of key public and private governance organisations and institutions.
2   Integrity mechanisms to ensure accurate and relevant proof of performance.
3   Robust reporting mechanisms for industries to account for their biodiversity protection performance at a national, industry-wide scale.
4   Facilities for private governance institutions to provide credible information to national governmental and whole-of-sector accounting against international environmental requirements such as the CBD and SDGs. At the same time, it is essential to retain the trust of farmers and programme managers around use of data and confidentiality.
5   Recognition measures for farmers that enable them to capitalise on good environmental performance and enable consumers to exercise civic judgement to preference good performers over bad.

References

ABARES (Australian Bureau of Agricultural and Resource Economics. (2019). *Agricultural commodities report: Sugar.* Retrieved from http://www.agriculture.gov. au/abares/research-topics/agricultural-commodities/mar-2019/sugar

ABRAPA (Associação Brasileira dos Produtores de Algodão –Brazilian Cotton Producers Association). (2016). *Sustentabilidade (Sustainability).* Retrieved from https://www.abrapa.com.br/Paginas/Sustentabilidade.aspx

ABSF (Australian Beef Sustainability Framework). (n.d.a). *Governance and principles.* Retrieved from https://www.sustainableaustralianbeef.com.au/governance-principles

ABSF (Australian Beef Sustainability Framework. (n.d.b). *Aligning with the UN sustainable development goals.* Retrieved from https://www.sustainableaustralianbeef. com.au/aligning-with-the-un-sustainable-development-goals

142 *Leticia Rodrigues da Silva et al.*

ABSF (Australian Beef Sustainability Framework). (2019). *Australian beef sustainability annual update 2019*. Retrieved from https://www.sustainableaustralianbeef.com.au/46221/documents/106732

ADIC (Australian Dairy Industry Council. (2016) *Australian dairy industry sustainability report 2016*. Retrieved from https://www.dairyaustralia.com.au/-/media/dairyaustralia/documents/industry/manufacturing/industry-sustainability/2016-australian-dairy-industry-sustainability-report.pdf?la=en&hash=322F4D5CA05E1D0E0D472AED5AA6244514DF7CA4

Advisory Committee (International Cotton Advisory Committee). (2019a). *International forum for cotton promotion*. Retrieved from http://staging.icac.org/cmte-cotton-industry/International-Forum-for-Cotton-Promotion-IFCP

Alberini, A., & Segerson, K. (2002). Assessing voluntary programs to improve environmental quality. *Environmental and Resource Economics, 22*, 157.

ASMC (Australian Sugar Milling Council). (2019). *Raw sugar production overview*. Retrieved from https://asmc.com.au/industry-overview/

Australian Parliament. (2015). *Australia's environment*. (Report of the Senate Environment and Communications References Committee). Canberra, ACT.

Australian Parliament. (2016). *Inquiry into the register of environmental organisations*. (Report of the House of Representatives Standing Committee on the Environment). Canberra, ACT.

Ayres, I. J., & Braithwaite, J. (1992). *Responsive regulation: Transcending the deregulation debate*. Oxford, UK: Oxford University Press.

BCI (Better Cotton Initiative. (n.d.). Where is better cotton grown? Retrieved from https://bettercotton.org/about-better-cotton/where-is-better-cotton-grown/

BCI (Better Cotton Initiative. (2018). *Better cotton principles and criteria, version 2.0 March 2018*. Retrieved from https://bettercotton.org/about-better-cotton/better-cotton-standard-system/production-principles-and-criteria/

BCI (Better Cotton Initiative). (2019). *Better cotton initiative 2018 annual report*. Retrieved from http://stories.bettercotton.com/2018-AnnualReport/index.html

Birks, S. (2012). Why the shadow of the law is important for economists. *New Zealand Economic Papers, 46* (1), 79–80.

Bonsucro. (2016). *Bonsucro production standard version 4.2 December 2016*. Retrieved from http://www.bonsucro.com/production-standard/

Bonsucro. (n.d.). *About Bonsucro*. Retrieved from http://www.bonsucro.com/what-is-bonsucro/

Buchanan, J. M., & Tullock, G. (1975). Polluters' profits and political response: Direct controls versus taxes. *American Economic Review, 65*, 139–147.

Cary, J., & Roberts, A. (2011). The limitations of environmental management systems in Australian agriculture. *Journal of Environmental Management, 92* (3), 878–885.

CGIAR, CCAFS. (n.d.). *Brazil's low-carbon agriculture (ABC) plan*. Climate Smart Agriculture. Retrieved from https://csa.guide/csa/brazil-s-low-carbon-agriculture-abc-plan

Companhia Nacional de Abastecimento (CONAB) (National Supply Company). (2018). *Indicadores da Agropecuária n° 12* (Agriculture Indicators No. 12). Retrieved from https://www.conab.gov.br/info-agro/precos/revista-indicadores-da-agropecuaria

Cotton Australia. (2019). *Economics*. Retrieved from https://cottonaustralia.com.au/australian-cotton/economics

Cotton Australia. (n.d.). *myBMP – The Australia Cotton Industry's sustainability standard*. Retrieved from https://cottonaustralia.com.au/uploads/publications/myBMP_background_doc_200218.pdf

Craik, W. (2018). Review of interactions between the EPBC Act and the agriculture sector. (Report). Canberra, ACT: Australian Department of the Environment and Energy. 0In%20Focus/Australian%20Dairy%20Industry%20In%20Focus%20 2016.pdf

Dairy Australia. (2019). *Australian dairy industry sustainability report 2018.* Retrieved from https://www.dairyaustralia.com.au/ourdairypromise

Dairy Sustainability Framework. (2014a). *FAQS.* Retrieved from https:// dairysustainabilityframework.org/dsf-membership/faqs/

Dairy Sustainability Framework. (2014b). *The dairy sustainability framework vision.* Retrieved from https://dairysustainabilityframework.org/the-gdaa/programmes-of-the-gdaa/the-dairy-sustainability-framework/

Dal Soglio, F., & Kubo, R. R. (2016). *Desenvolvimento, agricultura e sustentabilidade* (Development, agriculture and sustainability). Porto Alegre, Brasil: SEAD/ UFRGS.

EU (European Union). (2009). *Directive 2009/28/EC on the promotion of the use of energy from renewable sources.* Retrieved from https://eur-lex.europa.eu/legal-content/ EN/ALL/?uri=CELEX%3A32009L0028

Evans, M. C. (2016). Deforestation in Australia: Drivers, trends and policy responses. *Pacific Conservation Biology, 22,* 130–150.

FAO. (2006). *Livestock's long shadow: Environmental issues and options.* Retrieved from http://www.fao.org/3/a0701e/a0701e00.htm

FAO. (2019). *Gateway to dairy production and products: Milk production.* Retrieved from http://www.fao.org/dairy-production-products/production/en/

FAO & IDF. (2016). The dairy declaration of Rotterdam. Retrieved from http:// www.dairydeclaration.org/Portals/153/Dairy%20Declaration.pdf?v=1

Farmonline. (2014, May 26). *Taskforce to 'meat' sustainable goals.* Retrieved from https:// www.farmonline.com.au/story/3574803/taskforce-to-meat-sustainable-goals/

Faure, M. G. (2012). Instruments for environmental governance: What works? In P. Martin, L. Zhiping, Q. Tianbao, A. Du Plessis, Y. Le Bouthillier, & A. Williams (Eds.), *Environmental governance and sustainability.* Cheltenham UK: IUCN Academy of Environmental Law, Edward Elgar.

Glasbergen. P. (2007). Setting the scene: The partnership paradigm in the making. In P. Glasbergen, F. Biermann, & A. P. J. Mol (Eds.), *Partnerships, governance and sustainable development: Reflections on theory and practice* (pp. 1–28). Cheltenham, UK: Edward Elgar.

Goldsmith, S., & Eggers, W. D. (2004). *Governing by network.* Washington, DC: Brookings Institution Press.

GrazingBMP. (2019). *Grazing best management practices.* Retrieved from https://www. bmpgrazing.com.au

GRSBeef (Global Roundtable for Sustainable Beef). (2017). *Members.* Retrieved from https://grsbeef.org/page-1861857

GTPS (Grupo de Trabalho da Pecuária Sustentável – Brazilian Roundtable on Sustainable Livestock). (n.d.). *Objectives of GTPS.* Retrieved from http://gtps.org.br/ en/mission-and-objectives/

GTPS (Grupo de Trabalho da Pecuária Sustentável – Brazilian Roundtable on Sustainable Livestock). (2019). *Report of activities 2018.* Retrieved from http://gtps.org. br/biblioteca/gtps-relatorio-de-atividades-2018/

Gunningham, N., & Grabosky, P. (1998). *Smart regulation: Designing environmental policy.* Oxford, UK: Clarendon Press.

144 *Leticia Rodrigues da Silva et al.*

Gunningham, N., & Holley, C. (2016). Next-generation environmental regulation: Law, regulation, and governance. *Annual Review of Law and Social Science, 12*, 273–93.

Gunningham, N., & Sinclair, D. (2002). *Environmental partnerships: Combining sustainability and commercial advantage in the agriculture sector.* Canberra, ACT: Rural Industries Research & Development Corporation (RIRDC).

Hamman, E., & Deane, F. (2018). The control of nutrient run-off from agricultural areas: Insights into governance from Australia's sugarcane industry and the Great Barrier Reef. *Transitional Environmental Law, 7* (3), 451–468.

Hemme, T., & Otte, J. (Eds.). (2010). *Status and prospects for smallholder milk production: A global perspective.* Pro-Poor Livestock Policy Initiative. Rome: FAO.

Hepburn, S. (2015, August 19). Brandis' changes to environmental laws will defang the watchdogs. *The Conversation.* Retrieved from https://theconversation.com/brandis-changes-to-environmental-laws-will-defang-the-watchdogs-46267

Higgins, V., Dibden, J., & Cocklin, C. (2010) Adapting standards: The case of environmental management systems in Australia. In V. Higgins & W. Larner (Eds.), *Calculating the social: Standards and the reconfiguration of governing* (pp. 167–184). Hampshire, UK: Palgrave Macmillan.

Holley, C., & Lawson, A. (2015). Implementing law and collaborative governance. In P. Martin & A. Kennedy (Eds.), *Implementing Environmental Law* (pp. 238–259). Cheltenham, UK: Edward Elgar.

IDF (International Dairy Federation). (2018). *Annual Report 2017/18.*

Instituto Brasileiro de Geografia e Estatística (IBGE) (Brazilian Institute of Geography and Statistics). (2017). *Pesquisa Pecuária Municipal, produção brasileira de leite em 2017* (Municipal Livestock Research, Brazilian milk production in 2017). Retrieved from https://www.ibge.gov.br/estatisticas/economicas/agricultura-e-pecuaria/9107-producao-da-pecuaria-municipal.html?=&t=resultados

International Cotton Advisory Committee. (2019b). ICAC strategic plan 2019–2021. Retrieved from https://icac.org/About/AboutICAC?MenuId=2

ISO (International Sugar Organization). (2019a). *About sugar.* Retrieved from https://www.isosugar.org/sugarsector/sugar

ISO (International Sugar Organization). (2019b). *Devoted to improving conditions on the* Retrieved from *world's sugar market.* Retrieved from https://www.isosugar.org/

ITMF (International Textile Manufacturers Federation). (2014). Mission statement. Retrieved from https://www.itmf.org/

Kennedy, H. (2019, May 1). AgForce dumps best management practice data. *Queensland Country Life.* Retrieved from https://www.queenslandcountrylife.com.au/story/6101483/bmp-data-deleted-over-privacy-fears/

Khanna, M., & Damon, L. (1999). EPA's voluntary 33/50 program: Impact on toxic releases and economic performance of firms. *Journal of Environmental Economics and Management, 37* (1), 1.

Lawson, A. (2017). Farmers, voluntary stewardship and collaborative environmental governance in rural Australia. *Environmental and Planning Law Journal, 34* (4), 271–298.

Lawson, A., & Martin, P. (2018). Evaluating the governance potential of voluntary stewardship programs for farmers. *Environmental and Planning Law Journal, 35* (4), 331–354.

Maisonnave, F. (2019, April 14). Bolsonaro desautoriza operação em andamento do Ibama contra madeira ilegal em RO ('Bolsonaro disallows Ibama's ongoing operation against illegal timber in Rondônia State'), *Folha de São Paulo*. Retrieved from https://www1.folha.uol.com.br/ambiente/2019/04/bolsonaro-desautoriza-operacao-em-andamento-do-ibama-contra-madeira-ilegal-em-ro.shtml

Marshall, G. R. (2008). Nesting, subsidiarity, and community-based environmental governance beyond the local level. *International Journal of the Commons, 2* (1), 75.

Meat and Livestock Australia (MLA). (2018). Fast facts: Australia's beef industry. Retrieved from https://www.mla.com.au/globalassets/mla-corporate/prices--markets/documents/trends--analysis/fast-facts--maps/mla_beef-fast-facts-2018.pdf

Ministério da Agricultura, Pecuária e do Abastecimento (MAPA) (Brazilian Ministry of Agriculture, Livestock and Food Supply). (2017). *Plano de agricultura de baixo carbono* (ABC) ('Low carbon agriculture plan'). Retrieved from http://www.agricultura.gov.br/assuntos/camaras-setoriais-tematicas/documentos/camaras-setoriais/fibras-naturais/2017/16a-ro/plano_abc_16ro_fibras.pdf/view

Ministério da Agricultura, Pecuária e do Abastecimento (MAPA) (Brazilian Ministry of Agriculture, Livestock and Food Supply). (2019). *Programa leite saudável* ('Healthy milk program'). Retrieved from http://www.agricultura.gov.br/assuntos/sustentabilidade/programa-leite-saudavel

Ministério do Desenvolvimento, Industria e Comercio (MDIC) (Ministry of Development, Industry and Trade). (2018). *Base de dados do Comex Stat.* (Comex Stat Database). Retrieved from http://www.mdic.gov.br/index.php/comercio-exterior/estatisticas-de-comercio-exterior/base-de-dados-do-comercio-exterior-brasileiro-arquivos-para-download

Moura AMM. (2016). *Governança ambiental no Brasil: Instituições, atores e políticas públicas* (Environmental governance in Brazil: Institutions, actors and public policies), *Instituto de Pesquisa Econômica Aplicada – IPEA* (Institute of Applied Economic Research), Brasília. Retrieved from http://www.ipea.gov.br/portal/index.php?option=com_content&view=article&id=28192

myBMP. (2019). *About myBMP*. Retrieved from https://www.mybmp.com.au/What_is_different.aspx

Nason, J. (2019, May 7). Reef beef sinks Grazing BMP. *Beef Central*. Retrieved from https://www.beefcentral.com/news/reef-beef-sinks-grazing-bmp/#.XM_Yc63ih8o.email

Nestlé. (2019). *Cadeia do leite* (Milk supply chain). Retrieved from https://corporativo.nestle.com.br/csv/desenvolvimento-rural/cadeia-do-leite

Ostrom, E. (1990). *Governing the commons: The evolution of institutions for collective action*. Cambridge, UK: Cambridge University Press.

Paton, B. (2000). Voluntary environmental initiatives and sustainable industry. *Business Strategy and the Environment, 9*, 328.

Ponte, S., & Daugbjerg, C. (2015). Biofuel sustainability and the formation of transnational hybrid governance. *Environmental Politics, 24* (1), 96–114.

Potts, J., Lynch, M., Wilkings, A., Huppe, G., Cunningham, M., & Voora, V. (2014). *The state of sustainability initiatives review 2014: Standards and the green economy*. Winnipeg, Canada & London, UK: International Institute for Sustainable Development, International Institute for Environment and Development.

Productivity Commission. (2016). *Regulation of Australian agriculture*. (Report no. 79). Canberra, ACT. Retrieved from https://www.pc.gov.au/inquiries/completed/agriculture/report/agriculture.pdf

Pulsford, I., Lindenmayer, D., Wyborn, C., Lausche, B., Vasilijević, M., Worboys, G. L., & Lefroy, T. (2015). Connectivity conservation management. In G. L.

Worboys, M. Lockwood, A. Kothari, S. Feary, & I. Pulsford (Eds.), *Protected area governance and management* (pp. 43–80). Canberra, ACT: ANU Press.

Raízen. (2017). *ELO Elo Program*. Retrieved from https://relatoweb.com.br/raizen/2017/cotejo/180606/pt/impacto-positivo.html

Reinhardt, F. L., Stavins, R. N., & Vietor, R. H. K. (2008). Corporate social responsibility through an economic lens. *Review of Environmental Economics and Policy, 2* (2), 219–239.

RMAC. (2015). Meat industry strategic plan (MISP). (2020). *Red Meat Advisory Council*. Retrieved from https://rmac.com.au/wp-content/uploads/2016/12/MISP-2020-doc.pdf

Roth, G. (2011). Retaining the social licence: The Australian cotton industry case study. In J. Williams, & P. Martin (Eds.), *Defending the social licence of farming: Issues, challenges and new directions for agriculture*. Collingwood, Vic: CSIRO Publishing.

Russell, S., & Parsons, S. (2014). *A new tool for low-carbon agriculture in Brazil*. World Resources Institute. Retrieved from https://www.wri.org/blog/2014/05/new-tool-low-carbon-agriculture-brazil

Salles, R. (2019, April). *Audiência Pública da Comissão de Meio Ambiente e Desenvolvimento Sustentável da Câmara dos Deputados sobre os novos procedimentos e acordos do Ministério do Meio Ambiente* (Public Hearing of the Committee on Environment and Sustainable Development of the Chamber of Deputies on the new procedures and agreements of the Ministry of Environment). Retrieved from https://www2.camara.leg.br/atividade-legislativa/webcamara/videoArquivo?codSessao=76694

Sharma, S. (2001). Different strokes: Regulatory styles and environmental strategy in the north American iil and gas industry. *Business Strategy and the Environment, 10*, 344.

Smartcane. (2018). *Smartcane BMP: Position statement*. Queensland Cane Growers Organisation Ltd.

Smartcane. (2019). *Latest news*. Retrieved from https://smartcane.com.au/LatestNews/LatestNews.aspx

Smith, W. K., Nelson, E., Johnson, J. A., Polasky, S., Milder, J. C., Gerber, J. S., … Pennington, D. N. (2019). Voluntary sustainability standards could significantly reduce detrimental impacts of global agriculture. *Proceedings of the National Academy of Sciences of the United States of America, 116* (6), 2130–2137.

Stattman, S. L., Gupta, A., Partzsch, L., & Oosterveer, P. (2018). Toward sustainable biofuels in the European Union? Lessons from a decade of hybrid biofuel governance. *Sustainability, 10* (11), 4111.

Stavins, R. N. (2002). Experience with market-based environmental policy instruments. (FEEM Working Paper No. 52.2002; KSG Working Paper No. 00-004). Milan, Italy: Fondazione Eni Enrico Mattei (FEEM).

Textile Exchange. (2018). 2025 *sustainable cotton challenge*. Retrieved from https://textileexchange.org/2025-sustainable-cotton-challenge/

Torfing. J., Peters, B. G., Pierre, J., & Sørensen, E. (2012). Metagovernance: The art of governing interactive governance. In J. Torfing, B. G. Peters, J. Pierre, & E. Sørensen (Eds.), *Interactive Governance: Advancing the paradigm*. Oxford Scholarship Online. Retrieved from https://www.oxfordscholarship.com/view/10.1093/acprof:oso/9780199596751.001.0001/acprof-9780199596751

Tyrell, K., Denissen, A. K., Roger, I., Schonenberg, L., Holland, R., Peters, E., …, & Verhoestraete, E. (2017). *Sustainable cotton ranking 2017: Assessing company performance pesticide action network UK, Solidaridad and World Wildlife Fund*. Retrieved from https://www.sustainablecottonranking.org/

UN. (2015). *Transforming our world: The 2030 Agenda for sustainable development.* (A/Res/70/1). Retrieved from https://sustainabledevelopment.un.org/sdgs

UN Global Compact. (n.d.). Retrieved from https://www.unglobalcompact.org/

US Department of Agriculture (USDA). (2019, July). *World agricultural production.* (Foreign Agricultural Service Circular Series WAP7-19). Retrieved from https://usda.library.cornell.edu/concern/publications/5q47rn72z?locale=en

Williams, J., Alter, T., & Shrivastava, P. (2018). Systemic governance of sustainable agriculture: Implementing sustainable development goals and climate-friendly farming. *Outlook on Agriculture, 47* (3), 192–195.

Wyborn, C. (2015). Cross-scale linkages in connectivity conservation: Adaptive governance challenges in spatially distributed networks. *Environmental Policy and Governance, 25,* 1–15.

8 Biodiversity intelligence from satellites

Paul Martin, Evan Hamman,
Gabriel Leuzinger Coutinho, and
Márcia Dieguez Leuzinger

Abstract

Monitoring that the natural environment is being used in accordance with sustainability or conservation rules is often difficult or beyond the means of governments and other interested parties. Satellite technology provides a means for helping provide the data/information necessary for monitoring natural resource use. This chapter discusses the utilisation of satellite technology by Brazilian and Australian governments and NGOs. The Australian examples derive predominantly from use of satellite technology in the control of water use. Brazilian examples mostly concern how satellite technology has been used to track habitat destruction. Though satellite use is clearly useful in aiding governance, the challenge for both countries is to provide and enable satellite data to be used to the best effect.

Introduction

Data (whether it is called signals, intelligence, information, evidence or communications) is the feedstock of people's decisions. Decision-making frameworks and processes employ data to make decisions, and priorities and people attach value to different information and different possible outcomes when making decisions. Law and policy instruments provide signals of what people are expected to do, intending that these signals will trigger decisions and actions that comply. Communications, whether one way or multi-directional, are the key to the transactions that determine what people do with or to nature, and how resources flow or are used. Data is essential to understanding what is being managed and the systems that are involved, to monitoring the results of human actions, and to indicate how well governance is working and whether a change in approach is needed. By its very nature, modern environmental governance requires a lot of data, and many of the instruments used for managing the environment are data-hungry.

Environmental law follows the traditions of other regulatory regimes. When regulations fall under the traditions of criminal law, enforcement requires proof of a breach of a rule beyond a reasonable doubt, including that the wrongful act was carried out by the person charged and, often, that this caused material harm. Legal evidentiary requirements reflect citizen rights, and it typically costs a lot to prosecute possible environmental crimes. It is not unusual for a prosecution to fail and, even when a prosecution is successful, enforcement – with its many transaction costs – is difficult. Similarly, environmental civil cases face transaction cost challenges, including the costs of legal representation, evidence gathering and penalisation. Administrative arrangements can involve complicated data, administrative processes, documentation and recording, monitoring and reporting.

Market instruments also depend on many types of data, available at reasonable cost for the market to be efficient. Environmental markets require information to link buyers to sellers, to communicate the attributes and volumes being traded and to formalise and implement contracts. The 'transaction costs' of information can make regulatory or trading instruments non-viable in practice, which is one reason why market instruments can fail, notwithstanding the enthusiasm of their advocates. For market instruments and subsidies, the costs of monitoring implementation can be high, but without reliable monitoring, the risk of fraud or mistake can discourage investment, limiting the effectiveness of the instrument.

Monitoring a natural resource or natural systems is costly and can be technically difficult. This is particularly so when a vast area is involved or when what is being monitored is difficult to detect or measure (e.g. carbon sequestration soil, or loss of ephemeral or rare species). Science and the law impose standards of reliability, which adds cost and complexity, and when issues are politicised data requirements become more difficult to meet. When the data may be legally or politically contested, data costs and complexity increase. The transaction costs of environmental governance are, thus, a determinant of how effective governance can be (Martin, Williams, & Stone, 2008; Soares-Filho et al., 2016).

In this chapter, we consider the use of satellites to help regulate habitat destruction in Brazil and Australia. We will also consider the potential use of satellites in governing water markets in Australia. The chapter considers current and potential uses of satellite data and the institutional and regulatory changes needed to harness this potential.

The need for low-cost precision

Precise manual measurement and recording in the field, particularly when measurements are complex, typically takes a lot of time, involves labour, equipment, processing and transport, and can be very expensive. Automated measurement can be cheaper if a suitable method is available. Ultimately, the choice of technology reflects the purpose for which data is needed, the type of data and the decision-making rules or methods used and the costs. Because a technology could provide reliable data at low cost does not mean that it will be used. Economic and, particularly, political dynamics can have a significant influence. Innovations in technology, policy and analysis affect the economics of information. An example is the use of radar and cameras for traffic policing. To achieve savings using this technology, it has been necessary to adjust rules of evidence, shifting the onus from the police to the citizen, and to implement administrative systems for penalisation.

Many technologies could facilitate data capture and communications. These include innovative sensors and recording devices, which can be deployed using human agents, integrated with other equipment; for example ship-mounted video or data loggers to monitor fish catch, or using devices such as drones (unmanned vehicles) and satellites. In Australia and Brazil, satellites could improve the cost effectiveness of monitoring environmental conditions, detect actions that alter that condition, and so to improve regulatory, market or administrative instruments. Thus far, its use falls short of the potential, often because of institutional and political reasons. The increase in the number and capabilities of satellites suggests that intelligence improvements are possible if these obstacles can be overcome.

An example from Australia is the potential to reduce the transaction costs of governing water. Recently, instances of 'water theft' have undermined confidence in the water market in Australia's most economically significant river system, the Murray-Darling. The problem is compounded by the lack of reliable monitoring, including non-compliance by water users with their obligations to report water extraction, and covert drainage and water diversion works. Available satellite datasets, coupled with changed reporting obligations and enforcement rules, could lower the transaction costs and improve compliance (Alexandra & Martin, 2018). Notwithstanding that relevant satellite data has been available to water agencies for some time, implementation has been very slow (Galletta, 2018).

There are other examples of the innovative use of satellites by environmental organisations, to provide reliable environmental data at low cost. These include supervision of remote fisheries and of incursion into protected waters, identification of unauthorised habitat clearing and other environmental governance uses (Gibbens, 2018; Rose et al., 2015; Webster, 2018).

Satellites technologies

Satellite technology is a form of 'remote sensing'. Remote sensing essentially means finding or observing information about an object or place without physical proximacy (Campbell & Wynne, 2011, p. 6). For satellite sensing, a better definition is 'the practice of deriving information about the earth's land and water surfaces [by] using images acquired from an overhead perspective' (Campbell & Wynne, 2011, p. 6). Though private sector satellites are common, many are owned and operated by nations for defence, environmental, disasters monitoring and data-gathering purposes. Earth observation satellites are typically used for between 5 and 8 years then become space junk (Crowther, 2002). It is common for satellite programmes to launch more than one satellite (mission) into space. For example, the US Landsat programme began in 1972

Biodiversity intelligence from satellites   151

with Landsat 1. Landsat 8 was launched in 2013 and Landsat 9 is expected in 2020. Table 8.1 lists some satellite programmes for earth observation.

Ignoring space junk, there are almost 5,000 orbiting satellites, the number is increasing rapidly, and their coverage and their capabilities are improving. Many are for communications or monitor 'outer space', others monitor conditions on Earth. Their use depends on the capabilities of their sensors and processing technologies. Whether they are used effectively also depends on human capabilities and institutional matters, including rules, economics and political and judicial acceptability. It also depends on the availability of the captured data; for example, military satellites capture highly precise data that is not commercially available.

Table 8.1 Examples of satellite programmes utilised for earth observation

Satellite/ programme	First launch	Operator/developer	Purposes
Landsat	1972	US (NASA)	Moderate-resolution land remote sensing data in agriculture, geology, forestry, regional planning, education, mapping and global change research.
SPOT	1986	France, Belgium, Sweden	Climatology and oceanography, and monitoring human activities and natural phenomena.
ERS	1991	European Space Agency	Earth observation including measure ocean surface temperature and wind fields.
CBERS	1999	China, Brazil	Land and water resource monitoring and assessment, urban planning and disaster risk responses.
ASTER	1999	Japan, US (NASA)	Vegetation and ecosystem dynamics, hazard monitoring, geology and soils, land surface climatology, hydrology, land cover change.
QuickBird II	2001	US	Earth observation including map development, land and water monitoring and assessment including for insurance purposes.
Envisat	2002	European Space Agency	Wide variety of earth observation services including monitoring of changes in atmosphere, water, land, ocean and coasts, snow and ice and natural disasters.
UK2-DMC	2009	UK (British National Space Centre)	Earth observation services including land and water change and disaster management and monitoring.
DubaiSat	2009	UAE Space Program	Urban and infrastructure planning, land and water monitoring.
PAZ	2019	Hisdesat/ EADS CASA Espacio (Spain)	Earth observation services including evaluation of natural disasters and assistance in risk and crisis management.

Source: Author.

152 *Paul Martin et al.*

Sensors provide increasingly precise imaging of non-visible wave-lengths (e.g. infra-red, ultraviolet, radio, x-ray, microwave), spatial measures such as height or location and recording of video, temperature and sound. New sensor types are being developed, and combining datasets can provide rich intelligence. Some current natural resource management uses include using multi-spectrum scanners to monitor crops, tracking Earth surface and sea temperatures, monitoring forests and other vegetation, tracking vessels, monitoring events such as floods and fires, measuring atmospheric conditions and monitoring urban expansion or traffic.

Murray-Darling Basin case

Australian water policy is based largely upon the National Water Initiative, agreed by the Australian federal and six state governments in 2004 (COAG, 2004). The initiative applies to Australia's most economically important surface water system, the Murray-Darling river system. That river system flows through five states and territories. The Murray-Darling Basin Plan (the 'Plan') provides a coordinated management approach, with the *Water Act 2007* (Cth) providing a legislative basis. Some features of this law include: rights to extract water are tradeable and untied to land ownership; a sustainable limit of extraction is set based upon science; although extraction rights are for a nominated volume, availability is limited to an administratively declared limit that depends on seasonal conditions; water use must be reported to the relevant agencies and water for the environment is denominated in tradeable volumetric rights.

This complex governance system involves many thousands of transactions, all of which depend on data. Scientific data about the state of the river system informs the limits of extraction. Hydrological data is also used for this purpose and to understand how the river is operating. Economic and social data address the human needs, information about water infrastructures is recorded to manage the system and the market, and information is used to monitor the implementation and effects of the Plan (Martin & Shortle, 2010; Martin et al., 2008).

Many parts of the Murray-Darling catchment suffer extreme water shortages, and demands for agriculture at times exceed what credible scientists calculate to be sustainable extraction limits. Many aspects of the Plan are also politically contentious. There are serious disagreements between neighbouring states about the volumes taken from the upper catchment in the north of the system down to the opening to the ocean in the southern part (and all points in between). The disputes involve competing agricultural, environmental and tourism-related interests, the interests of the communities that depend on the river and the economic and political interests of the state governments. Disagreements have been exacerbated by media reports of water theft, unauthorised water impoundments or channels, and government staff 'turning a blind eye' to irresponsible or illegal activities.

Biodiversity intelligence from satellites 153

Data gathered by satellites can provide cost-effective information for making decisions about the system, primarily in two ways. The first involves governing the governance system itself (i.e. 'meta-governance' including administration and reporting, examined further in Chapter 11) and policy (e.g. conservation baselines, evaluation of programme performance, etc.). The second involves transaction data and 'legal enforcement', particularly in cases where what is being governed is spatially dispersed and found on private land. For example, such data can be useful where there are potentially fugitive or unidentifiable offenders, and where administrators and regulators lack resources to undertake onground monitoring.

Satellite data is currently being used by the Murray-Darling Basin Authority (and state and federal governments) for monitoring infrastructures, and to provide data about biodiversity (MDBA, 2017, appendix A, pp. 43–44). It has also been used to monitor unlawful extraction, though satellite data is not fully incorporated into the regulatory system where the potential for improvements in reliability and transactional efficiency has been identified (Alexandra & Martin, 2018; Galletta, 2018).

Data unreliability or unavailability generally comprise four broad types of water disputes: (1) tensions between water users and environmental interests and scientists over what level of water removal is 'sustainable'; (2) disagreements over what amount is being taken, in particular without legal authorisation; (3) concerns about unmetered and unreported taking of water, or metres and reports that are fraudulent or inaccurate and (4) disagreement over what amount of water is being returned to the environment, and whether the ecological benefits from this 'investment' are real or illusory.

For all these aspects of water governance, satellite data coupled with other forms of technology (unmanned aerial vehicles, artificial intelligence, robotics, etc.) and changes to administrative and reporting systems could lead to more cost-effective governance outcomes. Further, remotely sensed data, coupled with digital innovations such as blockchain and self-executing contracts, could improve water governance in the system, though competing political interests and the uncertainty of climate change (especially droughts and fish kills) will ensure that problems will continue for some time to come.

Monitoring habitat loss

Land-clearing rates in Brazil and Australia are among the highest in the world (Rebgetz, 2017). Thousands of hectares of forest are felled to make way for grazing, cropping, mining, urban sprawl, roads construction and timber. Over the last 150 years, the cumulative loss of biodiversity from clearing has been devastating for biodiversity (McAlpine, Fensham, & Temple-Smith, 2002; Reside et al., 2017). Brazil and Australia have political systems that are responsible for governing vast and rugged landmasses through the thicket of 'cooperative federalism' (Fenna, 2012; Souza, 2016). Both have hundreds of endemic plants, animals and fish found nowhere else on the planet. Both are considered to be 'mega biodiverse' (Mittermeier, 1997). Brazil faces problems of poverty and corruption in government decisions that are less evident (though not completely absent) in Australia (Green, 2012).

The nations have similar regulatory approaches to the issue of habitat destruction. Though state governments have primary responsibilities in day-to-day forest management, federal governments have undertaken obligations under multilateral environmental agreements (MEAs) such as the *Convention on Biological Diversity (CBD)* and the *World Heritage Convention (WHC)*. Because implementation of these MEAs occurs with the aid of both national and sub-national actors, reliable data that can surpass jurisdictional boundaries is essential.

The Australian state of Queensland (QLD), where most of Australia's land clearing for pasture occurs (Reside et al., 2017), uses satellite technology (Landsat and other data) to monitor vegetation extent and land clearing (see Queensland Government, 2019a, 2019b, 2019c, 2019d, 2019e). In the Brazilian state of Mato Grosso, the satellite-based Program for the Estimation of Deforestation in the Brazilian Amazon (PRODES) is used to monitor deforestation rates (Richards et al., 2017) and is also utilised for advocacy purposes by NGOs.

Mato Grosso land clearing

Mato Grosso is Brazil's third largest state (see Figure 8.1), with an area of 903,357.908 km^2. It is sparsely populated. Data from the Brazilian census in 2010 show a population of around three million people, which is predominantly urban (81.9 per cent).

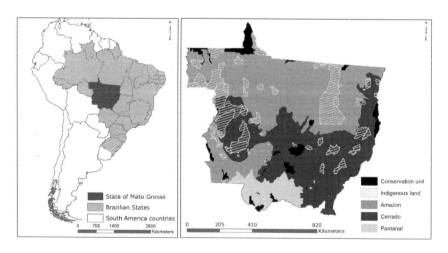

Figure 8.1 Left: Mato Grosso's location in South America; Right: Mato Grosso's biomes.
Source: Picoli et al. 2018 (with permission).

Mato Grosso was occupied in the 18th century. This occupation intensified when the Federal Government of Brazil sought to modernise farming and to integrate the central western regions with the rest of the country (Cunha, 2006). As a result, the population of the region increased from less than three million people in 1960 to more than seven million in 1980 (IBGE, 1990). Almost 17,000 km of paved roads were built from 1950 to 1989 (Dias, 2008). The government implemented subsidies, including tax breaks and low interest credits, to improve the region's economy (Becker, 2009).

There are three main biomes in the Mato Grosso state: the Cerrado (Brazilian savanna – 38.3 per cent), the Pantanal (wetlands – 7.2 per cent) and the Amazon Forest (54.5 per cent). Agriculture and livestock were responsible for 17.2 per cent and 3.1 per cent of Mato Grosso's GDP in 2014, respectively. In 2016, these activities were responsible for 25.36 per cent of Mato Grosso's GDP (IBGE, 2018).

This led to the 'modern era of deforestation' in the Amazon Forest (Fearnside, 2005). Until 1970, only 3 per cent of this biome had been cleared; Lemos and Silva (2012) estimated that 106,352 km^2 of the Amazon Forest were cleared in Mato Grosso prior to 1978. By 1985, the deforested area was 7.7 per cent; the Brazilian National Institute of Spatial Research (INPE) estimates that an area of 51,400 km^2 of the Mato Grosso's Amazon Forest was deforested between 1978 and 1988 (Fearnside, 1993). Dias (1994) notes that the anthropised landscape of the Cerrado area was 37 per cent in 1985. From 1980 to 1990, the land clearing of Mato Grosso's Cerrado occurred at an annual rate of 4,179 km^2 (Martini et al., 2009). The Pantanal was the least impacted biome of Mato Grosso. Until 1991, only 3.9 per cent of this biome had been cleared (Silva, 1998).

Around 40 per cent of Mato Grosso's area has been deforested (Governo de Mato Grosso, 2018b) despite the first *Forest Code (1934); second Forest Code (1965); third Forest Code (2012)* and the *National Environmental Policy Act (1981)*. Drivers of deforestation include commodity prices, exchange rates, infrastructures, migration and changes in governance policies following presidential elections (1994 and 2003 –2004) that caused instability in the institutions responsible for combating illegal deforestation in the Amazon (see peaks of deforestation in 1995 and 2003–2004 in Figure 8.2).

Thus, land clearing increased after 2002, driven by international soybean demand. This led to an increase in prices, encouraging expanded plantations, often in forest areas (Macedo et al., 2012). Mato Grosso's government changed in 2003, after the 2002 elections. Environmental protection was not a priority of the new governor, Blairo Maggi, one of the largest soybean producers in Brazil (Fearnside, 2006). The waves of deforestation that followed highlight the central role of interest competition facing biodiversity protection.

The decline in land clearing after 2004 was caused by four factors. First, international soybean prices fell from US$10.4 per bushel in 2004 to US$5.04 per bushel in 2006 (Macrotrends, 2018). Second, the Soy Moratorium (SoyM) was signed by major international soybean traders in 2006, who pledged not

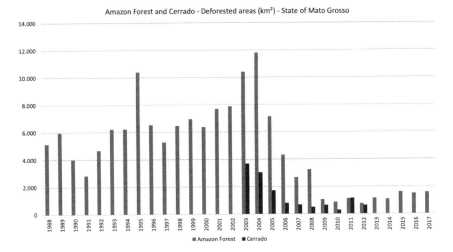

Figure 8.2 Deforested areas of the Amazon Forest and the Cerrado biomes in Mato Grosso by year.[1]
(Source: adapted from INPE, 2008).

to buy soy grown on Amazon Forest land cleared after 2006 (Gibbs et al., 2015). Satellite images from the PRODES project were used to identify those areas of forest cleared for soybeans (ABIOVE, 2010).

The third factor was the expansion of protected areas in Mato Grosso after 2004. There are 4.17 million hectares of protected areas in Mato Grosso's Amazon Forest. Approximately 72 per cent were protected between 2004 and 2007 (MMA, 2018). The final factor was government actions, such as the National Plan for Climate Change, the *Arco Verde* operation and the *Terra Legal* operation (Fearnside 2010; Nepstad, McGrath, & Soares-Filho, 2011).

From 2005 to 2016, agricultural deforestation in Mato Grosso occurred mainly around the BR-163 highway, which crosses the state from south to north (Picoli et al., 2018). Since 2013 deforestation rates have been increasing because of the relaxation of legislation, especially the *New Forest Code*, in 2012, and better international soybean prices. Recent political changes have led to an even more radical increase in forest clearing.

INPE began investigating remote sensing data to monitor the Amazon Forest in 1974 (Tardin, Santos, & Novo 1977). In 1988, US LANDSAT satellite data began to be used to monitor deforestation in the Amazon Forest. From 1988 to 2002 the process was analogous, the images from one year being compared with the images of the year before by the INPE staff, to identify deforestation. After 2003, computers were used. This process was called PRODES Digital (INPE, 2008).

The Brazilian Environmental Ministry (MMA) and the Brazilian Environmental Agency (IBAMA) support the PRODES project, and the Science,

Technology and Innovation Ministry of Brazil (MCTI) finances it (INPE, 2018). Brazil monitored only the deforestation of the Amazon Forest and the Atlantic Forest until 2002. IBAMA then expanded monitoring to other biomes like the Cerrado and the Pantanal through the *Projeto de Monitoramento do Desmatamento dos Biomas Brasileiros por Satélite* (PMDBBS – Brazilian Biomes Satellite Deforestation Program) (IBAMA, 2009). PMDBBS was financed by UNDP and MMA and ran until 2012.

For many years, satellite data was not used to improve environmental protection; rather than adapting environmental protection programmes, the Federal Government would simply develop a new programme to battle deforestation when the PRODES data showed that land clearing in the Amazon had risen considerably. Satellite data were, however, used by NGOs and the international community to pressure for environmental protection (Fearnside, 2005). This demonstrates the value of satellite monitoring as an aid to transparency in governance.

The System of Environmental Licensing of Rural Properties (SLAPR) initiated by the Mato Grosso government in 1999 pioneered government use of remote sensing to help control land clearing. Using SLAPR, the environmental licensing of a property occurs by georeferencing its perimeter, permanent preservation areas (APP) and legal reserves. Properties are monitored using satellite images. Enforcement actions may occur when illegal land clearing is detected (Insituto Socioambiental & Instituto Centro de Vida, 2006).

This programme reduced deforestation in 2000, as shown in Figure 8.2. Although deforestation increased in 2001 and 2002, the rate of increase in Mato Grosso was lower than in other states. Azevedo and Saito (2013), in their analysis of land clearing of the Amazon Forest in Mato Grosso between 2000 and 2007, note that after 2002 the use of satellites ceased and illegal deforestation increased from 72.5 per cent of total deforestation in 2002 to 98.4 per cent in 2007.

In 2004, INPE implemented a system for deforestation monitoring called DETER. This generated daily alerts to IBAMA to help plan inspection and control. The data were available to other government agencies and the public. The system had a lower resolution (250 m) than the PRODES system, but data was available daily. In 2015, the DETER technology was improved to provide greater resolution (56 m) and real-time monitoring. Monitoring was limited to the Amazon Forest until 2018, when the Cerrado was included (INPE, 2019).

In June 2019 an ambitious project was launched: MapBiomas Alerta. It is coordinated by the *Sistema de Estimativas de Emissões de Gases de Efeito Estufa do Observatório do Clima* (System of Greenhouse Gases Emissions of the Climate Observatory) and involves NGOs, universities and private companies. The MapBiomas Alerta validates and refines alerts of deforestation, degradation and regeneration of native vegetation using high-resolution images. It collects alerts from monitoring systems, including DETER, to locate deforestation in daily high-resolution images (3 m). For each validated alert, a report is automatically generated, with deforestation images correlated with the Rural Environmental Registry (CAR), Protected Areas, Rural Settlements and other geographical information. These reports should improve the effectiveness of agencies including MMA and IBAMA without additional expenditure. A trial from October 2018 to March 2019 showed Mato Grosso as the Brazilian state with the second most deforestation alerts (MapBiomas Alerta, 2019).

Satellite technology has not been used by Mato Grosso government to monitor site specific land clearing. Using remote sensing to help control land clearing through SLAPR was discontinued. However, annual disclosure has allowed environmental groups to apply political pressure. Satellite technology is also fundamental to MapBiomas Alerta and the SoyM lobby, which has slowed land clearing in Mato Grosso since 2006.

Queensland land clearing

Native vegetation clearing is a contentious issue in Australian biodiversity protection (Hamman, 2016, 2019a; Maron et al., 2015; McGrath, 2007; Neldner et al., 2017; Reside et al., 2017 Taylor, 2013). Policy is hotly debated between landholders, government and civil society at the state and federal level. Recent research has shown QLD clearing has removed hundreds of millions of hectares of native forest impacting many species (Cogger et al., 2003; McAlpine et al., 2002; Neldner et al., 2017; Possingham, Ryan, Baxter, & Morton, 2002; Taylor 2013). The clearing has been predominately for agriculture (Neldner et al., 2017; Seabrook, McAlpine, & Fensham, 2006), although mining and gas extraction, including infrastructure such as ports, railways, transmission lines and pipelines, have been a recent concern. The cumulative impacts of clearing are severe, including increased erosion in the catchment of the Great Barrier Reef World Heritage Area, discussed in Chapter 4 (Joo et al., 2012).

QLD first became a state in June 1859 after its separation from New South Wales. Thereafter, a thriving sugarcane and grazing industry arose. Australia became a federation in 1901, and the states largely retained control over land use (including vegetation). 'Crown Leasehold' tenure was utilised to develop rural QLD (pasture and agriculture) and approximately 70 per cent of rural and regional QLD is held under some form of pastoral lease (Wallace, Weir, & McCrimmon, 2015, p. 29).

While land clearing occurred in QLD throughout the 1800s and 1900s, the real damage began in the late 1970s with the introduction of new technologies and global commodity demand (Bradshaw, 2012). In the 1980s and 1990s, QLD was clearing between 200,000 and 350,000 ha p.a. In 1999 and 2000, approximately 750,000 ha was felled, up from 425,000 ha between 1997 and 1999 (Hamman, 2016). Much of the clearing occurred in a long and narrow belt of land known as the 'Brigalow Belt' – a strip of *acacia* woodland.

Most clearing was unregulated until 1995 when some restrictions were introduced under the *Land Act 1994* (Qld) (Hamman, 2019a; Maron et al.,

2015). Further controls were introduced with the *Vegetation Management Act 1999* (Qld) *(VMA)*, which required a permit to clear land (Hamman, 2016, 2019a; McGrath, 2007). The VMA was considerably tightened in 2006 including efforts to eliminate 'broadscale clearing' entirely (McGrath, 2007). Between 2006 and 2014, the rates of clearing reduced till about 2014 when relaxation of the laws allowed farmers to clear 'regrowth' and for 'high value agricultural' projects (Hamman, 2016, 2019a). In 2015–2016, woody vegetation loss in QLD was around 395,000 ha – the highest level since 2005–2006 (RMIT ABC Fact check, 2018).

Since 2012, approximately 1.2 million hectares of land have been cleared. A recent fact check report (RMIT ABC Fact check, 2018) summarised the figures as:

2012–2013: 261,000 ha
2013–2014: 295,000 ha
2014–2015: 298,000 ha
2015–2016: 395,000 ha

(Total: 1.2 million hectares)

This is 'the equivalent of around 814 international rugby fields being bulldozed every day for four years' (*ABC News*, 2018). As a recent review pointed out, '91% of the clearing of woody vegetation in 2014–2015 was to increase pasture for livestock grazing' (Neldner et al., 2017, p. 1).

Changes in woody vegetation in QLD are monitored using the US Government's Landsat programme. Landsat has been run for over 40 years in partnership between the US Geological Survey and the National Aeronautics and Space Administration (NASA) (US Government, 2019). The Landsat imagery informs the QLD Statewide Landcover and Trees Study known as SLATS (Hamman, 2019b; QLD Government, 2019a). Annual SLATS reports measure changes in woody vegetation, commencing in the 1980s (QLD Government, 2019b). The QLD Government (2019c) describes their use of the technology as follows:

Each satellite image or scene represents an area of approximately 33,000 km^2 on the ground – this means we need 99 scenes to cover the entire state of Queensland. Each Landsat satellite captures multiple images of the same area each year, passing over the same location every 16 days. Where possible, we select images from the winter dry season. Not only are these images less likely to be affected by cloud, this is also typically the time of greatest contrast between woody vegetation and grasses. Generally grasses tend to dry out in winter while woody vegetation remains relatively constant, making it easier to differentiate between the two cover types.

Annual SLATS reports are published by the QLD Government (2019d; Hamman, 2019b). Reports from 2010 to 2018 are available online and reports

160   *Paul Martin et al.*

dating back to the 1990s are available in hard copy. Uses of the reports include: analysis of land degradation; regional ecosystem mapping; assessment of carbon emissions and carbon farming opportunities; identification of land suitable for biodiversity offsets, and compliance monitoring (QLD Government, 2019d; Hamman, 2019b). Remote sensing is of most value in the winter period when there is least cloud cover restricting the images (WWF-Australia, 2015, p. 32).

QLD's SLATS programme helps to inform state and federal policy decisions (Hamman, 2019b). This includes providing accurate and timely intelligence to decide where clearing should be allowed and for what purposes. The accurate data allows the environmental regulator in QLD to understand what clearing is occurring, where and under what conditions (Goulevitch, 2013; Hamman, 2019b). This also allows decision-makers to consider cumulative impacts by integrating clearing data with other data, such as wetland loss, water pollution samples and species monitoring programmes. This helps to avoid laborious and costly field research.

The technology also contributes to transparency, public participation and good environmental governance. The raw Landsat imagery is freely available as are the SLATS reports. Media outlets, NGOs and the agricultural sector can be informed to address government policy, and utilise the raw data to argue their causes. NGOs, such as WWF-Australia (2015) have used the technology for independent reports on biodiversity loss. This creates a more level playing field for communities and more inclusive decision-making relating to policy-making processes.

The technology in QLD also assists with illegal clearing control (Hamman, 2019b). The data can be evidence of crimes illustrating land clearing. Cases against farmers for illegal clearing of native vegetation were virtually unheard of prior to the 2000s but are increasingly common (Goulevitch, 2013; Hamman, 2019a). The quality and the reliability of the Landsat imagery helps the regulator to prosecute offenders (Goulevitch, 2013). However, regulators may also need to ground-truth the data and provide further evidence from contractors that they carried out the clearing. Because satellite images on their own (pre- and post-clearing) may not satisfy the Court, legislative provisions were introduced to 'reverse the onus of proof' in criminal trials to facilitate prosecutions using Landsat images (Hamman, 2019a). Evidentiary certificates are also available to improve the chances of admissibility in the courtroom (Hamman, 2019b). Reversal of onus provisions were politically contentious and were recently removed, which may have made prosecution more difficult (Hamman, 2016, 2019b). Concerns about the evidential reliability of satellite imagery have also been raised in Court. (see, e.g. the case of *Baker v Smith* [2019] QDC 76).

Discussion and conclusion

Examination of the role of satellite technology in water market regulation and habitat protection gives rise to some observations about the use of such data. The raw data from government backed-satellites (e.g. NASA) is increasingly available to NGOs and scientists. In Australia, as the water governance and land-clearing examples show, its use is primarily by regulatory agencies for monitoring and, to a lesser degree, enforcement. In Brazil, government agencies also use satellite technology for monitoring and enforcement of environmental legislation, at both the federal and state level. In addition, NGOs and advocacy groups use spatial data to promote law and policy reform and to show deforestation rates for campaign and advocacy purposes. The availability and cost of the data and the expertise and methods in utilising it determine the degree to which both government and non-state actors can best deploy it.

In Australia, for example, QLD uses satellite data to aid land-clearing control, including to provide evidence for enforcement. In Brazil, although data is available, its use for enforcement is still limited. However, it has been used by the Public Prosecutor's Office as well as environmental agencies despite the fragile legality of the data. Civil society uses satellite data to advance their own arguments about environmental policy and implementation of international rules and norms; the disclosure of land clearing data has allowed environmental groups to pressure state and federal governments to combat deforestation, mainly in the Amazon Forest region. Satellite data has, for example, been an important tool for the Soy Moratorium, which has impacted the soy industry and thus helped to control one of the main causes of land clearing in Mato Grosso. The MapBiomas Alerta programme launched in 2019 provides another important tool to help government agencies to combat deforestation.

The lack of political interest in controlling deforestation in Brazil, however, undermines the value of these instruments. In 2019, the Environment Minister, Ricardo Salles, blamed the DETER and the PRODES systems for failures of the Amazon Forest deforestation control (Maisonnave, 2019). No evidence was produced for the allegations, and the lack of personnel and resources at IBAMA to use the data collected by DETER and PRODES to control deforestation was ignored. Brazil's president, Jair Bolsonaro, has criticised INPE for releasing data that showed a sharp increase in deforestation in 2019. Bolsonaro claimed that INPE was simply serving the interests of international NGOs. This eventually led to the resignation of INPE's Director, Ricardo Galvão, who had objected to the government's attempt to limit the disclosure and use of deforestation data (Ambrózio, 2019; Brant & Watanabe, 2019).

Given the increased availability of remotely sensed data, both Australia and Brazil have an opportunity to use technology to create a lower cost, more transparent systems of environmental intelligence, including integrating data from different technologies such as unmanned aerial vehicles and robotics. Legal and evidentiary difficulties, however, will need to be overcome for its more widespread use in environmental enforcement (see e.g. Purdy & Leung, 2012). The QLD experience in prosecuting illegal land clearing has shown satellite data can be challenged in Court, and that raw data must be supported

162   *Paul Martin et al.*

by a credible manual analysis to deal with contestable interpretations of what the images actually prove in regards a particular offence (Hamman, 2019b). When spatial data is used for land-clearing prosecutions in Australia, 'evidentiary certificates' have issued by departmental officers to assist courts to understand what the data says, and whether it can be trusted as evidence (Hamman, 2019b). In Brazil, the use of spatial data to monitor land-clearing can also serve as evidence for prosecuting illegal land clearing. In the scope of the 'Amazonia Protege' project, the Public Prosecutor's Office filed lawsuits based on satellite images generated by PRODES from August 2015 to July 2016. In São Paulo State, for example, the Environmental Secretariat (SMA), using the Satellite Image Environmental Monitoring, developed a methodology to identify and control illegal land clearing in 2013 that systematically monitors and integrates information. When irregularities are observed, the Environmental Military records the infraction notice. The system has been used to prevent environmental crimes.

There are many other legal and political limits to the legitimate use of remote sensing technologies (Purdy & Leung, 2012). Remote supervision does raise difficult questions, for example, about the individual landholder's right to privacy (Bartel, 2005). Once datasets are available, they can be combined to provide new intelligence, which may be threatening to some citizens. For example, recent animal rights campaign in Australia allowed the identification of individuals who owned facilities where animals are housed, raising concerns about safety and rights of those facility owners. These are legitimate concerns and must be addressed by policy-makers. Powerful stakeholders who oppose government supervision may use political tactics, and politicians and regulators may take a conservative stance in response to this pressure (Stavins, 2004).

Ultimately, with a rapidly growing free market for satellite data, and new initiatives and programmes being implemented by both the government and non-government sector, spatial intelligence is likely to become increasingly available. The governance challenge for countries like Australia and Brazil is how best to use such data reliably and responsibly in environmental law and governance. Changes to evidentiary rules to enable reliance on satellite imagery raise important technical and policy questions, and the political will of the government of the day will be an important consideration as to whether and how such data can be utilised effectively.

Note

1   The data for land clearing in the Cerrado biome was available only for the period between 2003 and 2012.

References

ABIOVE. (2010). *Soy moratorium: Mapping and monitoring of soy plantings in the Amazon biome in the third Year.* Retrieved from http://www.abiove.com.br/english/sustent/relatorio09/moratoria09_relatorio_jul10_us.pdf

Biodiversity intelligence from satellites 163

Alexandra, J., & Martin, P. (2018). 'Tax returns for water': Satellite-audited statements can save the Murray-Darling. *The Conversation.* Retrieved from https://theconversation.com/tax-returns-for-water-satellite-audited-statements-can-save-the-murray-darling-81833

Ambrózio, S. (2019, July 25). Ém crítica ao Inpe, Bolsonaro diz que não pode haver 'órgãos aparelhados' (Criticising INPE, Bolsonaro says that there cannot be politicized institutions). *O Estado de São Paulo.* Retrieved from https://sustentabilidade.estadao.com.br/noticias/geral,em-critica-ao-inpe-bolsonaro-diz-que-nao-pode-haver-orgaos-aparelhados,70002938711

Azevedo, A., & Saito, C. (2013). O perfil do desmatamento em Mato Grosso, após a implementação do licenciamento ambiental em propriedades rurais (Deforestation in Mato Grosso after the implementation of environmental licensing in rural properties). *CERNE, 19* (1), 111–122.

Bartel, R. (2005). When the heavenly gaze criminalises: Satellite surveillance, land clearance regulation and the human-nature relationships. *Current Issues in Criminal Justice, 16* (3), 322–339. doi: 10.1080/10345329.2005.12036328

Becker, B. (2009). *Amazônia: Geopolítica na virada do III milênio* (Amazon: Geopolitics at the turn of the third millennium). Rio de Janeiro, Brazil: Garamond.

Bradshaw, C. (2012). Little left to lose: Deforestation and forest degradation in Australia since European colonization. *Journal of Plant Ecology, 5* (1), 109–120. doi: 10.1093/jpe/rtr038

Brant, D., & Watanabe, P. (2019, August 2). Diretor do Inpe será exonerado após críticas do governo a dados de desmate (INPE director will be fired after government criticism of deforestation data). *Folha de São Paulo.* Retrieved from https://www1.folha.uol.com.br/ambiente/2019/08/diretor-do-inpe-sera-exonerado-apos-criticas-do-governo-a-dados-de-desmate.shtml

Campbell, J., & Wynne, R. (2011). *Introduction to remote sensing* (5th ed.). New York, NY: Guilford Press.

COAG (Council of Australian Governments). (2004). *Intergovernmental agreement on a National Water Initiative between the Commonwealth of Australia and the governments of New South Wales, Victoria, Queensland, South Australia, the Australian Capital Territory and the Northern Territory.* Department of Agriculture. Retrieved from http://agriculture.gov.au/water/policy/nwi

Cogger, H., Ford, H., Johnson, C., Holman, J., & Butler, D. (2003). *Impacts of land clearing on Australian wildlife in Queensland.* Sydney, Australia: WWW Australia.

Crowther, R. (2002). Space junk – Protecting space for future generations. *Science, 296,* 1241–1242.

Cunha, J. (2006). Dinâmica migratória e o processo de ocupação do Centro-Oeste brasileiro: O caso de Mato Grosso (Migratory dynamics and the occupation process of Brazilian Midwest: The case of Mato Grosso). *Revista Brasileira de Estudos de População, 23* (1), 87–107.

Dias, B. (1994). A conservação da natureza (The conservation of nature). In M. Pinto (Ed.), *Cerrado: Caracterização, ocupação e perspectivas* (Cerrado: Characterization, occupation and perspectives) (pp. 17–73). Brasília, Brazil: Editora Universidade de Brasília.

Dias, B. (2008). Conservação da biodiversidade no bioma cerrado: Histórico dos impactos antrópicos no bioma cerrado (Biodiversity conservation in the Cerrado biome: History of anthropic impacts in the Cerrado biome). In F. Faleiro, & A. Farias Neto (Eds.), *Savanas: Desafios e estratégias para o equilíbrio entre sociedade,*

164 *Paul Martin et al.*

agronegócio e recursos naturais (Savannas: Challenges and strategies for the equilibrium between society, agrobusiness and natural resources) (pp. 303–333). Planaltina, Brazil: Embrapa Cerrados.

Fearnside, P. (1993). Desmatamento na Amazônia: Quem tem razão nos cálculos – o INPE ou a NASA? (Deforestation in the Amazon: Who is right in the calculations – INPE or NASA?). *Ciência Hoje, 16* (96), 6–8.

Fearnside, P. (2005). Desmatamento, na Amazônia brasileira: História, índices e consequências (Deforestation in the Brazilian Amazon: History, indexes and consequences). *Megadiversidade, 1* (1), 113–123.

Fearnside, P. (2006). Desmatamento na Amazônia: Dinâmica, impactos e controle (Deforestation in the Amazon: Dynamics, impacts and control). *Acta Amazônica, 36* (3), 395–400.

Fearnside, P. M. (2010). Consequências do desmatamento da Amazônia (Consequences of deforestation in the Amazon), *Scientific American Brasil, 3* [special biodiversity ed.], 54–59.

Fenna, A., (2012). Centralising dynamics in Australian federalism. *Australian Journal of Politics & History, 58* (4), 580–590.

Galletta, S. (2018, October). Satellites could hold key to stopping water theft in Murray-Darling Basin. *Irrigation Australia*. Retrieved from https://www.irrigationaustralia.com.au/news/satellites-could-hold-key-to-stopping-water-theft-in-murray-darling-basin

Gibbs, H., Rausch, L., Munger, J., Schelly, I., Morton, D. C., Noojipady, P., … Walker, N. F. (2015). Brazil's soy moratorium: Supply-chain governance is needed to avoid deforestation. *Science, 347* (6220), 377–378.

Gibbens, S. (2018, March). How illegal fishing is being tracked from space. *National Geographic*. Retrieved from https://news.nationalgeographic.com/2018/03/illegal-fishing-ais-data-going-dark-protected-ocean-reserve- spd.html

Goulevitch, B. (2013). Ten years of using earth observation data in support of Queensland's vegetation management framework. In R. Purdy, & D. Leung (Eds.), *Evidence from Earth observation satellites: Emerging legal issues* (pp. 113–146). Leiden, The Netherlands: Brill Nijhoff.

Governo de Mato Grosso. (2018a). *Geografia* (Geography). Retrieved from http://www.mt.gov.br/geografia

Governo de Mato Grosso. (2018b). *Análise dos dados de destamatamento do Estado do Mato Grosso: Período de 2016/2017* (Analysis of deforestation data of the State of Mato Grosso: 2016/2017 Period). Cuiabá, Brazil.

Green, D. (2012). Corruption in Brazil. In C. Funderburk (Ed.), *Political corruption in comparative perspective: Sources, status and prospects* (pp. 41–70). Burlington, VT: Ashgate.

Hamman, E. (2016). Failed changes to Queensland's vegetation clearing laws: Implications for climate change, the Great Barrier Reef and Australian environmental policy. *Australian Environment Review, 31* (8), 303–307.

Hamman, E. (2019a). Clearing of native vegetation in Queensland: An analysis of finalised prosecutions over a 10-year period (2007–2018). *Environment and Planning Law Journal, 36* (6), 658–673.

Hamman, E. (2019b). The use of satellites in environmental regulation: Applications and implications for biodiversity conservation. *Australian Environment Review, 34* (5), 88–92.

IBAMA. (2009). *Projeto de monitoramento do desmatamento dos biomas Brasileiros por satélite* (Brazilian satellite biome deforestation monitoring Project). Retrieved from http://siscom.ibama.gov.br/monitora_biomas/index.htm

IBGE. (1990). *Estatísticas históricas do Brasil: Séries econômicas, demográficas e sociais 1550 a 1988* (Brazil historical statistics: Economic, demographic and social series 1550 to 1988). Rio de Janeiro, Brazil.

IBGE. (2018). *Sistema de contas regionais* (Regional account system). Retrieved from https://www.ibge.gov.br/estatisticas/economicas/contas-nacionais/9054-contas-regionais-do-brasil.html?=&t=downloads

INPE. (2008). *Monitoramento de floresta Amazônica por satélite* (Monitoring the Amazon forest by satellites. Retrieved from http://www.obt.inpe.br/OBT/assuntos/programas/amazonia/prodes/pdfs/apresentacao_prodes-1.pdf

INPE. (2018). *PRODES – Amazônia.* Retrieved from http://www.obt.inpe.br/OBT/assuntos/programas/amazonia/prodes

INPE. (2019). DETER. Retrieved from http://www.obt.inpe.br/OBT/assuntos/programas/amazonia/deter

Insituto Socioambiental and Instituto Centro De Vida. (2006). *Sistema de licenciamento ambiental em propriedades privadas rurais no estado de Mato Grosso: Análise de usa implementação* (Environmental licensing system on rural private properties in the state of Mato Grosso: Analysis of implementation). Brasília, Brazil: MMA.

Joo, M., Raymond, M. A. A., McNeil, V. H., Huggins, R., Turner, R. D. R., & Choy, S. (2012). Estimates of sediment and nutrient loads in 10 major catchments draining to the Great Barrier Reef during 2006–2009. *Marine Pollution Bulletin, 65*, 150–166.

Lemos, A., & Silva, J. (2012). Desmatamento na Amazônia legal: Evolução, causas, monitoramento e possibilidades de mitigação através do Fundo Amazônia (Deforestation in the Legal Amazon: Evolution, causes, monitoring and litigations possibilities through the Amazon Fund). *Floresta e Ambiente, 18* (1), 98–108.

Macedo, M. N., DeFries, R. S., Morton, D. C., Stickler, C. M., Galford, G. L., & Shimabukuro, Y. E. (2012). Decoupling of deforestation and soy production in the southern Amazon during the late 2000s. *Proceedings of the National Academy of Sciences of the United States of America, 109*, 1341–1346.

Macrotrends. (2018). *Soybean prices: 45 year historical chart.* Retrieved from http://www.macrotrends.net/2531/soybean-prices-historical-chart-data

Maisonnave, F. (2019). Salles critica Inpe e quer empresa privada para monitorar Amazônia (Salles criticizes INPE and wants private company to monitor Amazon). *Folha de São Paulo.* Retrieved from https://www1.folha.uol.com.br/ambiente/2019/06/salles-critica-inpe-e-quer-empresa-privada-para-monitorar-amazonia.shtml

MapBiomas Alerta. (2019). *What is map biomas alert.* Retrieved from http://alerta.mapbiomas.org/en?cama_set_language=en

Maron, M., Laurance, B., Pressey, B., Catterall, C. P., Watson, J., & Rhodes, J. (2015, March 18). Land clearing in Queensland triples after policy ping pong. *The Conversation.* Retrieved from https://theconversation.com/land-clearing-in-queenslandtriples-after-policy-ping-pong-38279

Martin, P., & Shortle, J. S. (2010). Transaction costs, risks, and policy failure. In C. D. Soares, J. E. Miller, H. H. Ashiabor, L. Kreiser, & K. Deketelaere (Eds.), *Critical issues in environmental taxation: International and comparative perspectives* (Vol. VIII [8], pp. 705–720). Oxford, UK: Oxford University Press.

Martin, P., Williams, J., & Stone, C. (2008). *Transaction costs and water reform: The devils hiding in the details* (Technical Paper, vol. 08). Sydney, Australia: CRC for Irrigation Futures.

Martini, P. R., Duarte, V., Shimabukuro, Y. E., & Arai, E. (2009) 'Zoneamento da cobertura vegetal do Estado do Mato Grosso (ortoretificado)' (Zoning of vegetal

166 *Paul Martin et al.*

cover in the state of Mato Grosso (orthorectified)). Retrieved from http://www
.dsr.inpe.br/panamazon/img/MT_Valdete1.pdf

McAlpine, C. A., Fensham, R. J., & Temple-Smith, D. E. (2002). Biodiversity conservation and vegetation clearing in Queensland: Principles and thresholds. *The Rangeland Journal, 24* (1), 36–55.

McGrath, C. J. (2007). End of broadscale clearing in Queensland. *Environment and Planning Law Journal, 24* (1), 5–13.

MDBA (Murray Darling Basin Authority). (2017). *Basin Plan Evaluation 2017.* Canberra, ACT.

Mittermeier, R. A. (1997). *Megadiversity: Earth's biologically wealthiest nations.* Prado Norte, Mexico: Agrupacion Sierra Madre.

MMA. (2018). Cadastro nacional de unidades de conservação (National register of conservation units). Retrieved from http://www.mma.gov.br/areas-protegidas/cadastro-nacional-de-ucs

Neldner, V. J., Laidlaw, M. J., McDonald, K. R., Mathieson, M. T., Melzer, R. I., Seaton, W. J. F. ... Limpus C. J. (2017). *Scientific review of the impacts of land clearing on threatened species in Queensland. Queensland Government, Brisbane.* Retrieved from https://environment.des.qld.gov.au/wildlife/threatened-species/documents/land-clearing-impacts-threatened-species.pdf

Nepstad, D., McGrath, D., & Soares-Filho, B. (2011). Systemic conservation, REDD, and the future of the Amazon Basin. *Conservation Biology, 25* (6), 1113–1116.

Picoli, M., Camara, G., Sanches, I., Simões, R., Carvalho, A., Maciel, A., ... Almeida, C. (2018). Big earth observation time series analysis for monitoring Brazilian agriculture. *ISPRS Journal of Photogrammetry and Remote Sensing, 145* (part B), 328–339.

Possingham, H., Ryan, S., Baxter, J., & Morton, S. (2002). *Setting biodiversity priorities.* (Report to the Prime Minister's Science, Engineering and Innovation Council (PMSEIC)). Canberra, ACT.

Purdy, R., & Leung, D. (Eds.). (2012). *Evidence from Earth Observation Satellites: Emerging Legal Issues.* Leiden, The Netherlands & Boston, MA: Brill Nijhoff.

QLD Government. (2019a). *Statewide land cover and trees study (SLATS).* Retrieved from https://www.qld.gov.au/environment/land/management/mapping/statewide-monitoring/slats

QLD Government. (2019b). *Statewide landcover and trees study Queensland series.* Retrieved from https://data.qld.gov.au/dataset/statewide-landcover-and-trees-study-queensland-series

QLD Government. (2019c). *Statewide land cover and trees study (SLATS):* Methodology. Retrieved from https://www.qld.gov.au/environment/land/management/mapping/statewide-monitoring/slats/slats-methodology

QLD Government. (2019d). *Statewide land cover and trees study (SLATS):* Reports and spatial products. Retrieved from https://www.qld.gov.au/environment/land/management/mapping/statewide-monitoring/slats/slats-reports#slats-most-recent-reports

QLD Government. (2019e). *Land cover change in Queensland* (2018). Remote Sensing Centre, Science Division, Queensland Government. Retrieved from https://www.qld.gov.au/__data/assets/pdf_file/0031/91876/landcover-change-in-queensland-2016-17-and-2017-18.pdf

Rebgetz, L. (2017, June 19). Land clearing rates in Queensland on par with Brazil, new study finds. *ABC News Online.* Retrieved from https://www.abc.net.au/news/2017-06-19/land-clearing-rates-qld-need-to-be-lowered-new-study/8628524

Reside, A. E., Beher, J., Cosgrove, A. J., Evans, M. C., Seabrook, L., Silcock, J. L., ... Maron, M. (2017). Ecological consequences of land clearing and policy reform in Queensland. *Pacific Conservation Biology, 23* (3), 219–230. doi: 10.1071/PC17001

Richards, P., Arima, E., VanWey, L., Cohn, A., & Bhattarai, N. (2017). Are Brazil's deforesters avoiding detection?' *Conservation Letters, 10* (4), 470–476.

RMIT ABC Fact Check. (2018, July 16). *Fact check: Is Queensland clearing land as fast as Brazil? ABC News.* Retrieved from http://www.abc.net.au/news/2017-12-01/fact-check-queensland-land-clearing-brazilian-rainforest/9183596

Rose, R. A., Byler, D., Eastman, J. R., Fleishman, E., Geller, G., Goetz, S., ... Wilson, C. (2015). Ten ways remote sensing can contribute to conservation. *Conservation Biology, 29* (2). doi: 10.1111/cobi.12397

Seabrook, L., McAlpine, C., & Fensham, R. (2006). Cattle, crops and clearing: Regional drivers of landscape change in the Brigalow Belt, Queensland, Australia, 1840–2004. *Landscape and Urban Planning, 78,* 373–385.

Silva, J. (1998). Levantamento do desmatamento no Pantanal brasileiro até 1990/91 (Survey of deforestation in the Brazilian Pantanal until 1990/91). *Pesquisa Agropecuária Brasileira, 33,* 1739–1745.

Soares-Filho, B., Rajão, R., Merry, F., Rodrigues, H., Davis, J., Lima, L., ... Santiago, L. (2016). Brazil's market for trading forest certificates. *PLoS One, 11* (4), e0152311. doi: 10.1371/journal.pone.0152311

Souza, C. (2016). *Constitutional engineering in Brazil: The politics of federalism and decentralization.* London, UK: Springer.

Stavins, R. N. (2004). *The political economy of environmental regulation.* Cheltenham, UK: Edward Elgar.

Tardin, A., Santos, A., & Novo, E. (1977). *Uso de dados do LANDSAT no estudo de impactos da implantação de projetos agropecuários da Amazônia* (Use of LANDSAT data to study the impacts of the implementation of Amazonian agricultural projects). Retrieved from http://www.obt.inpe.br/OBT/assuntos/programas/amazonia/prodes/pdfs/tardin-et-al-1977.pdf

Taylor, M. (2013). *Bushland at risk of renewed clearing in Queensland.* Sydney, Australia: WWF-Australia.

US Government. (2019). *Landsat>About Landsat.* Retrieved from https://landsat.usgs.gov/about-landsat

Wallace, A., Weir, M., & McCrimmon, L. (2015). *Real property law in Queensland.* Australia: Thomson Reuters.

Webster,L.(2018,February27).Ruralbeekeepersturntosatellitetrackingsystemstohalthive theft, *ABC News.* Retrieved from https://www.abc.net.au/news/rural/2018-02-27/beekeepers-call-for-better-security-amid-beehive-thefts/9449580

WWF-Australia. (2015). *Briefing: Bushland destruction rapidly increasing in Queensland.* Retrieved from https://birdsqueensland.org.au/downloads/fl024_bushland_destruction_rapidly_increasing_in_queensland_16sep15.pdf

9 The challenge of using drones

Paul Martin, Larissa Suassuna Carvalho Barros, Vivek Nemane, Gabriel Leuzinger Coutinho, and Márcia Dieguez Leuzinger

Abstract

Drones are mechanical devices that are, to varying degrees, mobile and can operate remotely from a human operator in aerial, terrestrial or water contexts. They can be used in varied ways to help protect the environment and can also facilitate or cause biodiversity harm. Drones are a mix of technologies for locomotion, sensing and communication, to which other technologies can be added. Each technology is rapidly evolving, and so are the capabilities and potential uses of drones. This chapter considers some benefits, costs and risks of drones' technology and examines how these might be better managed. In doing so the chapter considers biodiversity governance challenges that arise with technologies more generally, including (for example) equipment, chemicals and bio-tech.

Introduction

The word 'drones' usually conjures up unmanned aerial vehicles (UAV), but drones operate on land, in the air, under water and in space (Dalamagkidis, 2015). There is no recognised international categorisation system for drones (Hassanalian & Abdelkefi, 2017). Drones are used for many tasks, including surveillance and monitoring of biodiversity, mapping and herbicide spraying. Their benefits include savings, speed, convenience, surveillance without disturbance and the ability to gather large amounts of precise data.

Drones are used increasingly in science as sensors, and algorithm innovations improve their use in activities such as hydrology monitoring (Tauro, Porfiri, & Grimaldi, 2016) or as 'swarms' operating autonomously in un-mapped complex environments (McGuire et al., 2019). In Australia and Brazil, NGOs and citizens often use drone images of habitat destruction from forestry and infrastructure projects in activist campaigns, and the public and private organisations that are targets of these campaigns try to restrict these uses of drones. A notable international illustration is the police creation of a no-fly zone to limit the use of drones by First Nations people opposing the Dakota Access Pipeline in 2016 (US). In Australia, farmers are pressing for stronger legal restrictions on drones accessing private farms as part of a broader 'right to farm' policy, largely in response to animal activists using drones in political campaigns.

Almost any useful technology might also cause harm. Drones (for example) can interfere with navigation, breach personal rights or enable environmental crimes, such as poaching, and have been used for terrorist attacks as well as strikes against terrorists.

The consumer demand for drones has increased due to advances in drone technology platforms and its relatively easy access for recreational use. These particularly include autonomous navigation, autopilot features, beyond visual line of sight long-range operational capabilities and data collection. The commercial market for drones, with a forecast of a 35 per cent increase in the Asia Pacific region by 2024, has grown due to use and application of drones in industries and government services (Grand View Research, 2016).

This chapter considers some benefits, costs and risks of drones and examines how these might be better managed, especially with regard to biodiversity applications. Though the focus of this chapter is drones, we also consider some broader aspects of the interaction between changing technologies and biodiversity governance, including environmental governance issues of new, rapidly evolving technologies.

Drone technology evolution

A drone is a composite technology, with a platform having a locomotive capability suited to its aerial, watery or terrestrial context, driven by a power system. It typically has sensors for data capture or processing, has a communications system and may have mechanical 'tools'. Operation involves decision making, which may be partly independent of human intervention. Many technologies are being combined, creating new drone capabilities and uses, and all are evolving. Drones, overall, are improving their speed; duration in use; compactness; robustness; ubiquity; cheapness; interoperability; system integration; mechanical capabilities, sensor capabilities and quality; robotics; machine intelligence and ease of use.

Drone platforms can be made of diverse materials, including aluminium, composite materials (e.g. fibreglass, fibre carbon), plastics and even wood, depending on the drone's end-use, type and intended price (Hassanalian & Abdelkefi, 2017). The mobile component is defined by intended use. There are two main types of aerial drones: fixed-wing systems and multi-rotor systems. Multirotor systems are a subcategory of rotorcraft (i.e. helicopters), using multiple rotary blades to ensure stability (Vergouw, Nagel, Bondt, & Custers, 2016). There are many types of under-water drones, which may look like small submarines (e.g. Coxworth, 2010) or like multirotor aerial drones (e.g. Voss, 2018).

The propulsion system usually accounts for 40–60 per cent of the drone gross weight (National Research Council, 2000). It consists of an energy source and a mechanism to convert stored energy into machine work. The main energy sources are fossil fuels (i.e. kerosene, gasoline, methane), battery cells, fuel cells or solar cells. Different types of engines are used: fuel engines, such as gas engines and jet engines and electric motors. Small drones are generally powered by batteries and electric motors (Hassanalian & Abdelkefi, 2017; Vergouw et al., 2016; Wessley & Chauhan, 2017).

Drone configurations can include regular or high definition cameras; infrared cameras (e.g. to scan volcanoes (Harvey, Rowland, & Luketina, 2016), inspect equipment (Muntwyler, Schuepbach, & Lanz, 2015) and monitor vegetation (Reinecke & Prinsloo, 2017)); navigation using GPS and radar (Mejias, Lai, & Bruggemann, 2015) and atmospheric sensors to, for example, measure GHG concentrations, humidity or pressure (Everaerts, Lewyckyj, & Fransaer, 2004; Vergouw et al., 2016). Natural resource monitoring uses are proliferating, such as aerial inspection of sensitive areas, disaster monitoring and species surveillance. Drones are beginning to be used for anti-poaching actions and protected areas management, particularly in Africa. Payloads including cargo and mechanical tools can also be carried by drones.

Drones are increasingly used for military purposes, such as surveillance, intelligence data gathering, reconnaissance and strikes (Vachtsevanos & Valavanis, 2015). In the natural resource management context, emerging mechanical operations include the application of chemicals such as herbicides, pesticides and other poisons to control invasive species.

Cargo is expected to be the most common payload of drones (Vergouw et al., 2016). In Australia, Wing (Google's drone delivery company) has been approved to operate in Canberra (Porter, 2019). This drone delivery service has generated complaints about privacy, noise and impacts on the environment, including native wildlife and domestic animals (Department of Infrastructure, Transport, Cities and Regional Development, n.d.; Evans 2019). A resulting inquiry exposed legal lacunae, including overly complex regulation and the lack of an appropriate authority (Commonwealth of Australia, 2019). Given advances in robotics and payload capacity, logistical uses in remote areas seem likely. Cargo carrying capability is also relevant to potential illegal uses, such as wildlife smuggling.

A drone's control and communication system ensures that the drone is stable, even with external disturbances. It estimates the drone's state (i.e. velocity, altitude, position) to achieve this. Fine adjustments are increasingly autonomous, and some drones are fully autonomous when performing pre-programmed tasks. However, most drones are partially controlled by a human operator, requiring communication between the controller and the drone and, possibly, with other equipment or traffic control (Hassanalian & Abdelkefi, 2017; How, Frazzoli, Chowdhary, 2015; Vergouw et al., 2016). This is usually done by radio links, as with traditional aircraft. In some cases, a video signal can be used to transmit images. However, video communications are limited for commercial use (Hassanalian & Abdelkefi, 2017; Heppe, 2015).

Technology innovation studies demonstrate that there is a typical pattern of evolution from early concepts which often are inefficient, through to mature highly efficient configurations. This pattern can be seen with virtually all types of innovation, including policy innovation, and is also seen with composite innovations like drones (Abernathy & Utterback, 1978; Christensen, 1992). In the earliest stage, the concept and design are fluid, often with many alternative concepts vying for dominance. Over time many prove unviable, while some emerge as the paradigm, and few (perhaps only one) will survive to be mature and highly efficient.

Figure 9.1 is a conceptual illustration of this for drone technology. Drone sub-technologies are at various stages of maturity, and the overall integration of these into useful products is also maturing. Significant change and improvement, and many currently un-exploited uses, will become viable. This has implications for legal governance: regulation is likely to be infeasible until the specifics of the technology, its uses and its impacts are known. The balance of this chapter demonstrates the complexity that arises as society tries to govern technologies that are still immature.

Expanding uses

Drones are widely used in environmental and agricultural applications that affect biodiversity. Governments use drones for many purposes, including monitoring wildlife, wildfires and erosion; inspecting mines, landfills and protected areas; surveilling deforestation, poaching and fishing and managing protected areas (Cress et al., 2015; López & Mulero-Pázmány, 2019; Mulero-Pázmány et al., 2014). In the private sector, environmental uses

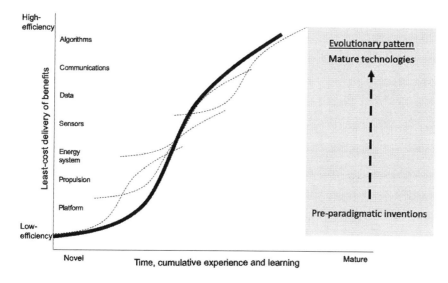

Figure 9.1 Composite evolution of drone technologies.
Source: Author.

of drones include monitoring environmental impacts of development, and day-to-day management of areas. Their real-time high-resolution images make it relatively easy to identify and thus mitigate or avoid environmental impacts (Lima, 2018; Mazur, Wisniewski, & McMillan, 2016). Drones are widely used in agriculture for monitoring crops (e.g. for bacteria and fungus damage) assessing soil before seeding, for planting (using drones to plant seeds), analysis of irrigation systems and to spray pesticides and fertilisers with precision (reducing the quantities used). In Australia, drones have been used to monitor remote water storages, fences and gates so that the farmer can remotely open or close valves, switches or gates. High-resolution drone images allow farmers to account for damages caused by disasters, for insurance purposes (Capolupo et al., 2015; Mazur et al., 2016; Sylvester, 2018).

Technological change of almost any type has implications for biodiversity. An example is using computer vision and machine learning to automatically count animals from drones, making it easier to conduct wildlife census (Andrew & Shephard, 2017; Seymour et al., 2017). Substantially autonomous drones will offer new options for continually monitoring protected areas, which is particularly a problem in developing countries (Muhumuza & Balkwill, 2013). Further technological advances will be needed before drones can operate autonomously in complex environments such as cities or forests, (Rejcek, 2018; Swearingen, 2019) but progress is rapid.

One limit to drone use is flight time. The current average flight time for conventional drones is 10–30 min. Advanced (particularly military) drones can fly for days or even months, but are not widely available (Dormehl, 2018). Generally, the main energy use is for propulsion. A development path to overcome this limitation is the production of machines that can rest in place (e.g. on the ground, roofs, walls or trees) while monitoring (Floreano & Wood, 2015).

New applications are constantly emerging. Innovative and cheap sensors can substantially increase the tasks that drones can perform. Combinations of big data, artificial intelligence and networked drones will further increase drone functionality. Additional mechanical functions, like idling in place, nano-chemical sprays and signal control of other machines (e.g. valves, switches) will expand how drones can be used (Floreano & Wood, 2015; López & Mulero-Pázmány, 2019).

We illustrate in the next items / sessions that the use of drone technologies can be beneficial or harmful to biodiversity. Governance will have to deal with optimising the beneficial uses of and controlling risks and harms from rapidly changing technologies where the current configurations give an incomplete picture of the future governance issues. Ideally, governance arrangements should be in place before issues emerge, but for many technologies, including drones, this does not happen. The need for future-oriented governance of risks also exists for other innovations that could benefit biodiversity but may also cause harm, such as biological and genetic engineering technologies (Ankeny & Hoffman, 2017).

Incremental adoption and learning

Naturally, the agencies in charge of protected areas wish to adopt technologies that assist them to cost-effectively carry out their duties, including protecting the integrity of the area and scientific studies of habitats and species. Their capacity to do so is limited by a lack of proven methods and experience to make optimal use of the innovation, under-developed policy frameworks, concerns about compliance with drone laws and a lack of funding. Adoption into use of an evolving technology by a public agency involves particular complexities, which we illustrate with the example of Chico Mendes Institute for Biodiversity Conservation (ICMBio, the Brazilian agency responsible for federal protected areas) adopting drones for protected area management.

ICMBio has been testing drones sporadically in recent years through independent and decentralised initiatives. These particularly include autonomous navigation, autopilot features, Beyond Visual Line of Sight long-range operational capabilities and data collection (Sayler, 2015). Data about these experimental uses is sparse but ICMBio (2018a; 2018b; 2018c) has recorded: (i) 2.4 per cent of federal protected areas use or have used drones for some biodiversity conservation application; (ii) 1.8 per cent of federal protected areas management plans have some norm concerning drones and (iii) 0.24 per cent of staff are trained for piloting drones. ICMBio has drafted an internal standard on the subject, which is awaiting approval. It contains guidelines on the most appropriate drone models for each biodiversity conservation application and rules for their use (ICMBio, 2018d).

The need to create a legal framework for the use of drones inside protected areas became evident when, in August 2018, ICMBio began examining the potential use of drones for management activities. The expectation was that they could work as a strategic tool for the management of protected areas, covering many management processes (ICMBio, 2018b). In November 2018, after planning, acquiring three drones and conducting a pilot training course, ICMBio started a test phase in Tapajós National Forest, a protected area in the Amazon. Lessons from the test were intended to support future acquisitions by identifying the best equipment for each type of mission (ICMBio, 2018c). In April 2019, ICMBio acquired 50 drones (ICMBio, 2019a).

The potential for drone applications in biodiversity conservation in Brazil is demonstrated by adoption data. An April 2019 ICMBio survey – only 15 months after the January 2018 survey – showed a tripling of use of drones: 7.5 per cent of federal protected areas use or have used drones for some environmental application (25 of 334). The uses identified in the January 2018 survey all concerned control of environmental crimes and infractions in protected areas. By the April 2019 survey, nearly half of the new utilisation of drone use were proactive actions for biodiversity conservation (7 of 17) (ICMBio, 2019b).

The most recently edited management plans in Brazil, such as the Iguaçu National Park Management Plan, now contain drone regulation, which requires drone overflights to have authorisation from the protected area administration (ICMBio, 2018a).

Some states have also started using drones for environmental monitoring and control. Piauí State was the pioneer, in 2015, followed later by Santa Catarina, Espírito Santo, Mato Grosso do Sul, Goiás and São Paulo. Drones are not only used for monitoring but also for biodiversity restoration. In 2016, the State Public Prosecutor's Office of Mato Grosso started a project in partnership with an NGO (*Instituto Ação Verde*) and the Federal University of Mato Grosso (UFMP): Water for the Future Project (*Projeto Água para o Futuro*). This project sought to identify, preserve and restore the urban springs in Cuiabá, the capital of Mato Grosso, and used remotely piloted aircraft system to map springs and confirm their condition (Moraes, Pansonato, & Barbosa, 2018). After mapping the springs and processing data, the State Public Prosecutor's Office investigates and adopts legal procedures to achieve repair of spring damage via a consensual or judicial solution.

In Australia, stakeholders comprising users from government, research sectors and hobbyists are also experimenting with or using professional drones for protection tasks, including for surveying, mapping and monitoring ecological habitat and biodiversity. The affordability, efficiency and practical utility of drones (especially in remote areas) can facilitate efficient conservation outcomes. Updating of policy and legal arrangements has also been identified as necessary to facilitate technological advancement and the beneficial uses of drones (State of Queensland, 2017). Currently, drones cannot be used in national parks other than for scientific research authorised under a specific permit. This caution by protected area managers is a rational response to an increasing awareness of risks and rights issues involving drones, and an uncertain and evolving state of legal arrangements.

Governance challenges

There are three main aspects of the governance of evolving technologies: control over possible adverse effects of legitimate uses; control over illegitimate uses and creating conditions to enable beneficial uses.

Human impact risk

The known human risks from drones include accidental impact (particularly concerning crowds, though malicious use cannot be ignored), surveillance or privacy-right intrusions and property trespass. Civil claims for personal and property injury are more likely as drone use increases (Stewart, 2016). Much of the risk focus is on UAVs, particularly the risks of drone impact with aircraft, which is addressed through aircraft regulation.

The risks from the use of aerial drones near airports are a particular concern. In 2018, Gatwick airport in the UK was shut down for 18 hours because an unknown operator flew drones in its airspace. Although this is illegal, agents had trouble preventing the unauthorised drone. Different control strategies have been tried or proposed, such as using cannons to launch nets, using other drones and even using trained eagles to attack hazardous drones. However, none seem to be a definitive solution (Hern, 2018).

In Brazil, the regulation of UAV human impact risk falls under the Brazilian Civil Aviation Regulation that covers the civil use of drones, updated in 2017 (*RBAC-E No. 94/2017*). The Civil Aviation Agency (ANAC) rules mean that a drone must not operate closer than 30 horizontal metres from people not involved in its use and not consenting to the operation. This rule does not apply where the drone is being used in accident response, or if there is a mechanical barrier to protect people who are not involved and not consenting. However, ANAC makes it clear that exposure to the risk is entirely the consenting person's responsibility (ANAC, 2019).

Under Brazilian regulations, it is unlawful to fly drones over sensitive areas, such as prisons and military installations, and over critical infrastructure, such as thermoelectric power plants and electrical substations. Violations attract severe penalties because of the danger (see ANAC, n.d.; UAV, n.da.).

In November 2015, the Brazilian Department of Airspace Control (DECEA) published a normative instruction that regulates access to Brazilian airspace by drones as complementary legislation to the Brazilian Aeronautical Code *ICA 100-40* (DECEA, 2015). Since 2016, the National Telecommunications Agency (ANATEL) has also begun to require the homologation of all drones that emit or operate on a radiofrequency basis to avoid interferences and other problems, based on an existing resolution – *ANATEL Resolution no. 242/2000* (ANATEL, 2016). In May 2017, ANAC created rules for the civil operations of drones through the Brazilian Civil Aviation Regulation – *RBAC-E no. 94/2017* (ANAC, 2019).

Drone technology and its uses, and rules to govern them, are evolving fast, with new uses constantly emerging and being trialled, and new issues emerging. Drones use multiple technologies configured for specific uses, which makes regulation complicated, in part because the configurations are 'flexible'. Approaches to regulating drone issues reflect legal path–dependency, a process of modifying earlier rules developed to deal with less sophisticated technologies and issues (illustrated in Hathaway, 2003; Le Gal, 2012). This constant process of 'catchup' is likely to contribute to uncertainty and leaves issues for later resolution, pending maturation of the technology and an accumulation of experience of problems and attempted solutions.

This phenomenon of early-stage confusion and incremental moves towards harmonised and systematic governance is seen in how new technologies with environmental implications are often dealt with in both Brazil and Australia. To illustrate this chaotic state, there are 15 Federal Bills currently in progress in the *Brazilian National Congress*, all commencing in the last five years. Lacking a comprehensive framework for systematic governance, some agencies in Brazil have asserted a role of regulating the use of drones, using whatever legal power they have. To illustrate, DECEA, ANATEL and ANAC all have

176   *Paul Martin et al.*

sought to fill the legal gap by issuing some standards in recent years (Passos de Freitas, 2017). This has also happened in Australia, with local governments and administrative bodies such as forestry corporations asserting that they have the power to create rules to control private uses of drones (though their legal authority to govern drones is often contestable).

In Australia, the Civil Aviation Safety Authority (CASA) regulates aircraft and airport safety and has created rules to protect the public from drones (CASA, 2018, n.d.). To a fair degree, these are similar to those in Brazil. The rules for private use of lightweight drones restrict operation to daylight within the operator's line of sight at a height below 120 m and no closer than 30 m to people, avoiding places where the drone could threaten public safety. Because around 15 per cent of new micro-drones demonstrate faults within six months, visual line of sight from the operator at all times is a common regulatory precaution (Martin, 2018). There are additional restrictions for commercial use and for larger drones (for links to CASA guidance see UAV Coach, n.db.). CASA rules, like those of the Brazilian ANAC, do not address civil issues like privacy and trespass.

Social interests

There are general privacy concerns about the recreational use of drones, for example to film people without their consent, but in the biodiversity conservation context, the main issue is the use of drones by civil activists to gather evidence, sending the drone into areas that they might otherwise not be able to enter on public or private land. Often, this is to obtain footage of habitat destruction to be used in political campaigns. This evidence-gathering is opposed by those who may be accused of wrong-doing, who may claim that this is an illegal or dangerous activity, or a violation of their citizen rights. Affected landowners tend to believe that aerial drone intrusions violate their private rights and assert a right to exclude drones from overflying their land. Some farmers even threatened to shoot down drones flying over their properties (Ashton, 2018). This private right claim is politically useful but legally far from certain. There are political attempts to restrict NGO use of drones which may violate sensitivities about privacy and other perceived intrusions.

Despite the protections for private rights in the Brazilian Constitution and legislation, the general law does not have human right norms regarding the use of drones. Because of the need to clarify the protection of perceived rights, a Law Project undertaken by the *National Congress (no. 9,425/2017)* is intended to establish licensing rules for drones to ensure respect for citizens' right to privacy and property, including rules covering image capture, especially of personal images.

Australian national and state legislation does include some privacy and anti-surveillance laws, but these are not comprehensive or harmonised. The use of camera, audio recording or other surveillance equipment on unmanned aircraft is partly governed by the national *Privacy Act 1988* (Cth). This regulates the handling of personal information about individuals. Australian 'Privacy Principles' only protect personal information about identified individuals or someone who could be reasonably identified from that information (*Privacy Act 1988* (Cth), s. 6). Because national government powers over individuals are constitutionally limited, acts by corporations (not individuals) are covered under this Commonwealth legislation. This generally limits most victims of a breach of privacy to the limited common law causes of action. The 'Eyes in the Sky' committee proposed a civil claim (tort) of breach of privacy for intrusive uses of drones (Commonwealth of Australia, 2014). The Australian government rejected this, endorsing common law remedies for trespass, nuisance, defamation and breach of confidence (Commonwealth of Australia, 2016).

The Australian Commonwealth and some states and territories laws regulate surveillance that uses devices, which can include drones. The fragmented state of surveillance control regulations reflects the early-stage state of a technology that is changing rapidly, with new uses and new issues arising. For example, the *Surveillance Devices Act 2004* (Cth) governs optical and listening devices but, in the state of New South Wales, surveillance laws also regulate data surveillance devices. In Queensland, surveillance laws only govern listening devices that record private conversations. Visual recording devices or location trackers that use video or still images do not fall under these controls, nor do they in the Australian Capital Territory and Tasmania. In an attempt to increase clarity about privacy, the Australian Government promotes a pamphlet about privacy laws to vendors of RPAS (Remotely Piloted Aircrafts). The aim is to encourage voluntary compliance by users, but it is unclear whether brochures have had the desired effect on drone user behaviour. In the absence of adequate laws, some Australian local governments have passed local regulations for privacy protection.

Lethal drones

Drones are widely used by military forces and increasingly by terrorists. EU Security Commissioner, Julian King, has warned that drones could be used for mass attacks such as dropping biological agents over crowds (Martin, 2019). In Venezuela, drones equipped with explosives were used in an assassination attempt on president Nicolás Maduro. Yemen rebels attempted an attack against an airport in Abu Dhabi, although the United Arab Emirates authorities deny the incident (Hudson, 2018). Saudi Arabia oil facilities were attacked by drones, affecting the international oil market (Safi & Borger, 2019). Other planned drone attacks have been frustrated by security services in the US and Europe (Grossman, 2018).

A technologically competent community of fishers and hunters has adapted drone technologies to improve their ability to kill animals in the wild. The first stage of this is the use of surface or under-water drones to locate target species and, sometimes, to herd them towards hunters. Commercial drones are available for hunting and fishing with capabilities such as infra-red detection for night or low light use. Drone use increases the efficiency of killing target creatures, whether legally or unlawfully, which is particularly a concern for the conservation of iconic species. Though not commercially available (and generally unlawful) the internet provides examples of civilian drones that have been weaponised, highlighting that this development is possible for hunting. Inventiveness and economic opportunity will continue to lead to more effective hunting drones, which will increase pressure on target species. They will be (and are being) used to increase pressure on harmful species such as feral pigs and deer, and there are few impediments to their being used for illegal purposes.

Autonomous decision making by machines is a further development that creates risks. The US Army is developing autonomous fighting drone technology and the British Ministry of Defence is funding research on it (Doward, 2018; Lee, 2018). Former Google employee, Laura Nolen, who worked in the US Army Project, Maven, argues that this technology should be banned because of the risks of serious accidents (McDonald, 2019). In 2018, the European Parliament called for an international ban on the development of weapons that kill without human intervention but a similar measure was not adopted by the UN (Psaledakis, 2018).

Ground based and aerial drones are being used to apply herbicides, pesticides and deliver poisons. Combining precise dosage and delivery, and potent (precisely targeted) chemicals can provide cost savings and effectiveness, reduces waste and control runoff or misapplication. Particularly for aerial drones, chemicals are best applied in micro-doses, reducing the weight to be carried. The precision use of drones to apply potent low-dose chemicals is not without risk, particularly if the delivery system is autonomous (increasing the potential of mis-delivery without direct human supervision). Chemicals registration approaches are being modified to cope with new formulations and delivery risks (Thornton, Hall, Luks, & Reeves, 2015), but autonomy without direct human supervision will further complicate risk regulation.

Biodiversity impacts

Some uses of drones raise questions about animal welfare, including the potential for drones to facilitate harmful activities, such as hunting, poaching and collecting, and the consequences of drones enabling more efficient and thus more harmful exploitation of native species, as already discussed.

Collisions and disturbance by drones are also known to harm native species, with collision risk illustrated by the fact that an Australian 2017 air traffic safety report indicates a significant increase in these incidents compared to reported bird strikes over the prior ten years (Australian Transport Safety Bureau, 2017). This, in turn, indicates major risk for bird population.

The challenge of using drones   179

There are increasing concerns about drone disturbance to wildlife, which has been demonstrated with wild bears, kangaroos and marine and other creatures (Brunton, Bolin, Leon, & Burnett, 2019; Mulero-Pázmány, et al., 2017). Drone users can cause distress and significant disturbance, particularly to sensitive or rare species; rules to address this concern are emerging. In Australia, whale and dolphin watching is an important tourist activity, and use of drones to observe them more closely has been identified as a cause of distress. The use of drones is permitted proximate to some whale and dolphin species (Natural Resource Management Ministerial Council, 2017) but risks remain of their displacement from their preferred habitats due to disturbance. The operation of drones near whales and dolphins must comply with the state or territory legislation, and the *EPBC Regulations* relevant to an aircraft marine parks (Natural Resource Management Ministerial Council, 2017). In the current regulatory regime, the compliance requirements under the *EPBC Regulations* are not consistent with the *Civil Aviation Act 1988* (Cth). Due to overlapping regulations, the operator requires permits from separate regulatory authorities. In addition to speed and safety concerns, the noise of drones can negatively impact the communication and navigation of whales and dolphins (Department of Environment and Energy, 2017).

Intentional damage

Drones will inevitably be used for illegal activities (as has occurred with the use of new technologies such as mobile phones and automobiles). In Brazil, drones have been used to deliver cell phones, drugs and weapons into prisons (Rodrigues, 2019). This has also occurred in Canada and the US (Johnson, 2019; Russon, 2013). Hackers have used drones to hack wireless, Bluetooth or R-F-I-D signals inside secure buildings (Larson & Sherman, 2018). In Australia, smugglers have used drones to monitor dock security or to trigger fire alarms to frustrate crime detection. In the US, drug cartels are using drones to monitor Border Patrol agents. Drones have been used to spy on police precincts and identify police informants (Hicks, 2018). It is easy to contemplate drones being used to frustrate environmental policing.

The ability of drones to efficiently gather data over large areas, to move things and to carry out activities remotely coupled with their capacity for covert use, gives them a great potential for illegal activities. The secret nature of these activities means that public information about what criminal innovations are happening or under development is scarce. Remote monitoring of rare or valuable species could facilitate poaching and illegal hunting, and drones are already used to smuggle illegal product or to facilitate avoidance of detection by authorities, but the extent of these uses in the biodiversity sphere is unknown.

Both poachers (Ecological Society of Australia, 2015) and biodiversity protectors are adopting technologies developed for warfare and, as military technologies improve, it can be expected that versions will be used for

180 *Paul Martin et al.*

both the exploitation of animals or their protection (for example, being used by para-military park rangers). There are cases of poachers shooting down drones from wildlife protection groups (Tillman, 2017). This can undermine the use of this technology for biodiversity protection because of the significant cost of losing a drone.

Drones and data

Drones are widely used for data gathering and, as drone data becomes more important, legal data issues will be more prominent. One issue is security against 'hacking' and cyber-attacks, and dealing with data misappropriation. Advances in meta-data analysis for policy and scientific reasons suggest that, if government agencies have rights to analyse private 'big data' for public purposes, this could yield valuable science and policy intelligence but access and ownership issues are politically sensitive. In Australia, after intense arguments, the *Telecommunications and Other Legislation Amendment (Assistance and Access) Act 2018* (Cth) enabled the government to access encrypted messages, including drone-captured data, but essentially for anti-terrorism purposes.

With increased autonomy (particularly machine-generated control algorithms), legal complexities can be anticipated about legal liabilities and about intellectual property rights to algorithms and data. Debates about rights to data gathered by drones are part of the larger discussion of 'data ownership', in the context of policy for 'big data' and precision in farming (see e.g. Weersink et al., 2018).

Conclusion

Earlier chapters make it clear that effective biodiversity protection will require a great deal of innovation. It will require economic innovation to overcome the 'missing market' problem that limits biodiversity conservation and restoration; it will call for new protective instruments, particularly those that can harness private incentives so that there is an economic and political basis for protecting the environment; and it will require cost-effective ways to carry out the many tasks involved in conservation and restoration. Technological innovation will help to meet some of the challenges, but (as has been the case in the past) technology can also create harms to nature. The characteristics of innovation itself create governance issues such as the challenge of governing ways of doing things that have not yet come into being, where their range of uses, outcomes (including impacts on nature) and unexpected impacts are not yet known.

In this chapter, we have explored this intersection between technological innovation and governance by examining drone technology. This technology is in the process of moving from a 'pre-paradigmatic' conceptual state towards being usefully applied to a number of practical problems. Because it is a composite technology, where its components are evolving new functionalities,

The challenge of using drones 181

drones come in many different forms and can be applied to an increasing array of uses. The limits to drone technology application cannot be known at this stage of development.

We have also discussed examples of drones providing considerable assistance in understanding and protecting nature. Their uses include sensing and data gathering, monitoring and carrying out mechanical or chemical tasks. The technology is being applied to supervise and police protected areas and to guard against irresponsible and wrongful activities. With greater mobility and autonomy, and new tools and instruments, the value of their use will increase. Drones are not the only technological innovations that should benefit biodiversity protection: transactional technologies, such as blockchain or data from improved sensors linked through the internet will provide better intelligence. In addition, researchers are investigating technologies, such as gene-shears, to help control harmful species (Prowse, Ross, Thomas, & Cassey, 2017; Zhang, 2016))

History demonstrates that innovation and risk are companions. The obvious risk is that technologies will not work, but another is that the technology will either cause harmful 'spillovers' or be misapplied, perhaps for antisocial purposes such as crime. The potential for accidental harm from drones is being realised as these machines become more common. The initial focus on the potential for aerial drones to collide with other aircraft has led to new rules to address this particular concern, but other risks are only becoming evident with experience. These include not only the risk of catastrophic failures or accidents to humans but also the potential for the technology to cause anguish or other psychological harms to people and to animals. Legal arrangements for these types of harm are only gradually emerging in response to experience and political dynamics. That environmental science and technology can face substantial political opposition is well-demonstrated with climate science, but this is also evident in political tensions over the use of drone technology by environmental activists.

The other lesson from history is that technological innovation intended to positive purposes may well be applied in perverse ways. With drones, the capacity to facilitate hunting, poaching or other damaging activities is increasingly obvious. This chapter, as well as highlighting issues with the particular technology, suggests the need for conservationists to engage early and well with the governance of the many technologies which are emerging that have implications for biodiversity. This is a new frontier, but it will become increasingly important.

References

Abernathy, W. J., & Utterback, J. M. (1978). Patterns of industrial innovation. *Technology Review,* 80 (7) (June/July), 41–47.

ANAC (Agência Nacional de Aviação Civil). (2019). *Drones.* Retrieved from http://www.anac.gov.br/assuntos/paginas-tematicas/drones

182   *Paul Martin et al.*

ANATEL (Agência Nacional de Telecomunicações). (2016). *Drones devem ser homologados para evitar interferências* (Drones must be approved to avoid interference). Retrieved from http://www.anatel.gov.br/institucional/ultimas-noticiass/2-uncategorised/1485-drones-devem-ser-homologados-para-evitar-interferencias

Andrew, M. E., & Shephard, J. M. (2017). Semi-automated detection of eagle nests: An application of very high-resolution image data and advanced image analyses to wildlife surveys. *Remote Sensing in Ecology and Conservation, 3* (2), 66–80.

Ankeny, R. A., & Hoffman, A. (2017, May). Gene drives may cause a revolution but safeguards and public engagement are needed. *The Conversation*. Retrieved from https://theconversation.com/gene-drives-may-cause-a-revolution-but-safeguards-and-public-engagement-are-needed-77012

Ashton, A. (2018, April 28). Horse riders and farmers threatening to shoot down drones spooking animals. *New Zealand Herald*. Retrieved from https://www.nzherald.co.nz/nz/news/article.cfm?c_id=1&objectid=12038754

ATSB (Australian Transport Safety Bureau). (2017). *Transport safety report: A safety analysis of remotely piloted aircraft systems*. Retrieved from https://www.atsb.gov.au/media/5773362/ar-2017-016a_final.pdf

Australian Law Reform Commission. (2014). *Serious invasions of privacy in the digital era (ALRC Report 123)*. Retrieved from htttps://www.alrc.gov.au/wp-content/uploads/2019/08/final_report.pdf

Brunton, E., Bolin, J., Leon, J., & Burnett, S. (2019). Fright or flight? Behavioural responses of kangaroos to drone-based monitoring. *Drones, 3* (2), 41.

Capolupo, A., Pindozzi, S., Okello, C., Fiorentino, N., & Boccia, L. (2015). Photogrammetry for environmental monitoring: The use of drones and hydrological models for detection of soil contaminated by copper. *Science of the Total Environment, 514,* 298–306.

Christensen. C. M. (1992). Exploring the limits of the technology S-Curve: Component technologies. *Production and Operations Management, 1* (4). doi: 10.1111/j.1937-5956.1992.tb00001.x

CASA (Civil Aviation Safety Authority). (2018). *Remotely piloted aircraft systems: Licensing and operation* (AC101-01). Retrieved from https://www.casa.gov.au/files/ac-101-01-v21

CASA (Civil Aviation Safety Authority). (n.d.). *Drones*. Retrieved from https://www.casa.gov.au/drones

Commonwealth of Australia. (2014). *Eyes in the sky: Inquiry into drones and the regulation of air safety and privacy*. Retrieved from http://search.ebscohost.com/login.aspx?direct=true&db=a9h&AN=85941828&site=ehost-live

Commonwealth of Australia. (2016). *Smart farming: Inquiry into agricultural innovation.* (Standing Committee on Agriculture and Industry report). House of Representatives'.

Commonwealth of Australia. (2019). *Inquiry into drone delivery systems in the ACT* (Standing Committee on Economic Development and Tourism, final report). Retrieved from https://www.parliament.act.gov.au/__data/assets/pdf_file/0007/1394485/9th-EDT-06-Inquiry-into-Drone-Delivery-Systems-in-the-ACT.pdf

Coxworth, B. (2010, January 8). *Neptune SB-1 radio-controlled submarine provides real-time underwater video*. Retrieved from https://newatlas.com/httpwwwgizmag comneptune-sb-113768/13768/

Cress, J. J., Hutt, M., Sloan, J., Bauer, M., Feller, M., & Goplen, S. (2015). *US geological survey unmanned aircraft systems (uas) roadmap 2014*. (US Geological Survey). Reston, VI: US Department of the Interior.

The challenge of using drones 183

Dalamagkidis, K. (2015). Definitions and terminology. In K. P. Valavanis, & G. J. Vachtsevanos (Eds.), *Handbook of unmanned aerial vehicles* (pp. 43–56). Dordrecht, The Netherlands: Springer.

DECEA (Departamento de Controle do Espaço Aéreo – Department of Airspace Control). (2015). ICA 100–140. Retrieved from https://www.decea.gov.br/drone/

Department of Environment and Energy. (2017). *Australian national guidelines for whale and dolphin watching.* [online]. Retrieved from https://www.environment.gov.au/marine/publications/australian-national-guidelines-whale-and-dolphin-watching-2017

Department of Infrastructure, Transport, Cities and Regional Development, ACT. (n.d.). *Drone delivery operations.* Retrieved from https://www.infrastructure.gov.au/aviation/environmental/aircraft-noise/act_drone_delivery_operations.aspx

Dormehl, L. (2018). 7 Drones that can stay airborne for hours — And the tech that makes it possible. Digital Trends, [10 September]. Retrieved from https://www.digitaltrends.com/cool-tech/drones-with-super-long-flight-times/

Doward, J. (2018, November 10). Britain funds research into drones that decide who they kill, says report. *The Guardian.* Retrieved from https://www.theguardian.com/world/2018/nov/10/autonomous-drones-that-decide-who-they-kill-britain-funds-research

Ecological Society of Australia. (2015). Poachers expected to use green drones to kill endangered wildlife. Retrieved from https://www.ecolsoc.org.au/poachers-expected-use-green-drones-kill-endangered-wildlife

Evans, J. (2019). *Google's drone delivery service launches in Canberra after being given green light to take to the skies.* Retrieved from https://www.abc.net.au/news/2019-04-09/google-drone-delivery-in-canberra-given-green-light/10983684)

Everaerts, J., Lewyckyj, N., & Fransaer, D. (2004). Pegasus: Design of a stratospheric long endurance UAV system for remote sensing. *The International Archives of the Photogrammetry, Remote Sensing and Spatial Information Sciences, 35* (Part B), 29–33.

Floreano, D., & Wood, R. J. (2015). Science, technology and the future of small autonomous drones. *Nature, 521* (7553), 460.

Grand View Research. (2016). *Consumer drone market analysis by product (Multi-Rotor, Nano), by application (Prosumer, Toy/Hobbyist, Photogrammetry) and segment forecasts to 2024.* Retrieved from https://www.grandviewresearch.com/industry-analysis/consumer-drone-market

Grossman, N. (2018, August 10). Are drones the new terrorist weapon? Someone tried to kill Venezuela's president with one. *The Washington Post.* Retrieved from https://www.washingtonpost.com/news/monkey-cage/wp/2018/08/10/are-drones-the-new-terrorist-weapon-someone-just-tried-to-kill-venezuelas-president-with-a-drone/

Harvey, M. C., Rowland, J. V., & Luketina, K. M. (2016). Drone with thermal infrared camera provides high resolution georeferenced imagery of the Waikite geothermal area, New Zealand. *Journal of Volcanology and Geothermal Research, 325,* 61–69.

Hassanalian, M., & Abdelkefi, A. (2017). Classifications, applications, and design challenges of drones: A review. *Progress in Aerospace Sciences, 91,* 99–131.

Hathaway, O. A. (2003). Dependence in the law: The course and pattern of legal change in a common law system. *Public Law and Legal Theory, 270.*

Heppe, S. B. (2015). Problem of UAV communications. In K. P. Valavanis & G. J. Vachtsevanos (Eds.), *Handbook of unmanned aerial vehicles* (pp. 530–576). Dordrecht, The Netherlands: Springer.

184 *Paul Martin et al.*

Hern, A. (2018, December 20). The drone crackdown: If a trained eagle can't stop them, what will? *The Guardian*. Retrieved from https://www.theguardian.com/technology/2018/dec/20/the-drone-crackdown-gatwick-if-a-trained-eagle-cant-stop-them-what-will

Hicks, M. (2018, May 4). *Criminal intent: FBI details how drones are being used for crime.* Retrieved from https://www.techradar.com/news/criminal-intent-fbi-details-how-drones-are-being-used-for-crime

How, J. P., Frazzoli, E., & Chowdhay, G. V. (2015). Linear flight control techniques for unmanned aerial vehicles. In K. P. Valavanis, & G. J. Vachtsevanos (Eds.), *Handbook of unmanned aerial vehicles* (pp. 530–576). Dordrecht, The Netherlands: Springer.

Hudson, B. (2018, August 5). Drone attacks are essentially terrorism by joystick. *The Washington Post*. Retrieved from https://www.washingtonpost.com/opinions/drone-attacks-are-essentially-terrorism-by-joystick/2018/08/05/f93ec18a-98d5-11e8-843b-36e177f3081c_story.html

ICMBio (Instituto Chico Mendes de Conservação de Biodiversidade). ICMBio. (2018a). Retrieved from https://sei.icmbio.gov.br/sip/login.php?sigla_orgao_sistema=ICMBio&sigla_sistema=SEI&infra_url=L3NlaS8=

ICMBio (Instituto Chico Mendes de Conservação de Biodiversidade. (2018b). *ICMBio inicia estudos para potencializar o uso de drone* (ICMBio begins studies to enhance the use of drone). Retrieved from http://www.icmbio.gov.br/portal/ultimas-noticias/20-geral/9890-icmbio-inicia-estudos-para-potencializar-o-uso-de-drone

ICMBio (Instituto Chico Mendes de Conservação de Biodiversidade). (2018c). *ICMBio testa drones na Amazônia* (ICMBio tests drones in the Amazon). Retrieved from: http://www.icmbio.gov.br/portal/ultimas-noticias/20-geral/10085-icmbio-testa-drones-na-amazonia

ICMBio (Instituto Chico Mendes de Conservação de Biodiversidade). (2018d). *Drones devem contribuir para fiscalizar UCs* (Drones should help oversee UCs). Retrieved from http://www.icmbio.gov.br/portal/ultimas-noticias/20-geral/9759-drones-devem-contribuir-para-fiscalizar-ucs

ICMBio (Instituto Chico Mendes de Conservação de Biodiversidade). (2019a). *Pregão eletrônico n° 5/2019* (Electronic Auction no. 5/2019). Retrieved from http://www.icmbio.gov.br/portal/images/stories/edital/ edital_pregao_eletronico_5_2019_srp.pdf

Johnson, L. (2019, September 29). A drone was caught on camera delivering contraband to an Ohio prison yard. *CNN*. Retrieved from https://edition.cnn.com/2019/09/26/us/contraband-delivered-by-drone-trnd/index.html

Larson, J., & Sherman, S. (2018, April 5). Hackers using drones to commit crimes. *ABC Arizona*. Retrieved from https://www.abc15.com/news/national/drone-hackers

Lee, P. (2018, April 11). Drones will soon decide who to kill. *The Conversation*. Retrieved from http://theconversation.com/drones-will-soon-decide-who-to-kill-94548

Le Gal, E. (2012). The effects of institutional path dependence, political dynamics and transaction costs on the potential for 'smart' regulatory innovation: An illustration with the biofuel weed risk case study. *Australasian Journal of Natural Resources Law and Policy, 15* (2), 219–254.

Lima, M. (2018). *A importância dos veículos aéreos não tripulados na coleta de imagens* (The importance of unmanned aerial vehicles in image collection). Retrieved from http://www.grupozago.com.br/importancia-dos-vants/

López, J., & Mulero-Pázmány, M. (2019). Drones for conservation in protected areas: present and future. *Drones, 3* (1), 10.

Martin, M. (2018, December 25). Know the rules before you fly your Christmas drone. *ABC*. Retrieved from https://www.abc.net.au/news/2018-12-25/drones-for-christmas-spark-safety-warning/10664092

Martin, N. (2019, August 3). Drones could be used in terror attacks. EU security chief fears, *Deutsche Welle*. Retrieved from https://www.dw.com/en/drones-could-be-used-in-terror-attacks-eu-security-chief-fears/a-49876427

Mazur, M., Wisniewski, A., & McMillan, J. (2016). *Clarity from above* (PwC global report on the commercial applications of drone technology). Warsaw, Poland: Drone Powered Solutions.

McDonald, H. (2019, September 15). Ex-Google worker fears 'killer robots' could cause mass atrocities. *The Guardian*. Retrieved from https://www.theguardian.com/technology/2019/sep/15/ex-google-worker-fears-killer-robots-cause-mass-atrocities

McGuire, K. N., De Wagter, C., Tuyls, K., Kappen, H. J., & de Croon, G. C. H. E. (2019). Minimal navigation solution for a swarm of tiny flying robots to explore an unknown environment. *Science Robotics, 4* (35). doi: 10.1126/scirobotics.aaw9710

Mejias, L., Lai, J., & Bruggemann, T. (2015). Sensors for missions. In K. P. Valavanis & G. J. Vachtsevanos (Eds.), *Handbook of unmanned aerial vehicles* (pp. 43–46). Dordrecht, The Netherlands: Springer.

Moraes, A. J. F., Pansonato, A., & Barbosa, G. N. (2018) *Procedimentos metodológicos do projeto Água para o Futuro utilizados nas nascentes urbanas de Cuiabá*. (Methodological procedures of the Water for the Future project used in the urban springs of Cuiabá). Cuiabá: EdUFMT. Retrieved from https://mpmt.mp.br/site/storage/webdisco/documentos/Anual/2018/07/19/procedimentos-metodologicos-do-projeto-agua-para-o-futuro-utilizados-nas-nascentes-urbanas-de-cuiaba.pdf

Muhumuza, M., & Balkwill, K. (2013). Factors affecting the success of conserving biodiversity in national parks: A review of case studies from Africa. *International Journal of Biodiversity, 2013*. doi: 10.1155/2013/798101

Mulero-Pázmány, M., Jenni-Eiermann, S., Strebel, N., Sattler, T., Negro, J. J., & Tablado, Z. (2017). Unmanned aircraft systems as a new source of disturbance for wildlife: A systematic review. *PloS One, 12* (6), e0178448. doi: 10.1371/journal.pone.0178448

Mulero-Pázmány, M., Stolper, R., Van Essen, L. D., Negro, J. J., & Sassen, T. (2014). Remotely piloted aircraft systems as a rhinoceros anti-poaching tool in Africa. *PloS One, 9* (1), e83873.

Muntwyler, U., Schuepbach, E., & Lanz, M. (2015, September). Infrared (IR) drone for quick and cheap PV inspection. In *Proceedings of the 31st European Photovoltaic Solar Energy Conference and Exhibition* (pp. 1804–1806).

National Research Council (2000). Uninhabited air vehicles: Enabling science for military systems. Washington, DC: *National Academies Press, 495*.

Natural Resource Management Ministerial Council. (2017). *Australian national guidelines for whale and dolphin watching*. Retrieved from Department of Environment and Energy http://www.environment.gov.au/marine/publications/australian-national-guidelines-whale-and-dolphin-watching-2017

Passos de Freitas, V. (2017). A regulamentação do uso de drones, o passado e o futuro (Drone regulation, past and future). *Revista Consultor Jurídico*. Retrieved from https://www.conjur.com.br/2017-dez-10/regulamentacao-uso-drones-passado-futuro

Porter, J. (2019). Google's wing drones approved to make public deliveries in Australia. *The Verge*, [9 April]. Retrieved from https://www.theverge.com/2019/4/9/18301782/wing-drone-delivery-google-alphabet-canberra-australia-public-launch

Prowse, T., Ross, J., Thomas, P., & Cassey, P. (2017, August 10). 'Gene drives' could wipe out whole populations of pests in one fell swoop. *The Conversation*. Retrieved from

186 *Paul Martin et al.*

http://theconversation.com/gene-drives-could-wipe-out-whole-populations-of-pests-in-one-fell-swoop-81681?utm_medium=email&utm_campaign=Latest from The Conversation for August 10 2017 – 80366442&utm_content=Latest from The Conversation for August 10 2017

Psaledakis, D. (2018, September 12). EU lawmakers call for global ban on 'killer robots'. *Reuters.* Retrieved from https://www.reuters.com/article/us-eu-arms/eu-lawmakers-call-for-global-ban-on-killer-robots-idUSKCN1LS2AS

Reinecke, M., & Prinsloo, T. (2017, July). *The influence of drone monitoring on crop health and harvest size.* In 1st International Conference on Next Generation Computing Applications (NextComp) (pp. 5–10). Port Louis, Mauritius: IEEE.

Rejcek, P. (2018). MIT's leading the pack with this cool new autonomous drone tech. *SingularityHub,* [31 May]. Retrieved from https://singularityhub.com/2018/05/31/mit-researchers-drive-new-advances-in-drone-technology/

Rodrigues, A. (2019, June 13). Crime usa de drone a macarrão para enviar drogas e celulares a prisões (Crime uses: From drone to noodles to send drugs and cell phones to prisons). *Folha de São Paulo.* Retrieved from https://www1.folha.uol.com.br/cotidiano/2019/06/crime-usa-de-drone-a-macarrao-para-enviar-drogas-e-celulares-a-prisoes.shtml

Russon, M. (2013, November 29). Drones used to deliver drugs to prisoners in Canada. *International Business Times.* Retrieved from https://www.ibtimes.co.uk/drones-delivers-drugs-prison-canada-contraband-inmates-526190

Safi, M., & Borger, J. (2019, September 19). How did oil attack breach Saudi defences and what will happen next? *The Guardian.* Retrieved from https://www.theguardian.com/world/2019/sep/19/how-did-attack-breach-saudi-defences-and-what-will-happen-next

Sayler, K. (2015). *A world of proliferated drones: A technology primer.* Washington, DC: The Center for a New American Security.

Seymour, A. C., Dale, J., Hammill, M., Halpin, P. N., & Johnston, D. W. (2017). Automated detection and enumeration of marine wildlife using unmanned aircraft systems (UAS) and thermal imagery. *Scientific Reports, 7,* 45127.

State of Queensland. (2017). *Queensland drones strategy.* Retrieved from https://www.premiers.qld.gov.au/publications/categories/plans/queensland-drones-strategy.aspx

Stewart, P. (2016). Drone danger: Remedies for damage by civilian remotely piloted aircraft to persons or property on the ground in Australia. *Torts Law Journal, 23* (3), 290–319.

Swearingen, J. (2019, March 26). A.I. is flying drones (very, very slowly). *The New York Times.* Retrieved from https://www.nytimes.com/2019/03/26/technology/alphapilot-ai-drone-racing.html

Sylvester, G. (2018). *E-agriculture in action: Drones for agriculture.* Bangkok, Thailand: FAO & International Telecommunication Union.

Tauro, F., Porfiri, M., & Grimaldi, S. (2016). Surface flow measurements from drones. *Journal of Hydrology, 540,* 240–245. doi: 10.1016/j.jhydrol.2016.06.012

Tillman, L. (2017, December 26). Poachers shoot down anti-poaching drone in the Gulf of California. *Los Angeles Times.* Retrieved from https://www.latimes.com/world/mexico-americas/la-fg-mexico-porpoise-drone-20171226-story.html

Thornton, M., Hall, G., Luks, F., & Reeves. (2015). *Nanotechnologies for pesticides and veterinary medicines: Regulatory considerations final report.* Canberra, ACT: APVMA.

The challenge of using drones 187

Vachtsevanos, G. J., & and Valavanis, K. P. (2015). Military and civilian unmanned aircraft. In K. P. Valavanis, & G. J. Vachtsevanos (Eds.), *Handbook of unmanned aerial vehicles* (pp. 93–104). Dordrecht, The Netherlands: Springer.

Vergouw, B., Nagel, H., Bondt, G., & Custers, B. (2016). Drone technology: Types, payloads, applications, frequency spectrum issues and future developments. In B. Custers (Ed.), *The future of drone use* (pp. 21–45). The Hague, The Netherlands: TMC Asser Press.

Voss, O. (2018, May 17). *The Geneinno Titan underwater drone will hit kickstarter soon.* Retrieved from https://www.cinema5d.com/geneinno-titan-underwater-drone-will-hit-kickstarter-soon/

Weersink, A., Fraser, E., Pannell, D., Duncan, E., & Rotz, S. (2018). Opportunities and challenges for big data in agricultural and environmental analysis. *Annual Review of Resource Economics, 10* (1), 19–37. doi: 10.1146/annurev-resource-100516-053654

Wessley, G. J. J., & Chauhan, S. (2017). Investigation on scaling of gas turbine engines for drone propulsion. *International Journal of Engineering Technology, Management and Applied*

Zhang, S. (2016). Save the Galapagos with GMO rats. What could go wrong? *Science.* Retrieved from http://www.wired.com/2016/06/save-galapagos-gmo-rats-go-wrong/

10 Funding biodiversity conservation

Davi Rossiter, Kip Werren, Paul Martin, and Larissa Ribeiro da Cruz Godoy

Abstract

Article 11 of the Convention on Biological Diversity is based on the acknowledgement that to implement biodiversity strategies, it is necessary to provide adequate funding to motivate and implement conservation and restoration action. This chapter discusses Australian and Brazilian investments in biodiversity actions, noting that funding allocations fall far short of what is required to maintain biodiversity. The chapter notes that the capacity of either government to fill the funding gaps is insufficient and innovative approaches are needed to motivate private investment. Thus far, neither country has prioritised funding innovations.

Introduction

It is a universally accepted truth that the pursuit of resources drives animal and human (and all other species) behaviour. Biological evolution is a process of adaptation to better access resources; the discipline of economics explains human behaviour in terms of a pursuit of resources to optimise individual or collective utility. The opportunity to secure wealth or to avoid losing wealth is a fundamental motivator of behaviour in a capitalist society and, as readers will have noted in the chapters concerning mining, agriculture and land-clearing, the pursuit of resources includes behaviour related to biodiversity.

Article 11 of the *Convention on Biological Diversity* (*CBD*) is based on the realisation that for people to implement national biodiversity strategies requires the possibility of economic rewards or the risk of economic penalties. The article states that 'each Contracting Party shall, as far as possible and as appropriate, adopt economically and socially sound measures that act as incentives for the conservation and sustainable use of components of biological diversity'.

Further, the drafters of the *CBD* were aware of the practical need for financial resources to implement biodiversity conservation and restoration. Signatory countries committed to ensure that sufficient investment would be available to motivate and then to do the work necessary to protect biodiversity. The *CBD* also recognises the need to reduce the financial disadvantage of less wealthy countries.

Thus, the Preamble for the *CBD* acknowledges:

> [T]hat substantial investments are required to conserve biological diversity and that there is the expectation of a broad range of environmental, economic and social benefits from those investments ... the objectives of this Convention, to be pursued in accordance with its relevant provisions, are the conservation of biological diversity, the sustainable use of its components and the fair and equitable sharing of the benefits ... taking into account all rights over those resources and to technologies, *and by appropriate funding*.
>
> (author emphasis)

The emphasis on resourcing is reinforced in article 20(1):

> Each Contracting Party undertakes to provide, in accordance with its capabilities, financial support and incentives in respect of those national activities which are intended to achieve the objectives of this Convention, in accordance with its national plans, priorities and programmes.

Further, article 21(4) states that 'the Contracting Parties shall consider strengthening existing financial institutions to provide financial resources for the conservation and sustainable use of biological diversity'.

Economic incentives in a market economy motivate the exploitation of nature. Government policies often promote such exploitation as a side effect of investment in infrastructures and industry development, or as a consequence of promoting investment and trade.

Over time, Australia and Brazil have transformed their ecosystems to supply the demand for infrastructure, food, fibre and fuel (Chapter 2). This has led to species extinction, deterioration of key services, such as water purification, and decreased protection from natural disasters due to the loss of buffers such as wetlands. Now, according to the International Union for the Conservation of Nature (IUCN) Red List (n.d.) of threatened species, Brazil has 7,444 threatened species and Australia has 8,488 threatened species. Australia and Brazil face common challenges in making biodiversity conservation feasible and attractive.

The expansion of agriculture into natural habitat continues to occur in Australia and Brazil, illustrating how economic incentives drive environmental destruction despite legal rules. Other private incentive-related impacts discussed in other chapters include the spread of invasive species, and animal and chemicals pollution (Chapter 2). The examination of mining risks (Chapter 3) shows how wealth motivations can undermine biodiversity protection norms. However, economic incentives are also important to private norms that moderate harmful consumerism, including eco-labels and industry or commercial voluntary standards, even if the incentive for these norms is often the hope of better market access and profits.

The National Biodiversity Strategies and Action Plans (NBSAP) website, under *Search NSABs and national reports* (n.d.), provide downloads of the Australian and Brazilian reports on strategies and action plans relevant to their *CBD* commitments. The actions proposed in these reports cannot happen (or not happen effectively) unless resources are available to fully implement them. No matter how often these documents declare that protective instruments and government structures will enable public agencies to effectively manage protected areas, control unlawful activities and limit environmental and social harms, unless resources are simultaneously provided to controlling agencies, nothing will happen.

It is not only the public agencies that require resources to implement biodiversity protection but also other stakeholders. A strategy that anticipates private land stewards or natural resource users that will change their practices to more sustainable ones is based on the belief that such stakeholders will be motivated (i.e. have incentives) and have the ability (i.e. have the knowledge and resources) to do what is expected of them. As biodiversity governance becomes more pluralist through the use of diverse market instruments, voluntary stewardship institutions, Indigenous management and increased role for non-government organisations, the range of actors who require motivation and capabilities to implement biodiversity strategies expands.

Positive conservation activities, such as restoring the environment, preventing or mitigating harmful social and economic activities and restoring habitat native fauna and flora, all require substantial resources. The pressures-and-conservation impact model developed by Waldron et al. (2017) demonstrates that spending on biodiversity conservation activities is pivotal for reducing biodiversity decline. Overall, if economic incentives motivate people contrary to conservation and if resources for conservation are not available, conservation simply will not happen.

In spite of commitments by Australia and Brazil upon becoming signatories to the *CBD*, and as this chapter highlights, insufficient funding makes it likely that many of the biodiversity strategies declared by Australia and Brazil cannot be effectively implemented. The historical failure of both countries to meet national strategies, whether Aichi or SDG targets, can often be traced to the chronic problem of an insufficient allocation of resources.

This chapter examines biodiversity conservation investment in both countries to explore the extent to which they are implementing *CBD* commitments. Though public data does not allow us to provide a reliable estimate of the biodiversity funding gap in either country, there is sufficient evidence to judge the extent to which these investment commitments are being met and implementation is happening, and to suggest what is required to ensure that they are.

Resource limitations

Significant resources are invested by governments and entrepreneurs who seek to utilise the natural environment for economic gain. The public and civil

Funding biodiversity conservation 191

organisations involved in managing the harms that arise are generally under resourced. Earlier chapters have discussed the effects of under-resourcing of biodiversity governance in mining (Chapter 3), habitat protection (Chapter 8), marine protection (Chapter 4), protected areas management and Indigenous rights to natural resources (Chapter 5). Both Australia and Brazil have large land and marine areas to supervise and, with few exceptions, the responsible agencies lack the funds or manpower to halt significant degradation of native biodiversity. In recent times, the funding reductions and increased responsibilities, discussed below, have added to these financial pressures.

Because it is often technically difficult to gather evidence and prosecute wrongdoers, the transaction costs of enforcement can overwhelm the limited allocated funds, and the institutional incentives for robust implementation of biodiversity regulations are often financially and politically weak; this is obvious with habitat protection but is true of most aspects of environmental policing. Though satellite and drones, new sensors and analytic technologies may improve the cost-effectiveness of intelligence gathering (Chapters 8 and 10), enforcement action will always require financial and human resources and political commitment. Along with market incentives and other non-policed instruments, incentives and resources are essential to promote land-holder stewardship, manage terrestrial and marine protected areas, evaluate and control development impacts and carry out all biodiversity governance activities. Insufficient economic incentives and resources for biodiversity protection are chronic with biodiversity governance.

As well as problems of public funding, the ability of resource users to implement sustainable practices is limited by the overwhelming economic impetus for resource exploitation compared with the limited economic incentives for conservation. Limitations are brought about by the unpredictable financial effects of commodity markets, climate or other episodic environmental events and self-interest (as discussed variously in Chapters 2, 3 and 4). In particular, because the Aboriginal, Torres Strait Islander, Indigenous and Traditional peoples are among the most socially and economically disadvantaged people in both jurisdictions, they often lack the ability to implement strategies. For any disadvantaged people, requirements such as travel to meetings, obtaining representation, education and healthcare, combined with institutional impediments and external pressures, can become insurmountable barriers to taking action. In these situations, rights to participate may exist in law but poverty and other disadvantages may make them ineffective (see Chapter 5).

The funding gaps

Ward and Lassen (2018) recently reported:

> A top-down study conducted at a global level estimated that USD 150 billion to USD 440 billion per year (0.08–0.25% of global GDP) would be needed by 2020 to achieve the CBD Strategic Plan, noting that some

192 *Davi Rossiter et al.*

synergies could be achieved by coordinating actions and thus reducing the total amount of funding required. Estimates by other credible experts back this figure up. John Tobin-de la Puente, cofounder of the Coalition for Private Investment in Conservation (CPIC) and a professor at Cornell University, suggested that USD 250 billion to USD 350 billion would be required each year to conserve healthy terrestrial and marine ecosystems on land and in the oceans, and restore the Earth's natural capital stock of clean air, fresh water and species diversity. Other estimates suggest that USD 300–400 billion in annual conservation finance is needed ... Currently, around USD 52 billion per year flows to conservation projects, the bulk from domestic government budgets and philanthropic sources, and as a co-benefit to investment in sustainable land management subsidies and green product certification.

(p. 21)

That report asserted (p. 22) that the US$200 to US$300 billion per annum needed to bridge the gap will have to come primarily from private sources. Another study on funds required to implement the Aichi targets found that 'current allocations of funding to biodiversity are between an eighth and a sixth of the levels required' (CBD High-Level Panel, 2014, p. 87).

Pizer, Morgenstern, and Shih (1998) and Martin, Cosby, and Werren (2017) discuss Australia's baseline requirement for biodiversity funding, set at about 2 per cent of GDP, noting, however, that the many national, temporal and species variables mean that such estimates are speculative.

Table 10.1 contrasts Australia and Brazil in terms of population, surface area and GDP. Though Australia enjoys a far higher GDP per person than Brazil, Brazil's GDP per hectare is higher. Both countries have many species and ecosystems that need protection, and these are dispersed over very large areas, with extensive agriculture being both the major economic land use and major causes of biodiversity loss (see Chapters 2 and 8). In both countries, the majority of the population live in coastal and urban areas and thus have large areas with sparse populations.

Table 10.1 Comparison of Australia and Brazil based on 2017 data

2017	Australia	Brazil	OECD average
Total population	24,450,561	209,288,278	
Total surface area km^2	7,692,060	8,515,767	
Population density: individuals per km^2	3.18	24.57	35.1
GDP US$	1,408,675,702,262	2,055,512,218,230	
GDP per capita US$	57,613	9,821	43,700
GDP per hectare US$	1,831	2,414	

Source: Table derived from UNdata. (n.d.). A World of Information. Retrieved from http://data.un.org/

The nature of biodiversity protection is that national funding capacity might be best assessed in terms of the funds available for unit of land to be protected rather than funds per person, which is the usual measure of national wealth. By this measure, it is clear that people, money and government resources are spread thinly over large rural areas, with Australia and Brazil in a group with less than US$3,000 GDP per hectare (Russian Federation, US$923; Canada US$1,650; Australia US$1,831; Argentina US$2,293, Iceland US$2,376; and Brazil US$2,414).

In neither Brazil nor Australia is it feasible for government to monitor what is happening or, often, is it possible for government to intervene – and the opportunities to fund biodiversity protection and restoration from local resources are limited. The scale – and thus the cost – of the required work, limited local funds and voter demands for better conservation, taken together, cause governments to rely on regulation in an attempt to force private lands conservation and restoration even when payments for environmental services (PES) might be more effective and equitable (Ball et al., 2019).

Implementing a PES system requires an environmental services buyer with sufficient income to pay for the required activities. Often, the only potential buyer is the government, who may avoid this role because of budget priorities. This can make a PES approach non-feasible in practice even if attractive in theory. International investment can sometimes help fill this gap, and Brazil has benefitted from international support, consistent with the requirements of article 20(2) of the *CBD*. For example under the REDD+ (MMA, 2016b) carbon credits scheme, biodiversity and social investment for Brazil are interwoven in an economic mechanism using payments for carbon sequestration to also fund social and biodiversity protection (see UN REDD Program website, n.d.).

Funding strategies

In both Brazil and Australia, government investment to protect and restore the environment, and to catalyse private investment is essential. Direct government environmental expenditure includes: acquiring and managing protected areas; regulation and enforcement; environmental monitoring and reporting; scientific research, education and extension; and biodiversity projects of government agencies (e.g. biosecurity and invasive species control, and restoration of habitats). Environment protection also requires government to recognise that policies that limit environmental impact assessment and provide environmentally perverse incentives and weak project level control undermine environmental governance (Rocha, 2017). Such policies and their implementation shape not only government actions but private investments that affect biodiversity. Regulations requiring habitat to be maintained on private lands, and taxation concessions for private environmental works, catalyse private conservation; taxation rules can support environmental philanthropy; public co-investment facilitates private conservation and restoration projects; regulatory hybrids support self-regulation; and laws that prohibit harm to biodiversity can motivate private investment (Martin et al., 2017).

Neither Australia nor Brazil has coherent and feasible environmental investment strategies to tackle the many practical resourcing and incentives challenges of government agencies, corporations or private citizens. Neither country has reported on strategies for biodiversity financing and incentives in their fifth reports on the implementation of the CBD (Department of the Environment, 2014; MMA, 2016a) because those strategies do not exist.

Partly in an attempt to bridge the funding gap, UNDP established the UN Development Program Biodiversity Finance Initiative (UNDP Biofin, n.d.) in which 35 countries participate in a structured approach, modified to suit each jurisdiction, to develop funding strategies for biodiversity conservation (UNDP, 2018). The Biofin process involves a review of policies and institutional arrangements, public and private expenditures (including projections) and estimation of what funds are needed to implement national plans (see, e.g. NBA, 2019). UNDP Biofin lists 68 categories of funding tactics. Actions are prioritised, and implementation and outcomes are monitored.

Brazil is a party to the UNDP Biofin but it has not created a business plan for the environment. Developing such a plan for Brazil or Australia would be complicated but a feasible funding strategy is essential to enable full implementation of national strategies. In neither country is government investment in biodiversity protection or exploitation consistently reported. Nor is any investment made in biodiversity protection categorised in a way that facilitates analysis of funds sources and uses or the funding gap. Private exploitation, conservation expenditures and voluntary and philanthropic investments are neither quantified nor reported. To estimate how much should be spent requires assumptions about what end-state for biodiversity must be achieved, how it can be achieved and what expenditure will be needed, but no national analysis of these fundamental matters is available.

Governments can (and do) attempt to force private landholders to undertake biodiversity activities using command and control mechanisms, such as laws that require landholders to control invasive species or retain habitat. This is a feature of biodiversity protection in both countries, particularly the protection of native habitat through legal controls over land-clearing. However, using regulation in this way has often led to political backlash and failure because of insufficient investment in enforcement and support. The approach also often involves administrative inefficiencies, for example in controlling permits. In addition, regulation is generally not well suited to forcing sustained positive action on private land and so can be intrinsically inefficient. For these reasons, economic incentives for private landholders may be more effective and efficient than regulation, but these are only possible if there are sources of funds to implement them. Innovations in taxation, philanthropy, investment institutions are needed to plug this large fiscal gap.

Despite experiments with new public/private investment models, to date neither the federal nor state governments in either country have shown much enthusiasm for a more strategic hybrid investment approach to biodiversity protection and restoration. The lack of innovation in funding strategies for the environment is a major impediment to more effective biodiversity protection in both countries.

As already noted, for neither Australia nor Brazil has it been possible to complete a comprehensive 'sources and uses of funds' analysis because of the many gaps in the available data and because of the lack of reliable environmental investment accounting. However, the following examination of what information is available is sufficient to support the inference that in neither country are sufficient incentives provided to motivate implementation of their biodiversity strategies, nor sufficient financial resources to do so.

Brazil

Brazil has an extensive and biologically rich land and marine area to govern, and there are many threats to its biodiversity. Brazil is not a wealthy country on a per capita basis, and it continues to be unable to invest what is required to protect its unique species. Its people and its government have a powerful incentive to develop the economy, and this provides a strong underlying negative incentive against biodiversity conservation. International environmental aid has been an important part of its efforts to protect nature.

International donations and loans generally flow to developing countries, mainly those with tropical forests. As already noted, this is consistent with the commitment of wealthier countries to support biodiversity conservation in poorer countries under the *CBD*. To elaborate, the Preamble to the *CBD* states:

> Acknowledging that the provision of new and additional financial resources and appropriate access to relevant technologies can be expected to make a substantial difference in the world's ability to address the loss of biological diversity,
>
> Acknowledging further that special provision is required to meet the needs of developing countries, including the provision of new and additional financial resources and appropriate access to relevant technologies,
>
> Noting in this regard the special conditions of the least developed countries and small island States,
>
> Acknowledging that substantial investments are required to conserve biological diversity and that there is the expectation of a broad range of environmental, economic and social benefits from those investments,
>
> Recognizing that economic and social development and poverty eradication are the first and overriding priorities of developing countries.

Within this framework, the *CBD* specifies principles for international support for developing countries in access to technology and information (art.

16, 17 and 18), and financial resources (art. 20 and 21). As a result Brazil has benefitted substantially from international support to implement biodiversity protection, including from Global Environmental Facility, the Deutsch Gesellschaft für International Zusammenarbeit, the UNDP, the UNEP, the Interamerican Development Bank, FAO, UNESCO and the EU (Godoy, 2015, p. 123; MMA, 2016a).

An example of an innovative investment programme is the *Programa Bolsa Verde* (Green Sponsorship Program), which serves a dual function of poverty reduction and payment for ecosystem services financed from the public budget. This federal programme is targeted at low income families who have an average monthly income below US$54 per person in current value (US$1.90 per day) and who live in areas that are important for environment conservation. An economic incentive of US$110 is paid every three months to stimulate the sustainable use of land, targeting individuals in land reform settlements and Traditional communities and farmers (MMA, 2013). The programme was established by *Federal Law no. 12.512/2011* and *Federal Decree no. 7.572/2011*. Its aims are rural poverty alleviation, preservation of natural resources and the conservation of ecosystems, and to engage individuals in educational activities.

This incentive benefitted 47,681 people at an annual cost of US$20,434,714 to the federal government. Seventy-eight per cent of the beneficiaries live in the Amazon biome. Based on satellite data, the Ministry of Environment reports that the programme has led to regeneration of 62,000 ha across all Brazilian biomes, including 45,000 ha in areas occupied for land reform programmes and 17,000 ha within protected areas (MMA, 2016a). However, a survey by MMA (2016c) of 1,000 people who benefitted from the programme found that, though they recognised the benefits of the programme and are aware of threats to ecosystems, they typically had not received information about the programme's context and goals. The beneficiaries lived in protected areas (conservation units) and land reform settlement areas managed by the federal government and invested around 10 per cent of the incentive on transaction costs. On average, the families had five members, with those in school age receiving education and many still lived in poverty. Most had electricity but no sewage facilities, waste treatment or water supply. Better monitoring and a link with the Rural Environmental Register (*Cadastro Ambiental Rural – CAR*) should improve effectiveness and reduce the management costs of *Bolsa Verde* (OECD, 2015, p. 39). Nevertheless, the *Programa Bolsa Verde* gradually lost resources and simply disappeared from the budget of 2018 (WWF, 2018).

Although there is wide recognition of the need to combine international financing with national government and private funding for more effective conservation, consistent with the aims of the Biofin initiative, little progress has been made other than a study of the benefits of and the need for further studies on the Ecological State Tax on the Circulation of Goods and Services (*Imposto sobre Circulação de Mercadorias e Serviços* 'Ecológico' – ICMS

'Ecológico'). The ICMS is a form of value-added tax on sales and services that are applied to: (i) the movement of goods, (ii) transportation services between several states or municipalities, as well as (iii) the telecommunications services. The tax revenue is transferred from the state government to local governments. The 'Ecological ICMS' is not a new 'ecological' tax, but it applies to environmental criteria that are included in state legislations to increase transfers to municipalities which adopt practices compatible with environmental conservation and preservation. Examples of environmental criteria are protected areas and Indigenous lands in the municipality's territory, the conservation and management of the soil and the control and combat of deforestation. The 'Ecological' ICMS can be understood as compensation mechanism for restrictions on land use to encourage the local government (Municipalities) to protect the environment (Biofin, 2018; Fonseca, 2014; Loureiro, 2002; Silva, 2005). However, in an analysis of the implementation of 'Ecological' ICMS in Pará State, Tupiassu, Fadel, and Gros-Désormeaux (2019) concluded that this mechanism rewarded the municipalities in which most of the deforestation occurs and contradicts with its compensatory and incentive functions. This study points to the need for evaluation of this instrument, taking into account the context of the Amazon region.

The innovative Brazilian Fund for Defense of Collective Rights (FDD) was created by *Federal Law no. 7.347/1985*, to compensate for damage to the environment that affects consumers, valuable artistic, aesthetic, historical, touristic or landscape assets and rights and other public interests. The FDD is administered by a council of seven representatives appointed by the government and three counsellors nominated by three NGOs, the Lawyers for a Green Planet Institute, Brazilian Institute for Consumers Rights and Public Policies and the National Forum of Non-Governmental Organizations for Consumers Defense (Leuzinger, Corrêa, & Rossiter, 2018).

The FDD is also available to support implementation, infrastructure and preservation of protected areas, recovery and preservation of natural areas, management and monitoring of species. The law permits the use of funds for eco-restoration, educational or scientific events, publications concerning the nature of infringements or damage caused, and for the modernisation of public agencies responsible for protecting the environment and other public goods. Even though FDD collected R$2.1 billion (approx. US$500 million) between 2012 and October 2017, it has allocated only R$21.7 million, a little over 1 per cent of the resources to its legal destinations; the rest of the money was allocated to primary surplus to the national treasury (Leuzinger et al., 2018).

The Brazilian Biodiversity Fund (FUNBIO) is a non-profit organisation created in 1996 as an innovative financial mechanism to implement the *CBD*. FUNBIO was initiated with a donation of US$10 million from the Global Environmental Facility. In its first round of funding, it provided US$2.4 million for ten initiatives related to natural forest management, conservation of natural ecosystems in private properties, sustainable management of fisheries resources, agriculture and biodiversity and management of protected

198 *Davi Rossiter et al.*

areas. Over 20 years, FUNBio has established partnerships with the private and public sectors and managed US$600 million in assets. It has invested into 310 protected areas covering 67 million ha and supported 270 projects from 232 different organisations (Leuzinger et al., 2018).

Brazil is more specialised in green technologies when compared to other BRICS (Brazil, Russia, India, China and South Africa) economies, although weak science-industry links, skills gaps and a complex incentive system hamper eco-innovation and the diffusion of environmental technology, goods and services. Various forms of trade protection, including local content rules, limit competition and increase environmental technology costs. Brazil makes substantial use of payments for ecosystem services (PES) and social programmes but faces implementation problems. Performance monitoring is often inadequate, regulations are heterogeneous, the effectiveness of public policies is not satisfactorily assessed, and licensing proceedings are burdensome and time consuming. Importantly, because of Brazil's substantial reliance on hydropower, with its implications for biodiversity, better integration between biodiversity conservation and energy policy is required. The OECD (2015) also indicates the need for greater use of green taxes and higher tax rates for carbon fuels, and for more effective implementation of biodiversity conservation targets (p. 18). The OECD further assesses that Brazil would benefit from better integration of environmental objectives into public investment programmes and economic policies generally (OECD, 2015, p. 19).

Australia

The Commonwealth Government of Australia is responsible for coordinating threatened species protection and recovery across states through a national framework policy. The Department of the Environment and Energy is responsible for administering the *Environment Protection and Biodiversity Conservation Act 1999* (Cth) (*EPBC Act*) and for implementing the Commonwealth's approach to threatened species management.

As has already been noted several times in this book, Australia's trend of biodiversity is poor and deteriorating. Calls for governments to increase their funding for the environment are common. However, given the scale of the funding gap for the environment, sufficient increases in public funding may be an unrealistic expectation since Commonwealth and state budgets are under pressure from terms of trade and slow economic growth, ageing population, increased demand for health care, infrastructure projects and servicing deficits. These demands mean that biodiversity conservation is often crowded out as a national priority. It is possible that government funding for biodiversity conservation will decline further.

The Australian Government has a national system of terrestrial and marine protected areas, consistent with the *in situ* biodiversity protection requirements of the *CBD*, and significant investment continues to be made to acquire and to manage these facilities. The national government also

Funding biodiversity conservation 199

conducts biodiversity campaigns, for example to control invasive species that have significant environmental impacts (e.g. feral camels and cats) and has invested substantial amounts in river and other water resources management to achieve both economic and biodiversity outcomes.

This investment is complementary to the biodiversity expenditures of state governments, which are primarily responsible under the *Australian Constitution* for landscape and riverine governance as well as operate national parks and other protected estates. In addition to federal and state investment, local governments have local protected areas and biodiversity projects and provide support for Landcare and Bushcare NGO groups to carry out on-ground works.

Many activities at all levels of government, such as road construction and maintenance, and other developments also incorporate biodiversity harm reduction components (e.g. wildlife corridors). Biodiversity protection and restoration require investment from all three levels of government, drawing on the budgets of many agencies and often involving co-investment in cash or in-kind from non-government sources. Such investment may be the cash-equivalent investment of labour, voluntary conservation areas or protective practices and cooperation. Though mixed nature of resourcing is not reliably or transparently recorded, over time, in any region, joint initiatives constitute a significant multi-party, multi-attribute approach to investment.

In 2001 Australia's national farming organisation, the Australian Conservation Foundation and the Australian Land and Water Research Organisation investigated the funding gap that then existed in biodiversity protection. It found that an investment of around AU\$6.6 billion (approx. US\$4.5 billion) per annum was needed, and AU\$3.7 billion was needed from public sources. At that time, the public investment being made was calculated at AU\$0.5 billion per annum (Madden et al., 2000). A later study for the Victorian state government (Martin & Werren, 2009) considered a number of prior studies and datasets and estimated that an amount roughly equivalent to Australia's defence budget (around 2 per cent of GDP) is required for terrestrial biodiversity conservation. Based on the 2017 GDP figure, this would represent around US\$28 billion per annum. A 2017 budget submission by the Australian Conservation Foundation and World Wildlife Fund (ACF & WWF, 2017) showed that not only have Commonwealth budget allocations for the environment declined, but institutional problems have also caused under-spending of the funds that have been allocated. They estimate that

> the total Federal Budget in 2020–2021 is projected to be 26 per cent larger than it was in 2013–2014. At the same time, environment and biodiversity spending is projected to be 41 per cent and 50 per cent lower respectively in 2020–2021 than 2013–2014 levels.

(p. 2)

Though a little attention has been paid to estimating the federal public funding gap, less has been paid to the funding gaps at the other levels of government and, particularly, to the deficiencies in private sector funding capacity to implement biodiversity protection.

The Australian Government (2019c) contends that:

> Responsibility for sustainable development and environmental steward-ship for current and future generations is shared across the community. Governments, businesses, Indigenous organisations, philanthropists, research and not-for-profit organisations and communities all have a role in this vital undertaking.

However, it is not clear what role the national government expects to have in funding biodiversity and it is even less clear what funding role is expected of the other levels of government, from industry, from NGOs and from private citizens.

Many NGOs, informal citizen groups and individuals are essential investors in biodiversity protection, through philanthropy, leveraging government grants, private investment and carrying out restoration and protection works. A decade ago, it was estimated that 8.1 million Australian adults (47 per cent) participated in nature conservation activities (e.g. planting or caring for native flora and fauna), and approximately one million Australian adults (6 per cent) participated in paid or voluntary work away from their home to conserve nature in 2011–2012 (ABS, 2013).

In the same period, around half a million Australian adults (484,000) participated in voluntary work with a nature conservation organisation (ABS, 2013). From 1992 to 2018, the total tax of deductible donations to environmental organisations amounted to AU\$2.2 billion (Australian Government, 2019c), with an upward trend in donations. Between 2009 and 2018 total tax deductible donations received by environmental organisations amounted to AU\$1.4 billion (Australian Government, 2019c).

Works by local government are important to conservation but are hampered by a lack of funds, administrative transaction costs and other difficulties in accessing funds from the two higher levels of government (see e.g. Martin & Low Choy, 2016, McKenzie & Pini, 2007). Local funding is particularly a problem for rural biodiversity protection because volatile commodity market conditions and volatile climate lead to unreliable cash flows for such areas. Funding from local sources is, thus, often intermittent but many biodiversity programmes require sustained funding to be effective. An example is the control of invasive species, where stop-start funding is not only often ineffective but can also contribute to invasive species dynamics that increase the impacts of harmful species (see Chapter 2).

The *Report on the review of the first five years of Australia's Biodiversity Conservation Strategy 2010–2030* (Biodiversity Working Group, 2016) highlighted a failure to engage all levels of government and the private sector, and two fiscal failings: weak accountability and the absence of adequate funding mechanisms to implement the strategy:

The Strategy lacked clear accountability for the implementation of actions. In many cases, the Strategy's actions are assigned to governments collectively, with broad reference to others such as the community and private sectors where applicable. Stakeholders commonly raised the framework for delivery, including funding responsibilities, as an issue with the Strategy's design as it is unclear who is responsible for action. Feedback received also advised the lack of accountability by government placed a greater strain on the under resourced conservation and land management sector.

(pp. 28–29)

As further discussed in Chapter 11, though the Commonwealth undertakes Australia's international environmental commitments, the states primarily manage land use, development approval, coastal areas and other matters that determine biodiversity outcomes. The Commonwealth does not have direct legislative power under the *Australian Constitution* for environmental issues; it uses other powers (trading and commerce (s 51(i)), taxation (s 51(ii)), quarantine (s 51(ix)), fisheries (s 51(x)), corporations (s 51(xx)), people of any race (s 51(xxvi)) and external affairs (s 51(xxix)) and cooperative arrangements which sometimes include delegations from the states to the Commonwealth to empower its interventions. To deal with this legal and practical complexity, the states and the Commonwealth use a cooperative federalism approach to national policies and strategies. Under these, the Commonwealth coordinates national action, negotiates with the states, and assumes the primary financial responsibility for many programmes substantially implemented through the states.

The ability of the Commonwealth to fund environmental programmes is a result of the Commonwealth's power to levy income and other taxes, fines and penalties, borrowing, fees for services, the sale of products and income from investments. The revenue of state governments comes from taxes on property, on employer' payroll, on a share of value-added taxes administered by the Commonwealth Government and from providing goods and services. The major source of revenue for local governments is taxes on property. The Commonwealth Government is fiscally dominant over other levels of government. The breakdown of the taxation revenue in the 2018 financial year was: Commonwealth Government AU$427,237 million (81 per cent); state governments AU$84,261 million (16 per cent); and local governments AU$18,122 million (3 per cent): a total of AUD $529,620 million (ABS, 2019).

Because of this 'vertical fiscal imbalance', the Commonwealth exercises substantial power over environmental programmes, particularly grants, delivered through the states and territories. Large scale programmes combine commonwealth and state funding, hybrid administration involving all three government levels and private partners, local government engagement and community investment and voluntary work. The Commonwealth also invests substantially in the national network of protected areas, including national parks and Indigenous Protected Areas, and in biodiversity protection and restoration on other Commonwealth lands and Indigenous Protected Areas, and marine ecosystems. Income tax deductions for environmental donations and for some biodiversity protection expenditures are also important for private biodiversity protection.

Environmental investments are affected by Commonwealth and state cost saving measures, change in policies and short term fiscal priorities. The administration of public programmes at all government levels involves transaction costs and impediments for organisations who access the limited financial support. There is evidence that the administrative transaction costs and programme uncertainty undermine citizen work for biodiversity and reform of this aspect of funding has received negligible attention (Martin & Low Choy, 2016).

The Commonwealth Government 'whole of government' environmental expenditure estimates for 2001–2002 to 2010–2011 is summarised in Figure 10.1 and is based on reports published from 2004 to 2007 (Department of the Environment, 2004, 2005, 2006, 2007).

Commonwealth projected environmental expenditure was estimated to peak at around AU$4.3 billion and has continued to decline since 2010.

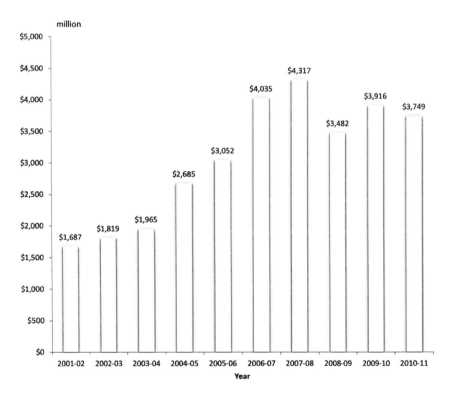

Figure 10.1 Commonwealth whole of government projected expenditure 2001–2002 to 2010–2011.
Source: Adapted from data in Department of the Environment, 2004, 2005, 2006, 2007.

However, because there is no reliable comparable data, it is unclear how much has been spent, though overall funding is clearly inadequate.

The Commonwealth government has a lead role in funding many environmental programmes; for example through the Biodiversity fund (AU$1 billion), the Natural Heritage Trust (AU$1 billion), and restoration of rivers in the Murray Darling Basin (AU$15 billion, though this investment is focused on sustainable eco-services rather than biodiversity *per se*). The Commonwealth Government's payments to support state environment services for 2018–2019 is estimated to be AU$803.4 million (Australian Government, 2019a).

The contribution of local and state government departments to natural resource management, including management of protected areas, was estimated in 2014 at around AU$4.9 billion per annum (ABS, 2014).

Despite inconsistent and confusing reporting and investment overlaps, the OECD has extrapolated that the shared jurisdictional public expenditure on biodiversity has persisted between AU$400 million and AU$500 million per year since 2010 (OECD, 2019). That report also notes, by way of contrast, that public expenditure on road transport infrastructure is around AU$13 billion per year.

Awareness of the need for private sector funding and hybrid environmental investment strategies is increasing. The Commonwealth Government's threatened species strategy aims to attract external funds to complement public investment (Australian Government, 2015). The strategy highlights that to halt the decline of Australia's threatened species, four things must be achieved: controlling feral cats, safe havens for species most at risk, improving habitat, and emergency intervention to avoid extinctions. The Commonwealth Government created the *Threatened Species Prospectus* (Australian Government, 2017) to attract private and philanthropic investment to the recovery of threatened species through a partnership between national and state government organisations, and non-government conservation and community groups.

The prospectus seeks non-government investment in 51 recovery projects of more than AU$50 million. The Australia National Audit Office has calculated that by 2018 this initiative had raised AU$5,564,958 (non-government contribution: AU$3,658,116 (65.73 per cent) and Government contribution: AU$1,906,842 (34.27 per cent)) (Auditor-General, 2018). While a useful start towards a coordinated investment approach, even AU$50 million would be inadequate to fund Australia's threatened species recovery.

Moves towards public/private funding 'cocktails' are slowly arising in some states. For example, the New South Wales Office of Environment and Heritage biodiversity investment strategy has instituted a Biodiversity Conservation Trust, aiming for private leverage of government investment of AU$240 million over five years, and AU$70 million in ongoing annual funding. The aim is to increase the private conservation estate and to provide biodiversity protection and connectivity between protected ecosystems (NSW Office of Environment and Heritage, 2018). The programme involves three categories of conservation area, reflecting the degree of legal permanence

204 *Davi Rossiter et al.*

and the level of support. It links to the state's biodiversity offset scheme under which developers can be required to fund offsetting protected areas.

Protected areas funding

Both countries have substantial protected area systems and funding to expand and to manage the system is a significant concern.

Australia's National Reserve comprises legally recognised parks, reserves and protected areas on public, private and Indigenous managed land. In 2016, the National Reserve System included 10,590 terrestrial protected areas under the jurisdiction of the Commonwealth and states governments (Department of the Environment and Energy, 2016). There are also local government parks and reserves. The National Reserve System covers 150,918,390 ha (19.63 per cent) of the Australian land mass.

Between 1996 and 2013, the Commonwealth provided approximately AU$200 million to assist in the purchase of 371 properties (around 10 million hectares) to add to the National Reserve System. This Programme was not extended past 2013 (Department of the Environment and Energy, 2019).

It is arguable that expanding protected areas may not be the most efficient investment approach to protecting biodiversity. Adams, Iacona and Possingham (2019) argue:

> The rapid expansion of the global protected area network suggests that countries are investing heavily in expansion to meet protected area targets, but there is a lack of evidence that these investments are being matched with appropriate management funding. Furthermore, many regions have established protected area networks with significant management issues; in these regions, it is probably best for investments to be in management before any further expansion. Our model results show that management provides immediate biodiversity benefits that, for many realistic scenarios, are more valuable than the future benefits achieved by expansion, and thus suggest that management should be considered just as important as, if not more important than, acquisition.
>
> (pp. 410–411)

Moreover, the:

> [S]etting aside and managing areas in the National Reserve System will not, of itself, ensure that all biodiversity conservation objectives are met. Successful biodiversity conservation requires protected areas to be established and well-managed in conjunction with the full range of conservation measures applied to other lands across the landscape.
>
> (Natural Resource Management Ministerial Council, 2009)

The estimated budgetary expenditure of the Director of National Parks (including expenditure on the Commonwealth Marine Reserves network) for employee wages, depreciation and supplies in the 2018–2019 year is AU$79 million (Australian Government, 2019b). We were unable to collate expenditure on the management of protected areas by local and state government departments.

Brazil's investment in protected areas management is low compared to other countries, at an average of AU$1.43 per hectare (overall funding remaining the same though the protected area has substantially increased). Australia spends around AU$19.64 per hectare. A 2009 study indicates that AU$208 million p.a. was needed to fund federal protected areas, with additional funds needed to compensate land owners for compulsory acquisition (Godoy, 2015, pp. 92–95).

Payments by visitors for access to conservation reserves is a possible private financing mechanism for biodiversity conservation that might be expanded, but this does require effective supervision and management. Protected areas in Brazil were visited by 4.8 million people in 2011, 4.1 million in 2010 and 2009 and 3.5 million in 2008 (Godoy, 2015, p. 105). Visitation may be theoretically possible for all categories of protected areas, but this must respect their ecological vulnerability and legal framework. Sustainable ecotourism could contribute funds for *in situ* conservation, as can access charges, user charges for recreational or athletic events, fees for camping areas, parking and housing and other services.

The Amazon Region Protected Areas Program (ARPA) is coordinated by Brazil's Ministry of Environment, with administrative and financial management assigned to FUNBIO. Its fundamental purpose is to expand the national system of protected areas. ARPA is financed by the Global Environmental Facilities, WWF-Brazil and Germany and the Amazon Fund through the Brazilian Development Bank. Norway was the main donor of the Amazon Fund and, by the end of 2016, the country has contributed 97.4 per cent of US$2.8 billion. In 2017, the Norwegian government cut its annual contribution to less than half to this fund because of increasing deforestation in Brazil (WWF, 2018). And, finally, in 2019, Norway followed Germany and completely suspended donations to the Amazon fund after the explosion on the rates of deforestation (Boffey, 2019).

The Protected Areas Fund (FAP) is another private institution for biodiversity conservation. It is an endowment fund managed by FUNBIO, capitalised through donations that are invested, with profits used to finance protected areas separately or as connected parks. A further example is the Rio de Janeiro State Fund to support native forest protection, a private financial mechanism developed by FUNBIO to target US$20 million to 40 national, state and local government protected areas. This and other examples are explained on the FUNBIO website.

Conclusions

The preceding chapters have examined aspects of agricultural, marine, mining and protected area management and, in all chapters, deficiencies in funds

206 *Davi Rossiter et al.*

feature as constraints for effective implementation of biodiversity policies and rules. In neither Brazil nor Australia is it possible to credibly assert that the *CBD* commitments to sufficient economic incentives for biodiversity protection and to provide funds to implement national biodiversity strategies have been met.

This chapter indicates that the capacity of either government to fill the funding gap from taxation revenues is insufficient to the need. Innovative approaches are needed in order to obtain leverage from the economic power of business and civil society. As yet, neither country has prioritised funding innovations, though it is clear that without these it will not be possible to implement other plans and thus achieve important biodiversity and social goals.

The UNDP Biofin programme provides a tangible illustration of the type of strategies that are needed by both countries to deal with the fiscal challenge of biodiversity protection. Whether within this programme or otherwise, a feasible investment strategy for biodiversity is essential to improving outcomes for nature in ways that are both feasible and fair.

References

ABS (Australian Bureau of Statistics). (2013). *Community engagement with nature conservation Australia 2011–2012.* Canberra, ACT. Retrieved from https://www.abs.gov.au/ausstats/abs@.nsf/0/B58ED9EDEB6CF1BECA257B39000F3870?Opendocument

ABS (Australian Bureau of Statistics). (2014). *Discussion paper: Towards an environmental expenditure account Australia; and Data Cube.* Canberra, ACT. Retrieved from https://www.abs.gov.au/AUSSTATS/abs@.nsf/DetailsPage/4603.0.55.001August%202014?OpenDocument

ABS (Australian Bureau of Statistics). (2019). *Taxation Revenue, Australia, 2017–2018.* (Catalogue No. 5506.0). Retrieved from https://www.abs.gov.au/ausstats/abs@.nsf/mf/5506.0

ACF & WWF (Australian Conservation Foundation & World Wildlife Fund). (2017). *Ongoing underinvestment in environmental protection puts all Australians at risk* (Pre-Budget Submission). Canberra, ACT: Department of the Treasury.

Adams, V., Iacona, G., & Possingham, H. (2019). Weighing the benefits of expanding protected areas versus managing existing ones. *Nature Sustainability, 2,* 404–411.

Auditor General. (2018). *Funding models for threatened species management.* Retrieved from https://www.anao.gov.au/work/performance-audit/funding-models-threatened-species-management

Australian Government. (2015). *Threatened species Strategy.* Retrieved from https://www.environment.gov.au/system/files/resources/51b0e2d4-50ae-49b5-8317-081c6afb3117/files/ts-strategy.pdf

Australian Government. (2017). *Threatened species prospectus.* Retrieved https://www.environment.gov.au/system/files/resources/86e2d7df-6523-44b4-bb7a-692576bd0d67/files/threatened-species-prospectus.pdf

Australian Government. (2019a). *Final budget outcome 2018–2019.* Retrieved from https://archive.budget.gov.au/2018-19/fbo/FBO_2018-19_web.pdf

Australian Government. (2019b). *Budget 2018–2019: Portfolio budget statements 2018–2019.* (Budget Related Paper No. 1.6: Environment and Energy Portfolio).

Retrieved https://www.environment.gov.au/system/files/resources/0349e89d-e187-415e-8568-8561177f3591/files/2018-19-pbs.pdf

Australian Government. (2019c). *A decade of donations for the environment: The register of environmental organisations (REO) Report*. Retrieved http://www.environment.gov.au/system/files/resources/9f4fe939-02f2-402e-b553-f5d2a9319327/files/reo-report-2019.pdf

Australian Farm Institute (2019). Managing agriculture's ecosystem services. *Farm Policy Journal, 16* (3).

Biodiversity Working Group. (2016). *Report on the review of the first five years of Australia's Biodiversity Conservation Strategy 2010–2030*. Canberra, ACT: Department of the Environment and Energy.

Biofin (Biodiversity Finance Initiative). (2018). *Brazil financial solutions for nature*. Brasília, Brazil: MMA.

Boffey, D. (2019, August 16). Norway halts Amazon fund donation in dispute with Brazil. *The Guardian*. Retrieved from https://www.theguardian.com/world/2019/aug/16/norway-halts-amazon-fund-donation-dispute-brazil-deforestation-jair-bolsonaro

CBD High-Level Panel. (2014). *Resourcing the Aichi Biodiversity Targets: An assessment of benefits, investments and resource needs for implementing the Strategic Plan for Biodiversity 2011–2020* (Second Report of the High-Level Panel on Global Assessment of Resources for Implementing the Strategic Plan for Biodiversity 2011–2020). Montreal, Canada.

Department of the Environment. (2014). *Australia's fifth national report under the Convention on Biological Diversity*. Canberra, ACT. Retrieved from https://environment.gov.au/biodiversity/international/fifth-national-biological-diversity-report

Department of the Environment and Energy. (2016). *Collaborative Australian protected areas database (CAPAD)*. Retrieved from https://www.environment.gov.au/land/nrs/science/capad/2016

Department of the Environment and Energy. (2019). *National Reserve System protected area requirements*. Retrieved from https://www.environment.gov.au/land/nrs/about-nrs/requirements

Department of the Environment and Heritage. (2004, May 11). *A sustainability strategy for the Australian continent: Environment budget statement 2004–2005* (Statement by the Honourable Dr David Kemp, MP Minister for the environment and Heritage). Retrieved from https://archive.budget.gov.au/2004-05/ministerial/environment.pdf

Department of the Environment and Heritage. (2005). *Environment budget overview 2005–2006*. Retrieved from http://www.environment.gov.au/archive/about/publications/budget/index.html

Department of the Environment and Heritage. (2006). *Environment budget overview 2006–2007*. Retrieved from http://www.environment.gov.au/archive/about/publications/budget/index.html

Department of the Environment and Water Resources. (2007). Protecting Australia's future: Environment budget overview 2007–2008: A long-term plan to protect and enhance Australia's natural Environment, water resources and cultural heritage. Retrieved from http://www.environment.gov.au/archive/about/publications/budget/index.html

Fonseca, R. A (2014). *O ICMS ecológico no estado de Minas Gerais* (The ecological ICMS at Minas Gerais state). (Doctoral dissertation). Universidade Federal de Lavras, Minas Gerais.

208 *Davi Rossiter et al.*

Godoy, L. R. (2015). *Compensação ambiental e financiamento de áreas protegidas* (Environmental compensation and financing of protected areas). Porto Alegre, Brazil: Fabris.

IUCN Redlist. (n.d.). Retrieved from https://www.iucnredlist.org/

Leuzinger, M. D., Corrêa, D. B. D. R., & Rossiter, M. F. C. (2018). Governance of Brazilian public environmental funds: Illegal allocation of resources collected to the fund for defense of collective rights. *OIDA International Journal of Sustainable Development, 11* (7), 11–24.

Loureiro, W. (2002). *Contribuição do ICMS ecológico à conservação da biodiversidade no Estado do Paraná* (Contribution from ecological ICMS to the conservation of biodiversity at Paraná State). (Doctoral dissertation). Universidade Federal do Paraná, Curitiba, Paraná.

Madden, B., Hayes, G., Duggan, K., The Virtual Consulting Group, & Griffin nrm Pty Ltd. (2000). *National investment in rural landscapes An investment scenario for NFF and ACF with the assistance of LWRRDC.* Canberra, ACT: Commonwealth of Australia. doi: 10.1017/CBO9781107415324.004

Martin, P., Cosby, A., & Werren, K. (2017, February 7). The environment needs billions of dollars more: Here's how to raise the money. *The Conversation.* Retrieved from https://theconversation.com/the-environment-needs-billions-of-dollars-more-heres-how-to-raise-the-money-70401

Martin, P., & Low Choy, D. (2016). *Recommendations for the reform of invasive species management institutions.* Canberra, ACT: Invasive Animals CRC Pestsmart. Retrieved from http://www.pestsmart.org.au/wp-content/uploads/2016/05/Recommendations_InstitutionsReptv2.pdf

Martin, P., & Werren, K. (2009). *An industry plan for the Victorian environment?* (Discussion paper). Melbourne, Australia: Victorian Govt, Department of Sustainability and Environment.

McKenzie, H., & Pini, B. (2007). *Factors impeding and facilitating natural resource management by local government.* Canberra, ACT: Rural Industries Research and Development Corporation.

MMA (Ministério do Meio Ambiente do Brasil). (2013). *Environmental conservation support program/Bolsa Verde* (Eradicating extreme poverty and conserving the environment). Brasília.

MMA (Ministério do Meio Ambiente do Brasil. (2016a). *5° Relatório Nacional para a Convenção sobre Diversidade Biológica de 2014* (5th national report on the Convention on Biological Diversity for 2014). Brasília. Retrieved from http://www.mma.gov.br/informma/item/10772-quinto-relat%C3%B3rio

MMA. Ministério do Meio Ambiente do Brasil. (2016b). *ENREDD+: National strategy for reducing emissions from deforestation and forest degradation, and the role of conservation of forest carbon stocks, sustainable management of forests and enhancement of forest carbon stocks.* Brasília.

MMA (Ministério do Meio Ambiente do Brasil). (2016c). *Monitoramento e difusão do programa Bolsa Verde: Relatório final de 2015* (Monitoring and reach of program Bolsa Verde: final report for 2015). Brasília.

Natural Resource Management Ministerial Council (2009). *Australia's strategy for the National Reserve System 2009–2030.* Canberra, ACT: Australian Government.

NBA (National Biodiversity Authority). (2019). *Biodiversity finance plan.* (Working Document). GoI-UNDP project on Biodiversity Finance Initiative (BIOFIN).

Retrieved from https://www.biodiversityfinance.net/knowledge-product/india-biodiversity-finance-plan

NBSAPs (National Biodiversity Strategies and Action Plans). (n.d.) *Search NBSAPs and national reports*. CBD. Retrieved from https://www.cbd.int/nbsap/default.shtml

NSW Office of Environment and Heritage. (2018). *Biodiversity conservation investment strategy 2018*. Retrieved from www.environment.nsw.gov.au

OECD. (2015). *OECD environmental performance reviews: Brazil*. Paris, France: OECD Publishing. doi: 10.1787/9789264240094-en

OECD. (2019). *OECD environmental performance reviews: Australia 2019*. Paris, France: OECD Publishing. doi: 10.1787/9789264310452-en

Pizer, W., & Morgenstern, R., & Shih, J. S. (1998). *The cost of environmental protection* (Discussion Papers, dp-98-36). Resources For the Future.

Rocha, Lilian R. L. (2017). *Desmatamento e queimadas na Amazônia (Deforestation and burning fires at Amazon)*. Curitiba, Brazil: Juruá.

Silva, S. T. (2005) Reflexões sobre o 'ICMS Ecológico' (Analysis of 'Ecological' ICMS). In S. A. S, Kishi, S. T. Silva, & I. V. P. Soares (Eds.), *Desafios do Direito Ambiental no Seculo XXI: estudos em homenagem a Paulo Affonso Leme Machado*. (Challenges of environmental law in the 21st century: Studies in honor of Paulo Affonso Leme Machado) (pp. 753–776). São Paulo, Brazil: Malheiros.

Tupiassu, L., Fadel, L. P. S. L., Gros-Désormeaux, J. R. (2019). ICMS Ecológico e desmatamento nos municípios prioritários do estado do Pará (Ecological ICMS and deforestation in Pará's Municipalities). *Revista Direito GV, 15* (3). doi: 10.1590/2317-6172201928

UNdata. (n.d.). *A world of information*. Retrieved from http://data.un.org/

UNDP: The Biodiversity Finance Initiative. (n.d.). *BIOFIN catalogue of finance solutions*. Retrieved from http://www.biodiversityfinance.org/finance-solutions

UNDP: The Biodiversity Finance Initiative. (2018). *The BIOFIN workbook 2018: Finance for nature*. New York, NY.

UN REDD Program. (n.d.). Retrieved from https://www.un-redd.org

Waldron, A., Miller, D. C., Redding, D., Mooers, A., Kuhn, T. S., Nibbelink, N., … Gittleman, J. L. (2017). Reductions in global biodiversity loss predicted from conservation spending. *Nature, 551* (7680), 364–367. doi: 10.1038/nature24295

Ward, A., & Lassen, M. (2018). *Scoping paper: Expanding finance opportunities to support private land conservation in Australia*. Trust for Nature. Retrieved from https://www.trustfornature.org.au/images/uploads/newsEvents/Publications/Conservation-Finance-Scoping-Paper-2018/Conservation-Finance-Scoping-Paper-30-October-2018.pdf

WWF (World Wildlife Fund). (2018). *Financiamento público em meio ambiente: um balanço da década e perspectivas* (Public Financing for the environment: A review of the decade and prospects). Brasília. Retrieved from. https://d3nehc6yl9qzo4.cloudfront.net/downloads/financiamentomma_final2_web.pdf

11 Governing the governance system

Paul Martin, Amy Cosby, and Carolina Dutra

Abstract

Australia and Brazil are megadiverse countries that are committed to operating a natural resource governance system to implement their international commitments under the Convention on Biological Diversity. However, both countries are facing severe loss of biodiversity with similar challenges. The overall system of governance demands more attention in order to improve its capacity and this chapter analyses how Australian and Brazilian biodiversity governance systems are working using the lens of meta-governance. The national priorities and complex arrangements regarding habitat protection, invasive species control and surface water management in Australia and rainforest protection in Brazil will be considered. 'Meta-governance' can be understood as how a governance system is managed. Based on empirical evidence about meta-governance problems that demonstrate their ineffectiveness, this chapter proposes some realistic recommendations to overcome the gaps identified.

Introduction

A minimal expectation of environmental governance is that the international commitments made by a country are efficiently implemented through local institutions. This requires appropriate instruments (laws, policies, programmes) and credible organisational arrangements (agencies, programmes and governance systems) applied and modified with integrity (Martin, Boer, & Slobodian, 2016).

The UN Information Portal on Multilateral Environmental Agreements (n.d.) lists 11 global treaties concerning biodiversity and 52 regional treaties and protocols for international environmental governance. Many are 'soft norms' with no specific commitments for the States Parties. There are also provisions in trade, intellectual property and human rights instruments with implications for biodiversity; for example, protection of free trade or international investment may facilitate environmentally harmful enterprises, or the accidental introduction of harmful invasive species.

As well as being Parties to the *Convention on Biological Diversity (CBD)* (1992), the *Cartagena Protocol* (2003) and Aichi Biodiversity Targets (CBD, 2010),

Australia and Brazil have also ratified a number of multilateral environmental agreements related to biodiversity conservation: the *Convention on the Conservation of Migratory Species of Wild Animals (CMS)*, *Convention on International Trade in Endangered Species of Wild Fauna and Flora (CITES)* (1975), *Convention on Wetlands of International Importance Especially as Waterfowl Habitat (Ramsar Convention)* (1987), *Convention Concerning the Protection of the World Cultural and Natural Heritage (UNESCO-WH)* (1972). In the case of Nagoya Protocol, Brazil and Australia have signed it but have not already ratified it. In this chapter, our focus is predominantly on biological diversity and, thus, primarily on the *CBD* and related instruments, but our observations about meta-governance are relevant to other conventions.

Despite international commitments and local arrangements, Australia and Brazil suffer serious biodiversity declines. In their regular *CBD* reports, both countries highlight many programmes and laws (Department of the Environment, 2014; MESBF, 2015), and their national strategies indicate many actions (MoE, 2017; NRMMC, 2010) but, in both countries, aspects of biodiversity are in crisis.

In this chapter, we suggest that the fundamental problem is the failure to implement standards of governance which are expected of public or private organisations: the existence of sound strategies, implementation with integrity, monitoring and performance reporting, continuous improvement and feasible approaches to resourcing those strategies. The absence of these management requirements will undermine the effectiveness of any public policy. Before beginning the discussion on meta-governance, the next sections outline the meaning of a number of key terms used in the chapter. The sections that then follow discuss meta-governance, the challenges of biodiversity challenges and the strategies employed by Australia and Brazil to meet those challenges.

Key terms

- Governance: the legitimate exercise of ongoing control (also management, supervision) over the operation of a social system (e.g. a country, community or organisation) to direct how it behaves and ensure its integrity.
- Institutions: public and private rules and the organisations that create, interpret or apply them. This includes public and private, national and international arrangements.
- Environmental governance: governance directed towards the sustainable, equitable and efficient use of the environment conducted by institutions using methods that may include laws, social norms, incentives and social or cultural interventions.
- Environmental law: methods of environmental governance that use norms supported by the authority of the State, including government regulation and administrative rules, private contract and international agreements.

212 *Paul Martin et al.*

Meta-governance

The CBD aims for conservation, sustainable use of biodiversity and equitable sharing of benefits from genetic resources. The *CBD* can be seen in two ways. The most common is that it is a collection of individual requirements that include principles of environmental law. Implementation is about meeting each commitment or applying each principle as a distinct requirement. The alternative interpretation is that the states that have ratified it agreed to implement comprehensive systems for environmental governance, with specific commitments and principles being part of this system, as well as a commitment to implement a comprehensive and disciplined governance framework to ensure transparency, adequate resourcing and other governance elements so that biodiversity is protected and used fairly.

'Meta-governance' connotes how a governance system is managed, controlled or directed (see Muelman, 2008, pp. 66–86; Muelman & Niestroy, 2015). A natural resource governance system comprises rules, strategies and organisational structures to direct how natural resources are used and conserved, and how the costs and benefits are allocated. One aspect is the legal institutions and instruments that work with other socio-economic interventions to direct government and private activities. Such a system requires investment and the effective and efficient allocation of resources indicated by the *CBD*'s Preamble and articles 11, 20 and 21. Also specified in the *CBD* is the need for objective evaluation and disciplined continuous improvement using a scientific approach, that is, objective analysis of empirical evidence, and transparency concerning the analysis and results (articles 7, 21, 23(4), 24, 25, 26 and Annex 1).

Corporate and public sector good governance has five essential ingredients, some envisaged by the texts of the *CBD*.

1 A sound strategy: A 'formula' to allocate resources within the anticipated context to achieve priority objectives is contemplated by *CBD* article 6(a) and (b). *CBD* strategies and key documents of signatory countries are lodged with the Secretariat. There is no peer review or good practice standards for these strategies, though the Secretariat does provide guidance for reports.

2 Adequate resources: Anticipated by *CBD* article 11 (incentives for biodiversity conservation) and article 20, which require each signatory state to provide 'in accordance with its capabilities, financial support and incentives' to implement its plans. There is no assessment of whether these fiscal requirements have been met.

3 Clear accountability for implementation and outcomes: National accountability is relevant but so too is accountability for subordinate roles and responsibilities. There is no independent review of national strategy implementation. National Aichi Targets and the UN Sustainable Development Goals (SDGs) could eventually support objective performance

reviews. As elaborated upon below, many datasets contain relevant information and some provide comparative information on governance (e.g. the Global Integrity Reports) (Global Integrity, n.d.), the World Bank Worldwide Governance Indicators (WB, n.d.), the SDG Country Profiles and the Yale Environment Performance Index (EPI, 2019). However, there is no international verification of implementation.

4   Risk management: Human endeavours can fail, demonstrated by failures in biodiversity protection. Failure can mean that the outcomes fall short or that perverse outcomes arise (Martin & Williams, 2010). In engineering or business, there are well-known methods (including international standards) for risk management but public policy risk management is under-developed. There is no requirement for States Parties of the *CBD* to manage risks to their biodiversity strategies.

5   Arrangements to ensure accountability, transparency and efficient resourcing: Good governance requires that responsibilities are clearly allocated to appropriate groups, and there is an independent audit of assessed performance and reports.

In this chapter, we consider whether these elements of governance are evident in the implementation of biodiversity protection laws.

The governance challenge

Australia is a sparsely settled, wealthy country with a rich environmental heritage, partly because European settlement occurred barely 200 years ago. It has a reliable legal and political system and many environmental institutions. Other chapters highlight aspects of Australia's environmental governance: ratification of international environmental conventions and statements of intent; laws, policies, incentives and economic instruments; private standards and codes; active non-government organisations and an ethos that values Australia's biodiversity. Notwithstanding, a biodiversity disaster is underway, indicated by the number of species under threat of extinction – at least 63 mammal species, 52 bird species, 125 fish species and 108 higher plant species (WB, 2019). It is reasonable to question Australia's environmental governance and, thus, whether the meta-governance that should ensure the reliability, integrity and continuing improvement of that system is adequate.

Brazil is the largest country in South America and the fifth largest in the world. It hosts varied ecosystems, including Amazon and Atlantic rainforests and Cerrado (savanna), and has the greatest biodiversity of the megadiverse countries. It is an upper-middle income country with an uneven population density and, like Australia, the coastal zone is the most heavily populated. The promotion of sustainable development is constrained by socio-economic inequality – partly due to slavery and the consequences of its abolition – and

214 *Paul Martin et al.*

problems with the supply of essential services (access to water, sanitation, health, education, public security, housing, energy, etc.) (Oxfam, 2017). Its environmental heritage faces serious threats from historical land use, cycles of exploitation and industrialisation. The country has public corruption issues (ranking 105th out of 108 countries on the perceptions of corruption index, with Australia being 77th (Transparency International, 2018)) and a political system that privileges (wealthy) private interests. These characteristics entrench inequality, further disempowering poor, Indigenous and Traditional peoples (Transparency International, 2018). Brazil has the 10th highest Gini rating for inequality at 51.3, which is only slowly improving (Australia is 102nd with a rating of 34.7, which is gradually worsening (Index Mundi, n.d.)). Socio-economic-political problems taint environmental management.

The chapters in this book highlight that Brazil has many public and private environmental organisations. It has often been a pioneer in international environmental conventions and declarations; constitutionalising social and environmental rights, with abundant laws, policies, incentives and economic instruments at all levels of government; it has private standards and codes of conduct in some industries; active international organisations and NGOs; and its population is generally proud of its natural heritage and wishes that government would partner more effectively with its citizens for biodiversity protection (Gesisky, 2018). Like Australia, these positive aspects of biodiversity protection have not created good outcomes for nature. There are 175 bird, 80 mammal, 93 fish and 558 higher plant species under threat of extinction (WB, 2019). The continuing decline indicates problems of accountability, effectiveness and efficiency of governance.

Biodiversity strategies

The boundaries and components of biodiversity governance are not 'cut and dried'. Social justice, health, welfare, trade, industry, housing, relationships with animals and other issues impact on or are affected by nature; for example, mines governance is interwoven with human habitation and welfare, and riverine and terrestrial biodiversity; economic and industrial systems are interwoven with farming's impacts; culture and recreation either negatively or positively impact/protect coastal systems; environmental laws interact with finances and social, economic and environmental systems, and thus their governance, are deeply interwoven. Other chapters describe law and policy strategies and instruments that are consistent with arrangements envisaged by international commitments. In implementation of the *CBD* principles, both countries have made progress in converting international commitments into formal laws and policies, and there has been reasonable progress 'on paper' with institutional arrangements, but there are failings in providing sufficient resources and taking the necessary actions for the implementation of policies and strategies. (Martin, Leuzinger, & Silva, 2016)

Other evaluations point to governance issues, though none assess how well environmental governance *per se* is managed:

- The Yale Environmental Performance Index (EPI, 2019) provides an overall score and rating which, arguably, indicates meta-performance (inferring meta-governance). Australia is ranked 21st of 180 countries with a score of 74.12. Brazil is ranked 69th with a score of 60.70.
- The SDG scorecard (Sustainable development reports, n.d.) provides metrics for the 17 SDGs notably: SDG 6 (water and sanitation), 7 (energy), 11 (cities and communities), 12 (consumption and production), 13 (climate), 14 (life below water) and 15 (life on land), with the last two emphasising biodiversity. In 2017, Australia's index score was 73.9, rated 38/162 countries, and Brazil's scored was 70.6, rated 57/162. It was assessed that both Australia and Brazil face challenges with governance of life on land and under water, and Brazil was assessed as showing moderate improvements on marine issues.
- The Biodiversity Indicators Partnership (BIP, 2019) provides links to indicator datasets on Aichi Targets, the SDGs and other agreements, for various themes (e.g. agriculture, species, marine biodiversity) and for governance (finance, research and knowledge; policies and conservation actions). It provides access to country indicators.
- Environmental governance is affected by overall governance, including the efficiency of democratic institutions, citizen participation and corruption. The World Bank Governance Indicators website (WB, n.d.) provides a national assessment under six categories: citizen participation, political and social stability, the effectiveness of government, regulation, the rule of law and corruption. Table 11.1 summarises the findings of five of the categories.

There are many international environmental governance instruments (see, e.g. UN Information Portal on Multilateral Environmental Agreements, n.d.). Many have principles or flexible norms that suggest what the state 'could' do, reflecting a content of 'soft norms'. A smaller number create specific binding obligations. Instruments in trade, intellectual property and human rights also have environmental implications; for example, free trade or international investments may contribute to the spread of invasive species or of land clearing for agriculture, constraining implementation of environmental obligations.

The efficiency of environmental governance is affected by jurisdictional complexity (stronger coordinating mechanisms are needed when structures are fragmented and complicated) and by meta-governance to monitor and direct government agencies. Biodiversity governance occurs at national, regional and local level. In Australia, responsibilities are shared by a federal government, eight states and territories and 565 local councils, with 56 regional natural resource management organisations. In Brazil, the national environmental system (SISNAMA) involves federal agencies, 26 states and

Table 11.1 World Bank Governance Indicators for Australia and Brazil (2019)

Indicator	Country	Year	Governance Score (−2.5 to + 2.5)[a]	Percentile Rank (0 to 100)[b]	Standard error[c]
Political stability and absence of violence/ terrorism	Australia	2008	0.96	80.29	0.26
		2013	1.03	83.41	0.23
		2018	0.98	82.86	0.21
	Brazil	2008	−0.31	33.65	0.24
		2013	−0.26	36.97	0.23
		2018	−0.36	31.90	0.21
Government effectiveness	Australia	2008	1.79	95.63	0.23
		2013	1.64	94.79	0.22
		2018	1.60	92.79	0.22
	Brazil	2008	−0.09	52.43	0.20
		2013	−0.09	50.71	0.19
		2018	−0.45	36.06	0.18
Regulatory quality	Australia	2008	1.77	96.60	0.24
		2013	1.80	97.16	0.22
		2018	1.93	98.08	0.22
	Brazil	2008	0.05	54.37	0.18
		2013	0.07	54.50	0.17
		2018	−0.31	39.90	0.18
Rule of law	Australia	2008	1.77	95.19	0.17
		2013	1.78	95.77	0.15
		2018	1.72	92.79	0.16
	Brazil	2008	−0.32	46.15	0.14
		2013	−0.08	52.58	0.13
		2018	−0.28	44.23	0.14
Control of corruption	Australia	2008	2.04	96.13	0.17
		2013	1.79	93.84	0.14
		2018	1.81	92.79	0.14
	Brazil	2008	0.01	59.22	0.15
		2013	−0.08	55.92	0.13
		2018	−0.42	40.38	0.12

Source: Adapted from WB. (2019). *Worldwide Governance Indicators*. Retrieved from http://info.worldbank.org/governance/wgi/Home/Reports

a Higher score corresponds to better governance.
b Rank of country among all countries.
c Lower values indicate better precision.

the Federal District, as well as 5,570 municipalities. In both countries, there are overlaps and gaps in responsibility, and politics complicates protection and investment in the environment.

National, state and regional government regulation of land use, natural resources use, animal welfare, food and other agricultural product standards, waste disposal, intellectual property, corporate regulation, transportation and many other institutional arrangements all affect biodiversity. Laws that have apparently little or nothing to do with the environment have an underestimated role. Taxation, for example, provides incentives or tax deductions for resource exploitation, production infrastructures or environmental protection. Property and civil rights, Indigenous rights, Minority rights, and contracts all play a part in private transactions. Administrative law is fundamental to environmental approval of impactful developments and much government action. Unfortunately, governance is rarely influenced by systematic empirical assessment of whether instruments work and what collateral effects arise. As shown in Table 11.2, different approaches have been taken to policy instruments by Australia and Brazil at national, state, local government and private sector levels.

Under the Australian federation, constitutional authority for natural resources primarily lies with the states. The Commonwealth Government's involvement is mainly through the *Environmental Planning and Biodiversity Conservation Act 1992 (EPBC Act)*, through funding programmes (See Chapter 10) and through coordinated arrangements, such as the National Water Initiative (APEEL, 2017a). The Commonwealth Government has authority over marine issues, national protected areas, preventative biosecurity and international investment. Many other overlapping matters require coordination but there is no standing body for nationally coordinated environmental governance. A Council of Australian Governments (COAG) is responsible for federal and state coordination on selected issues, exemplified by the *National Water Initiative* (COAG, 2004) but no longer has an environment coordination group. The ECOLEX (n.d.) legislation database (not specific to biodiversity) for Australia counts over 3,600 environmental instruments, including some redundant and procedural matters.

Brazil is also a federation with three levels of government with legal authority for natural resources: (a) environmental legislation is the duty of federal

Table 11.2 Australian and Brazilian examples of policy instruments for the environment

Instrument	Australian examples	Brazilian examples
Taxes Fees Charges	• Excise taxes on petroleum products • Great Barrier Reef: Charges on tourist-related services and structures • Environment protection fees	• Contribution for intervention in economic domain (excise tax on fuels) • Royalties on oil and gas • Energy development charge
Tradeable permits	• Renewable energy certificates • Emissions reduction fund • National water market	N/A
Deposit-refund systems	• Deposit-refund system for beverage containers • Cash for containers	N/A
Environmental subsidies	• Caring for Our Country • Green loans programme • National solar schools programme	N/A
Voluntary approaches	• Australian packaging covenant • Bush tender • Land for wildlife	N/A

Source: Adapted from OECD. (n.d.). *Database on policy instruments for the environment.*

congress (creating overall rules), state and federal district parliaments (supplementing federal law) and municipal by-laws. As for the Australian case, the ECOLEX (n.d.) environmental legislation database lists Brazil's environmental laws: 2,671 instruments. The resulting complexity is exemplified by the Brazilian system of environmental reserves, with different types of protected areas created by all levels of government.

The many instruments and administrative transactions create concerns about 'red tape' or 'green tape'. Unfortunately, red tape reform often results in broad deregulation rather than opportunities to both reduce red tape and strengthen biodiversity protection by administrative streamlining. Efficiency criticisms of 'green tape' and restrictive regulation show that environmental safeguards impose two types of cost: intentional restrictions of activities to protect biodiversity and the costs of restoration and protection; and transactions costs. Incidental transaction costs, such as the costs of securing and administering government grants or coordinating programmes, or the administration and reporting involved with resource development and resource use licences, affect efficiency. Other forms of transaction costs are the government costs of supervision and enforcement of rules, and the cost of subsidies and their administration. Both public and private regulations impose both types of transactions costs.

Though commentators lump intended opportunity costs and obligations with transaction costs as 'green tape', this is imprecise. To label intentional constraints as 'inefficiencies' ignores the role of government to impose constraints on self-interest in the public interest and treats one possible social goal (wealth) as paramount. Incidental transaction costs and the opportunity costs of unnecessary or ineffective constraints can be more credibly criticised.

The *CBD* embeds the principle that harm-doers should meet the cost of preventing and remediating preventable harms and – by implication – beyond this, protection and restoration are the economic responsibility of all citizens (see Chapter 3). Other chapters in this book highlight how self-interests and politics often distort *CBD* principles in ways that privilege some stakeholders.

CBD articles 11 and 20 acknowledge that private incentives and resources are essential, but neither Australia nor Brazil has integrated public/private biodiversity funding strategies. The involvement of business is increasing, driven by politics, consumer demand, corporate responsibility and social licence initiatives (e.g. the UNEP finance and insurance programmes, the World Business Council for Sustainable Development and industry environmental standards and certification programmes listed in the Ecolabel Index (Ecolable, 2019)). Chapter 7 examines hybrid – government–private – governance in Australia and Brazil.

All levels of government in both countries promote economic exploitation of nature while attempting to govern harms. Rezoning of land to industrial or residential development, extractive industry development and export promotion for primary products increase pressures on biodiversity. Environmentally harmful subsidies are a policy problem not addressed as part of Australia or Brazil's biodiversity protection strategies.

Australia's meta-governance

Australia reflected its ten *Aichi Biodiversity Targets* in its *Strategic Plan for Biodiversity 2011–2020* (NRMMC, 2010). It planned that, by 2015, Australia would have: increased citizen participation and the involvement of Indigenous people, doubled its ecosystem services markets; added 600,000 km^2 of habitat for conservation, and 1,000 km^2 of landscapes and aquatic systems restored for connectivity; reduced invasive species impacts; have science priorities for biodiversity; reviewed federal and state conservation instruments and established a biodiversity monitoring and reporting system. Targets for habitat or species were not specified. That plan largely ignores state and local government agents, civil society and business; the plan also ignores how Australia will fund incentives and resourcing (Martin, Cosby, & Werren, 2017).

An evaluation of the first five years of implementation of the national biodiversity strategy, involving the three levels of government, reported 'good progress on some of its ten measurable time-bound targets' but did not evaluate relevant programmes to inform the 2011–2020 strategy. The report concluded that the targets were inadequate and did not communicate effectively or provide adequate guidance to those who should be involved. It found that not enough attention was paid to non-rural contexts and urban people. The report also found that 'the Strategy has not effectively influenced biodiversity conservation activities', partly because of a lack of oversight and coordination; insufficient attention to implementation and responsibility, and an unrealistic approach to monitoring and reporting. The authors noted the failure to address commitments and principles from the *CBD*, particularly to ensure economic incentives and funding (Department of the Environment, 2014, p. 27).

A 2013 review praised Australia's network of protected reserves (or protected areas) but stated that 'while Australia's nominally 'protected' areas increase in area, the trajectory of real commitment to conservation is in decline, along with Australia's biodiversity' (Ritchie et al., 2013). In the same year, the Australian Senate enquiry into biodiversity protection highlighted 44 areas where improvement was needed (Environment and Communications References Committee, 2013), noting the need to: harmonise national and state processes; reduce transaction costs; increase monitoring and evaluation; institute a comprehensive biosecurity system; refine the regulatory system; engage all government, private sector, including commercial actors; better target frontline funding and conduct better reviews and audits.

Two years later, an analysis of Australia's threatened species management identified weaknesses in protection and recovery management, and resource allocation (McDonald et al., 2015). It identified a gap between processes and scientific good practice (notably concerning risk) and funding problems. Along with process reform, it recommended a relatively small increase in funds, and greater transparency to improve protection.

The comprehensive *National State of Environment Report 2016* (Metcalfe & Bui, 2017) used scientific data about Australia's environment.[1] The study provides 72 report cards reflecting almost 1,200 specific assessments. The report, unfortunately, neither documents nor critiques the programmes of the three levels of government, civil society and industry, nor evaluates governance, including whether continuous improvement in policy and practice occurs. It does, however, assess biodiversity management in the form of a dashboard showing a status grade and a five-year trend, a degree of confidence in the grade and trend, and, where possible, a comparison between the two periods for biodiversity management. The evaluated performance varies widely between issues (i.e. protected areas, threatened species, management of climate and pollution issues, natural resource use, habitat conservation, grazing pressure and invasive species) but performance on all but a few is rated at the unsatisfactory end of the scale.

Publishing in the same year, the Australian Panel of Experts in Environmental Law (APEEL, 2017a) analysed Australia's environmental laws. Nine reports assessed marine, coastal and terrestrial biodiversity, environmental governance core principles and institutional arrangements, climate, community engagement and the role of private enterprise (Farrier et al., 2017; Fowler, Makuch, Richardon, & Walmsley, 2017; Fowler, Wilcox, Martin, Holley, & Godden, 2017; Lindsay, Jaireth, & Rivers, 2017; Richardson, 2017). Fifty-seven reforms were proposed to legal environmental governance (APEEL, 2017b). The analysis and recommendations indicate failures to translate principles of the *CBD* and other instruments into Australian laws, weaknesses in organisational arrangements and insufficient resources and political commitment.

All these reports indicate that Australian governments have 'cherry picked' their international commitments, ignoring many and adopting others to a limited degree. Australia does not plan to create the type of governance system that the *CBD* envisages, and lacks incentives and resources to improve biodiversity outcomes. Though a basic monitoring and evaluation system exists, scientific opinion suggests that this is insufficient. Evaluation is inadequate, addresses only some organisations and actions and ignores public/private interactions. Partly as a result, accountability is weak and performance is not transparent. Governance risks are not managed. The organisational structure of biodiversity governance is fragmented and coordination is limited, particularly for the major threats to biodiversity identified in Australia's 2010 biodiversity conservation strategy.

Chapter 8 details habitat loss in Australia and Brazil. An unfavourable assessment of the effectiveness, efficiency and fairness of government habitat protection undertaken by Ritchie et al. (2013) reports: laws allow an increase in exploitative uses – including logging, grazing by livestock, mining, commercial development and hunting and fishing; and Australian state governments have reversed curbs on the clearing of native vegetation outside protected areas. Adams and Moon (2013) report that remnants of native ecosystems persist on private and leasehold land and in unreserved marine areas, providing a complement to protection in reserves in Queensland (QLD) and Victoria, but laws controlling vegetation clearing have been relaxed, accelerating the loss of regional biodiversity, and conservation covenants are often tenuous. Pressey et al. (2000) note that there have been excisions of conservation land for mining, and the government of New South Wales (NSW) was considering relaxing anti-clearing laws, even though the authors demonstrated that 85 per cent of the state's native vegetation with high conservation priority was on private land. In addition, legal aid funding in NSW was wound back making it more difficult to hold the state government to environmental account (Smith, 2013).

Australia's water governance involves tensions between economic and environmental (private and political) interests, that is, primary production, domestic and industrial use, pollution and habitats. It involves managing dams and weirs, scientific and technical issues and socio-economic complexities. Management is principally the responsibility of the states and territories. However, because of the interconnectivity and increasing awareness of the 'tragedy of the commons' (Harden, 1968) in 2004, the Australian state and federal governments created the *National Water Initiative: A blueprint for water management* (COAG, 2004).

Of particular interest is the *Water Act 2007* (Cth) regulating the nationally significant Murray Darling Basin system across five states. The *Murray Darling Basin Plan* (Department of Agriculture, n.d.) is a framework for coordinated federal and state action with a budgeted investment of A$13 billion (almost US$9 billion). The plan uses tradeable water entitlements within science determined limits. This has helped reduce over-allocation but the amount of water saving for the environment and governance effectiveness, integrity and efficiency are open to debate. Water for the environment has been consistently reduced to meet agricultural and rural community demands, leading to large fish kills (MDBA, 2019). Governance has become focused on the competing interests between the environment and consumption; among different regions; between experts and agencies; among states and between states and the Commonwealth. Due to a major drought, there are proposals to further weaken environmental safeguards (Davis & Burns, 2019; Loussikian & Rabe, 2019)

The management of the Murray Darling Basin does have good governance attributes. The *Water Act 2007* (Cth) coordinates state and national government action intended to implement Australia's international commitments and incorporates a science-informed (market based) strategy to pursue environmental and socio-economic outcomes. Implementation involves specific commitments, scientific monitoring and review, clear accountabilities involving all levels of government, industry and civil society, and uses economic incentives and substantial investments. However, many critiques suggest that governance in practice falls well short of the ideal (and that even good governance may not avoid deterioration in biodiversity, given climate change) (Murray Darling Basin Royal Commission, 2019).

Australian governance of invasive species has many weaknesses, and harm from exotic weeds, animals and disease is increasing. Effective biodiversity

222 *Paul Martin et al.*

protection will require prevention of new incursions and control of established harmful species. The national government is principally responsible for international biosecurity and first-response. State governments and the community are expected to control established species. State agencies and civil organisations primarily focus on species that affect production. The many plans and programmes are fragmented and under-resourced (particularly for established environmental harm species). The *Overview* of the *National State of Environment Report 2016* (Commonwealth of Australia, 2017–2018, p. 15) identifies governance problems including insufficient resourcing and inadequate monitoring and data and tardy responses. Frontline citizen invasive species control is impeded by administrative complexity, shifting priorities and unreliable support, weak accountability and limited participation. The governance of invasive species involves many state and national strategies and fragmented by jurisdiction along the invasion curve. The official mantra of 'shared responsibility' is not based on a social consensus and, often, the motivation and capacity to embrace roles are lacking. Accountability, even for regulated responsibilities, is weak. The meta-governance of invasive species management needs reform.

A more positive view is provided by the OECD *Environment Performance Review: Australia 2019* (OECD, 2019) and Australia's fifth implementation report for the CBD (Department of the Environment, 2014). The OECD report considers issues such as the carbon intensity of energy systems but does not consider threatened species and sustainable use of biodiversity. It highlights progress in protected areas and Indigenous engagement but notes ongoing declines in biodiversity. It particularly points to the need for investment, federal/state coordination and greater citizen decision-making. The 50,000 abandoned mines needing rehabilitation and contaminated sites are discussed, as is progress in engaging the business sector. Australia's 2014 Fifth National Report under the *CBD* focuses on biodiversity status, threats and implications for people, the biodiversity strategy and action plan and implementation, 'mainstreaming' biodiversity and progress against Australia's Aichi and Millennium Development Biodiversity metrics. The report notes that 'in general, population size, geographic range and genetic diversity are decreasing in a wide range of species across all groups of plants, animals and other forms of life' but does not detail the extent nor the trend. The report presents a positive picture of national initiatives without discussing strategic problems identified in other studies. The report neither considers other levels of government and civil society organisations, nor the role of business.

The fifth report does highlight targets where Australia has made progress – essentially those under the direct control of government, such as protected areas and government programmes. It does not discuss targets that require other stakeholders to take effective action, where progress has often been uninspiring. The response to a question on what has been learned from implementation is sanguine, highlighting a focus on managing total systems, on the benefits of local engagement, leadership in protected areas and baseline data and environmental metrics. Self-criticism (or even reporting criticisms) is not reported. Omitting critiques minimises serious challenges of coordination, incentives and resources and fragmentation to Australia's implementation of the *CBD*, for which better strategies are required.

The Australian government has circulated a first draft of the next national strategy; it is limited in scope (Biodiversity Working Group, 2018). The draft has been criticised for being a public-relations approach, with a lack of commitments or plans and a failure to address the failings of earlier strategies or the principles of the *CBD* (Ritchie, Christensen, Bateman, & Nimmo, 2018).

Australia does have much to be proud of in its legal, market and social instruments. However, implementation (particularly resourcing) is insufficient to meet the challenges, as highlighted in earlier chapters. As Jackson et al. (2017, p. 57) note, the lack of a robust meta-governance framework contributes to:

- Lack of a cohesive policy and legislative framework that deals with the complex and systemic nature of the issues to provide authority for actions to protect and maintain Australia's unique natural capital.
- Poor collaboration and coordination across sectors, levels of government (national, state and territory and local councils) and managers (public and private), over time.
- Inadequacy of data and long-term monitoring.
- A lack of follow-through from policy to action.
- Insufficient resources for environmental management and restoration.
- Inadequate dealing with cumulative impacts.

Brazil's meta-governance

In 2002, Brazil adopted its initial *National Biodiversity Policy* using existing laws (i.e. the *Forest Code* (*Federal Law no. 4.771/1965*, revoked by *Federal Law no. 12.651/2012*, the *New Forest Code*), the *National System of Conservation Units* (*SNUC Law, Federal Law no. 9.985/2000*) and new laws such as the *Biosafety Law* (*Law no. 11.105/2005*),the *National Strategy for Invasive Alien Species* (*CONABIO Resolution no. 05/2009*) and the *Biodiversity Law* (*Federal Law no. 13.123/2015*). Formulation of the 2020 biodiversity goals involved a consultation process initiated in 2011 which underpinned the Brazilian Panel on Biodiversity to promote synergy between institutions, disseminate knowledge and support decision-making for the *Aichi Targets*.

In 2017, Brazil adopted its recent strategy (MMA, 2017), with 20 national targets:

1 By 2020, at the latest, Brazilian people are aware of the values of biodiversity and the steps they can take to conserve and use it sustainably.
2 By 2020, at the latest, biodiversity values, geo-diversity values and socio-diversity values have been integrated into national and local development

224 *Paul Martin et al.*

and poverty reduction and inequality reduction strategies, and are being incorporated into national accounting, as appropriate, and into planning procedures and reporting systems.

3 By 2020, at the latest, incentives harmful to biodiversity, including the so-called perverse subsidies, are eliminated, phased out or reformed in order to minimise negative impacts. Positive incentives for the conservation and sustainable use of biodiversity are developed and applied, consistent and in harmony with the *CBD*, taking into account national and regional socio-economic conditions.

4 By 2020, at the latest, governments, private sector and stakeholders at all levels have taken steps to achieve or have implemented plans for sustainable production and consumption to mitigate or prevent negative impacts from the use of natural resources.

5 By 2020, the rate of loss of native habitats is reduced by at least 50 per cent (in comparison with the 2009 rate) and, as much as possible, brought close to zero, and degradation and fragmentation are significantly reduced in all biomes.

6 By 2020, all stocks of any aquatic organism are managed and harvested sustainably and legally, and apply ecosystem based approaches so that overharvesting is avoided, recovery plans and measures are in place for depleted species, fisheries have no significant adverse impacts on threatened species and vulnerable ecosystems, and the impacts of fisheries on stocks, species and ecosystems are within safe ecological limits, when scientifically established.

7 By 2020, the incorporation of sustainable management practices is disseminated and promoted in agriculture, livestock production, aquaculture, silviculture, extractive activities and forest and fauna management, ensuring conservation of biodiversity.

8 By 2020, pollution, including from excess nutrients, has been brought to levels that are not detrimental to ecosystem function and biodiversity.

9 By 2020, the National Strategy on Invasive Alien Species is fully implemented, with the participation and commitment of states and the elaboration of a National Policy, ensuring the continuous and updated diagnosis of species and the effectiveness of Action Plans for Prevention, Contention and Control.

10 By 2015, the multiple anthropogenic pressures on coral reefs, and other marine and coastal ecosystems impacted by climate change or ocean acidification are minimised so as to maintain their integrity and functioning.

11 By 2020, at least 30 per cent of the Amazon, 17 per cent of each of the other terrestrial biomes and 10 per cent of the marine and coastal areas, especially areas of particular importance for biodiversity and ecosystem services, are conserved through protected areas foreseen under the SNUC Law and other categories of officially protected areas such as Permanent Protection Areas, legal reserves and Indigenous lands with

native vegetation, ensuring and respecting the demarcation, regularisation and effective and equitable management, so as to ensure ecological interconnection, integration and representation in broader landscapes and seascapes.

12 By 2020, the risk of extinction of threatened species has been significantly reduced, tending to zero, and their conservation status, particularly of those most in decline, has been improved.

13 By 2020, the genetic diversity of microorganisms, cultivated plants, farmed and domesticated animals and of wild relatives, including socio-economically as well as culturally valuable species, is maintained, and strategies have been developed and implemented for minimising the loss of genetic diversity.

14 By 2020, ecosystems that provide essential services, including services related to water, and contribute to health, livelihoods and well-being, are restored and safeguarded, taking into account the needs of women, Traditional peoples and communities, Indigenous peoples and local communities and the poor and vulnerable.

15 By 2020, ecosystem resilience and the contribution of biodiversity to carbon stocks has been enhanced through conservation and restoration actions, including restoration of at least 15 per cent of degraded ecosystems, prioritising the most degraded biomes, hydrographic regions and ecoregions, thereby contributing to climate change mitigation and adaptation and to combatting desertification.

16 By 2015, the *Nagoya Protocol on Access to Genetic Resources and the Fair and Equitable Sharing of Benefits Arising from their Utilization* is in force and operational, consistent with national legislation.

17 By 2014, the national biodiversity strategy is updated and adopted as policy instrument, with effective, participatory and updated action plans, which foresee periodic monitoring and evaluation.

18 By 2020, the Traditional knowledge, innovations and practices of Indigenous peoples, family rural producers and Traditional communities relevant for the conservation and sustainable use of biodiversity, and their customary use of biological resources are respected in accordance with their uses, customs and traditions, national legislation and relevant international commitments, and fully integrated and reflected in the implementation of the *CBD*, with the full and effective participation of Indigenous peoples, family rural producers and Traditional communities, at all relevant levels.

19 By 2020, the science base and technologies necessary for enhancing knowledge on biodiversity, its values, functioning and trends, and the consequences of its loss, are improved and shared, and the sustainable use of biodiversity, as well as the generation of biodiversity-based technology and innovation are supported, duly transferred and applied. By 2017, the complete compilation of existing records on aquatic and terrestrial fauna, flora and microbiota is finalised and made available through permanent

226 *Paul Martin et al.*

and open access databases, with specificities safeguarded, with a view to identifying knowledge gaps related to biomes and taxonomic groups.

20 Immediately following the approval of the Brazilian targets, resources needs assessments are carried out for the implementation of national targets, followed by the mobilisation and allocation of financial resources to enable, from 2015 on, the implementation and monitoring of the *Strategic Plan for Biodiversity 2011–2020*, as well as the achievement of its targets.

Roles and responsibilities are defined. Implementation of the *National Biodiversity Action Plan* (MMA, 2005) and the *National Biodiversity Targets* (MMA, 2017a) are the responsibility of the Secretariat of Biodiversity of the Ministry of Environment. The National Biodiversity Commission (CONABIO) (created by *Federal Decree no. 4.703/2003* and modified by *Federal Decree n. 4.987/2004*) identifies priority areas for the conservation, sustainable use and sharing of benefits from Brazilian biodiversity (see *Federal Decree no. 5.092/2004* and MMA *Administrative Ruling no. 126/2004*, updated by MMA Administrative Ruling no. 9/2007 and CONABIO Administrative Ruling no. 463/2018). Other public bodies have responsibilities for biodiversity management, with the plan being part of the broader national environmental policy. CONABIO, however, has been dis-established by *Federal Decree no. 9.759/2019* that extinguished collegiate organs at the Federal level and limited the creation of new ones, having an impact at environmental democracy.

Brazil has plans for protected areas, monitoring and combatting deforestation under the *SNUC Law*. Its protected area categories include Permanent Protection Areas and legal reserves (regulated by the *New Forest Code of 2012*), and Indigenous and Traditional lands, pursuing interconnectivity, integration and representation of ecosystems (Brazil's National Target 11, Aichi Target 11). The categories broadly serve the same functions as the IUCN Protected Area Categories.

Brazilian Federal agencies have been re-organised around the following functions: advice (legal, communication, institutional relations, internal control, etc.); management (international relations, forest and sustainable development, biodiversity, environmental quality and ecotourism); normative/decision-making (National Environmental Council, National Legal Amazon Council, National Forestry Commission, Public Forestry Management Committee, Genetic Heritage Management Council, Benefit-sharing Fund Management Committee, etc.) and executive (IBAMA, Chico Mendes Institute and Botanical Garden Research Institute of Rio de Janeiro). The Secretariat of Biodiversity has Departments of Conservation of Ecosystems, Conservation and Management of Species, Protected Areas, Genetic Heritage and Support to the Genetic Heritage Management Council (established by *Federal Decree nº 9,672/2019*). Reports have identified that the country is progressing in environmental protection but rigorous policy implementation remains essential (OECD, 2015), but recent political statements undermine confidence in this (Atkins, 2018; Watts, 2019).

The Ministry of the Environment has 576 permanent employees, 195 Environmental Trust positions and 142 outsourced staff, with 201 employees in the Forest Service within the Ministry of Agriculture (MMA, n.d.). States and municipalities structure their biodiversity functions in various ways (consolidated data on human resources is not available).

The resources allocated by Brazil for conservation of the environment continue to be insufficient, particularly in recent years. Between 2013 and 2018, the budget for the Ministry of the Environment fell from R$5 billion to R$3.7 billion. This is around one-fifth of the Ministry of Agriculture's and one-tenth of the Ministry of Mines and Energy annual budget (WWF, 2018).

There is a great imbalance between government income from exploiting natural resources and funding for environmental protection. Between 2008 and 2018, the Federal Government raised about R$400 billion from water, oil and other minerals while the budget to the MMA to protect these resources was less than R$64 billion, less than one-fifth of the income (WWF, 2018). This trend was observed regarding states and municipalities' budgets, whose expenditure between 2008 and 2018 was about R$13.1 billion per year, with 42 per cent applied in human resources and 25 per cent in environmental investments. There are no consistent approaches; for example, Sao Paulo city spends three times more than Pará state, which is covered by the Amazon biome (WWF, 2018). The agency most affected by 2018 funding cuts was the Chico Mendes Institute for Biodiversity Conservation (ICMBio), responsible for protected areas. Its budget fell by 44 per cent compared to 2017 (WWF, 2018).

An important environmental initiative is The Amazon Fund established in 2008 by *Decree no. 6,527*. It is a worldwide Results–Based Funding instrument for Reducing Emissions from Deforestation and Forest Degradation (Amazon Fund (n.d.). *Home.* n.d.; REDD+ Brasil, 2016). Its governance comprises two Committees (Guidance, with state, federal and civil society actors; and Technical, with science specialists) managed by the Brazilian Development Bank, and independently evaluated (Amazon Fund, *Monitoring Evaluations,* n.d.). Recent changes made by MMA caused an impasse with environmental agencies, civil society and Norway and Germany, the main donors (Amazon Fund, *Donations,* n.d.). A donation cut of 50 per cent from Norway (MMA, 2019) was triggered by increased deforestation in the Amazonian biome. According to the Brazilian National Institute for Space Research (INPE), deforestation of the Amazon has increased since 2018 by 278 per cent (INPE, 2019). Pereira et al. (2019) discuss the impacts of political influence on environmental policies and Freitas et al. (2018) highlight reduced environmental standards triggered by amendments to the *New Forest Code of 2012*.

According to *Annual Budget Law (Federal Law no. 13.808/2019)*, the national budget for the Ministry of the Environment is R$2.8 billion, of which R$1.7 billion is for human resources and the balance to implement federal policies. In February 2019, this budget was further reduced by 20 per cent, hampering programmes to the following extent: 95 per cent for climate change; 83 per cent for solid waste management; 69 per cent for biodiversity management;

26 per cent for protected areas; 19 per cent for research, species conservation and speleological heritage and 20 per cent in fire control (*Federal Decree no. 9,741/2019*).

Brazil's 6th report the implementation of the *CBD* scheduled originally for 2018 was being prepared by the National Biodiversity Commission (MMA, n.d.) which was dis-established by *Federal Decree no. 9.759/2019*. These reports provide useful information, but (as is the case with the Australian reports) put a 'spin' on government performance (Martin et al., 2016). There is no objective critique of the effectiveness of the National Biodiversity Policy programmes, and scientific or management data to enable evaluation is very limited. The Brazilian Biodiversity Information System (SiBBr) technical information on the conservation and sustainable use of biodiversity resources is incomplete. This system is managed by PNUD (Programa de las Naciones Unidas para el Desarrollo) and financed under project 'Technical Support to Eligible Parties to Produce the Sixth National Report to the CBD (6NR – LAC II)' with US$100,000.00. The Biodiversity Portal (funded by Germany), which provides data from information catalogued by ICMBio for protected areas and is based on the Atlas of Living Australia, provides scientific data but does not address governance (ICMBio, n.d.). Studies by non-government organisations (e.g. WWF, IUCN, SOS Mata Atlântica, Imazon e Greenpeace) and by Brazilian and foreign scholars provide independent and largely critical insights. A dataset about relevant scientific production regarding Brazilian biodiversity can be accessed from Global Biodiversity Information Facility (GBIF, n.d.). Biota Project, focused on Sao Paulo State, has also international projection on this concern (FAPESP, n.d.). Empirical analysis of biodiversity governance is not available from these platforms. This subject is addressed in general terms (e.g Moura, 2016) or with a specific focus (e.g. Martin et al., 2016).

The 2015 OECD Environmental Performance Review identified positive features of Brazilian governance, including the creation of an environmental protection regime, and comprehensive laws. However, it noted that implementation was inadequate, due to economic weakness and inequality; fragmented institutions and insufficient coordination, variations in the capacity of public institutions; the urban need for services such as water, waste management and transport; large scale land clearing and habitat destruction; and a lack of human resources for protected areas. The OECD recommended:

- Rationalise the multitude of coordination bodies to improve policy coherence.
- Streamline environmental funds and monitor them for transparency and efficiency.
- Strengthen subnational implementation and enforcement capacity.
- Develop a uniform system for environmental data, including on environmental law implementation and economic aspects of environmental policies.

Governing the governance system 229

- Require strategic environmental assessment of territorial plans and development programmes.
- Clarify the environmental licensing procedures and build administrative capacity.
- Strengthen the capacity of environmental inspectors at all levels of government and engage local communities in compliance monitoring.

Brazil's political compass has shifted away from advancing the interests of Indigenous and other minority peoples and protecting biodiversity towards economic growth. Institutional arrangements to protect biodiversity have been weakened, leading to habitat clearing and incursions into Indigenous and Quilombola (Traditional) peoples' lands. On 19 June 2019, 77 environmental law professors signed a public letter that identified ten significant institutional changes that undermine Brazil's environmental governance arrangements. These include transferring environmental protection to agencies with an economic use focus, reduced legal safeguards, downgrading environmental monitoring, reduced funds, reduced protected areas and changing their emphasis towards economic uses. These professors called on civil society, the legal community and the judiciary and the National Congress to halt the erosion of biodiversity protection (APRODAB, 2019).

Should Brazil de-prioritise its international environmental commitments, biodiversity faces profound difficulties without significant international action. Legal institutions face a culture of corruption and political compromise, with powerful economic and political interests benefiting from natural resources exploitation. Recent structural changes embed conflicts of interest within government organisations responsible for biodiversity protection. The risk that biodiversity protection will fail is high, and meta-governance safeguards are weak.

Conclusions

Though scholars may debate definitions of 'governance' or what constitutes meta-governance, governance always refers to systems to govern (alt. 'control', 'direct', etc.) a social entity (e.g. corporation, government, etc.) so that it operates efficiently and with integrity to achieve its legitimate purposes. Good governance generally requires a formula for focusing all efforts to achieve the purposes of the entity (a strategy), resources to implement that formula managed within a rational structure that allocates roles and responsibilities, accountability and transparency to ensure efficiency and integrity, and management of risk. Corporations and public agencies are also expected to ensure stakeholder participation and transparency. Meta-governance is the oversight and improvement of all these elements of good governance.

Other chapters in this book show that Australia and Brazil's biodiversity institutions involve complex public and private rules and organisations, policies and strategies, incentives and supports. They suggest a commitment to international environmental agreements but they also show that the performance of this system is not protecting the natural heritage. Every biodiversity challenge involves complex socio-ecological dynamics with many actors and changing contexts; distinct governance approaches (including many laws, administrative and private rules) are used; implementation of governance arrangements is limited by insufficient science and resources and socio-political complexities; and the outcomes are variable (at best) and unsatisfactory (generally).

There are gaps in adopting international commitments, notably the absence of strategies for non-government actors (particularly the business sector) or with subordinate governments, and a failure to align economic incentives and to ensure economic and human resources for implementation. Ratified international instruments that contain environmental principles (i.e. the precautionary principle and the recognition of minority interests in nature) had driven the adoption of these principles into local law. However, their translation into the practice has been weakened by the administration or judicial interpretation. Robust meta-governance would make it transparent whether these principles have been effectively adopted into local laws, policies and programmes.

Both countries use many instruments and programmes, and much useful work and substantial investment have occurred. Without this, biodiversity loss would have been far worse. The three levels of government in each country have agencies, rules and programmes to manage the use or conservation of biodiversity. However, neither country has adequate coordination and harmonisation, and both lack robust and transparent evaluation of national, state and local programmes. In both countries, confidence in environmental governance has sometimes been shaken by indications of weak integrity in public agencies. Coordination and integrity are aspects of implementation where better supervision would give confidence to the community and contribute to effective governance.

Underperformance is often because there are not enough resources for public agencies, business or civil society organisations to do what is needed. A lack of private incentives to invest in protecting biodiversity adds to this problem. Neither country has made a serious attempt to systematically address these problems. Though it is unrealistic to believe in a simple solution, there is a strong case for tackling these fundamental economic-ecological governance problems.

This chapter and the other chapters in this book highlight that biodiversity governance in both countries has many failings. There are many 'wicked problems', but some are conceptually straightforward even if difficult in practice to deal with. No international or domestic body has meta-governance responsibility, which makes it easier to 'paper over' serious problems. This reduces the impetus towards effective solutions and desperately needed improvement in biodiversity governance.

Note

1 The 344 datasets are retrieved from https://soe.environment.gov.au

References

Adams, V. M., & Moon, K. (2013). Security and equity of conservation covenants: Contradictions of private protected area policies in Australia. *Land Use Policy, 30*, 114–119.

APEEL (Australian Panel of Experts on Environmental Law. (2017a). Blueprint for the next generation of Australian environmental law. (2017). Sydney, Australia: APEEL. Retrieved from http://apeel.org.au

APEEL (Australian Panel of Experts on Environmental Law). (2017b). *The future of Australian environmental laws* (Overview Paper). Melbourne, Australia. Retrieved from http://apeel.org.au/papers

APRODAB (Brazilian Association of Environmental Law Professors. (2019, June 19). *Letter in defence of the environment, environmental law and national environmental policy*. Retrieved from https://www.revista-pub.org/post/letter-in-defense-of-the-environment-environmental-law-and-national-environmental-policy

Atkins, E. (2018, October 10). Jair Bolsonaro's Brazil would be a disaster for the Amazon and global climate. *The Conversation*. Retrieved from https://theconversation.com/jair-bolsonaros-brazil-would-be-a-disaster-for-the-amazon-and-global-climate-change-104617

Biodiversity Working Group. (2018*). Australia's strategy for nature 2018–2030: Australia's Biodiversity conservation strategy and action inventory – Draft*. Canberra, ACT: Australian Government. Retrieved from http://environment.gov.au/biodiversity/conservation/strategy/draft-revision

BIP (Biodiversity Indicators Partnership). (2019). UNEP WCMC. Retrieved from https://www.bipindicators.net

Boffey, D. (2019, August 16). Norway halts Amazon fund donation in dispute with Brazil. *Guardian* (online).

CBD. (2010). Aichi Biodiversity Targets. Retrieved from https://wwww.cbd.int/sp/targets/

COAG (Council of Australian Governments). (2004). *Intergovernmental agreement on a National Water Initiative between the Commonwealth of Australia and the governments of New South Wales, Victoria, Queensland, South Australia, the Australian Capital Territory and the Northern Territory*. Department of Agriculture. Retrieved from http://agriculture.gov.au/water/policy/nwi

Commonwealth of Australia. (2017–2018). *Australia: State of the Environment 2016: Overview*. Retrieved from https://soe.environment.gov.au

Davis, J., & Burns, A. (2019, October 13). As rivers and dams dry up, groundwater emerges as a new battleground in fight for water. *ABC News*. Retrieved from https://www.abc.net.au/news/2019-10-13/groundwater-the-new-frontier-for-corporations/11593610

Department of Agriculture. (n.d.). *The Murray Darling Basin Plan*. Retrieved from http://www.agriculture.gov.au/water/mdb/basin-plan

Department of the Environment. (2014). *Australia's fifth national report under the Convention on Biological Diversity*. Retrieved from https://environment.gov.au/biodiversity/international/fifth-national-biological-diversity-report

232 *Paul Martin et al.*

Ecolable. (2019). *Ecolable index.* Big Room Inc. Retrieved from http://www.ecolabelindex.com

ECOLEX. (n.d). *The gateway to environmental law.* IUCN, UNEP, FAO. Retrieved from https://www.ecolex.org/result/?type=legislation

Environment and Communications References Committee. (2013). *Effectiveness of threatened species and ecological communities' protection in Australia.* Retrieved from http://www.aph.gov.au/Parliamentary_Business/Committees/Senate/Environment_and_Communications/Completed_inquiries/2010-13/threatenedspecies/report/index

EPI (Environmental Performance Index). (2019.). *Global metrics for the environment.* Yale Centre for Environmental Law and Policy. Retrieved from https://epi.envirocenter.yale.edu/

FAPESP (Fundação de Amparo á Pesquisa do Estado de São Paulo). (n.d.). *Biota-FAPESP.* Retrieved from http://www.fapesp.br/biota/

Farrier, D., Godden, L., Holley, C., McDonald, J., & Martin, P. (2017). *Terrestrial biodiversity conservation and natural resources management* (Technical paper No. 3). Melbourne, Australia: APEEL. Retrieved from http://apeel.org.au

Fowler, R., Makuch, Z., Richardon, B., & Walmsley, R. (2017a). *The foundations of environmental law: Goals, objects, principles and norms.* (Technical Paper No. 1). Melbourne, Australia. Retrieved from http://apeel.org.au

Fowler, R., Wilcox, M., Martin, P., Holley, C., & Godden, L. (2017b). *Environmental governance.* (Technical Paper No. 2). Melbourne, Australia: APEEL. Retrieved from http://apeel.org.au

Freitas, F. L. M., Sparovek, G., Berndes, G., Persson, U. M., Englund, O., Barreto, A., & Mörtberg, U. (2018). Potential increase of legal deforestation in Brazilian Amazon after Forest Act revision. *Nature Sustainability, 1,* 665–670.

GBIF. (n.d.). *Brazil.* Retrieved from https://www.gbif.org/country/BR/summary

Gesisky, J. (2018). *Survey reveals that Brazilians wish to be closer to nature, but they think nature is not being protected as it should.* WWF. Retrieved from https://www.wwf.org.br/?67262/Survey-reveals-that-Brazilians-wish-to-be-closer-to-nature-but-they-think-nature-is-not-being-protected-as-it-should

Global Integrity. (n.d.). *Resources.* Retrieved from https://www.globalintegrity.org/resources/

Harden, G. (1968). The tragedy of the commons. *Science, 162* (3859) [December], 1243–1248.

ICMBio. (n.d.). *Portal da Biodiversidade.* Retrieved from http://www.icmbio.gov.br/portal/portaldabiodiversidade

Index Mundi. (n.d.). *GINI index (World Bank estimate) – Country Ranking.* Retrieved from https://www.indexmundi.com/facts/indicators/SI.POV.GINI/rankings

InforMEA. (n.d.). *Treaties and MEAs in Biological diversity.* Retrieved from https://www.informea.org/en/topics/biological-diversity

INPE (National Institute for Space Research) (2019). *Dashboard: Deforestation.* Retrieved from http://terrabrasilis.dpi.inpe.br/

Jackson, W. J., Argent, R. M., Bax, N. J., Clark, G. F., Coleman, S., Cresswell, I. D ... Wienecke, B. (2017). *Australia State of the Environment 2016: Overview, independent report to the Australian Government Minister for the Environment and Energy, Australian Government Department of the Environment and Energy.* Canberra, ACT: Australian Government.

Governing the governance system   233

Lindsay, B., Jaireth, H., & Rivers, N. (2017). *Democracy, and the environment*. (Technical Paper No. 8). Melbourne, Australia: APEEL. Retrieved from http://apeel.org.au

Loussikian, K., & Rabe, T. (2019, October 13). Drought-busting laws to fast- track approvals for critical projects amid $ 1b cash boost. *Sydney Morning Herald*. Retrieved from https://www.smh.com.au/politics/nsw/drought-busting-laws-to-fast-track-approvals-for-critical-projects-amid-1b-cash-boost-20191012-p5302f.html

Martin, P., Boer, B., & Slobodian, L. (2016). *Framework for assessing and improving law for sustainability: A legal component of a natural resource governance framework*. Bonn: Germany: IUCN.

Martin, P., Cosby, A., & Werren, K. (2017). The environment needs billions of dollars more: Here's how to raise the money. *The Conversation*. Retrieved from http://theconversation.com/the-environment-needs-billions-of-dollars-more-heres-how-to-raise-the-money-70401

Martin, P., Leuzinger, M. D., & Silva, S. T. (2016). Improving the effectiveness of legal arrangements to protect biodiversity: Australia and Brazil. *Revista de Direito Internacional, 13*, 25–36.

Martin, P., & Williams, J. (2010). *Policy risk assessment* (Technical Report No 03/10). CRC for Irrigation Futures. Retrieved from https://hdl.handle.net/1959.11/16257

McDonald, J. A., Carwardine, J., Joseph, L. N., Klein, C. J., Rout, T. M., Watson, J. E. M., … Possingham, H. P. (2015). Improving policy efficiency and effectiveness to save more species: A case study of the megadiverse country Australia'. *Biological Conservation, 182*, 102–108. doi: 10.1016/j.biocon.2014.11.030

MDBA (Murray Darling Basin Authority). (2019). *Fish deaths in the lower Darling*. Australian Government. Retrieved from https://www.mdba.gov.au/managing-water/drought-murray-darling-basin/fish-deaths-lower-darling

MESBF (Ministry of Environment and Secretariat of Biodiversity and Forests). (2015). *Brazil: Fifth National Report to the CDB* (January). Retrieved from mma.gov.br/informma/item/10772-quinto-relatório

Metcalfe, D. J., & Bui, E. N. (2017). *Australia state of the environment 2016 (SOE 2016)*. (Independent report to the Australian Government Minister for the Environment and Energy). Canberra, ACT. Retrieved from https://soe.environment.gov.au/

Meuleman, L. (2008). Public management and the metagovernance of hierarchies, networks and markets: *The feasibility of designing and managing governance style combinations*. Springer Science & Business Media.

Meuleman, L., & Niestroy, I. (2015). Common but differentiated governance: A metagovernance approach to make the SDGs work. *Sustainability, 7* (9), 12295–12321. doi: 10.3390/su70912295

Ministry of Climate and Environment. (2019). *Norway continues the dialogue with Brazil about the Amazon Fund*. Government of Norway. Retrieved from https://www.regjeringen.no/en/aktuelt/norway-continues-the-dialogue-with-brazil-about-the-amazon-fund/id2662831

MMA (Ministry of Environment). (2005). *Action plan to implementation of the national biodiversity plan – PAN-Bio*. Retrieved from https://www.MoE.gov.br/estruturas/chm/_arquivos/panbio%20final.pdf

MMA (Ministry of Environment). (2017). *National biodiversity strategy and action plan, 2016–2020*. Retrieved from https://www.cbd.int/doc/world/br/br-nbsap-v3-en.pdf

234 Paul Martin et al.

MMA (Ministry of the Environment). (n.d.a). *Comissão Nacional da Biodiversidade* (National Biodiversity Commission). Retrieved from http://www.mma.gov.br/biodiversidade/comissao-nacional-de-biodiversidade

MMA. (Ministry of the Environment. (n.d.b). *Servidores do Ministério do Meio Ambiente* (Ministry of Environment employees). Retrieved from http://www.mma.gov.br/mma-em-numeros/servidores

Moura, A. M. M. M. (Ed.). (2016). *Governança ambiental no Brasil: Instituições, atores e políticas públicas* (Environmental governance in Brazil: Institutions, actors and public policies). Brasília, Brazil. Retrieved from http://www.ipea.gov.br/portal/images/stories/PDFs/livros/livros/160719_governanca_ambiental.pdf

Muelman, L. (2008). *Public management and the metagovernance of hierarchies, networks and markets.* Heidleberg, Germany: Physica-Verlag.

Murray-Darling Basin Royal Commission Report. (2019). Adelaide, SA: SA Government.

NRMMC (Natural Resources Management Ministerial Council). (2010). *Australia's biodiversity conservation strategy 2010–2030.* Canberra, ACT: Department of the Environment and Energy. Retrieved from http://www.environment.gov.au/biodiversity/strategy/index.html

OECD (n.d.) *Database on policy instruments for the environment.* Retrieved from https://pinedatabase.oecd.org/Default.aspx?isid=74584dbb-b542-4635-a844-388cbf728257

OECD. (2015). *OECD environmental performance reviews: Brazil.* Retrieved from https://www.oecd.org/env/oecd-environmental-performance-reviews-brazil-2015-9789264240094-en.htm

OECD. (2019). *OECD environmental performance reviews: Australia 2019.* Paris: OECD Publishing. doi: 10.1787/9789264310452-en

Oxfam Brazil. (2017). *Inequalities in Brazil: The divide that unites us.* Retrieved from https://www.oxfam.org.br/sites/default/files/arquivos/relatorio_a_distancia_que_nos_une_en.pdf

Pereira, E. J. A. L., Ferreira, P. J. S., Ribeiro, L. C. S., Carvalho, T. S., & Pereira, H. B. B. (2019). Policy in Brazil (2016–2019) threatens conservation of the Amazon rainforest. *Environmental Science & Policy, 100* [October], 8–12.

Pressey, R. L., Hagar, T. C., Ryan, K. M., Schwarz, J., Wall, S., Ferrier, S., & Creaser, P. M. (2000). Using abiotic data for conservation assessments over extensive regions: quantitative methods applied across New South Wales, Australia. *Biological Conservation, 96,* 55–82.

REDD+ Brasil. (2016). *The Amazon Fund.* MoE. Retrieved from http://redd.MoE.gov.br/en/finance/the-amazon-fund

Richardson, B. (2017). *The private sector, Business law and environmental performance.* (Technical Paper No. 7). Melbourne, Australia: APEEL. Retrieved from http://apeel.org.au

Ritchie, E. G., Bradshaw, C. J. A, Dickman, C. R., Hobbs, R., Christopher, N., Johnston, E. L., … Woinarski, J. (2013). Continental-scale governance failure will hasten loss of Australia's biodiversity. *Conservation Biology, 27* (6), 1133–1135.

Ritchie, E., Christensen, B., Bateman, B., & Nimmo, D. (2018). Australia's draft 'Strategy for nature' doesn't cut it. Here are nine ways to fix it. *The Conversation.* Retrieved from http://theconversation.com/australias-draft-strategy-for-nature-doesnt-cut-it-here-are-nine-ways-to-fix-it-92345

Smith, J. (2013). Legal aid cuts threaten environmental justice. *EDO NSW Weekly Bulletin, 8141.*

Sustainable Development Reports. (n.d.). *Reports.* Retrieved from https://www.sdgindex.org/reports/

Transparency International. (2018). *Home.* Retrieved from https://www.transparency.org

UN. (n.d.). *Sustainable development goals (SDGs).* Retrieved from https://www.un.org/sustainabledevelopment/sustainable-development-goals/

UN Information Portal on Multilateral Environmental Agreements. (n.d.). Retrieved from https://www.informea.org/

Watts, J. (2019, June 5). Deforestation of Brazilian Amazon surges to record high. *The Guardian Online.* Retrieved from https://www.theguardian.com/world/2019/jun/04/deforestation-of-brazilian-amazon-surges-to-record-high-bolsonaro

WB (World Bank) (n.d.). *Worldwide governance indicators.* Retrieved from https://datacatalog.worldbank.org/dataset/worldwide-governance-indicators

WB (World Bank). (2019). *Data country and species datasets.* Retrieved from https://data.worldbank.org

WWF. (2018). *Financiamento público em meio ambiente; Um balanço da década e perspectivas* (Public financing of the environment: A review of the decade and prospects). Retrieved from http://www.amazonfund.gov.br/en/monitoramento-e-avaliacao/independent-evaluations/

12 Strategies to improve outcomes

Paul Martin, Márcia Dieguez Leuzinger, Solange Teles da Silva, and Gabriel Leuzinger Coutinho

Abstract

This chapter provides the central findings from this book, based on the evidence presented in previous chapters. It highlights that the effectiveness of law and policy instruments depends on a comprehensive institutional architecture, consisting of organisations, processes, coordination mechanisms and resources. An effective meta-governance system is needed to ensure that implementation is backed by sound strategies, transparent public accountability and sufficient resources. Effectiveness also requires genuine community engagement. The chapter presents proposals for fundamental improvement.

Introduction

Australia and Brazil have sometimes been pioneers in conservation, implementing major initiatives and new ideas to advance biodiversity protection and environmental social justice. Brazil was a pioneer in constitutional protection of the environment with the 1988 Brazilian Constitution – Appendix A) specifying:

> Everyone has the right to an ecologically balanced environment, which is a public good for the people's use and is essential for a healthy life. The Government and the community have a duty to defend and to preserve the environment for present and future generations.
>
> (art. 225)

Sub-clauses of the constitution establish the government's obligations and address aspects of implementation that align with the requirements of the *Convention on Biodiversity (CBD)*.

Australia has also often shown its commitment to biodiversity, exemplified by its substantial network of terrestrial and marine protected areas, its comprehensive National Water Initiative that addresses both surface and ground-water systems, and its many national, state and local laws and policies (Productivity Commission, 2017).

Beyond the actions of national governments, biodiversity in both countries benefits from delegated or independent non-government actions consistent with the *CBD* requirements. Examples are: in northern Brazil in 2016, the Pará State in the Amazonian Region had a programme to encourage the sustainable use of biodiversity, to guide public policies and to attach economic value to biodiversity (*Programa Paraense de Incentivo ao Uso Sustentável da Biodiversidade – Biopará*) *(SECTET, n.d.)*; and the 'Sinal do Vale', founded in 2011, is a local-global learning centre located at Mata Atlantica biome in Rio de Janeiro State which promotes solutions for the local community for soil and forest regeneration, classified as an 'incubator for nature conservation' (IUCN, n.d.). In Australia, a good example is citizen-led action, such as the national Landcare programme, which is significant to biodiversity protection. Though not linked formally to the *CBD*, Landcare is often harnessed for government conservation programme delivery, and this has had both positive and negative consequences for citizen-based Landcare (Alexandra, Bonacci, & Riddington, 2007; Marshall, 2008; Tennent & Lockie, 2013).

When reading the *CBD* performance reports for either country one could be led to believe that the only actions that are relevant are those carried out by the national government. State, regional and non-government initiatives are given minimal attention in the reports. This downplays the fact that it is difficult, if not impossible, to achieve effective implementation of the *CBD* commitments by governments without effectively engaging all levels of government (federal, regional and local) and the non-government sector. One of the conclusions highlighted by this book is that there is currently insufficient engagement of, and coordination between, all the levels of government and the non-government sector in the implementation of the *CBD*, in both countries.

Politics and regression

The discussions of the varied topics in this book highlight that, periodically, the governments in both countries regress in environmental law and policy, weakening their prior commitments to biodiversity protection or the interests of the poor and marginalised people who depend on and protect biodiversity. In practice, regression takes many forms. Sometimes it involves repealing or narrowing protective laws. At other times it occurs indirectly through limiting enforcement or by defunding environmental programmes. No less significantly, it also occurs in practice by the promotion and support for harm-doing activities by government agencies or the private sector.

There are ample examples of how Brazil has reduced socio-environmental legal protections. This process began in 2003 with two provisional measures (113 and 131) that liberalised the commercialisation of genetically modified Roundup Ready soybeans. This was followed by *Law no.11.105/2005* (*Biosecurity Law*) that withdrew from IBAMA the competence for the licensing of transgenics and then by the *12.651/2012* (*New Forest Code*), which reduced environmental restoration requirements for illegal damage to habitats (Soares et al., 2014, pp. 363–364) and it continued with provisional measures (Presidential provisional measures which have legal effect, e.g. *558/2012* and *756/2016*) to reduce protected areas. Proposed laws are expected to further

238   *Paul Martin et al.*

reduce biodiversity safeguards (see, e.g. von Schoenfeld, Santos, & Uchoas, n.d.). Though the Brazilian constitution recognises the rights of Indigenous people to live in their traditional territories, consistent with international commitments, the Minister of Justice, in 2017, added an administrative step to the land right process – a decision by a specialised technical group – that makes the exercise of this constitutional right more difficult (*Ordinance* (trans. "Portaria") *no. 68/2017*). This Ordinance was revoked by *Ordinance no. 80/2017*, but the specialised technical group that it created to deal with Indigenous lands demarcations continued to exist. In another example of practical regression, the Brazilian President approved provisional measures for mining sector reform (*Provisional Measures 789.790 & 791/2017*) that weakened protections against mining impacts, adversely affecting Indigenous peoples' land interests and the natural environment. These were passed without consultation with Indigenous people.

Australia's national and state governments also periodically downgrade environmental protection, mainly to reduce impediments to economic interests in natural resources. Though Brazil's land-clearing record is more widely publicised, Australia suffers an equivalent rate of (primarily tropical) habitat loss. The 2016 State of Environment Report indicates a gradual slowing in Australia's rate of land clearing since the 1900s but this is against the background of an inexorable decline in the remaining intact habitat (Bradshaw, 2012). As that amount declines, the importance of what remains increases with scarcity. Control of habitat destruction in Australia is mainly through state laws, but both state and federal development controls can apply to projects that may have significant impacts (see Chapter 3). Two issues illustrate how political factors drive regression. The first is controls on agricultural land clearing and the second is development approval, particularly of major projects in sensitive environments.

Under the *Environment Protection and Biodiversity Conservation Act 1999* (Cth) (*EPBC Act*) the Commonwealth Government has authority for nine matters of national environmental significance, and the government can intervene to address 'key threatening processes'. Land clearing is one of the 21 listed key threatening processes under the *EPBC Act*, and a listing as a key threatening process gives the Commonwealth legal power to create a Threat Abatement Plan to address the process (see Department of the Environment and Energy, n.d.). The national government has decided that no Threat Abatement Plan will be prepared for land clearing, leaving this issue substantially in the hands of the states.

Land clearing control in two states illustrates how political volatility affects whether habitat protection is effectively addressed by the states. Under a more environmentally oriented (Labor) government in Queensland (QLD), according to the 2016 State of Environment Report (Metcalfe & Bui, 2017):

> [T]he introduction of a ban on broadscale clearing that came into effect in 2006, and the extension of clearing controls to high-value regrowth in 2009, land clearing fell to a historical low of 78,378 hectares in 2009–2010.
>
> (p. 20)

Then, after a change to a development-focused state government:

> Major reforms to the Vegetation Management Act 1999 were introduced in 2013 to allow landholders to clear vegetation not cleared since 31 December 1989 .... By 2013–14, clearing had increased to 296,324 hectares. This compares with the average annual rate of land clearing before the 2006 ban of 448,000 hectares per year. A recent report by the World Wildlife Fund ... on clearing rates in Queensland found that:
>
> - clearing of non-remnant native vegetation increased from about 54,000 ha in 2009–2010 to about 183,000 ha in 2013–2014
> - clearing of remnant vegetation nearly doubled from about 52,000 ha in 2012–2013 to about 95,000 ha in 2013–2014, and has nearly quadrupled since 2009–2010
> - about 700,000 ha of high-value regrowth lost protection in 2013, and are currently being cleared
> - about 125,000 ha of remnant vegetation, including about 12,000 ha of endangered ecosystems, have been remapped as exempt from protection on regulatory maps since 2012.
>
> Land cleared in Queensland's reef catchments increased by 229 per cent from 2008–09 to 2013–14, from 31,000 hectares per year to 102,000 hectares per year. A 113 per cent increase from 2010–11 to 2012–13 coincided with the policy change to reduce compliance activities.
>
> (p. 20)

With the re-election of a Labor government in QLD, the controls were re-introduced (*Vegetation Management and Other Legislation Amendment Bill 2018* (QLD)) and the rate of land clearing reduced. In the adjoining state, New South Wales (NSW), the political tide has turned in the opposite direction, with the election of a Liberal/National Party coalition government committed to reducing impediments to agriculture. The *Biodiversity Conservation Act 2017* (NSW) now allows landholders to self-assess whether they need to apply for permission to clear bushland, a significant reduction in legal controls. Media reports indicate that the rate of habitat loss has accelerated (Davies, 2018a, 2018b).

Undermining existing laws

Regression does not necessarily require changes to the law; it can occur through budget and staff reductions of environmental agencies or policy decisions, such as deciding to limit enforcement. Though, officially, the law and policy may be unchanged and programmes ostensibly continue, in practice, implementation is weakened. The effects of political volatility on implementation in practice are demonstrated by water governance in Australia. The commitment to bring the Murray-Darling River System

240 *Paul Martin et al.*

within sustainable limits of extraction as required by the *Water Act 2007* (Cth) has been eroded by political compromises (largely in response to severe droughts). The volume of water originally calculated required to restore river health was around 4,000 ML/yr, later reduced to 3,200 ML/yr as the target within the Murray-Darling Basin Plan. This has been further reduced to a current 2,700 ML/yr goal, and the independent supervisory commission has been removed. Respected scientists indicate a significant risk that the plan will fail to meet environmental objectives, and have proposed a rescue plan (Wentworth Group of Concerned Scientists, 2017a, 2017b). At the time of writing (when a major drought is underway), political pressure to harvest environmental water reserves for agriculture and to bypass biodiversity impact assessment rules for water infrastructures is happening at federal and state levels, and further compromises are happening.

Defunding can also be a form of regression. A report by WWF-Brazil and Association Contas Abertas (2018) using public data reports a decrease in Brazilian public spending on environmental policies since 2014. In 2018, 44 per cent of funds for the ICMBio, the federal environmental agency in charge of the protected areas management, were deferred. Community programmes are also affected. For example the 2018 budget provides no funding for the Bolsa Verde' programme, which has provided R$300.00 (about US$ 70) every three months to impoverished families, who depend on natural resources in 'sustainable use' protected areas in order to incentive them to conserve biodiversity (WWF, 2018, p. 9).

In Australia because of transfers between the three levels of government and across agencies and because of how expenditures are reported, it is not possible to reliably quantify the public environmental investment declines over recent years. Anecdotal NGO reports indicate a significant deterioration in funding and staff support for biodiversity conservation and restoration. A 2017 budget submission by the WWF Australia and the Nature Conservation Council states that the federal government intended to reduce environment spending below 60 per cent of the 2013–2014 budget (additional to reductions over recent years), and the federal environment department was to reduce biodiversity protection staffing by approximately a third under a 25 per cent budget cut (Morton 2017; WWF/Australian Conservation Foundation, 2017).

In both countries, de-prioritisation of *CBD* commitments may be concealed by non-disclosure or by claims that efficient environmental protection and economic goals are being achieved by deregulation, administrative changes or reallocation of resources. There is no reliable mechanism for transparency about environmental funding in either country.

The Preamble to the *CBD* affirms that states have sovereignty over their biological resources, with article 3 stating:

> States have, in accordance with the Charter of the United Nations and the principles of international law, the sovereign right to exploit their own resources pursuant to their own environmental policies, and the

responsibility to ensure that activities within their jurisdiction or control do not cause damage to the environment of other States or of areas beyond the limits of national jurisdiction.

A government's political decision to de-prioritise the environment is, to that extent, not inconsistent with *CBD* provisions. However, periods of regression prejudice previously won environmental gains, causing a government to fail to implement its *CBD* commitments. Mechanisms to safeguard against political 'backsliding' and erosion of the integrity of implementation commitments of governments would be sensible even accepting that national sovereignty must be respected under the *CBD*.

It has been proposed that a principle of 'non-regression' within the *CBD* would help to address this problem (IUCN, 2015, art. 10; IUCN World Commission on Environmental Law, 2016, princ. 12). Our examination of implementation in this book suggests that an effective non-regression principle would require a comprehensive approach to covert regression, poor implementation, administrative arrangements, resourcing and the implementation actions of non-federal governments and agencies. There is also a risk that a poorly conceived non-regression principle could impede genuine reforms that require removing or streamlining arrangements to replace these with ones that are expected to work better. An effective non-regression principle would require a sophisticated implementation infrastructure, perhaps analogous to that for the *Aarhus Convention* that deals with principles of citizen engagement (Ebbesson et al., 2014).

Architectures, not just instruments

Related to the effects of politics on implementation is the role of the institutional 'architecture' of governance. This is the rules, jurisprudence, political and organisational arrangements that constitute the legal parts of biodiversity governance. Though the jurisprudential traditions of Brazil and Australia are different, the development of legal governance has followed similar patterns. Both countries have ratified the *CBD* and related instruments, and created environmental laws and implementation arrangements that have features in common. Both countries have had to respond to the challenges of continually declining megadiversity and the need to address the interests of Traditional and Indigenous peoples. Both countries have a tension between economic growth and biodiversity protection.

Both countries have a three-tier federated structure. Australia's federation is eight states and territories (Australia also has eight dependent territories) and 561 local government areas. Brazil's federation is 26 states, the Federal District and 5570 municipalities. The constitutions and jurisprudential traditions of the two countries are different. Notably, the Brazilian constitution has a statement of rights and the Australian constitution lacks a specific statement of rights in Australia. That is, the Brazilian constitution includes *Title*

II – Fundamental Rights and Guarantees, particularly article 5°, LXXIII, and the right to protect the environment under article 225 23; but citizen rights in Australia rely on the common law and rights and obligations under specific legal instruments. Environmental protection is not a Commonwealth power under the Australian constitution. Nevertheless, there are similar patterns in the implementation of the *CBD*.

The governance of the environment in both countries is fragmented, and the fragmentation may be increasing. Among the causes are increasing demands for land and natural resources, including for conversion of 'virgin' habitat to agricultural, mining and urban use and competition between uses. A landscape that was once a simple mosaic of native vegetation and grazing, for example, may now host many different land uses. These include public tenures (i.e. roads, forestry and conservation tenures and special uses like military reserves), private land (i.e. various types of agriculture and industry and residential land use) and special uses (i.e. Indigenous and Traditional people's land and resource rights, protected water catchments and sites of national or international significance). Some uses are incompatible, and many have competing objectives and are advocated using political rights and social power. The public interest in how lands are used or managed, particularly concerning issues like Indigenous justice, landholder stewardship, public access and use and animal welfare, has to be taken into account. These dynamics affect the governance system, as the legacy of history and institutional arrangements intersects with contemporary interests to create complicated rules, organisations, strategies and administrative arrangements (Hathaway, 2003; Leach, et al., 2007; Martin & Becker, 2011).

The first level of governance fragmentation is between national, state and local governments and between agencies at all three levels. Each level of government passes laws dealing with their responsibilities, resulting in many instruments and administrative arrangements. Government agencies have natural resource management or biodiversity policies and strategies that are independent of the arrangements of other agencies. This is evident in peri-urban landscapes where there is an intersection of public agencies responsible for urban development and agriculture or environmental protection arrangements. Environmental agencies also implement non-regulatory governance, such as protection or restoration projects and infrastructures, protected areas management, subsidy schemes, community or industry engagement and many other interventions. At all levels, government agencies are also involved in environmental harm-doing and natural resource consumption, through licences, zoning, development control or development promotion and monitoring and enforcement.

Government functions are carried out by agencies with specialised policies and programmes: agriculture, urbanisation, environment protection, social justice, economic development, protected areas and other activities that directly or indirectly affect biodiversity. In both countries, fragmentation creates transaction costs and complexity, which impede effective *CBD* implementation (Martin & Shortle; 2010; Martin, Williams, & Stone, 2008; Ruhl, 1996). These can cause problems of coordination, agency competition and conflict, fragmentation and dissipation of limited resources, confusion of stakeholders and unclear accountability.

The characteristics of biodiversity protection add to the difficulties. Many biodiversity losses are caused by the accumulation of small harms – a 'death of 1000 cuts' for the environment. Though strategies may aspire to a 'whole of landscape' or system approach, regulation and policing, impact assessment and incentive or subsidy schemes usually address narrow issues. This reduces the ability of the governance system to deal effectively with cumulative harms.

The building of infrastructure, particularly dams and roads in wilderness areas such as the Amazonian Region, illustrates the systems' characteristics of environmental degradation. These infrastructures open up areas for human access and facilitate uses that are inconsistent with biodiversity. These secondary consequences of infrastructure development are poorly considered when developments are designed and so not well managed, leading to the loss and fragmentation of habitats (Lees et al., 2016). An example is the Belo Monte Dam on the Xingu River, the development of which did not take into account cumulative harms (Panel of Experts, 2009). A recent report by the Australian Panel of Experts in Environmental Law highlighted that, in Australia, the same failure to account for cumulative impacts contributes to under-managed harms (Farrier et al., 2017).

Though, in principle, citizens in both countries have rights to assert or defend environmental interests, political and economic power imbalances reduce this equality in practice. This is demonstrated in both countries – in this book particularly with the examples of agricultural and mining interests being able to subvert or avoid biodiversity protection laws (Chapters 2, 3, 10 & 11).

Power relations in natural resource governance are difficult to deal with, they are a 'vicious' systems problem involving many sub-problems, and each proposed solution may create another problem. Managing political and economic power also involves philosophical and practical challenges. Contests over natural resources highlight the tension between the promotion of economic growth and development, and protecting those who lack economic power, future generations and the intrinsic worth of the environment.

Power dynamics have many governance effects. Stakeholders in damaging uses of nature often oppose biodiversity protection, and a strong political desire to reduce governments' shares of GDP adds to the pressure for governments to limit their involvement in protecting nature. Power battles involving private interests trigger tensions within government as ministries and agencies pursue competing public (and sometimes private) goals, and compete for economic and political capital. Powerful actors with competing interests undermine biodiversity protection politically or operationally by creating 'political economy' problems (see e.g. Rickards, Wiseman, & Kashima, 2014; Ruhl, 2012; Wimmer, de Soysa, & Wagner, 2003). In both jurisdictions, our cases show 'agency capture' instances; and 'public choice'

244 *Paul Martin et al.*

bargaining (and corruption for which we have not produced evidence) can compromise implementation of biodiversity conservation strategies.

In both countries shifts in governance power and responsibility from the public to the private sector are happening, though this trend is given limited attention in the literature (see Chapters 7 & 11, and Green, 2014). Industry creates and implements governance rules, consumer preferences lead to eco-brands or market standards that impose requirements on industries, and NGOs exercise political power to shape governance. Industry and the citizen sector have more resources than does government, some of which is applied to the environment through their purchasing and investment, including for environmental outcomes. Both countries' biodiversity strategies and reports on implementation of the *CBD* pay little attention to actions other than those of national governments. However, the convention contemplates a systematic approach, which suggests the need to pay attention to private incentives and funding to implement *CBD* obligations. The increasing importance of public/private partnerships in conservation was highlighted by the *2012 Rio +20 Declaration*, and this is reinforced by the Sustainable Development Goals (*SDGs*). The private sector has a fundamental role in shaping incentives and in providing or directing resources, which is why *CBD* implementation must aim to maximise non-government leadership while controlling harmful non-government activities. Neither Australia's or Brazil's biodiversity strategies embrace the private sector's potential role, other than as the mere subject or respondent of public sector-led initiatives.

The need for an effective public/private approach is emphasised by pressure on government budgets, compared to the growth in the private economy, and increasing demands for public investment. Attempts to overcome this fiscal problem using private sector engagement and investment have mainly involved market instruments and 'market-like' programmes, and sometimes strategies to build private investment and engagement in biodiversity protection, but these innovations are not well integrated into national strategies (OECD, 2007; Pirard, 2012, pp. 59–68; Stavins, 2002, pp. 355–435).

Industry and NGOs are involved in many sustainability activities through philanthropy, industry codes and standards, corporate environmental stewardship and public good investment and product and business accreditation and environmental branding. Though this public/private activity is not enough to overcome the impediments to environmental progress, it shows the potential of a deeper partnership approach.

Payments for environmental services (PES) can tie economic incentives to the actual delivery of outcomes, though many implementations pay for inputs and activities rather than paying for results (Alston, Andresson, & Smith, 2013, pp. 139–159; Hejnowicz, Raffaelli, Rudd, & White, 2014, pp. 83–97). There has been an increase in these instruments in Brazil under the international REDD+ scheme and local arrangements (Fearnside, 1999; Pagiola, Von Glehn, & Taffarello, 2013). An opportunity for Brazil, as a developing country with iconic biodiversity, is the ability to attract international funds, which is less available for Australia as a developed economy.

The *CBD* and related instruments imply environmental governance involving government, industry and citizen action within a system that provides sufficient incentives and resources to implement effective protection. The provisions of the *CBD* point to the need for an effective national strategy to achieve this, requiring a coordinated approach spanning all sectors and all levels and forms of government.

The 'Future We Want' Rio declaration (UN, 2012) clearly emphasised that the implementation of sustainable development will depend on the active engagement of both the public and the private sectors:

> We recognize that the active participation of the private sector can contribute to the achievement of sustainable development, including through the important tool of public-private partnerships. We support national regulatory and policy frameworks that enable business and industry to advance sustainable development initiatives, taking into account the importance of corporate social responsibility. We call upon the private sector to engage in responsible business practices, such as those promoted by the United Nations Global Compact.

Though, in both countries, governments have moved towards market instruments, in neither country is public/private biodiversity collaboration emphasised in the national strategy. This lack of engagement of the larger economy and its associated power structures in protecting biodiversity is a significant weakness.

Weak accountability and continuous improvement

The *CBD* has administrative requirements for transparency and, potentially, international accountability in the implementation of *CBD* commitments, requiring national strategies and regular implementation reports. The *CBD* webpage provides links to country commitments, strategies and performance. Country-specific Aichi Targets and SDG metrics could provide a basis for stronger accountability and transparency. Other evaluations, such as irregular Organisation for Economic Co-operation and Development (OECD) Environment Performance evaluations (OECD, n.d.), report from the International Union for the Preservation of Nature (IUCN) and other international reports add to this potential. Each country conducts its own evaluations of biodiversity outcomes, and environmental NGOs, policy and academic researchers provide additional performance data and opinions. However, this intelligence is not organised to provide systematic critical evaluation consistent with a disciplined continuous improvement approach.

Both Australia and Brazil have provided five official reports on implementation of the *CBD*, from 1998 to 2016. The sixth report is under preparation.

246 *Paul Martin et al.*

These are discussed in Chapter 11. Neither country's reports provide a comprehensive and objective review of performance. Though each acknowledges declines in biodiversity, the reports do not provide critical analysis of where governance arrangements need to improve to achieve better outcomes.

The underlying rationale for the *CBD* signatory reports should be to drive continuous improvement based on evidence. Both countries have disheartening outcomes, despite initiatives and policy experiments, such as new market instruments and community engagement programmes. However, neither country provides evidence-based reports of what has been learned, nor do their biodiversity strategies reflect a systematic scientific approach to improvement.

'Localised' interpretations or restatements of *CBD* and other international principles have led to unique approaches to implementation. One example is interpretations of the Precautionary Principle. Another is the categorisation of protected areas, where each country has tailored its approach. Australia, for example, reports Indigenous Protected Areas (IPAs) as constituting almost 45 per cent of Australia's National Reserve System. Though IPAs are managed for conservation, fitting IUCN Protected Area categories 5 and 6, these lands are owned by Indigenous people and managed generally under collective native title. They could be removed from the IPA system should the Traditional Owners decide to do so, but they are reported as part of the public conservation estate as if they were unambiguously protected for the environment.

In Brazil, the IUCN Protected Area classification has been modified. As discussed in Chapter 5, the term 'protected area' is a species of specially protected territorial space. Since 2006, protected areas include only Conservation Units (UCs), Indigenous and Quilimbola lands. UCs have 12 management categories. Federal UCs are created and managed by ICMBio, which has this specific mission. Within the 12 management categories there are five that offer full protection (IUCN categories I, II, III & IV), which do not allow direct use of natural resources) and seven offering sustainable use (IUCN categories V & VI). Those management categories are listed within *SNUC Law (Federal Law no. 9.985/2000)*, with different features and goals.

Besides conservation units, there are other types of protected areas, created by different laws. For example, the *2012 Forest Code (Federal Law no.12.651/2012)* provides two types: permanent preservation areas and legal reserves. Botanical gardens, zoos, ecological parks, among others, are protected areas that are not UCs. These have special protection because the 1988 constitution established that once a protected area is created it can only be modified or extinguished by a specific law.

The concern about local reinterpretation of *CBD* principles is for the integrity of reporting and compliance, and the potential for localisation to mask non-adherence. A lack of independent standards for assessing how countries implement *CBD* principles makes it hard to compare performance, and weakens the impetus for improvement.

The national biodiversity strategies and the national country reports on implementation of the *CBD* should be pivotal to continuing improvement. The implementation reports should identify what outcomes have been achieved compared to objective benchmarks or performance targets; the governance causes of the outcomes, including performance shortfalls and specific plans for performance improvement. It would then be possible to consider progress over time. Reports and strategies should be subject to constructive critical review from the CBD Secretariat or an independent body. Perhaps reflecting the political history of the convention and related instruments and the sensitivity of countries to any loss of sovereignty or the risk of political embarrassment, such a disciplined approach to improving biodiversity governance is not part of the *CBD* regime.

We anticipate that, in the future, specific reporting of achievement of the Aichi Targets and SDGs will create a stronger impetus for continuous improvement. However, underperforming governments are likely to want to avoid embarrassment, so slow progress towards disciplined, systematic and accountable improvement is likely without international accountability and transparency reforms.

Citizen participation arrangements need improvement

Our investigations of both countries *CBD* implementation suggests problems with implementation of principles for community engagement, which require cultural respect, access and benefit sharing provisions for Indigenous and Traditional peoples. Overall, environmental and social impact rules exist and provide opportunities for citizens to be involved in decisions. In Brazil, these rights are based in the constitution and, in both countries, environmental and planning laws mandate processes for community engagement. Effective environmental activist and advocacy groups work with citizens to use these rights. Both countries have rights for Indigenous people to be consulted on many matters important to their welfare and cultures. In both countries, courts have enforced consultative and substantive obligations on governments and developers in favour of citizens, and there is a myriad of examples of diligent implementation (see e.g. Bubna-Litic et al., 2016).

However, there are policies and practices that do inhibit effective community participation, and *de facto* derogate from the rights that exist on paper. In Brazil, the newly elected president issued a Decree that extinguished many committees and created new guidelines, rules and limitations for federal public administration committees (Decree no. 9,759/2019). This has weakened or removed institutional arrangements that previously supported citizen participation. Other examples from both countries include:

- Legislating some matters as non-appealable or non-reviewable administrative or ministerial decisions; or imposing restrictions on appeal or review.

248 *Paul Martin et al.*

An Australian example is the limiting appeal rights under the *Water Act 2007* (Cth) to holders of water licences, for a limited set of matters.

- Failing to implement legislated requirements. An example from Brazil is implementation of *Presidential Decree no. 4,340/2002*, which requires civil society-based management councils. Only 149 of 844 conservation units for sustainable use have these and of the full protection units, 118 of 149 comply.
- Failing to take citizen views into account, even if those views are clear. An example from Brazil is the process of creating conservation units (UCs) where public consultation is mandatory other than for biological reserves and ecological research stations. This is to help manage the risk that new UCs may exclude traditional land users. For federal UCs, ICMBio conducts public hearings but consultation imposes no obligation on ICMBio to take community views into account.
- Legal and administrative arrangements which designate some development as 'nationally significant' or 'state significant', with reduced citizen rights of review or objection. Chapter 3's discussion of the Australian Adani example illustrates how this can abrogate citizen rights.
- Using consultation or other practices that limit engagement or participation so it becomes non-feasible for citizens to participate, or makes engagement ineffective.

The central feature of citizen participation is the extent of power held by the citizen compared to that of institutional power-holders such as government agencies or corporations. The engagement continuum ranges from informing citizens of decisions, through to full empowerment where citizens make the decisions that affect them (Arnstein, 1969). Empowerment results from formal arrangements and from the quality and integrity of implementation. There are many possible engagement processes but no validated best practice in either country or an institutional guardian of engagement quality.

Citizen engagement is emphasised in Australia's current 2010–2030 Biodiversity Strategy (Ministerial Council, 2010): Priority for action 1: Engaging all Australians in Natural Resources Management (p. 71). The engagement strategy proposes three tactics for engaging all Australians: mainstreaming biodiversity; Indigenous engagement and strategic investments and partnerships. The performance targets do not focus on biodiversity outcomes or the effectiveness of engagement, and the tactics proposed do not address known engagement impediments, including bureaucratic complexity, insufficient resources and the lack of legal standing. Performance benchmarks and action accountabilities are non-specific. The draft of the proposed replacement strategy, *Australia's strategy for nature 2018–2030: Australia's biodiversity conservation strategy and action inventory* (Biodiversity Working Group, 2018), has a goal to 'connect people with nature' and another 'to build and share knowledge' but contains no reference to participatory approaches or community decision-making. Unlike in Brazil, there is no constitutional protection for the environment or citizen rights to the environment. Many laws limit or circumvent citizen rights (Lindsay, Jaireth, & Rivers, 2017).

Citizen engagement is often restricted by a lack of resources. Depending on the issues, the process and how the issues arise, money, skills and other resources for effective participation may not be available. This problem is significant when consultation on planned developments or other approvals involves specialist technical knowledge. An example is the approval of genetically modified crops and new chemicals; both countries have a science-based risk management process for approving the release of such innovations (Hayek, 1942; Kinchy, Lee Kleinman, & Autry, 2008) but when citizens lack the technical knowledge or money to pay for independent experts or for technical research their ability to participate effectively is minimal.

Neither Australia nor Brazil is signatory to the *Aarhus Convention*, with its binding commitments and implementation arrangements for community participation that include legal rights, judicial and administrative mechanisms and other arrangements. Implementation of this convention is evaluated and transparently reported (Dellinger, 2012; for Australia, see Lindsay et al., 2017). Brazil has signed the Escazu Convention, the first Regional Agreement on Access to Information, Public Participation and Justice in Environmental Matters in Latin America and Caribbean Region. However, throughout the negotiation process Brazil lobbied for a non-binding instrument, which suggests that ratification may not be immediate.

Meta-governance is inadequate

With increased natural resource demand and declining availability, and the proliferation of resource uses and technologies tensions over resource development projects like mines or dams are complicated. Community engagement and objective assessment can be bypassed because of political considerations, which calls into question the integrity of biodiversity governance.

Transparent self-evaluation by government of their implementation of the national biodiversity strategy is limited despite NGO and industry criticisms of government action. There is a tendency for governments to minimise or at least channel criticisms, and this weakens accountability. Independent environmental agencies, empowered to provide for 'full and frank' evaluations of environmental governance performance, would provide greater transparency and support continuous improvement and integrity (see Fowler et al., 2017; Shearman, 2018).

Corruption can undermine biodiversity protection, and 'agency capture' and political path dependence are pervasive issues that are hard to address (Rickards et al., 2014). In both Australia and Brazil, examples from mining and habitat destruction show that political compromises of environmental protection rules can facilitate harm to the environment (Chapters 5 & 8).

250   *Paul Martin et al.*

The signatories to the *CBD* have formally committed to creating incentives and ensuring adequate resources to implement biodiversity strategies. However, a lack of resources explains many of the failures of biodiversity governance. The capacity of private landholders (particularly small-scale farmers and Indigenous or Traditional communities) is limited, and neither country has an investment strategy for the environment (Chapter 10). The lack of a viable funding plan to implement biodiversity protection is a deficiency in the biodiversity strategies of both countries.

The cost of detecting landscape harm, restoring a landscape, species recovery and species protection can be very high. Australia and Brazil have large areas needing protection and many vulnerable species. The investment required is substantial. Pressures on public finance and political pressures on environmental protection have meant that, in both countries, government environmental agencies have had their budgets reduced. More resources might come from new sources, including taxation, industry investment, philanthropy and in-kind work carried out by landholders and other members of civil society, but innovation in how biodiversity is funded is not an explicit priority in either country.

For example, in Brazil, the Ministry of Environment 2018 budget was the lowest for the previous five years. In 2013, the expenses of the Ministry and its agencies (ANA, IBAMA, ICMBio) was R$5.056 billion (about US$1.3 billion). In 2017, this had been reduced to R$3.953 billion (less than US$1 billion) and in 2018, to around R$3.5 billion. ICMBio was the most affected agency, receiving R$708 million compared to R$1.256 billion in 2017 (WWF, 2018, pp. 8–9). As the number of conservation units they administer has increased, the budgetary gap has grown. An analogous situation exists in Australia. Over the longer term, there has been a growing funding gap for the environment, and declines in public funding have made this worse (Martin, Cosby, & Werren, 2017; Morton, 2017). In both countries, agencies have not always been able to spend what they have been allocated because of fiscal, programme and political constraints. In Brazil, mandatory 'contingency reserves' amounted to R$422.5 million in 2018 (Cardoso, 2018), and Australia's under-spending is substantial (ACF & WWF, Australia, (2017), particularly Chart 1 Decline in actual and forecasted Federal Environment Department appropriations).

Other pressures can compromise implementation of conservation strategies. Powerful economic and political forces can undermine biodiversity protection and competing community values can make implementation of environmental policy difficult. Without a sufficiently strong social consensus in favour of the environment, the pressure for political compromise and the fear of political backlash can undermine the willingness of public servants to implement policies. The combination of insufficient funds and manpower, unfavourable political contexts, strong opposition from some interests coupled with the scale of the biodiversity protection challenge, impedes implementation of biodiversity protection.

Looking to the future

Demands for natural resources are likely to increase because of population growth, *per capita* consumption, commercial and technological change and the consequences of past mismanagement. It is likely that, as supply and demand combine to drive the economic value of resources, political pressures to compromise environmental protection will intensify. There will need to be significant improvement in biodiversity governance instruments and institutions if the outcomes from environmental protection are to improve.

Further innovation in governance is needed. Our analysis in this book shows the need for transparent evaluation and reporting, and for stronger integrity mechanisms, better participatory processes and safeguards against social injustice and unfairness. Our analysis also points to gaps in economic incentives and resources for implementation of biodiversity protection and restoration strategies (Chapter 11).

In both countries, authority, responsibility and resources are fragmented across organisations, levels of government, programmes and policies. As the issues themselves become far more complicated, more systematic responses are needed and current structures are unlikely to provide these.

There is pressure to minimise the Government share of the economy in both countries. Industry increasingly implements environmental and social justice 'good citizenship' rules, independent of government. The private sector will become more important through market instruments and by entrusting industry with governance responsibility. In some instances, this is evolving towards 'hybrid governance', where governments delegate some regulatory roles to private citizens and industry (Chapter 7).

A hybrid model has many things in its favour, when it can be made to work. The economic capacity of industry and the citizenry dwarfs that of government, and marketplace incentives offer a motivational power that the public sector cannot match. Industries understand the activities and participants in their sectors, which should enable efficient governance and can operate without the political complexities that impede governments.

However, the significant risks must be addressed. Neither jurisdiction has a strategy for shared environmental governance that provides a reliable framework for responsibility and authority. Over and above concerns about 'greenwash', these 'experiments' with markets and regulatory partnerships are not yet evolving into a coordinated strategic approach. Unsuccessful innovations could undermine the role of government and the capacity of the public sector to protect the public interest. As with public environmental governance generally, adequate evaluation and public reporting of governance performance is lacking.

That serious implementation problems exist, as demonstrated in the preceding chapters, without attracting transparent self-criticism by the countries themselves or by the convention parties, is a concern. Achieving significant improvement does require honest reflection and a strong commitment to better performance.

252 *Paul Martin et al.*

We anticipated, at the commencement of the study reported on in this book, that we would arrive at a mix of domestic and international issues. What we have found is that most issues span both dimensions. Our research points to four essential improvements in international and domestic biodiversity governance that should be addressed at both levels.

The first is the need for disciplined, comprehensive and transparent performance review and accountability. The preceding chapters show many situations where *CBD* commitments and the laws and policies that are meant to translate these into domestic application are not being implemented or not being implemented effectively. As discussed, this is for a many reasons, including political impediments, organisational and administrative failings and insufficient resources for government and citizen actors to do what is necessary. However, the community is not provided with reliable objective reporting of how governance arrangements are working, and, as a result, government is not pursuing the disciplined continuous improvement approach to biodiversity protection that is essential to achieve better results.

This problem should be addressed at two levels. First, national governments need to create better environmental governance frameworks: clear strategies that systematically address all their obligations and which address all levels of government and private stakeholders, objective review of implementation and results, funding plans that address the needs for the plans that are announced, transparent performance accountability for both implementation responsibilities and results and strong safeguards against potential failures of integrity. Second, the *CBD* Secretariat, with the support of the international community, needs stronger processes to evaluate and report signatory state implementation of all *CBD* and related commitments, and to promote disciplined continuous improvement. The Aichi Targets and SDGs could provide a useful tool to focus improvement, though caution is needed to ensure that what is evaluated is directly relevant to the specific commitments that have been made.

Community engagement in biodiversity protection has many aspects. One is increasing community awareness and supervision of implementation of biodiversity strategies. We were surprised to find, in our study for this book, that few experts or other stakeholders we spoke to had reviewed their country's national reports of *CBD* implementation and environmental. It was also surprising that NGOs do not publish public assessments of the implementation of *CBD* commitments. NGO evaluation of *CBD* reports could provide an additional impetus for improvement in national biodiversity governance.

There are many opportunities to improve citizen participation in both countries. As we noted, neither Australia nor Brazil is party to the *Aarhus Convention*, with its well-developed and documented principles and implementation arrangements, process guidelines and legal instruments. Even if there are political or legal barriers to joining this convention, adopting many of its principles, processes and legal arrangements would be one way of addressing the failures of citizen participation in biodiversity protection in both countries.

To satisfy the *CBD* commitments, ensuring that incentives and resources are aligned in support of national programmes is fundamental to achieving the better environmental and social outcomes that are the underlying purpose of these international agreements. Neither country has an investment plan for the environment, or an economic strategy for the environment. Countries are not required to address these fundamental, pragmatic aspects of the *CBD* but they should be.

This book has provided detailed evidence about the implementation of the *CBD* and related instruments in two countries. It shows that progress has been made but that that progress is insufficient to solve the major problems of sustainability. It further shows that biodiversity governance failure is endemic as is the underperformance of international and domestic instruments. It provides recommendations designed to have a systemic effect on improving implementation of international and domestic policies.

The need to improve implementation is fundamental, and our hope is that this book will add to the impetus towards governance solutions that will work.

References

ACF & WWF (Australian Conservation Foundation & World Wildlife Fund). (2017). *Ongoing underinvestment in environmental protection puts all Australians at risk* (Pre-Budget Submission). Canberra, ACT: Department of the Treasury.

Alexandra, J., Bonacci, M., & Riddington, C. (2007). *Public-private partnerships for reforestation.* Canberra, ACT: RIRDC.

Alston, L. J., Andresson, K., & Smith, S. M. (2013). Payment for environmental services: Hypotheses and evidence. *Annual Review of Resource Economics, 5* (1), 139–159. doi: 10.1146/annurev-resource-091912-151830

Arnstein, S. R. (1969). A ladder of citizen participation. *Journal of the American Institute of Planners, 35* (4), 216–224.

Biodiversity Working Group. (2018). *Australia's strategy for nature 2018–2030: Australia's Biodiversity conservation strategy and action inventory – Draft.* Canberra, ACT: Australian Government. Retrieved from http://environment.gov.au/biodiversity/ conservation/strategy/draft-revision

Bradshaw, C. J. A. (2012). Little left to lose: Deforestation and forest degradation in Australia since European colonization. *Journal of Plant Ecology, 5* (1), 109–120. doi: 10.1093/jpe/rtr038

Bubna-Litic, K., Goreham, E., Pope, T., Becker, K., & Craig A. (2016). Australia: Participation principle and marine protected areas. In P. Martin, B. Boer, & L. Slobodian (Eds.), *Framework for assessing and improving law for sustainability* (pp. 17–31). Gland, Switzerland: IUCN.

Cardoso, A. (2018, January 19). *Orçamento para o Meio Ambiente em 2018: pior do que parece* (Environmental budget 2018: Worse than it sounds. *INESC.* Retrieved from https://www.inesc.org.br/orcamento-para-o-meio-ambiente-em-2018-pior-do-que-parece/

Davies, A. (2018a, August 4). Clearing of native vegetation in NSW jumps 800 % in three years. *The Guardian.*

254 *Paul Martin et al.*

Davies, A. (2018b, July 9). Illegal land clearing in NSW may be accelerating, complaints data suggests. *The Guardian.*

Dellinger, M. (2012). Ten years of the Aarhus Convention: How procedural democracy is paving the way for substantive change in national and international environmental law. *Colorado Journal of International Environmental Law and Policy, 23* (February 2012), 311–364.

Department of the Environment and Energy. (n.d.a). *Species profile and threats database.* Retrieved from http://www.environment.gov.au/cgi-bin/sprat/public/publicgetkeythreats.pl

Department of the Environment and Energy. (n.d.b). *Indigenous protected areas.* Retrieved from http://www.environment.gov.au/land/indigenous-protected-areas

Ebbesson, J., Gaugitsch, H., Jendrośka, J., Stec, S., & Marshall, F. (2014). *The Aarhus convention: An implementation guide.* Geneva, Switzerland: UN Economic Commission for Europe.

Farrier, D., Godden, L., Holley, C., McDonald, J., & Martin, P. (2017). *Terrestrial biodiversity conservation and natural resources management* (Technical paper No. 3). Melbourne, Australia: APEEL. Retrieved from http://apeel.org.au/s/APEEL_Terrestrial_biodiversity_conservation_NRM.pdf

Fearnside, P. M. (1999). Biodiversity as an environmental service in Brazil's Amazonian Forest: Risks, value and conservation. *Environmental Conservation, 26* (4), 305–332.

Fowler, R., Wilcox, M., Martin, P., Holley, C., & Godden, L. (2017). *Environmental governance.* Melbourne, Australia: APEEL. Retrieved from http://apeel.org.au/s/APEEL_Environmental_governance-9688.pdf

Green, J. (2014). *Rethinking private authority: Agents and entrepreneurs in global environmental governance.* Princeton, NJ: Princeton University Press.

Hathaway, O. A. (2003). Dependence in the law : The course and pattern of legal change in a common law system. *Public Law and Legal Theory, 270.*

Hayek, F. A. (1942). Scientism and the study of society. *Economica, 9* (35), 267–291.

Hejnowicz, A. P., Raffaelli, D. G., Rudd, M. A., & White, P. C. L. (2014). Evaluating the outcomes of payments for ecosystem services programmes using a capital asset framework. *Ecosystem Services, 9,* 83–97.

IUCN. (2015). *Draft international covenant on environment and development: Implementing sustainability 5th edition* (31 Rev. 4). Gland, Switzerland: IUCN.

IUCN World Commission on Environmental Law (2016). *World declaration on the environmental rule of law.* Rio de Janeiro, Brazil: IUCN.

IUCN (n.d.) *Incubator for nature conservation: Sinal do Vale.* Retrieved from https://www.iucn.org/theme/environmental-law/our-work/protected-areas-pas/incubator-nature-conservation-inc/sinal-do-vale

Kinchy, A. J., Lee Kleinman, D., & Autry, R. (2008). Against free markets, against science? Regulating the Socio-Economic Effects of Biotechnology. *Rural Sociology, 73* (2), 147–179.

Leach, M., Bloom, G., Ely, A., Nightingale, P., Scoones, I., Shah, E., & Smith, A. (2007). *Understanding governance: Pathways to sustainability.* (STEPS Working Paper 2). Brighton, UK: STEPS Centre. doi: 10.1039/b810642h

Lees, A. C., Peres, C. A., Fearnside, P. M., Schneider, M., & Zuanon, J. A. S. (2016). Hydropower and the future of Amazonian biodiversity. *Biodiversity Conservation, 25,* 451–466. doi: 10.1007/s10531-016-1072-3

Lindsay, B., Jaireth, H., & Rivers, N. (2017). *Democracy, and the environment* (Technical Paper No. 8). Melbourne, Australia. Retrieved from http://apeel.org.au/s/APEEL_democracy_and_environment.pdf

Marshall, G. (2008). *Community-based, regional delivery of natural resource management: Building system wide capacities to motivate voluntary farmer adoption of conservation practices.* Canberra, ACT: RIRDC.

Martin, P., & Becker, J. (2011). A tale of two systems: Conflict, law and the development of water allocation in two common law jurisdictions. *International Journal of Rural Law and Policy, 1,* 1–18.

Martin, P., Cosby, A., & Werren, K. (2017, February 7). The environment needs billions of dollars more: Here's how to raise the money. *The Conversatio.* Retrieved from https://theconversation.com/the-environment-needs-billions-of-dollars-more-heres-how-to-raise-the-money-70401

Martin, P., & Shortle, J. S. (2010). Transaction costs, risks, and policy failure. In C. D. Soares, J. E. Miller, H. Ashiabor, L Kreiser, & L. Deketelaere (Eds.), *Critical issues in environmental taxation: International and comparative perspectives* (pp. 705–720). Oxford: Oxford University Press.

Martin, P., Williams, J., & Stone, C. (2008). *Transaction costs and water reform: The devils hiding in the details* (Technical Paper, vol. 08). Sydney, Australia: CRC for Irrigation Futures.

Metcalfe, D. J., & Bui, E. N. (2017). *Australia state of the environment 2016 (SOE 2016).* (Independent report to the Australian Government Minister for the Environment and Energy). Canberra, ACT. doi: 10.4226/94/58b6585f94911

Ministerial Council. (2010). *Australia's biodiversity conservation strategy 2010–2030.* Canberra, ACT: Ministerial Council.

Morton, A. (2017, December 13). Environment funding slashed by third since Coalition took office. *The Guardian.*

OECD. (2007). *Instrument mixes for environmental policy.* Paris, France: OECD Publishing.

OECD. (n.d.). *Environmental performance reviews.* Retrieved from http://www.oecd-ilibrary.org/environment/oecd-environmental-performance-reviews_19900090

Pagiola, S, Von Glehn, H. C., & Taffarello, D. (2013). Brazil's experience with payment for environmental services. *PES Learning Paper, 1.*

Panel of Experts. (2009). *Belo Monte experts panel report.* International Rivers. Retrieved from https://www.internationalrivers.org/resources/belo-monte-experts-panel-report-3947

Pirard, R. (2012). Market-based instruments for biodiversity and ecosystem services: A lexicon. *Environmental Science & Policy, 19–20,* 59–68.

Productivity Commission. (2017). *National water reform.* (Report no. 87). Canberra, ACT.

Rickards, L., Wiseman, J., & Kashima, Y. (2014). Barriers to effective climate change mitigation: The case of senior government and business decision makers. *Wiley Interdisciplinary Reviews: Climate Change, 5* (6), 753–773.

Ruhl, J. B. (1996). Complexity theory as a paradigm for the dynamic law-and-society system: A wake-up call for legal reductionism and the modern administrative state. *Duke Law Journal, 45* (5), 851–928.

Ruhl, J. B. (2012). The political economy of climate change mitigation policies. *Minnesota Law Review, 97,* 206–277.

256 *Paul Martin et al.*

Schoenfeld, A., von, Santos, M., & Uchoas, L. (n.d.). *Legislação socioambiental brasileira numa encruzilhada* (Brazilian socio-environmental legislation at a cross-roads). Heinrich Böll Stiftung. Retrieved from https://br.boell.org/pt-br/flexibilizacao-da-legislacao-socioambiental-brasileira

SECTET (Secretaria de Ciência, Tecnologia e Educação Profissional e Tecnológica do Estado do Pará) (n.d.) *Programa Biopará: politica pública para pesquisa e desenvolvimento de cadeias produtivas da biodiversidade paraense* (Biopará Program: Public policy for research and development of Paraense biodiversity production chains) Retrieved from http://www.sectet.pa.gov.br/sites/default/files/Programa%20BIOPAR%C3%81-ilovepdf-compressed.pdf

Shearman, D. (2018, March 26). Why Australians need a national environment protection agency to safeguard their health. *The Conversation.*

Soares-Filho, B., Rajão, R., Macedo, M., Carneiro, A., Costa, W., Coe, M., … Alencar, A. (2014). Cracking Brazil's Forest Code. *Science, 344,* 363–364.

Stavins, R. N. (2002). Experience with market-based environmental policy instruments. In *Handbook of Environmental Economics, 1* (52), 355–435.

Tennent, R., & Lockie, S. (2013). Vale landcare: The rise and decline of community-based natural resource management in rural Australia. *Journal of Environmental Planning and Management, 56* (4), 572–587. doi: 10.1080/09640568.2012.689617

UN. (2012). *The future we want.* Resolution 66/288 of the United Nations Conference on Sustainable Development in Rio de Janeiro. doi: 10.1093/oxfordhb/9780199560103.003.0005

Wentworth Group of Concerned Scientists. (2017a). *Review of water reform in the Murray-Darling Basin.* Retrieved from https://wentworthgroup.org/2017/11/review-of-water-reform-in-the-murray-darling-basin/2017/

Wentworth Group of Concerned Scientists. (2017b). *Five actions necessary to deliver the Murray-Darling Basin Plan 'in full and on time'.* Sydney, Australia. Retrieved from http://wentworthgroup.org/wp-content/uploads/2017/06/Five-actions-to-deliver-Murray-Darling-Basin-Plan-Wentworth-Group-June-2017.pdf

Wimmer, A., de Soysa, I., & Wagner, C. (2003). *Political science tools for assessing feasibility and sustainability of reforms.* Bonn, Germany: University of Bonn, Center for Development Research.

WWF-Australia & ACF (Australian Conservation Foundation). (2017). *Ongoing underinvestment in environmental protection puts all Australians at risk.* Pre-Budget Submission to the Department of the Treasury.

WWF (2018). *Financiamento público e meio ambiente: um balanço da década e perspectivas* (Public financing and environment: A review of the decade and prospects). Retrieved from https://d3nehc6yl9qzo4.cloudfront.net/downloads/financiamentomma_final2_web.pdf

Appendix A
Legislation list

Australian Laws

Aboriginal Heritage Act 2006 (VIC)
  Biodiversity Conservation Act 2017 (NSW)
  Civil Aviation Act 1988 (Cth)
  Coastal Management Act 1995 (VIC)
  Commonwealth of Australia Constitution Act 1900 (Cth) (*Australian Constitution*)
  Conservation and Land Management Act 1984 (WA)
  Conservation and Land Management Act 1984 (WA)
  Crown Land (Reserves) Act 1978 (VIC)
  Crown Land Management Act 2016 (NSW)
  Crown Lands Act 1989 (NSW)
  Dairy Produce Act 1986 (Cth)
  Environment Legislation Amendment Bill 2013 (Cth)
  Environment Planning and Assessment Act 1979 (NSW)
  Environment Protection and Biodiversity Conservation Act 1999 (Cth) (*EPBC Act*)
  Environment Protection and Biodiversity Conservation Regulation 2000 (Cth)
  Environmental Protection – Great Barrier Reef Protection Measures – and Other
Legislation Amendment Bill 2019, (the *2019 Bill*))
  Environmental Protection Act 1994 (QLD)
  Environmental Reform (Consequential Provisions) Act 1999 (Cth)
  EPBC Regulation 2000 (Cth)
  Geographic Place Names Act 1998 (VIC)
  Heritage Act 1995 (VIC)
  Land (Planning and Environment) Act 1991 (ACT)
  Land Act 1994 (QLD)
  Land Rights Act (Traditional Owners Settlement) 2010 (VIC)
  Land Rights Act 1976 (NT)
  Land Rights Act 1976 (NT)
  Land Rights Act 1983 (NSW)
  Land Rights Act 1983 (NSW)
  Land Rights Act 1991 (QLD)
  Land Rights Act 1991 (QLD)

258   *Legislation list*

Mineral Resources Act 1989 (QLD)
Mineral Resources Development Act 1990 (VIC)
Mineral Resources Development Act 1995 (TAS)
Mining Act 1971 (SA)
Mining Act 1978 (WA)
Mining Act 1980 (NT)
Mining Act 1992 (NSW)
Native Title Act 1993 (Cth)
Privacy Act 1988 (Cth)
Surveillance Devices Act 2004 (Cth)
Telecommunications and Other Legislation Amendment (Assistance and Access) Act 2018 (Cth)
Vegetation Management Act 1999 (Qld) (*VMA*)
Vegetation Management and Other Legislation Amendment Bill 2018 (Qld)
Water Act 2002 (Qld)
Water Act 2007 (Cth)

Brazilian laws

Federal Laws (unless otherwise indicated in brackets with abbreviation of state)

1988 Constituição Federal (Brazilian Federal Constitution of 1988) (CF/88)

• Constitutional Transitory Dispositions 1988

10.696/2003
10.831/2003 (Organic Agriculture Law)
11.105/2005 (Biosecurity Law)
11.947/2009
11.428/2006 (Atlantic Forest Law)
12.512/2011 (Access to Information Law)
12.651/2012 (New Forest Code)
13.105/2015 (New Code of Civil Procedure)
13.123/2015 (Access to Genetic Resources and Associated Traditional Knowledge Law)
13.808/2019 (Annual Budget Law)
14.661 (SC)
2.393/1995 (RJ)
23.291/2019 (MG)
4.771/1965 (Forest Code - revoked)
6.001/1973 (Indigenous Law)
7.347/1985 (Public Civil Processes Law)
7.572/2011
8.078/1990 (Code of Consumer Protection and Defense (CDC))

8.978/1990
9.433/1997 (*National Water Resources Policy Law*)
9.456/1997 (*Protection of Cultivars Law*)
9.605/2008 (*Environmental Crimes Law*)
9.984/2000 (*Creation of National Water Agency Law*)
9.985/2000 (*National System of Protected areas (SNUC Law)*)
National Environmental Policy Act (1981)

Federal (Presidential) Decrees

2.519/1998 (*Ratification of CBD*)
23.793/1934 (*Forest Code*)
4.339/2002 (*Biodiversity*)
4.340/2002 (*SNUC regulation*)
4.703/2003 (*National Program for Biodiversity Decree*)
4.887/2003 (*Quilombolas Decree*)
4.987/2004 (*Biodiversity (revoked)*)
5.758/2006 (*National Plan for Protected Areas (NPPA)*)
5.092/2004 (*Identification of Priority Areas for Conservation*)
6.527/2008 (*Amazon Fund*)
7.572/2011 (*Payment* (Bolsa verde) *for Protection of the Protection of The Forest*)
84.017/1979 (*Regulation of National Parks*)
9.312.2018 (*Creation of 2 Marine Protected Areas*)
9.313/2018 (*Creation of 2 Marine Protected Areas*)
9.672/2019 (*Restructuring of MMA*)
9.741/2019 (*Expenditure Regulation for 2019*)
9.759/2019 (*Extinguish and Establish Guidelines for Public Participation in Government Issues*)

Other

CONABIO *Administrative Ruling no. 463/2018*
Chilean *Law no. 20.930/2016 (Derecho real de conservación)*
Federal Draft Bill no. 1.551/2019
State Draft Bill no. 3.575/2016
MoE Administrative Ruling no. 126/2004 (Recognise priority areas for conservation)
Federal Draft Bill no. 1.551/2019
Federal Draft Bill no. 9425/2017
Provisional Measure no. 870/2019 (Reorganised federal executive power)
Federal Draft Bill 6.969/2013
Provisional Measure 558/2012
Provisional Measure 756/2016
Provisional Measure 789/2017
Provisional Measure 790/2017
Provisional Measure 791/2017

260   *Legislation list*

Provisional Measure no 80/2017
Provisional measure 2.186-16/2001
RBAC-E No. 94/2017
RBAC-E No. 94/2017
Resolution No. 242/2000
ICA 100–40

Appendix B
International material

Agreement on the Conservation of Albatrosses and Petrels. Entered into force February 1, 2004. ATS [2008] 19. (*ACAP*).

Aichi Biodiversity Targets. (2010). In *Strategic Plan for biodiversity 20122-2020.* Retrieved from https://www.cbd.int/sp/targets/ (*Aichi Targets*).

Cancun Declaration on Mainstreaming the Conservation and Sustainable Use of Biodiversity for Well-Being. 2016. COP 13, Cancún, Mexico. Retrieved from www.cbd.int/cop/cop-13/hls/cancun declaration-en.pdf

Cartagena Protocol on Biosafety to the Convention on Biological Diversity. Entered into force September 11, 2003. UNTS, vol. 2226, p. 208. (*Cartagena Protocol*).

Convention Concerning the Protection of the World Cultural and Natural Heritage. Entry into force December 17, 1975. UNESCO. Retrieved from https://www.refworld.org/docid/4042287a4.html

Convention Concerning the Protection of the World Cultural and Natural Heritage. 1972. UNESCO. Retrieved from https://whc.unesco.org/en/conventiontext/ (*UNESCO-WH*).

Convention for the Conservation of Antarctic Marine Living Resources. Entered into force April 7, 1982. ATS [1982] 16.

Convention for the Conservation of Antarctic Seals. Entered into force March 11, 1978. UKTS, no. 45.

Convention on Access to Information, Public Participation in Decision-Making and Access to Justice in Environmental Matters. Entered into force October 31, 2001. UNTS, vol. 21161, p. 447. (*Aarhus Convention*).

Convention on Access to Information, Public Participation in Decision-Making and Access to Justice in Environmental Matters. Entered into force October 30, 2001. UNTS, vol. 2161, p. 447. (*Aarhus Convention*).

Convention on Biological Diversity. Entered into force December 29, 1993. UNTS, vol. 1760, p. 79. (*CBD*).

Convention on Conservation of Migratory Species of Wild Animals. Entered into force November 1, 1983. ATS [1991] 32. (*Bonn Convention* or *CMS*).

Convention on International Trade in Endangered Species of Wild Fauna and Flora. Entered into force July 1, 1975. UNTS, vol. 993, p. 243. (*CITES*).

Convention on the Conservation of Migratory Species of Wild Animals. Entered into force November 1, 1983. UNTS, vol. 1651. (*CMS*).

262   *International material*

Convention on Wetlands of International Importance Especially as Waterfowl Habitat (Ramsar Convention). Entered into force December 21, 1975. UNTS, vol. 996, p. 245.

Convention on Wetlands of International Importance Especially as Waterfowl Habitat. Entered into force December 21, 1975. UNTS, vol. 996, p. 245. *(Ramsar Convention).*

Declaration of the United Nations Conference on the Human Environment. 1972. Retrieved from https://www.ipcc.ch/apps/njlite/srex/njlite_download.php?id=6471 *(Stockholm Declaration).*

Indigenous and Tribal Peoples Convention, 1969. Entered into force September 5, 1991. ILO, C169. *(ILO 169).*

International Convention for the Control and Management of Ships' Ballast Water and Sediments. Entered into force September 8, 2017. Retrieved from http://www.imo.org/en/About/Conventions/ListOfConventions/Pages/International-Convention-for-the-Control-and-Management-of-Ships'-Ballast-Water-and-Sediments-(BWM).aspx *(Ballast Water Management Convention)*

International Convention for the Prevention of Pollution from Ships, as Modified by Protocol of 1978). Entry into force October 2, 1983. Retrieved from http://www.imo.org/en/About/Conventions/ListOfConventions/Pages/International-Convention-for-the-Prevention-of-Pollution-from-Ships-(MARPOL).aspx *(MARPOL 73/78)*

International Convention for the Regulation of Whaling. Entry into force November 10, 1948 IUCN (ID: TRE-000074).

Kyoto Protocol to the United Nations Framework Convention on Climate Change). Entered into force February 16, 2005. UNTS, vol. 2303, p. 162. *(Kyoto Protocol).*

Nagoya Protocol on Access to Genetic Resources and the Fair and Equitable Sharing of Benefits Arising from their Utilization to the Convention on Biological Diversity. Entry into force October 12, 2014. Retrieved from https://treaties.un.org/pages/ViewDetails.aspx?src=IND&mtdsg_no=XXVII-8-b&chapter=27&-clang=_en *(Nagoya Protocol)*

Nagoya-Kuala Lumpur Supplementary Protocol on Liability and Redress to the Cartagena Protocol on Biosafety. Entered into force March 5, 2018. Retrieved from https://bch.cbd.int/protocol/supplementary/

Protocol on Environmental Protection to the Antarctic Treaty. Entered into force January 14, 1998. UNTS 2941. *(Antarctic-Environmental Protocol* or *Madrid Protocol).*

Regional Agreement on Access to Information, Public Participation and Justice in Environmental Matters in Latin America and the Caribbean. Opened for signature 4 March 2018. UN Doc. LC/PUB.2018/8/-*. *(Escazú Agreement).*

Rio Declaration on Environment and Development. (1992). Retrieved from UNESCO website http://www.unesco.org/education/pdf/RIO–E.PDF

SDGs (Sustainable Development Goals). (2015). In *Transforming our world: The 2030 agenda for sustainable development*. Retrieved from https://sustainabledevelopment.un.org/

UN Convention on the Law of the Sea. Entered into force November 16, 1994. UNTS, vol. 1883, p. 3; 1834, p. 3; 1834, p. 3. (*Law of the Sea*).

UN Declaration on the Rights of Indigenous Peoples. 2007. A/RES/61/295. Retrieved from https://www.un.org/development/desa/indigenouspeoples/declaration-on-the-rights-of-indigenous-peoples.html (*UNDRIP*)

UNs Convention to Combat Desertification. Entered into force December 26, 1996. UNTS, vol. 1954, p. 3.

World Heritage Convention. 1972. Retrieved from https://www.iucn.org/theme/world-heritage/about/world-heritage-convention (*WHC*)

Appendix C
Cases

Bulga Milbrodale Progress Association Inc v Minister for Planning and Infrastructure and Gloucester Resources Limited v Minister for Planning [2019] NSWLEC 7
Marsh v Baxter [2014] WASC 187. (CIV 1561 of 2012)
Scott v Avery 5 HLC 811 [1843–1860] All E.R. Rep. 1 HL (UK)
Warkworth Mining Limited [2013] NSWLEC 48 (*Bulga Case*)
Warkworth Mining Limited v Bulga Milbrodale Progress Association Inc [2014] NSWCA 105

Index

Note: **Bold** page numbers refer to tables; *italic* page numbers refer to figures and page numbers followed by "n" denote endnotes.

Adams, V. 204, 220
Adani Carmichael case 48, 52–53
aerial drones 169, 174, 176, 178, 181; *see also* drone technologies
agriculture: biodiversity loss 125, 140; bio-social issues authors 16; commodification of agricultural products 40; contamination 34–35; expansion of 32, 189; financial constraints 35–36; habitat loss 32; industry sustainability initiatives 127, **129**; internationalisation of 40; invasive species 32–34; modern commodity agriculture 26; production efficiency 26, *26–28*; public programmes 36–37; socio-ecological issues 38–39; water, climate and biodiversity 37–38
agrochemicals: application of 40; Brazil 34–35, 40, 133; new 40; problems of spillover effects 112; use of 32
Aichi Biodiversity Targets 116, 210, 219
Aichi Targets 13, 17, 32, 39, 75, 190, 192, 215, 223, 226, 245, 247, 252
Akiba v Commonwealth case 97
Amazon: Amazon Fund 227; 'Amazonia Protege' project 162; Amazon Region Protected Areas Program (ARPA) 205; biodiversity in 31; Blue Amazon 78, 107; Brazilian 32, 40, 154; coral reef 77; deforestation of 13, 32, 155–157, *156*, 161; INPE 156; land clearing 157; Mato Grosso's 155, 156; 'Rubber Cycle' 90; Tapajós National Forest 173
ANAC *see* Civil Aviation Agency (ANAC)
Anangu Law 99

ANATEL *see* National Telecommunications Agency (ANATEL)
architectures: Amazonian Region 243; biodiversity protection, characteristics of 243; *CBD* implementation 244; constitutions and jurisprudential traditions 241–242; environmental governance 242, 245; 'Future We Want' Rio declaration 245; governance power and responsibility 243–244; government functions 242–243; payments for environmental services (PES) 244–245; politics, effects of 241; power relations in natural resource governance 243; public/private approach 244
Arco Verde operation 156
Aronson, J. 59
Atlas of Marine Protection 68
Australia: Aboriginal and Torres Strait Islander peoples 18; agricultural water infrastructures and demands 31; beef case studies 134–135; biodiversity banking instruments 37; biodiversity conservation 198–199; biodiversity governance 6–12; citizen engagement 248–249; collaborative biodiversity governance 102; Commonwealth 177; Commonwealth Government 201–203, *202*, 217; comparative agricultural statistics 30, **30**; control of habitat destruction 238; 'cooperative federalism' 153; cotton case studies 131; Cotton Research and Development Corporation

266   *Index*

(CRDC) 131; Dairy Australia 136–137; dairy case studies 136–137; *Dairy Produce Act 1986* 136; *DairySAT* 137; effectiveness of environmental protection 10–11; environmental governance 213; environmental laws 63; environmental organisations 200; *Environment Protection and Biodiversity Conservation Act 1999* 198; exotic cane beetle 33; farming 30; federal public funding gap 199–200; fifth national report on implementation of the *CBD* 11, 13–14; five-day workshop 14; funding strategies 198–204; *GrazingBMP* 135; Indigenous Protected Areas (IPAs) 246; industry-led cotton and sugar initiatives 127; international agreements for marine conservation 70, **71–72**; invasive animal problems 33; James Hardie case 58; land-clearing rates 153; largest agricultural landholders 30, **31**; local funding 200; Mariana case 58; marine governance (*see* marine governance, Australia); meta-governance (*see* meta-governance, Australia); mine approval (*see* mining approvals, Australia); national and state governments 238; national farming organisation 199; National Reserve System 97; NGOs and citizens 168–169; policy instruments for environment 217, **217**; 'Privacy Principles' 177; protected areas (*see* protected areas, Australia); public and private rules and organisations 229; public governance structures 140; public/private funding 'cocktails' 203; QLD Canegrowers Organisation 133; Red Meat Advisory Council 134; *Report on the review of the first five years of Australia's Biodiversity Conservation Strategy 2010–2030* 200–201; risk-based programmes 137; Royal National Park 100; Smartcane BMP 132, 133; stakeholders 174; State of Environment Report, 2016 9–10; state of environment reports (SOEs) 9; sugar case studies 133; surfing reserves (*see* surfing reserves, Australian); *Water Act 2002* 131; water policy 152; whale and dolphin watching 179; World Bank Governance Indicators 215, **216** Australian Beef Sustainability Framework (ABSF) 134–135

Australian Cane Farmers Association 133 Australian Conservation Foundation 199, 240 *Australian Constitution* 199, 201, 241–242 Australian Dairy Industry Council (ADIC) 136 Australian Land and Water Research Organisation 199 Australian Laws 257–258 Australian Panel of Experts in Environmental Law 39, 73, 220, 243 *Australian State of Environment Report 2016* 29 Azevedo, A. 157

Balée, W.L. 95 Bauman, T. 99 beef case studies: Australia 134–135; Brazil 135 Bells Beach Surfing Recreation Reserve 110, 119 Bernardo, C.T.S. 59 *Biodiversity Conservation Act 2017* (NSW) 239 biodiversity governance: in Australia 6–12; biodiversity protection 3; in Brazil 6–9, 12–14; complexity and subjectivity 2; environmental governance 9; environmental programmes 1; evidence-based policy approach 2, 4; issues 1; 'zones of autarchy' 1 Biodiversity Indicators Partnership 215 biodiversity intelligence from satellites: monitoring habitat loss 153–160; Murray-Darling Basin case 152–153; need for low-cost precision 149–150; satellites technologies 150–152; 'water theft' 150 *Biodiversity Law* 223 biodiversity loss 12, 16–17, 22, 25–26, 31–33, 32, 37, 40, 50, 73, 85, 125, 140, 160, 192, 230, 243 biodiversity protection: Australian Senate enquiry 219; Australian surfing reserves 109–111; Brazilian surfing reserves 111–112; community engagement 252; conservation innovation 106–107; corruption 249; effectiveness of 3, 6; financial constraints 26; funding gap 199; implementation of 6–7, 37, 190, 196, 200, 213, 250, 251; innovative citizen-led initiatives 105; MSP

76; national funding capacity 193;
perspectives on surfing reserves 112;
'political economy' problems 243; rural
17, 35–36, 39, 200; surfing reserves
106–109; World Surfing Reserves
(WSRs) 112, **113–115,** 116–117
biodiversity strategies: *CBD* principles
214, 218; environmental governance
215; policy instruments for
environment 217, **217;** 'red tape' or
'green tape' reform 218; taxation
216–217
Biosafety Law 223
Blignaut, J. 59
blockchain contract 16, 40, 153, 181
Blue Amazon 78, 107
Brazil: ABR (Algodão Brasileira
Responsável – Responsible Brazilian
Cotton) 131–132; agricultural
certification 41; agricultural economy
26–28; Aichi targets 13; Amazon
Region Protected Areas Program
(ARPA) 205; beef case studies
135; biodiversity conservation 173;
biodiversity governance 6–9, 12–14;
Biosecurity Law 12; *CBD* principles
195–196; *Code of Consumer Protection
and Defense (CDC)* 56; collaborative
biodiversity governance 102;
comparative agricultural statistics
30, **30;** concerns 12; contingency
reserves 250; cooperative federalism
153; cotton case studies 131–132;
dairy case studies 137–138;
ELO social indicators 133–134;
environmental and planning laws
247; environmental legislation
217–218; Escazu Convention 249;
Fifth National Report 3, 13–14;
Fifth National Report to the CDB
29; Food Acquisition Program 36;
funding strategies 195–198; GTPS
135; habitat clearing 32; habitat loss
220; Healthy Milk programme 137;
ICMS 196–197; Iguaçu National
Park Management Plan 173–174;
Imaflora and Solidaridad Foundation
133; international agreements for
marine conservation 70, **71–72;**
international donations and loans 195;
Itatiaia National Park 100; IUCN
Protected Area classification 246;
land-clearing rates 153, 238–239;
'legal reserve' 32; livestock production

31; Mariana and Brumadinho cases
48; marine governance (*see* marine
governance, Brazil); meta–governance
(*see* meta–governance, Brazil); mine
disasters 53–61; mineral sector 62;
Mining Code 1967 49; Ministry of
Environment 196, 250; national
environmental system (SISNAMA)
215–216; National Institute for Space
Research 13; *National Plan for Low
Carbon Emissions in Agriculture (Plano
ABC)* 137–138; National Report
on implementation of *CBD* 12;
National School Meal Program 36;
Nestlé's Good Farm Practices 138;
New Code of Civil Procedure of 2015,
adoption of 9; new road networks 31;
NGOs and citizens 168; payments
for ecosystem services (PES) 59, 198;
post-disaster management 61; poverty
and corruption 154; Programa Bolsa
Verde (Green Sponsorship Program)
196; protected areas (*see* protected
areas, Brazil); public and private
rules and organisations 214, 229;
public governance structures 140;
Raízen's ELO Programme 132,
133; REDD+ scheme 37; reduced
socio-environmental legal protections
237; rights of Indigenous people
238; *SNUC Law* 12; sugar case
studies 133–134; sugar sector 127;
threats to biodiversity 12; *TTAC* 55;
UN agreement to extend Brazil's
jurisdiction 85n1; UNDP Biofin 194;
user of agrochemicals 34–35; World
Bank Governance Indicators 215, **216**
Brazil, Russia, India, China and South
Africa (BRICS) 198
Brazilian Amazon 32, 40, 154
Brazilian Biomes Satellite Deforestation
Program (PMDBBS) 157
Brazilian Civil Aviation Regulation 175
Brazilian Environmental Agency 156
Brazilian Environmental Ministry 156
Brazilian Federal Constitution 1988 89
Brazilian Forest Service (BFS) 39
Brazilian laws: Federal (Presidential)
Decrees 259; Federal Laws 258–259
Brazilian National Congress 175
broadacre farming 29, 41
Brumadinho tailings dam disaster, case of
48, 53, **54,** 60–61
Bulga case 50–52, 53

268 *Index*

Captain Cook's declaration 96
Cartagena Protocol (2003) 210
cattle grazing 25, 135
cell-grazing 35
Cerrado biome *156*, 162n1
Chico Mendes Institute for Biodiversity
  Conservation (ICMBio) 78–80, 79,
  91–93, 101, 173–174, 226–228, 240,
  246, 248, 250
CIF *see* Inter-Federation
  Committee (CIF)
Cintra, A.C.A. 56
Civil Aviation Act 1988 179
Civil Aviation Agency (ANAC) 175–176
Civil Aviation Safety Authority
  (CASA) 176
civil procedure law 56
civil society organisations 102, 222, 230
class actions *see* collective actions
climate change 12, 17, 29, 39, 73–75,
  83–84, 153, 224–225, 227
collective actions 56, 58, 130
co-management, Australia: native title
  and statutory rights 96–98; Uluru-Kata
  Tjuta National Park 98–100
combine or 'hybridise' government
  and non-government governance
  approaches 126
communications 9, 15, 20, 59, 131, 148,
  150–151, 169–170, 179
*Conservation and Land Management
  Act 1984* 100
conservation units (UCs) 12, 13, 77, 80,
  81, 91–94, 95, 112, 196, 246, 248, 250;
  'full protection' 78, 79; 'sustainable use'
  78, 79
contamination 21, 26, 29, 33–35, 38;
  genetic 33
Convention on Biological Diversity
  (CBD) 3, 89, 154, 188, 210, 236;
  Aichi Targets and SDGs 247;
  commitments 11–12, 22, 50, 206,
  237; implementation of 245–246;
  incentives and resources 253; 'localised'
  interpretations or restatements 246;
  Nagoya Protocol 18; national biodiversity
  strategies 247; principles 15, 48, 246;
  propositions 4; 'report card' 5; *Rio
  Declaration*, questions 5; Secretariat
  requirements 11, 252; signatory reports
  246; *in situ* and *ex situ* biodiversity
  conservation 125–126; strategies to
  improve outcomes 245; summary data
  7, **8**; *UN Declaration on the Rights of
  Indigenous Peoples*, 2007 18

co-regulation or collaborative governance
  see hybrid governance
corporate social responsibility (CSR)
  initiatives 130, 245
corporatisation 17, 30
Cosby, A. 192
cotton case studies: Australia 131; BCI's
  principles 130–131; best management
  programme (BMP) 131; Brazil
  131–132; International Forum for
  Cotton Promotion (IFCP) 130;
  International Textile Manufacturers
  Federation (ITMF) 130; '2025
  Sustainable Cotton Challenge' 130
Council of Australian Governments
  (COAG) 152, 217, 221
Craik, W. 138–139
CRISPR (clustered regularly interspaced
  short palindromic repeats) modified
  genetics 40
cropping 28–29, 138, 153
cross-breeding 33
cyber-attacks 180

dairy case studies: Australia 136–137;
  Brazil 137–138; Dairy Australia and
  FEPALE 136; 2016 *Dairy Declaration*
  136; Dairy Sustainability Framework
  (DSF) 136; Global Dairy Agenda of
  Action (GDAA) 136
da Silva, T. 6
data ownership 180
Deane, F. 139
DECEA 175
decision-making processes 10–11, 20,
  51, 101, 140, 148–149, 160, 222–223,
  226, 249
deforestation: of Amazon 13, 32, 154, 155,
  157, 227; in Brazil 161, 205, 226; illegal
  134, 157; in Mato Grosso 156; rates
  154, 156, 161
defunding 237, 240
De Groot, R.S. 59
Dermot, S. 99
DETER 157, 161
De Wit, M. 59
Dinamarco, C.R. 56
drone technologies 16, 20–21; beneficial
  uses and controlling risks 172;
  biodiversity impacts 178–179; Cargo
  170; composite evolution of 171, *171*;
  computer vision and machine learning
  172; configurations 170; control and
  communication system 170; and data
  180; data capture or processing 169;

Index 269

environmental and agricultural applications 171–172; environmental monitoring and control 174; evolution 169–171; expanding uses 171–172; fixed-wing systems and multi-rotor systems 169; habitat destruction, images of 168; human impact risk 174–176; hydrology monitoring 168; incremental adoption and learning 173–174; innovation studies 170–171; intentional damage 179–180; international categorisation system 168; lethal drones 177–178; for military purposes 170; propulsion system 169–170; 'right to farm' policy 169; sensors, innovative and cheap 172; social interests 176–177; terrorist attacks 169

eco-labels 41, 189
ECOLEX 217–218
'Ecological' ICMS 197
Economic Exclusive Zone (EEZ) 77–78
ecosystem services 75, 84–85, 196, 219, 224
eco-use and ecotourism 106, 205, 226
energy extraction 84
Environmental Defenders Office (EDO) 51
environmental disasters 53, 60, 150
environmental governance approaches: architectures 242, 245; Australia 213; biodiversity governance 9, 215; Brazil 229
environmental harm 21, 35, 60, 107, 222, 242
environmental laws 41, 148–149, 211
environmental organisations 51, 138, 150, 200, 214
environmental protected areas 18, 78, 79, 112
environmental protection 6–7, 9–10, 12–13, 19, 38, 40–41, 49, 70, 73, 81, 107–108, 112, 116, 138, 155, 157, 226–229, 238, 240, 242, 249–251
environmental volunteering 41
European environmental rules 41
exotic species 33
Extractive Reserves (Resex) 78–79, 93–94, 100
'Eyes in the Sky' committee 177

Faganello, C.R.F. 60
farming 29, 107; aggregation 17; -based programmes 36; biodiverse or organic 35; broadacre 29, 41, 135; corporations 30; expansion 6, 17; farmland biodiversity 40–41; farm sectors to Brazil and Australia 127, **128**; industrial 16, 25; low carbon 138, 160; low-cost farmland 31; modern 31; organisations 29; ownership 30; 'smart farming' technologies 31
Federal Foreign Investment Review Board 48
Federal Law No. 13.123/2015 39
Federal Public Attorney's Office (MPF) 57
fertigation 31
financial constraints 26, 35–36
fisheries 68–70, 72–75, 77, 81–82, 84, 90, 111, 135, 150, 197, 201, 224
Folegatti, M.V. 60
funding biodiversity conservation: Australia 198–204; Brazil 195–198; Brazilian Biodiversity Fund (FUNBIO) 197–198, 205; Brazilian Fund for Defense of Collective Rights (FDD) 197; BRICS 198; comparison of Australia and Brazil 192, **192**; Contracting Party 189; direct government environmental expenditure 193; economic incentives 189; environmental investment strategies 194; funding gaps 191–193; funding strategies 193–195; incentive-related impacts 189; national funding capacity 193; PES 193; private investments 193–194; private landholders 194–195; protected areas funding 204–205; resource limitations 190–191; 'sources and uses of funds' analysis 195; stakeholders 190; UN Development Program Biodiversity Finance Initiative 194

genetically modified (GM) crops 31, 249; corn 33; Roundup Ready soybeans 237; soybean varieties 33
genetically modified organisms (GMOs) 33–34
genetic engineering 33, 172
Global Environmental Facility 196, 197
Global Roundtable for Sustainable Beef (GRSBeef) 134
governance system: Australia's meta-governance 219–223; biodiversity strategies 214–218; Brazil's meta-governance 223–229; governance challenge 213–214; meta-governance 212–213

government agencies 21
G2 Programme 59
Great Artesian Basin 38
Great Barrier Reef 29, 53, 68, 76–77, 82–84, 107, 133, 135, 139, 158
Great Barrier Reef Marine Park, case of 68
Grinover, A.P. 56
Gupta, A. 140

habitat destruction 20, 148–149, 154, 168, 176, 228, 238, 249
habitat loss: in Australia and Brazil 32, 220; in Brazilian Amazon 40; broadacre agriculture on 26; Mato Grosso land clearing 154–158; Queensland land clearing 158–160
habitat protection 15, 32, 68, 76, 160, 191, 220, 238
hacking 179, 180
Hamman, E. 139
Hardie, J. 58
herbicide resistance 31, 33, 34, 168, 170, 178
Historical Anthropological Cultural Zone (HACZ) 95
hybrid arrangements 125–126, 140–141
hybrid governance 18–19, 126–127, 130, 137, 138, 140, 251

Iacona, G. 204
IBAMA (Brazilian Institute of Environment and Natural Renewable Resources) 55, 58, 156–158, 161, 226, 250
indigenous and traditional people's stewardship, Brazilian: *Access to Information Law* 91–92; co-management 93–94; conservation units (UCs) 91–94; *Constitutional Transitory Dispositions 1988* 90; contributions to conservation 95–96; cultural rights 93; environmental legislation 90–91; *ILO 169* or articles 215 and 216 93; indigenous populations 89; land rights 90, 91; non-indigenous Traditional populations 89–90; Resex and RDS 93–94, 100–101; *Rio de Janeiro Law 2.393/1995* 94–95; *Serra do Mar State Park* 95; *SNUC Law* 93; 'territorial interfaces' 92, **92**
Indigenous Land Use Agreements (ILUAs) 97, 100

Indigenous Protected Areas (IPAs) 96–97, 100, 106, 118, 201–202, 246
intelligence gathering, cost-effectiveness of 191
Inter-Federation Committee (CIF): legal concerns 57; Technical Chambers (CTs) 56
intergenerational equity, principle of 5, 50
Interim Measure no. 870/2019 39
International Union for the Conservation of Nature (IUCN) 3, 15, 79, **80,** 88, 91, 99–101, 118, 226, 228, 245, 246; comparative research, state parties 101; Management Principles 99; Red List 189
International Union for the Preservation of Nature (IUCN) 67, 245
invasive species 12, 26, 29, 32–34, 40, 69, 170, 189, 193–194, 199–200, 210, 215, 219–222
investigations: biodiversity governance 14; *CBD* implementation 247; evidence-based investigation 14; individual reports 14; policy evaluation 14; synthesis workshop 15–16
Investor Mining and Tailings Safety site 62
irrigation 29, 34, 37–38, 112, 133, 172

Jackson, W.J. 223
James Hardie case 53, 55, 58, 62
joint management *see* co-management, Australia

Kayapó Indigenous tribes, study of 95
Kennedy, A. 51

landcare programmes 36, 137, 199, 237
landholder good stewardship 19
land rights 90–91, 96–97, 100, 238
Lassen, M. 191
Lazarow, N. 119
Lease Back Agreements 100
legislation list: Australian Laws 257–258; Brazilian laws 258–261
lethal drones: community of fishers and hunters 177–178; dropping biological agents 177; ground based and aerial drones 178; risks of serious accidents 178; *see also* drone technologies
Leuzinger, M.D. 6, 14
Luciano, D. 47

Mabo case (Mabo and others v. Queensland) 96
management plans (MPs) 52, 75, 77–81, 94–95, 99, 173
Mariana disaster 53, 54, 58, 61
marine areas 13, 16, 68–69, 73, 75–77, 79, 84, 116, 191, 195, 200
marine biodiversity conservation and international agreements: Australia and Brazil 70, **71–72**; Estuarine biodiversity issues 69, *70;* government agencies 69–70, *70;* issues 68–69
marine governance, Australia: Australian Panel of Experts in Environmental Law 73; biodiversity loss 73; Dolphin Safe 73; *Marine state of environment report 2016* 72; Marine Stewardship Council 73; *State of the marine environment report* 72–73; 5th report under *CBD* 72, 73
marine governance, Brazil: *Aichi Targets* 75; *Australian State of the marine environment report 2016* 75; conventions on climate change *(UNFCCC)* 74–75; desertification 75; effectiveness of public policies 74; *Law of the Sea* 75; MPAs 75; *National Biodiversity Strategy and Action Plan* 74; shared public/private management 74; 5th report 74
marine protected areas 17; Australia's marine governance 70–73; Brazil's marine governance 74–75; conservation of marine biodiversity 67–68; implementing Australia's protected areas 82–84; implementing Brazil's protected areas 75–82; marine biodiversity conservation and international agreements 68–70
marine protection 68, 77, 82, 85, 191
Marine Spatial Planning (MSP) 68, 73, 76, 82, 85, 116
Marsh v Baxter case 34
Martin, P. 6, 14, 192
Mato Grosso land clearing: agricultural deforestation 156; agriculture and livestock 155; deforestation in Amazon 155; DETER 157; INPE 156; land clearing 155–156; location in South America 154, *154*; MapBiomas Alerta 157; 'modern era of deforestation' 155; permanent preservation areas (APP) 157; PRODES Digital 156, 157; satellite technology 158; System of Environmental Licensing of Rural Properties (SLAPR) 157

Medeiros, E. 57
Medical Research and Compensation Foundation 58
'mega biodiverse' 154
meta-governance: corporate and public sector good governance 212–213; corruption 249–250; inadequate 249–250; issues 21
meta-governance, Australia: Aichi and Millennium Development Biodiversity metrics 222; *Aichi Biodiversity Targets* in its *Strategic Plan for Biodiversity 2011–2020* 219; APEEL 220; 2014 Fifth National Report 222–223; habitat loss 220; national biodiversity strategy 219; *National State of Environment Report 2016* 219–220; OECD *Environment Performance Review: Australia 2019* 222; of protected reserves 219; 'shared responsibility' 222; threatened species management 219; water governance 221
meta-governance, Brazil: Amazon Fund 227; *Annual Budget Law* 227–228; Brazilian Biodiversity Information System (SiBBr) 228; Brazilian Federal agencies 226; environmental governance arrangements 229; environmental protection 227; implementation of *CBD* 228; Ministry of the Environment 227; *National Biodiversity Policy* 223; national targets 223–226; 2015 OECD Environmental Performance Review 228–229; roles and responsibilities 226; *SNUC Law* 226
Mickwitz, P. 14
Milanez, B. 57, 59
mine disasters, Brazil 53–61; federal agencies regulating mining 54, **55**; Mariana and Brumadinho 53, **54**
minimum-tillage planting 35
mining 16, 17, 191; acts for the states 49; complex issues 49; extraction 47; governance frameworks 48–50; mine approval in Australia 50–53; mine disasters in Brazil 53–61; political systems 48
mining approvals, Australia: *Adani Carmichael case* 48, 52–53; *Bulga case* 50–52
'missing market' problem 33, 35, 180
MMA 156–158
'model law' 102

272 *Index*

Moon, K. 220
Morgenstern, R. 192
multilateral environmental agreements (MEAs) 154
Murray-Darling Basin case 150; data unreliability or unavailability 153; hydrological data 152; National Water Initiative 152; water governance 153
Murray Darling Basin Plan 221
Murray-Darling River System 38, 239–240
Mutitjulu Aboriginal community 98

Nagoya Protocol, case of 18, 38, 211
National Biodiversity Action Plan 226
National Biodiversity Commission (CONABIO) 223, 226
National Biodiversity Strategies and Action Plans (NBSAP) 190
National Biodiversity Targets 39, 226
National Congress 82, 176, 229
National Department of Mineral Production (DNPM) 54
National Environmental Policy Act (1981) 155
National IPA programme 100
National Irrigation Policy 37
National Mining Agency (ANM) 54, 61
National Plan for Climate Change 156
National Program for the Strengthening of Family Agriculture (PRONAF) 36
National Reserve System 73, 97–98, 117–119, 204, 246
National Strategy for Invasive Alien Species 223
National Surfing Reserves (NSRs) 107, 109–110, **111,** 117, 119
National System of Conservation Units (SNUC) 12, 77, 78, 90–91, 93–95, 223–224, 226, 246
National Telecommunications Agency (ANATEL) 175
National Water Initiative (NWI) 37, 152, 217, 222, 236
National Water Resources Policy 37
Native Title Act 1993 96
Natural Resource Governance Framework (NRGF) 3
natural resources: or natural systems 149; use of 95
non-government organisations (NGO) 41, 105
'non-regression,' principle of 241

ocean governance system 68
offshore mining 84
Oosterveer, P. 140
organic certification 34
Organisation for Economic Co-operation and Development (OECD): Environment Performance evaluations 245
outcomes, strategies to improve: architectures 241–245; *CBD* commitments 245; citizen participation arrangements 247–249; genetically modified Roundup Ready soybeans 237; 'good citizenship' rules 251; hybrid model 251; innovation in governance 251; meta-governance is inadequate 249–250; politics and regression 237–239; undermining existing laws 239–241; weak accountability and continuous improvement 245–247

partnered governance of biodiversity: beef case studies 134–135; cotton case studies 130–132; dairy case studies 136–138; farm stewardship programmes 139; Great Barrier Reef (GBR) 139; National Environmental System (SISNAMA) 138; National Environment Council (CONAMA) 138; National Farmers Federation 139; *Paris Agreement on Climate Change* 138; QLD *Environmental Protection Act 1994* 139; receptiveness to partnered arrangements 138–140; Smartcane BMP and Grazing BMP 139; sugar case studies 132–134
partnership innovations 19
Partzsch, L. 140
Payment for Ecosystem Services (PES) schemes 36–37, 59, 60
pesticide resistance 21, 33–35, 131–133, 170, 172, 178
Pizer, W. 192
policy implementation 41, 226
polluter pays principle (PPP) 5, 17, 36, 50
Possingham, H. 204
precautionary principle 4, 5, 17, 50, 53, 230, 246
Pressey, R.L. 221
private conservation reserves 19, 41
private funding 19, 73, 196, 203

private governance 12, 41, 141
private regulation of agriculture 41
PRODES Digital 156–157
Program for the Estimation of Deforestation in the Brazilian Amazon (PRODES) 154, 156–157, 161–162
Programme to Recover Permanent Preservation Areas (APP) 59
protected areas (PAs) 16, 158; categorisation of 246; IUCN categories and guidelines 88
protected areas, Australia 82–84; Great Barrier Reef Marine Park Authority (GBRMPA) administers 82–84; MPAs 76–77; onshore mineral and energy export facilities 83; *State of the marine environment report* 77, 83; 5th report 77
protected areas, Brazil: 'Blue Amazon' 78; *Brazilian Constitution* 77; definition 77; documented plans of federal marine conservation units 79, *81*; Environmental Marine Protected Area (APA) 79–80; 'full protection' conservation units 78; IUCN Categories for Protected Areas 79, **80**; management council of federal marine conservation units 79, *81*; marine and coastal protected areas 79; MPAs 76, 78–79; network of use and protection zones 80–81; oil spills 82; Sustainable Development Goals objective 14 75–76; 'sustainable use' units 78
Protected Areas Fund (FAP) 205
protected areas funding: funding strategies 204–205; National Reserve System 204
protected areas management 18, 173, 191, 205, 240, 242
Protector Recipient Principle (PRP) 60
public funding 9, 35, 140, 191, 199, 250
public/private hybrids in environmental regulation 16
public programmes 26, 29, 36–37

Queensland land clearing (QLD) 220; for agriculture 158; 'Brigalow Belt' 158; 'Crown Leasehold' tenure 158; Government 52; illegal clearing control 160, 161–162; *Land Act 1994* 158–159; SLATS 159–160; US Government's Landsat programme 159; *Vegetation Management Act 1999* 159

Reiblich, J. 119
Reinhardt, F.L. 127
Reload Areas of Doce River Watershed 56
remote sensing 150, 156–158, 162
Renova Foundation 58; environmental and socio-economic programmes 57; legal concerns 57
Restoration of Permanent Preservation Areas (APP) 56
Ritchie, E.G. 220
robotics 40, 153, 161, 169–170
Rodrigues, G.A. 57
Rodriguez, J.R. 2
RPAS (Remotely Piloted Aircrafts) 177
rural biodiversity 17, 29, 35–36, 39–40, 200
Rural Environmental Registry (CAR) 158, 196
Rural Settlements 158

Saito, C. 157
salinisation process 34
Samarco Company 54–55, 60
Santana, P.C. 14
satellite sensing, definition 150
satellites technologies 16, 20; in Australia and Brazil 161; Earth observation satellites 150; private sector satellites 150; satellite programmes 151, **151**; sensors 152; US Landsat programme 150–151
Save the Waves Coalition 'surfonomics' programme 112
Science, Technology and Innovation Ministry of Brazil (MCTI) 156–157
SDG scorecard (Sustainable development reports) 215
sectoral self-regulation 41
Shih, J.S. 192
shipping 69, 84
Short, A.D. 107
'smart farming' technologies 31
'smart' livestock farm 31
SNUC Law see National System of Conservation Units (SNUC)
social justice and management of protected areas: Brazilian indigenous and traditional people's stewardship 89–96; co-management in Australia 96–100; comparing Australia and Brazil 100–101; third World Parks Congress 89

274 *Index*

socio-ecological issues 26, 38–39
de Souza, L.R. 14
Soy Moratorium (SoyM) 155–156, 158, 161
State Environmental Agency 95
Stattman, S.L. 140
Stavins, R.N. 127
Stockholm Declaration on the Human Environment (1972) 50
sugar case studies: Australia 133; Brazil 133–134; International Sugar Organization (ISO) 132; Organic, Fairtrade, Rainforest Alliance and Bonsucro 132
surfing reserves: *Aichi Biodiversity Targets* 116; Australian 109–111; and biodiversity 107–109; Brazilian 111–112; category of Crown Land 117; *CBD* 116; and conservation innovation 106–107; conservation of megadiversity 109; IPAs 118–119; IUCN protected area 118; Local Environmental Plans 117; passive-use recreation 108–109; perspectives on 112; Save the Waves Coalition 116; *Strategy for the National Reserve System* 119; surf breaks 108, 116, 117–118; surfers 108; surf tourism development 108; use of voluntary easement (VE) 119–120; WSRs (*see* World Surfing Reserves (WSRs))
surfing reserves, Australian: Angourie reserve 110–111; Bells Beach Surfing Recreation Reserve 109–110; National Surfing Reserves (NSRs) 109–110, **111**; New South Wales (NSW) 110
surfing reserves, Brazilian: *Brazilian Constitution, 1988* 118; Conservation Units (UCs) 112; Save the Waves Coalition 'surfonomics' programme 112; World Surfing Reserve 111; WSR assessment criteria 112
Sustainable Development Goals (SDGs) 17, 32, 126
Sustainable Development Reserves (RDS) 93–94, 100

tailings dams, upstream 61
Terra Legal operation 156
Transaction and Conduct Adjustment Agreement *(TTAC)* 55; compensation programme 56; Doce River watershed 58; negotiation process 57; restoration/rehabilitation measures 56; Samarco Company 60
transaction costs 20, 41, 48, 54, 85, 149–150, 191, 196, 200, 202, 218, 219, 242
TÜV Süd 61

Uluru-Kata Tjuta National Park 96; evaluation 99–100; local laws 98–99
UNDP Biofin programme 206
UN Information Portal on Multilateral Environmental Agreements 210
unmanned aerial vehicles (UAV) 153, 161, 168, 174–176

Vale Group 57
Vietor, R.H.K. 127
voluntary easement (VE), use of 119–120

Waldron, A. 190
Ward, A. 191
waterways, pollution of 29
welfare brands, environmental and animal 41
Werren, K. 192
World Surfing Reserves (WSRs) 112, **113–115,** 116–117; biodiversity conservation 107; environmental protection 107–108
World Wildlife Fund 67, 130, 199, 239
WWF/Australian Conservation Foundation 240
WWF-Brazil and Association Contas Abertas 240

Yale Environmental Performance Index 215